ORDER OUT OF CHAOS

THE MEDIEVAL MEDITERRANEAN

PEOPLES, ECONOMIES AND CULTURES, 400-1500

EDITORS

Hugh Kennedy (St. Andrews)
Paul Magdalino (St. Andrews)
David Abulafia (Cambridge)
Benjamin Arbel (Tel Aviv)
Mark Meyerson (Toronto)
Larry J. Simon (Western Michigan University)

VOLUME 65

ORDER OUT OF CHAOS

Patronage, Conflict and Mamluk Socio-Political Culture, 1341-1382

BY

JO VAN STEENBERGEN

BRILL
LEIDEN · BOSTON
2006

This book is printed on acid-free paper.

Library of Congress Cataloging-in-Publication Data

Steenbergen, J. van.
Order out of chaos : patronage, conflict, and Mamluk socio-political culture, 1341-1382 / by Jo Van Steenbergen.
p. cm. — (Medieval Mediterranean, ISSN 0928-5520 ; 65)
Includes bibliographical references and index.
ISBN-13: 978-90-04-15261-8
ISBN-10: 90-04-15261-X (alk. paper)
1. Mamelukes—History. I. Title.

DS97.4.S84 2006
956'.015—dc22

2006048451

ISSN 0928–5520
ISBN-13: 978-90-04-15261-8
ISBN-10: 90-04-15261-X

PRINTED IN THE NETHERLANDS

To Maya
and to Jonas, Marie and Anna

CONTENTS

Acknowledgments ix
Abbreviations-Transliteration xi
Introduction 1

Chapter One Legitimate Power 15
a. The socio-political elite 16
b. The Sultanate 22
c. The Amirate 33
d. Conclusion 49

Chapter Two Effective Power 53
a. Observations 53
b. Patrons and Clients 57
c. Kinship 76
d. Households and Networks 94
e. Networks of Effective Power between 1341 and 1382 100

Chapter Three Struggle for Power 123
a. Observations 123
b. Motives 128
c. Strategies 137
d. Order out of Chaos: 1341–1382 146

Conclusion 169

Appendix 1: The Qalawunid Sultanate, 1279–1382 175
Appendix 2: Effective Power holders between 1341 and 1382 177
Appendix 3: Struggle for Power between 1341 and 1382 189

Bibliography 197
Index 203

ACKNOWLEDGMENTS

I would like to express my strong appreciation for the inspiration, guidance and support I received from Urbain Vermeulen, who supervised the thesis that preceded this study and to whom I owe my entrance into academic life, my interest in the Mamluk regime and my enthusiasm for the history of the Islamic Middle East. Likewise, I am grateful to former colleagues at the Oriental Studies Department of the Katholieke Universiteit Leuven (Belgium), where most of the research for this study was conducted.

I must also thank the School of History of the University of St Andrews (UK), where this book was actually written and where it benefited a lot from a unique and challenging scholarly environment. I am especially indebted to my colleagues and fellow-historians from the Middle Eastern Studies Department: Angus Stewart, Ali Ansari, Hugh Kennedy and Robert Hoyland. Without their valuable comments, suggestions, guidance, support and assistance this project would have been so much harder to bring to an end. Angus Stewart in particular deserves to be mentioned, for he read through the bulk of the manuscript and prevented me from making too serious errors. Other colleagues and friends who should be mentioned and thanked for their assistance, feedback and suggestions at the various stages of the research and writing process are my external examiners Dionisius Agius and Heinrich Biesterfeldt, as well as Robert Irwin, Anne Broadbridge and Maaike van Berkel, and Yves Van den Broek. It goes without saying that I am solely responsible for any mistakes and shortcomings contained in this study.

A number of institutions and organisations need to be thanked for their support: the Fund for Scientific Research-Flanders (Belgium) for its financial support in the period 1998–2003, the Netherlands-Flemish Institute in Cairo (Egypt) for its hospitality and institutional assistance ('madam' Shahdan, 'madam' 'Azza, Mushir, Ghali, Khalid and Fathi in particular), and the Dār al-Kutub in Cairo, Cambridge University Library, the Bodleian, the British Library and the Forschungs- und Landesbibliothek Gotha.

And last but not least, my family needs to be mentioned. I owe them immense gratitude for their support and understanding, and for enduring a long sequence of deadlines. In particular my beloved Maya deserves special thanks, for her assistance, encouragement and criticism, for her many sacrifices, and for not giving up when she had to compete with the Mamluks so often. Thank you, Maya.

ABBREVIATIONS

**AI*	*Annales islamologiques*
**BSOAS*	*Bulletin of the School for Oriental and African Studies*
**EI*^{2}	*Encyclopaedia of Islam, New Edition*, 12 vols., Leiden-Paris, 1960–2004
**IJMES*	*International Journal of Middle Eastern Studies*
**JESHO*	*Journal of the Economic and Social History of the Orient*
**JRAS*	*Journal of the Royal Asiatic Society*
**JSS*	*Journal of Semitic Studies*
**MSR*	*Mamlūk Studies Review*
**SI*	*Studia Islamica*

TRANSLITERATION

Transliteration follows the practice of *Mamlūk Studies Review*. In principle, Arabic words are italicised. Names not commonly known in English take diacritics, but are not italicised. Words used throughout the book and therefore not requiring diacritical marks, or italicisation, include sultan, amir, mamluk, Mamluk and Qalawunid, except when they are used in official titles. The term mamluk refers to a social category, to an individual who is a manumitted military slave, whereas, if capitalised, Mamluk refers to the regime that dominated Egypt and Syria from the mid-thirteenth to the early sixteenth centuries.

In general, Mamluk amirs are identified by their personal names and any further commonly used part of their name (e.g. Qawṣūn, but Yalbughā al-Khāṣṣakī) and sultans are referred to by their honorific, but without the honorific's first element (al-malik), followed by their personal names (e.g. al-Nāṣir Muḥammad, al-Manṣūr Abū Bakr). Full names of the sultans and of most of the amirs that are mentioned in this book can be found in Appendices 1 and 2.

INTRODUCTION

> I could not say much of the Mamalucs, of whom I knew no auther [*sic*] that has written in particular: neither did they deserve that any should. For they were a base sort of people, a Colluvies of slaves, the scum of all the East, who, having treacherously destroyed the Jobidae, their Masters, reigned in their stead; and bating that they finished the expulsion of the Western Christians out of the East (where they barbarously destroyed Tripoli and Antioch, and several other Cities) they scarce did anything worthy to be recorded in History.[1]

Ever since the extreme negativism of this early eighteenth-century approach to the Syro-Egyptian Mamluk regime (ca. 1260–1516/17 CE),[2] Mamluk studies have progressed steadily, and important steps have been taken to start acknowledging the intrinsic value of this regime's long and crucial contribution to Middle Eastern history.[3] Nevertheless, the pace of scholarship in general, and Mamluk scholarship in particular, is slow, and several periods in Mamluk history remain unexplored, especially from the perspective of their social and political development. This is particularly true for the years between the death of the Mamluk regime's most successful sultan al-Malik al-Nāṣir Muḥammad (r. 1293–1294; 1299–1309; 1310–1341) in June 1341 and the accession to the throne of the amir Barqūq (d. 1399) towards the end of November 1382.

This still rather obscure period of forty years has gained a reputation primarily as an episode of social, economic and political chaos and upheaval, in which the twelve scions that succeeded al-Nāṣir Muḥammad to the throne never managed to equal the unparalleled welfare and *grandeur* his reign came to stand for. On the contrary, abundant accounts

---

[1] Anonymous, *The Life of Reverend Humphrey Prideaux, D.D., Dean of Norwich*, London 1748, p. 268 (from P.M. Holt, "The Position and Power of the Mamluk Sultan", *BSOAS* 38/2 (1975), p. 237).

[2] Dates in this study will be Common Era only.

[3] This is best epitomised by the fact that, since 1997, the field of Mamluk studies now even has its own bi-annual journal, *Mamlūk Studies Review*, one of the several ongoing Mamluk projects by the University of Chicago Middle East Documentation Centre, that were initiated by Bruce Craig and played a key role in the recent blossoming of the field.

of failed harvests, famines, pestilence and plague on the one hand, and of seemingly endless conflicts in the cities and in the countryside on the other, were considered a significant indication of the dire straits the regime and especially its subjects were in. As a result, several economic and socio-political phenomena that left their marks on the second half of Mamluk history are claimed—and often undoubtedly correctly so—to have their origins somewhere during these forty years. Scholarship, however, has remarkably enough never focused on this crucial episode. This was largely due to the fact that, for a long time, source material from unstable and confusing times such as these was not deemed useful for any historiographical narrative. Already in 1896, William Muir doomed the study of the period for many decades, when he—as did many after him—concluded that, indeed, this was nothing but an unattractive era of transition that lacked any order worthy of a historian's attention:

> 1341–1382 AD. For the next forty years the Sultanate was held by the house of Nâsir; in the first score by eight of his sons successively, and in the second by his grandsons; from first to last a miserable tale. They rose and fell at the will of the Mameluke leaders of the day, some mere children; the younger, indeed, the better, for so soon as the puppet Prince began to show a will of his own he was summarily deposed, or he was made away with, few of such as reached maturity dying a natural death. The Emirs rose and fell: each had his short day of power; then deposed and plundered, exiled or strangled, others succeeded but to share their fate. There were short intervals of able rule; but for the most part, murders, torture, execution, crime, and rebellion were throughout the period rife. The tale is sad and unattractive, and will be disposed of as briefly as the history admits of.[4]

It was only in 1980, therefore, in an unpublished PhD-dissertation, that a detailed chronological narrative of the period was attempted. But even its author, Werner Krebs, felt obliged to admit that his subject was of minor importance only and had so far been justly neglected.[5]

---

[4] W. Muir, *The Mameluke or Slave Dynasty of Egypt. A History of Egypt from the Fall of the Ayyubite Dynasties to the Conquest by the Osmanlis. AD 1260–1517*, London 1896 (repr. Amsterdam 1968), pp. 86–103 (quote from p. 86). For similar approaches, see e.g. S. Lane-Pool, *A History of Egypt in the Middle Ages*, London 1901 (1914), pp. 317–322; G. Wiet, *L'Égypte arabe. De la conquête arabe à la conquête ottomane. 642–1517 de l'ère chrétienne*, in G. Hanotaux (ed.), *Histoire de la Nation Égyptienne*, Tome IV, Paris 1937, pp. 499–510; M.J. Surūr, *Dawlat Banī Qalāwūn fī Miṣr. Al-Ḥāla al-Siyāsīya wa al-Iqtiṣādīya fī ʿahdihā bi-wajh khāṣṣ*, Cairo 1947, pp. 53–66.

[5] W. Krebs, *Innen- und Außenpolitik Ägyptens. 741–784/1341–1382*, unpublished Ph.D. thesis, University of Hamburg 1980. See p. 1: "Wir bekennen: Die Jahre des

It actually took another few years before the publication of more concise and slightly more positive reconstructions of the period's history, as smaller chronological units, though, incorporated within the larger surveys of pre-modern Middle Eastern history, by Peter Holt and Robert Irwin respectively.[6] Yet again, Irwin felt obliged to admit that a proper reconstruction of the period's socio-political history in particular still remained confusing and troublesome:

> Study of this confused epoch is complicated by the difficulty in determining who really exercised the power in the Sultanate. Not all of al-Nāṣir Muḥammad's descendants were degenerates or minors—putty in the hands of powerful emirs—but plainly in cases where that was so, it would be necessary to identify the background and intentions of emirs and, since abrupt switches in policy resulted from the frequent coups and murders at the top, it is difficult to find a narrative thread that will make sense of it all.[7]

Individual aspects of the period's socio-political history fared somewhat better in attracting scholarly attention. Ḥayā Nāṣir al-Ḥājjī made detailed reconstructions of the lives of two major characters from the period's political scene, the amir Qawṣūn (d. 1341) and the sultan al-Ashraf Shaʿbān (d. 1377); David Ayalon, Jean-Claude Garcin, Amalia Levanoni, Peter Holt and Ulrich Haarmann focused on specific areas of social and political activity, mostly, however, in a larger conceptual or historical framework (eunuchs, the region of Upper Egypt, mamluks, the sultanate, and mamluks' scions respectively); William Brinner identified the nominal character of the caliph's and sultan's reigns between the years 1363 and 1412; and, most recently, Amalia Levanoni, again,

---

Propheten 741 bis 784 zählen nicht zu den bemerkenswertesten Perioden des Vorderen Orients, haben auch, innerhalb des reichlichen Vierteljahrtausands mamlukischer Herrschaft [. . .] nur eine geringe Bedeutung [. . .] nicht zu Unrecht wurde sie von der islamkundlichen Forschung [. . .] ausgespart und von der Mamlukenforschung der letzten Jahrzehnte recht vernachlässigt".

[6] P.M. Holt, *The Age of the Crusades. The Near East from the Eleventh Century to 1517*, (A History of the Near East), London-New York 1986, pp. 121–128; R. Irwin, *The Middle East in the Middle Ages: The Early Mamluk Sultanate 1250–1382*, London-Sydney 1986, pp. 125–151.

[7] Irwin, *The Middle East*, p. 125. Similar feelings prevailed in Holt, "Mamluks", *EI*², VI, p. 323: 'It would be otiose in this article to recount in detail the political history of the later Kalawunids.' and in later, equally more general, surveys of Mamluk or pre-modern Middle Eastern history (e.g. U. Haarmann, 'Der arabischen Osten im späten Mittelalter 1250–1517", in U. Haarmann (ed.), *Geschichte der arabischen Welt*, München 1987, pp. 243–244; Linda S. Northrup, "The Bahri Mamluk Sultanate, 1250–1390", in Carl F. Petry (ed.), *The Cambridge History of Egypt, Volume 1, Islamic Egypt, 640–1517*, Cambridge 1998, pp. 253, 287–288).

questioned the source material's ethnocentric judgement of the 1382 transition to the reign of Barqūq.[8]

Though all of undeniably crucial importance and often of outstanding scholarship, finding 'a narrative thread that will make sense of it all', as Irwin put it, has remained problematic until today. This is largely due to the fact that narrative historiography is not the most suitable approach to generate historical insight into the multitude of socio-political events and individuals that coloured the period. When the available source material provides information on much more than a thousand individuals that were all more or less politically involved, and on seventy-four socio-political conflicts in just four decades, it becomes evident that a mere narrative listing of facts and figures can only result in a situation in which one can no longer see the forest for the trees, and chaos appears prevalent.[9] So far, unfortunately, the results of this deficient approach have only been rather extreme

---

[8] See Ḥ. Nāṣir al-Ḥājjī, "al-Aḥwāl al-Dākhilīya fī salṭanat al-Ashraf Shaʿbān b. Ḥusayn b. Muḥammad b. Qalāwūn, 764–778 h./1362–1376 m.", *ʿĀlam al-Fikr* 3/3 (1983), pp. 761–822; Ḥ. Nāṣir al-Ḥājjī, "al-Amīr Qawṣūn: ṣūra ḥayya li-niẓām al-ḥukm fī salṭanat al-mamālīk", *al-majalla al-ʿarabīya li-l-ʿulūm al-insānīya* 8/32 (1988), pp. 6–55; D. Ayalon, "The Eunuchs in the Mamluk Sultanate", *Studies in Memory of Gaston Wiet*, Jerusalem 1977, pp. 267–295 (repr. in D. Ayalon, *The Mamluk Military Society*, London 1979, III), esp. pp. 282–294; J.-Cl. Garcin, *Un centre musulman de la haute Égypte médiévale: Qūs*, Cairo 1976; A. Levanoni, *A Turning Point in Mamluk History: The third reign of al-Nāṣir Muḥammad ibn Qalawun (1310–1341)*, (*Islamic History and Civilization: Studies and Texts* 10), Leiden 1995, pp. 81–132; A. Levanoni, "Rank-and-file Mamluks versus amirs: new norms in the Mamluk military institution", in Th. Philipp & U. Haarmann (eds.), *The Mamluks in Egyptian Politics and Society*, Cambridge 1998, pp. 17–31; Levanoni, "The Mamluk Conception of the Sultanate", pp. 381–384; A. Levanoni, "al-Malik al-Ṣāliḥ", *EI*², VIII, pp. 986–987; A. Levanoni, "al-Maqrīzī's Account of the Transition from Turkish to Circassian Mamluk Sultanate: History in the Service of Faith", in H. Kennedy (ed.), *The Historiography of Islamic Egypt (c. 950–1800)*, (*The Medieval Mediterranean. Peoples, Economies and Cultures, 400–1453* 31), Leiden 2001, pp. 93–105; P.M. Holt, "al-Nāṣir", *EI*², VII, pp. 992–993; P.M. Holt, "Shaʿbān", *EI*², IX, pp. 154–155; U. Haarmann, "The Sons of Mamluks as Fief-Holders in Late Medieval Egypt", in Tarif Khalidi (ed.), *Land Tenure and Social Transformation in the Middle East*, Beirut 1984, pp. 141–168; U. Haarmann, "Arabic in Speech, Turkish in Lineage: Mamluks and their Sons in the Intellectual Life of Fourteenth Century Egypt and Syria", *JSS* 33 (1988), pp. 81–114; U. Haarmann, "Joseph's Law—the careers and activities of mamluk descendants before the Ottoman conquest of Egypt", in Th. Philipp & U. Haarmann (eds.), *The Mamluks in Egyptian Politics and Society*, Cambridge 1998, pp. 55–84; W.M. Brinner, "The Struggle for Power in the Mamluk State: Some Reflections on the Transition from Bahri to Burji Rule", *Proceedings of the 26th International Congress of Orientalists, New Delhi, 4–10 January 1964*, New Delhi 1970, pp. 231–234. Additionally, there is J. Wansbrough, "Ḥasan", *EI*², III, p. 239.

[9] For a list of those conflicts, see Appendix 3. In all, information was retrieved on one thousand four hundred and thirty sultans, amirs and mamluks who all played, at the very least, an institutional socio-political role between the years 1341 and 1382.

generalisations, like the following quite remarkable summary of the period's political history by the pioneer of Mamluk studies, David Ayalon:

> Coalitions and combinations of forces [. . .] were generally of a most temporary nature, and the stability of each sultan's rule was to a large extent dependent on his ability to take full advantage of the rivalry among the various units. A detailed presentation of the vast material supplied on this topic by Mamluk sources is of no special interest [. . .].[10]

No period in history deserves such a blanket rejection of its own historical dynamism. In fact, Stephen Humphreys, in a recent review article on Mamluk politics, made a case for giving priority to the study of this period's political dynamics in particular.[11]

Therefore, the study presented here aims to heed this call and to contribute to the filling of a vacuum in academic research that has existed for far too long. To this end, it proposes to search for the dynamics of action and reaction that shaped the period's politics and moulded their social background, and that will enable, eventually, a reconstruction of its political development that will claim to make more 'sense of it all'.

Ultimately, it may even be postulated that, rather than being of no special interest, this episode and the information it reveals on the Mamluk political process in general should be considered of more interest than any other episode in Mamluk history. This is due to the fact that, for the majority of years between 1341 and 1382, the dynamics of that process were not 'cloaked' under any institutional disguise and therefore were more significant and revealing than ever.

---

[10] See D. Ayalon, "Studies on the Structure of the Mamluk Army", *BSOAS* 15 (1953), p. 218. For a similar critique on Ayalon's judgement, see W.W. Clifford, "State Formation and the Structure of Politics in Mamluk Syro-Egypt, 648–741 AH/1250–1340 CE", unpublished Ph.D. thesis, University of Chicago 1995, p. 17. For similar, though less extreme generalisations on the timeframe, see I.M. Lapidus, *Muslim Cities in the Later Middle Ages*, Cambridge (Mass.) 1967, pp. 20–21; R. Chapoutot-Remadi, "Liens et relations aux sein de l'élite mamluke sous les premiers sultans Bahrides, 648/1250–741/1340", unpublished Ph.D. thesis, Université de Provence. Aix-Marseille I 1993, pp. 67, 82; Levanoni, *Turning Point*, pp. 79, 116.

[11] See R.S. Humphreys, "The Politics of the Mamluk Sultanate: A Review Essay", *MSR* 9/1 (2005), p. 223. For a similar call, see also Tsugitaka Sato's statement, concluding his book on the *iqṭāʿ* system, that "the fate of both Egyptian and Syrian society after the reign of Sultan al-Nāṣir needs further, and more careful study from a comprehensive view based on the contemporary sources" (Tsugitaka Sato, *State and Rural Society in medieval Islam. Sultans, muqtaʿs and fallahun*, (*Islamic History and Civilization. Studies and Texts* 17), Leiden-New York-Koln 1997, p. 239).

This study will maintain that in the political process—as especially Ira Lapidus and Michael Chamberlain have previously argued in more general terms—Mamluk institutions, including the sultanate, came second only to the individuals that populated them, and to the social and political interaction they generated among themselves in particular.[12] This is why detailed prosopographical analysis of this socio-political interaction in the years between 1341 and 1382 lies at the basis of this study.[13] The results of that analysis, enabling the first solid interpretation of the period's political culture and development, are presented here via a reconstruction of that interaction from three perspectives: institutions, individuals, and conflicts.

In keeping with a long tradition of Middle Eastern military government, mamluks gained their momentum of political power and dominance on the thirteenth-century battlefields of Egypt and Syria, a military momentum that would remain an essential characteristic of the regime they initiated. Being rooted in the military corps of the last Ayyubid sultan, al-Ṣāliḥ Ayyūb, this regime continued to derive its authority and legitimacy primarily from its coercive force. However, at the same time, the generally defensive nature of that momentum eventually—as will be detailed below—turned the men of that regime from a military force, who were equally involved in politics and government, into a body politic, whose background and authority continued to be militarily defined, but whose concerns were social and political rather than military. In particular, the long first half of the fourteenth century and the internal and external status quo that pertained to most of the third reign of al-Nāṣir Muḥammad b. Qalāwūn (r. 1293–1294; 1299–1309; 1310–1341) should be deemed largely responsible for this 'politicisation'—or perhaps rather 'demilitarisation'—of the Mamluk military regime.[14] As a result, despite the fact that

---

[12] See I.M. Lapidus, *Muslim Cities in the Later Middle Ages*, Cambridge (Mass.) 1967; Michael Chamberlain, *Knowledge and Social Practice in Medieval Damascus, 1190–1350*, (*Cambridge Studies in Islamic Civilization*), Cambridge 1994; and additionally also Clifford, "State Formation". The insights offered by these three studies in particular have been of fundamental importance for the present work. For a call to implement such 'middle range theories of social interaction', see W.W. Clifford, "*Ubi Sumus*? Mamluk History and Social Theory", *MSR* 1 (1997), pp. 45–46.

[13] A reduced sample of the results of this prosopographical research may be found in Appendix 2, where the period's main political characters are listed. Recently, Stephen Humphreys equally made a call for more prosopographical research like this (Humphreys, "The Politics of the Mamluk Sultanate", p. 228).

[14] In this context, Northrup, for instance, notices a parallel 'de-mamlukization' (Northrup, "The Bahri Mamluk sultanate", p. 262).

the thirteenth-century military institutional framework, from which this body politic continued to stem, remained an essential element in the nature of the political process, it came to be superseded by socio-political *modi operandi* that went far beyond the military.

As noted above, this growing divergence between the institutional framework and socio-political practice is one of the main parameters of this study. Especially in the period immediately after Muḥammad's reign, this split became a major characteristic of the socio-political process, occasionally even defined as "the breakdown of the established political system".[15] At the same time, despite this divergence, it will equally be maintained that both remained two sides of the same coin. While institutions came second to practice only, neither can be properly analysed without the other, for only together did they engender interaction, power, and political development.

Therefore, this study's first chapter will focus on that subordinate, yet indispensable institutional framework of Mamluk politics and on the part it still played in Mamluk society between 1341 and 1382. Consisting of mostly military institutions whose authority and prerogatives were largely derived from the sultanate and its unremitting caliphal legitimisation, the exercise of political power as described in this chapter will be conveniently captured under the heading of 'Legitimate Power'.

The use of this terminology actually helps to picture both the association with and the distinction from this study's second chapter, on the period's socio-political practice, similarly captured under such a heading: 'Effective Power', as it were Legitimate Power's superior *alter ego*.[16] This chapter will focus on individuals and the nature of their socio-political relationships. It will analyse how the institutional framework was used to enhance and create power via the set-up of comprehensive households and supplementary networks of supporters, and it will establish what variants of this Effective Power there were in the period between 1341 and 1382.[17]

---

[15] Humphreys, "The Politics of the Mamluk Sultanate", p. 223.

[16] For the use of the term 'Effective Power' in this context, see also Northrup, "The Bahri Mamluk sultanate", p. 287. It will be used to represent a social type of power, for 'the ability to get things done' irrespective of any type of institutions and as essentially generated in the interaction between individuals.

[17] For, yet again, Stephen Humphreys' recent call for such a reconstruction of Mamluk households, see Humphreys, "The Politics of the Mamluk Sultanate", p. 227.

And finally, the third chapter will continue in this vein and analyse how these households and networks competed for power during those four decades. It will, therefore, focus on the motives and strategies behind the period's seventy-four socio-political conflicts and situate them again within the balancing processes of Effective Power.[18] Hence, it will become possible to use insights thus gained to conclude with a reconstruction of the period's political history, demonstrating how an alternative predominant order of Effective Power relapsed repeatedly into the period's five moments of socio-political chaos, a cycle only the amir Barqūq managed to break in 1382.

The sources

There are, of course, some drawbacks and limits inherent in this study's approach to the political history of the period between 1341 and 1382 that need to be acknowledged and taken into consideration.

Though individuals, groups, and their socio-political behaviour are this study's subject, the deeper emotional and behavioural grounds for actions performed and decisions taken mostly cannot and will not be incorporated in the analysis. As a work of history, and an 'exploratory essay',[19] far more emphasis will be put on the how and what of socio-political processes than on their why, and if this has resulted in an occasional overemphasis on the less emotional, material character of these processes, then this can only be acknowledged.

An important reason for such an emphasis, is, of course, the nature of the source material that allows for such insights to be gained. Since the majority of them are chronicles, and they all provide narratives, which are of an unremittingly personal character, one generally needs to be wary of putting too much confidence in the factual accuracy of their accounts.[20] And when an analysis of political processes and,

---

[18] As mentioned above, these seventy-four conflicts and their main characteristics are listed in Appendix 3.

[19] For the term 'exploratory essay', see Chamberlain, *Knowledge and Social Practice*, p. 3.

[20] See e.g. N.O. Rabbat, "Representing the Mamluks in Mamluk Historical Writing", in Kennedy (ed.), *The Historiography of Islamic Egypt*, pp. 59–75; U. Haarmann, "al-Maqrīzī, the master, and Abū Ḥāmid al-Qudsī, the disciple—whose historical writing can claim more topicality and modernity?", in Kennedy (ed.), *The Historiography of Islamic Egypt*, p. 149; A.F. Broadbridge, "Academic Rivalry and the Patronage System in Fifteenth-Century Egypt: al-ʿAynī, al-Maqrīzī, and Ibn Ḥajar al-ʿAsqalānī",

very often covert, behaviour has to be based on such material, one needs to be even more careful. As suggestive as the abundance of their illustrations of those processes may be, they can never be considered exhaustive, nor, strictly speaking, representative of an obscure political process that remains largely shrouded in the clouds of premodern history. At the same time, however, the sources' involvement also means that whatever their meddling with the stories they narrate, in order to present them convincingly, they always had to embed them within those social and political processes that were familiar to themselves, their audience, and the social environment this study hopes to revive. Whatever those stories' historical accuracy, therefore, they instinctively or subconsciously reflected the processes this study is actually looking for. Moreover, as will be detailed below, the coherent, plagiaristic nature of Mamluk historiography even suggests that such involvement translated rather into omitting certain facts than in totally transforming or making up historical accounts.[21] It may therefore be safely assumed that the period's source material allows not just for—though inherently conjectural—quite convincing interpretations, but also for the reconstruction of a general line of political developments that is derived from information on events and main characters that were ubiquitous in the period's source material and therefore as close as one can get to Mamluk historical reality.[22]

One drawback which follows from this, and which seriously affected this study and the rendering of its analysis in this book, is the overwhelming wealth of material which is available and which so far largely prohibited any narrative attempt to present a coherent picture of the period's history. This material spans many years, it reflects an eventful and unstable history, and it is very diverse in nature, in particular with respect to the processes of socio-political conduct that

MSR 3 (1999), pp. 85–107; A.F. Broadbridge, "Royal Authority, Justice, and Order in Society: The Influence of Ibn Khaldūn on the Writings of al-Maqrīzī and Ibn Taghrī Birdī", *MSR* 7/2 (2003), pp. 231–245; R. Irwin, "al-Maqrīzī and Ibn Khaldūn, Historians of the Unseen", *MSR* 7/2 (2003), pp. 217–230.

[21] See e.g. D.P. Little, *An Introduction to Mamluk Historiography*, Wiesbaden 1970.

[22] Because of this repetitive character of Mamluk narrative historiography, the following approach has been adopted to condense the critical apparatus: if possible, only a reference's presumably original or nearly original source or sources are mentioned, in chronological order; if more source material exists, this is simply indicated by the adding of 'e.g.', for example. For a similar approach, see R. Amitai-Preiss, *Mongols and Mamluks. The Mamluk-Ilkhanid war, 1260–1281*, (*Cambridge Studies in Islamic Civilisation*), Cambridge 1995, p. 6.

defined that fragmented history. It has, therefore, been considered inescapable to represent this wealth and variety through the reproduction of an often wide range of examples that may, occasionally, interfere with, or even interrupt the general flow of the argument. This has been deemed unfortunate, but at the same time equally necessary to render the analysis as comprehensive as possible and to give full credit to the riches of the period's political history.

The abundant narrative historiographical material that, despite some lack of historical accuracy, remains extremely illustrative and informative of the Mamluk political processes and developments in the period between 1341 and 1382, was transmitted chiefly in two distinct formats: biographical dictionaries and chronicles.[23] Of major importance for this study in the first category were two dictionaries written by the Syrian contemporary scholar and administrator Khalīl b. Aybak al-Ṣafadī (1297–1363): the multi-volume comprehensive continuation of a predecessor's work, the *Kitāb al-Wāfī bi-al-Wafayāt*, and the condensed and more focused *Aʿyān al-ʿAṣr wa Aʿwān al-Naṣr*. Both contain an unmatched wealth of information on the individuals al-Ṣafadī often had received direct information on or was personally involved with, until shortly before his death in 1363. His *Sitz-im-Leben* as a mamluk's son, as an important Syrian administrator and as an acquaintance to many a Syrian political character turned him into a privileged and involved witness, and a very useful source for this study.[24] On the basis of the *Aʿyān*, but with the addition of a lot of new information for the period after 1363, the Egyptian scholar Ibn Ḥajar al-ʿAsqalānī (1372–1448) wrote his own well-known dictionary, *al-Durar al-Kāmina fī Aʿyān al-miʾa al-thāmina*.[25] And similarly, the later

[23] Only this study's main sources and their coherence will be presented here; for their full bibliographic details, and a complete list of the primary sources used, see the Bibliography.

[24] See e.g. D.P. Little, "al-Ṣafadī as Biographer of his Contemporaries", in D.P. Little (ed.), *Essays on Islamic Civilization: presented to Niyazi Berkes*, Leiden 1976, pp. 190–211 (repr. in D.P. Little, *History and Historiography of the Mamluks*, London 1986, I); F. Rosenthal, "al-Ṣafadī", *EI*², VIII, pp. 759–760; D.P. Little, "Historiography of the Ayyubid and Mamluk epochs", in C.F. Petry (ed.), *The Cambridge History of Egypt, Volume 1, Islamic Egypt, 640–1517*, Cambridge 1998, pp. 431–432.

[25] See e.g. F. Krenkow, "The Hidden Pearls. Concerning the Notables of the Eighth Islamic Century", *Islamic Culture* 2 (1928), pp. 527–539; A.A. Rahman, "The life and works of Ibn Hajar al-Asqalani", *Islamic Culture* 45 (1971), pp. 203–212, 275–293; 46 (1972), pp. 75–81, 171–178, 265–272, 353–362; 47 (1973), pp. 57–74, 159–174, 255–273; F. Rosenthal, "Ibn Ḥadjar al-ʿAsḳalānī", *EI*², III, pp. 776–778.

historian Ibn Taghrī Birdī (1411–1469) wrote his own valuable continuation of al-Ṣafadī's work, *al-Manhal al-Ṣāfī wa al-Mustawfī baʿda l-Wāfī*, and often exceptionally facilitated the historian's job by referring to the sources he had copied from.[26]

As mentioned above, copying from predecessors' accounts, generally without acknowledgements, is also what made up considerable parts of many contemporary or near-contemporary chronicles. And actually, from that perspective, quite insightful observations can be made on the narrative traditions that determined the historiography of the period between 1341 and 1382, as it may be found in Mamluk chronicles written roughly in the century after 1341.

Generally, a major geographical distinction can be discerned between chronicles compiled in Syria and those written down in Egypt.[27] The Syrian side of this specific period's historiographical tradition is mainly represented by a number of Damascene chronicles, which are all continuations of the works of the Damascene scholar al-Dhahabī (d. 1347). Especially the works of Muḥammad Ibn Shākir al-Kutubī (d. 1362), the *ʿUyūn al-Tawārīkh*, and of his contemporary Ibn Kathīr (c. 1300–1373), the *al-Bidāya wa al-Nihāya*, are of interest for the local and more general social and political insights they offer, up to the year 1359 and 1366 respectively. Although each of the latter two works occasionally contains reports and stories that are not to be found in the other, they do offer many identical accounts of the events of these years, often almost matching word for word and indicative of their deep interdependence.[28]

The Egyptian 'school' on the other hand—wealthier in information for this study since the centre of political gravity largely remained in Egypt—clearly consisted of more than only one historiographical tradition, even within some of the individual chronicles that covered it. Until the reports of the year 1354, it is very likely that the origin of many narratives can be traced back to one largely lost contemporary chronicle, the *Nuzhat al-Nāẓir fī Sīrat al-Malik al-Nāṣir* by the

[26] See e.g. A. Darraj, "La vie d'Abu l-Mahasin Ibn Tagri Birdi et son oeuvre", *AI* 11 (1972), pp. 163–181; G. Wiet, *Les Biographies du Manhal Safi*, (*Mélanges de l'Institut d'Égypte* 19), Cairo 1932; W. Popper, "Abū al-Maḥāsin", *EI*², I, p. 138.

[27] See L. Guo, "Mamluk Historiographical Studies: The State of the Art", *MSR* 1 (1997), pp. 29–32.

[28] See *GAL*, II, pp. 46–48; SII, pp. 45–47; F. Rosenthal, "al-Kutubī", *EI*², V, pp. 570–571; H. Laoust, "Ibn Kathīr Historien", *Arabica* 2 (1955), pp. 87–103; H. Laoust, "Ibn Kathīr", *EI*², III, pp. 817–818.

well-connected military man and historian al-Yūsufī (1297–1358).[29] Donald Little has demonstrated how this definitely was the case for reports by others—especially the contemporary al-Shujāʿī's *Tārīkh* as well as the early fifteenth-century annalistic chronicles by al-Maqrīzī (1364–1442) and by al-ʿAynī (1361–1451), the *Sulūk* and the *ʿIqd al-Jumān*—on the end of the reign of al-Nāṣir Muḥammad, claiming at the same time quite convincingly that, even despite today's loss of al-Yūsufī's text beyond the report on the year 1338, this dependence could safely be extended until the accounts of the year 1345.[30] But, as this year was only chosen since it was, by chance, the last to have been preserved from al-Shujāʿī's history, and since those chronicles, in particular the most elaborate and detailed among them, al-Maqrīzī's *Sulūk*, show no significant change from the pre-1345 period in the nature and presentation of its historical material, it seems safe to assume that such interdependence with—if not dependence on—al-Yūsufī's *Nuzha* continued until the last year reported in it, namely 1354.[31]

Beyond 1354, however, such interdependence becomes less straightforward to determine. Only from the reports on the year 1363 onwards do some parallels re-appear, especially when remarkably detailed lists of promotions and appointments start to pop up in the narratives of al-Maqrīzī and al-ʿAynī, as well as in those of the contemporary author Ibn Duqmāq (ca. 1350–1407)—in his *Jawhar al-Thamīn* and, as from the year 1367, similarly in his *Nuzhat al-Anām*[32]—

[29] On this author, see Ibn Ḥajar, *Durar*, IV, p. 381: '[. . .] he compiled a large history in about fifteen volumes, which he called *Nuzhat al-Nāẓir fī Sīrat al-Malik al-Nāṣir*, beginning with the regime of al-Manṣūr [Qalāwūn] and coming to an end in the year 1354 [. . .]'. For a partial reconstruction of this very detailed history, for the years between 1333 and 1338, see al-Yūsufī, *Nuzhat al-Nāẓir fī Sīrat al-Malik al-Nāṣir*, A. Hutayt (ed.), Beirut 1986. See also Little, "Historiography of the Ayyubid and Mamluk Epochs", pp. 426–427.

[30] Little, "Four Mamluk Chronicles", pp. 252–268. See also Little, "Historiography of the Ayyubid and Mamluk Epochs", p. 427.

[31] In this study, the most striking parallels between texts are occasionally referred to in the footnote apparatus by inserting 'identical in . . .' for a word for word match in two sources, or 'similiar in . . .' for less literal parallels.

[32] The manuscript of the *Nuzhat al-Anām* used for this study was the most complete one preserved (Bodleian Ms. Marshall 36); this hitherto unknown manuscript contains the report of the years 1367 until 1378 and was copied according to the colophon in 1386; until now, it was only catalogued as the untitled work of an obscure 'al-Bayrūtī'; the fact that it was the second extant copy of the *Nuzha* was revealed after close examination and comparison with the only other extant manuscript, dated 1382 (Gotha Ms. Orient A 1572) (an alleged third manuscript, Ms. Cairo Dār al-Kutub 1740 *tārīkh*, turned out to be missing from the Cairo Dār al-Kutub).

and of Ibn Ḥajar, after 1372, the first year to be recorded in his chronicle, the *Inbā' al-Ghumr*. As with the earlier tradition, this later Egyptian narrative strand would also certainly need further specialised research. For the time being, however, the road such research is very likely to take is indicated by some explicit remarks to that extent. In his own chronicle, the Egyptian historian Ibn Bahādur al-Mu'minī (d. 1473) claims that al-ʿAynī, in his *ʿIqd al-Jumān*, mentions his extensive borrowing from a great number of histories, among which "the history of al-Yūsufī [. . .], [. . .] of Ṣārim al-Dīn Ibrāhīm b. Duqmāq and [. . .] of the judge Nāṣir al-Dīn Ibn al-Furāt [. . .]."[33] Secondly, Ibn Ḥajar, in the introduction to his chronicle that includes the period between 1372 and 1382, also refers very explicitly to his methodology and sources:

> Most of what is mentioned in [my chronicle], have I either seen with my own eyes, taken over from [people] I consulted, or found in the writings of those I trust among my predecessors and peers, like the great history of the *shaykh* Nāṣir al-Dīn Ibn al-Furāt, whom I have studied a lot of Hadith with, and like [the work] of Ṣārim al-Dīn Ibn Duqmāq, whom I met a lot. Most of what I transmit is from his writings and from the writings of Ibn al-Furāt via [Ibn Duqmāq's], [as well as from the works of] [. . .] Ibn Ḥijjī, [. . .] al-Maqrīzī, [. . .] and others.[34]

All the preceding clearly hints at the existence of more than one major historiographical tradition for the period between 1341 and 1382: at least one in Syria, and two subsequent ones in Egypt.[35] And within the latter, the history of al-Yūsufī on the one hand, and allegedly also those of Ibn Duqmāq and, especially, of Ibn al-Furāt (1334–1405) on the other were of vital importance. It is therefore extremely unfortunate that the parts of Ibn al-Furāt's *Tārīkh al-Duwal wa l-Mulūk*

---

[33] See Ibn Bahādur al-Mu'minī, *Kitāb Futūḥ al-Naṣr fī Tārīkh Mulūk Maṣr*, MS. Cairo Dār al-Kutub 4977 *tārīkh*, fol. 1.

[34] Ibn Ḥajar, *Inbā' al-Ghumr*, I, pp. 2–3.

[35] An outsider among these traditions actually was Ibn Khaldūn (1332–1406), who stayed in Egypt after 1382 and who had close contacts among the socio-political elite, an element which allegedly fed greatly into the history of the era he recorded in volume five of his *Kitāb al-ʿIbar* and which, despite his own *Sitz-im-Leben* that undoubtedly needs to be taken into consideration, still remains very similar in contextual character to and as insightful as the narratives of the Egyptian historiographical traditions of the 1370s and 80s. These historical accounts of his so far do not seem to have received even part of the attention his Muqaddima has been given. On Ibn Khaldūn's activities in Egypt, see W.J. Fischel, *Ibn Khaldūn in Egypt: his public functions and his historical research, 1382–1406: a study in Islamic historiography*, Berkeley 1967.

that deal with the period between 1341 and 1382 are not known to have been preserved.[36]

Of greater importance for this study than the exact nature of this interdependence, though, remains the fact that the prevalence of such traditions resulted in an occasionally even complementary uniformity in the period's source material, deeply rooted in the society it evoked. In their own historical process, these contemporary traditions, and especially the way their constituents reconfirm, contradict and complement each other, gave shape to a near-contemporary critical mass of material that enables us to come very close to the historical processes and realities they claim to be narrating.

[36] Zie G. Flügel, *Die Arabischen, Persischen und Türkischen Handschriften der Kaiserlich-Königlichen Hofbibliothek zu Wien*, vol. II, Wien 1865, p. 49; C. Brockelmann, *Geschichte der Arabischen Litteratur*, 2 vols. & 3 suppls., Leiden 1943–1949 & 1937–1942, vol. II, pp. 61–62; SII, p. 49; *Tārīkh Ibn al-Furāt*, vols. IV–V, H.M. al-Shammaʿ (ed.), Basra 1967; vols. VII–IX, Q. Zurayq, N. ʿIzz al-Din (eds.), Beirut 1936–1942.

CHAPTER ONE

LEGITIMATE POWER

In the quest for Mamluk political culture in the period from 1341 to 1382, for the social and political dynamics of Mamluk power and government, a first point to be considered and defined is the institutional parameters of that power and government. This chapter will set this scene and, from such an institutional perspective, will focus on those that were involved in the political process of acquiring and executing socio-political power: the socio-political elite as defined by the sultanate and the amirate.

Though institutions were perhaps not as fundamental to the Middle East as they were to other societies,[1] they undeniably continued to be quite a ubiquitous and crucial factor in the Mamluk sultanate and its political process. The concern with which the Mamluk regime continued to nurture the institution of the caliphate well into the fifteenth century is but one example that attests to this. And the same goes for many politico-military institutions, including the sultanate: though often superseded by a detached socio-political process—especially in the period between 1341 and 1382 with its several puppet sultans—they retained their value as a framework for identification, domination and, not in the least, remuneration.

No institution, no socio-political culture, can however be analysed properly without knowing whom it applied to. Before reconstructing that institutional framework, therefore, that loose body of individuals that operated within it and used it to develop their socio-political involvement will be identified, that is, the actors that created power and executed government. Originally constituting the core military manpower society relied on for its defence, it was these actors who, as mentioned above, were transformed into a body politic while retaining their military character. Since this military character, which

---

[1] See e.g. Chamberlain, *Knowledge and Social Practice*, pp. 4–5, where he claims that the survival of documents and archives in Europe, and their overall loss in the Middle East, attest to this contrasting difference in the importance both societies attached to these documents in the framework of social identity and social survival.

had gradually developed into a definite military structure, continued to be the major source for their domination over Mamluk society, politico-military institutions remained their framework for operation—even between 1341 and 1382—and for identification as a socio-political elite, at least in the chronicles and biographical dictionaries, and therefore in Mamluk society as it may be reconstructed today.

The Socio-political Elite

On the basis of contemporary observers' reports, roughly three categories of people are generally distinguished within the Mamluk social environment: a wide variety that made up the common people, an intermediate category of mostly cultural and economic notables, and a third layer that was of an exclusively military and urban character and that included the socio-political elite.[2] Whereas the extremely diverse body of common people provided most of the labour force that guaranteed an income to the other social groups, this category never even conceived of trying to translate that crucial but inferior economic position into any significant social or political weight.[3] Nevertheless, between 1341 and 1382, largely unidentifiable urban gangs from this group occasionally became politically involved when they were called upon by political heavy-weights in the course of some of the era's many socio-political conflicts. This happened especially in the early 1340s, and then again during most of the reign

[2] For discussions of the composition of Mamluk society, see A. Sabra, *Poverty and Charity in Medieval Islam. Mamluk Egypt, 1250–1517*, (*Cambridge Studies in Islamic Civilization*), Cambridge 2000, pp. 10–11; Lapidus, *Muslim Cities*, pp. 7, 79–82; Staffa, *Conquest and Fusion. The Social Evolution of Cairo, A.D. 642–1850*, Leiden 1977, pp. 6–7; C.F. Petry, *The Civilian Elite of Cairo in the Later Middle Ages*, Princeton 1981, p. 3; B. Martel-Thoumian, *Les civils et l'administration dans l'état militaire mamluk (IXe/XVe siècle)*, (*Publicatons de l'Insitut Français de Damas* 136), Damas 1991, p. 329; B. Shoshan, *Popular Culture in medieval Cairo*, (*Cambridge Studies in Islamic Civilization*), Cambridge 1993 (1996), p. 3; N. Rabbat, "Representing the Mamluks in Mamluk Historical Writing", in Kennedy (ed.), *The Historiography of Islamic Egypt*, pp. 60–61.

[3] See Lapidus, *Muslim Cities*, pp. 165, 170; D. Ayalon, "The Muslim City and the Mamluk Military Aristocracy", *Proceedings of the Israel Academy of Sciences and Humanities* 2 (1968), p. 325 (repr. in D. Ayalon, *Studies on the Mamlûks of Egypt (1250–1517)*, London 1977, VII); B. Shoshan, "The 'Politics of Notables' in Medieval Islam", *Asian and African Studies: Journal of the Israel Oriental Society* 20 (1986), pp. 183–184; Shoshan, "Grain Riots and Moral Economy: Cairo 1350–1517", *Journal of Interdisciplinary History* 10/3 (1980), pp. 470–473, 478; Shoshan, *Popular Culture*, pp. 56–66; Sabra, *Poverty and Charity*, pp. 136, 166–167.

of al-Ashraf Shaʿbān (d. 1377) and when the amir Barqūq subsequently rose to prominence.[4] This political involvement, however, never exceeded the level of direct action, of plundering, looting, throwing stones, and, especially, providing manpower in violent confrontations. Though some relatively obscure groups within the common people could thus be useful to influence government, policy making and the power process, they were always used and engaged by others who were the real policy makers, and there was never any attempt made to change that situation.

The same goes for the political involvement of the intermediate group of military, cultural and economic notables. Auxiliary forces in- and outside the urban environment, including a secondary corps called the *ḥalqa*, can equally be linked to some of the era's major political conflicts, but again only in a similar capacity to that of the urban gangs.[5] As for the legal-religious scholars, the *ʿulamāʾ*, and the

[4] In September 1341, *ḥarāfish* are reported to have taken part in a rebellion of mamluks of the sultan, ending in their severe punishment (al-Shujāʿī, *Tārīkh*, pp. 152–154); by the end of that year, these *ḥarāfish* seem to have taken revenge when they assisted in the taking of the amir Qawṣūn's palace outside the citadel, subsequently plundered and stripped by mamluks and 'common people' alike (see al-Shujāʿī, *Tārīkh*, pp. 184–186; al-Maqrīzī, *Sulūk*, II/3, pp. 588–589; 591–593); one year later, in December 1342, 'common people' were again reported to have been involved in the rebellion of an unsuccessful pretender to the throne (al-ʿAynī, *ʿIqd al-Jumān*, pp. 68–69); when sultan al-Ashraf Shaʿbān got caught up in a number of conflicts involving unruly Yalbughāwīya-mamluks between 1366 and 1367, his resultant victory over them is partly accredited to the support he received from 'the common people', a relationship which he supposedly continued to cherish until his murder in 1377 (see al-Nuwayrī, *Kitāb al-Ilmām*, VI, p. 18; Ibn Khaldūn, *Kitāb al-ʿIbar*, V, p. 460; Ibn Duqmāq, *Nuzhat al-Anām*, fols. 37–38v; al-Maqrīzī, *Sulūk*, III/1, pp. 135, 136, 151, 152–153, 173–174; al-ʿAynī, *ʿIqd al-Jumān*, pp. 146, 153–154; Ibn Taghrī Birdī, *Nujūm*, XI, pp. 77–78); in 1379, the amir Barqūq is reported to have embarked upon a successful campaign to gain similar support from the common people, most notably gangs like the *zuʿr* and the *ʿabīd*, who subsequently assisted him to overcome two conflicts with peers in 1379 and 1380 (see Ibn Khaldūn, *Kitāb al-ʿIbar*, V, p. 469; al-Maqrīzī, *Sulūk*, III/1, pp. 352, 365–366, 382, 383–384; Ibn Ḥajar, *Inbāʾ al-Ghumr*, I, pp. 299, 310–311; II, pp. 2–3). On these gangs, see Lapidus, *Muslim Cities*, pp. 82–85; W.M. Brinner, "The Significance of the ḥarāfīsh and their 'Sultan'", *JESHO* 6 (1963), pp. 190–215; W.M. Brinner, "Ḥarfūsh", *EI²*, III, p. 206; Staffa, *Conquest and Fusion*, p. 7; Petry, *The Civilian Elite of Cairo*, p. 3; Rabbat, "Representing the Mamluks", pp. 60–61; Shoshan, *Popular Culture*, pp. 4–6; Sabra, *Poverty and Charity*, pp. 12–15, 135; Haarmann, "Joseph's Law", p. 61; I. Perho, "Al-Maqrīzī and Ibn Taghrī Birdī as Historians of Contemporary Events", in Kennedy (ed.), *The Historiography of Islamic Egypt*, p. 107; I. Perho, "The Sultan and the Common People", *Studia Orientalia: Societas Orientalis Fennica* 82 (1997), pp. 145–157; R. Irwin, "Futuwwa: Chivalry and Gangsterism in Medieval Cairo", *Muqarnas* 21 (2004), pp. 161–170.

[5] This of course leaves aside some of the major tribal uprisings that were directed

clerks employed in the regime's many administrations, the *kuttāb*, their—especially stipendiary—subordination to that real socio-political elite left them little room for any serious political involvement of their own.[6] Nevertheless, these notables occasionally again became involved, when key administrators (and especially their administrative prerogatives) were at the centre of political conflict in July 1344, February 1346, June 1348, and between December 1352 and February 1353.[7] Additionally, there was the odd influential scholar, like a certain Shams al-Dīn Muḥammad b. ʿAlī b. al-Naqqāsh (1320–1362), whose scholarship made him gain substantial standing and influence with sultan al-Nāṣir Ḥasan (d. 1361).[8] Even they, however, remained largely subordinate to the socio-political intentions and ambitions of the others, motives this intermediate social category had never really been party to. When analysing the socio-political process that took shape between 1341 and 1382, this study will therefore not focus on them either.

Those individuals whose intentions and ambitions were largely responsible for this era's socio-political processes are traditionally grouped in a third category, one that shared a strong military background, an unparalleled coercive force that kept them at the top of society. They were those endowed with military rank and income, many hundreds of amirs and the sultan, who, with their personal military corps, were the dynamic centre of Mamluk military and political affairs, and, in fact, of Mamluk society at large. It has to be acknowledged, however,

---

against the regime's control, necessitating military deployment from Cairo or Aleppo, but not affecting the regime's internal socio-political situation in any distinguishable way (see Garcin, *Qūs*, pp. 382–389; R. Irwin, "Tribal Feuding and Mamluk Factions in Medieval Syria", in Chase F. Robinson (ed.), *Texts, Documents and Artefacts: Islamic Studies in honour of D.S. Richards*, (*Islamic History and Civilization. Studies and Texts* 45), Leiden 2003, pp. 251–264.

[6] See Lapidus, *Muslim Cities*, pp. 3, 44, 59, 77–78, 130–141, 185–191; Chamberlain, *Knowledge and Social Practice*, pp. 38, 40; Staffa, *Conquest and Fusion*, pp. 4–5, 6, 124–126, 386–387, 389; Petry, *The Civilian Elite of Cairo*, pp. 3, 312; Martel-Thoumian, *Les civils et l'administration*, pp. 11–12, 329, 422–429, 434–435; B. Martel-Thoumian, "Les élites urbaines sous les Mamlouks circassiens: quelques éléments de réflexion", in U. Vermeulen & J. Van Steenbergen (eds.), *Egypt and Syria in the Fatimid, Ayyubid and Mamluk Eras, III*, (*Orientalia Lovaniensia Analecta* 102), Leuven 2001, pp. 273–274, 281, 286, 305; J. Berkey, *The Transmission of Knowledge in Medieval Cairo: a Social History of Islamic Education*, Princeton 1992, pp. 13–14; Rabbat, "Representing the Mamluks", pp. 60–61, 66; Shoshan, "The 'Politics of Notables'", pp. 180–181, 183–184, 186, 190.

[7] See al-Maqrīzī, *Sulūk*, II/3, pp. 663–664 (for 1344), 693–694 (for 1346), 760 (for 1348), 882–883 (for 1353).

[8] See e.g. al-Maqrīzī, *Khiṭaṭ*, III, p. 124; al-ʿAynī, *ʿIqd al-Jumān*, p. 129.

that, politically, the vast majority of them, again, hardly achieved anything beyond providing substantial manpower in times of conflict, and that, socially, they lived in a—especially stipendiary—subservient situation that was very comparable to many of the notables.[9] Nevertheless, their position was still different from those notables to the extent that, in principle, each one of them had the potential to rise above that low profile and to enter the socio-political elite of amirs that enjoyed superior political and social status, that is, authority, power, and commensurate wealth.

As already argued above, these military men's political status largely originated from the role they came to play between 1250 and 1260, through their victories over Crusaders and Mongols, when they managed to incorporate the sultanate into their ranks and to safeguard and re-unite Egypt and Syria under their suzerainty.[10] Since their background as mamluks was military in nature, as was the role they came to play after 1250 and the political tradition they inherited, Mamluk politics came to be an exclusively military affair, limited to mamluk amirs in particular. By 1341, however, there had not been any external threats worthy of any large-scale military operations since the last failed Ilkhanid attack against Syria in 1312, and the resultant interregional status-quo was not to change until Timur's invasion in 1400.[11] Under the surface, though, things were not always that stable between 1341 and 1382, resulting in the organisation of a number of military expeditions of varying sizes, against rebellious *nā'ib*s in Syria, against the former sultan Aḥmad in al-Karak between 1342 and 1344, against unruly tribes in Egypt and Syria in the years 1347, 1353–1354, 1359–1360 and 1365–1366, and against the Kingdom

[9] See esp. Chamberlain, *Knowledge and Social Practice*, pp. 92–93.

[10] See e.g. Levanoni, "The Mamluks' Ascent to Power in Egypt", *SI* 72 (1990), pp. 121–144; Irwin, *The Middle East in the Middle Ages*, pp. 26–61; Amitai-Preiss, *Mongols and Mamluks. The Mamluk-Ilkhanid war, 1260–1281*, (*Cambridge Studies in Islamic Civilization*), Cambridge 1995, pp. 48–77.

[11] On these invasions, the interregional calm in between them, and its repercussions on the sultanate, see e.g. P.M. Holt, "Succession in the early Mamluk Sultanate", in E. von Schuler (ed.), *XXII. Deutscher Orientalistentag. Wurzburg 1985: Ausgewahlte Vortrage*, (*Zeitschrift der Deutschen Morgenlandischen Gesellschaft*, Supplement VII), Stuttgart 1989, pp. 144–147; Holt, *The Age of the Crusades*, pp. 110–111, 114–115, 179; Irwin, *The Middle East in the Middle Ages*, pp. 118–121. On that status quo, even called '*pax mamlukia*' see also R.St. Humphreys, "Egypt in the world system of the later Middle Ages", in Petry, *Cambridge History of Egypt. Vol. 1*, pp. 453–454; C.F. Petry, *Protectors or Praetoriansī: The Last Mamluk Sultans and Egypt's Waning as a great Power*, New York 1994, pp. 29–35.

of Lesser Armenia and a Turkmen vassal on Syria's northern frontier in 1360, 1366, 1375 and 1377. These campaigns were, however, mostly erratic, *ad hoc*, and of a rather limited scale, involving a *nā'ib* and his local troops, or a handful of amirs, their mamluks and some auxiliary forces only. Therefore, in the middle of the fourteenth century, many years of absence of any serious military challenge had generally turned the military into a social and political body first and foremost, one that continued, however, to be defined along the same military-institutional lines of sultanate and amirate.

This politicisation, or rather relative demilitarisation, of the social group of amirs—especially the high-ranking elite among them—in the course of the fourteenth century is best reflected in the fact that not just the sultanate, but also the amirs' ranks were opened up to many a non-mamluk, who may have lacked a mamluk's military prowess, but not necessarily his social and political skills.[12] As a result, even these ranks' specific privileges, including dress code, horse riding, acquiring a corps of mamluks and obtaining a highly desirable *iqṭāʿ* income, were no longer the exclusive domain of mamluks. One extreme example of this phenomenon is mentioned by al-Maqrīzī, when he states that sultan al-Ṣāliḥ Ismāʿīl (d. 1345) made one of his palace eunuchs an amir, with "a *khāṣṣakīya*, servants, and mamluks that rode in his service, so that he gained high status [among the regime's senior amirs]".[13] Instead of indicating this eunuch's military, let alone mamluk, status, his endowment with military rank and privilege reflected the considerable degree of social and political success and prestige eunuchs like him had come to enjoy.

One group the military ranks were opened up to, especially in the period between 1341 and 1382, were the mamluks' offspring, the *awlād al-nās*. Not just al-Nāṣir Muḥammad's descendants, but also many a mamluk's scions—even at one instance down to the fourth generation—acquired military rank and income.[14] To some extent, this was linked

---

[12] See Haarmann, "Joseph's Law", pp. 83–84; Haarmann, "The Sons of Mamluks as Fief-holders", pp. 141–145, 162–163; Levanoni, *Turning Point*, pp. 48–52; D.S. Richards, "Mamluk amirs and their families and households", in Th. Philipp & U. Haarmann (eds.), *The Mamluks in Egyptian Politics and Society*, Cambridge 1988, p. 39; J. Van Steenbergen, "Mamluk Elite on the Eve of al-Nāṣir Muḥammad's death (1341): A Look Behind the Scenes of Mamluk Politics", *MSR* 9/2 (2005), pp. 182–183.

[13] Al-Maqrīzī, *Sulūk*, II/3, p. 679; addition in square brackets from Ibn Taghrī Birdī, *Nujūm*, X, p. 97.

[14] The amir Khiḍr b. ʿUmar b. Aḥmad b. Baktamur al-Sāqī was an amir in the

to the second reign of al-Nāṣir Ḥasan (1355–1361), whose predilection for the promotion of *awlād al-nās* is generally acknowledged, by the contemporary sources and in modern historiography alike. Ibn Duqmāq, for instance, remarks that

> [al-Nāṣir Ḥasan] strived to promote *awlād al-nās*. Most of them were promoted during his reign, during which nine of the [. . .] [highest ranking amirs] belonged to the *awlād al-nās* [. . .], while he also made some amirs of forty and ten. [On top of that], he summoned the *awlād al-nās* who had been expelled [from Cairo] back from Syria to Egypt [. . .]. For he used to say: never ever have I heard about a mamluk's son who revolted against the sultan.[15]

Such predilection, however, seems not to have been entirely a novelty, as may be seen from al-Ṣafadī's biographical note on the amir Maliktamur al-Ḥijāzī (d. 1347):

> In the end, he gathered the sons of the amirs around him, to mount with him, dismount in his service, eat from his table and receive his favours and gifts.[16]

Actually, the majority of the period's *awlād al-nās* amirs were indeed promoted well before or after Ḥasan's reign, irrespective of his policies and therefore illustrative of the unrestricted social mobility that characterised fourteenth-century Mamluk society. Their elite status, on the other hand, can be linked to his second reign only.

Another illustration of how demilitarisation and social integration came to be introduced into the Mamluk military ranks may be found in the recurrent appearance of amirs who lacked both mamluk and *awlād al-nās* backgrounds.[17] They included a variety of characters, like leading members from different tribes in Egypt and Syria, local

---

mid-1370s (see Ibn Duqmāq, *Nuzhat al-Anām*, fol. 108; Ibn al-Jīʿān, *al-Tuḥfa*, p. 151). Levanoni states that she counted 257 *awlād al-nās* amirs (Levanoni, *Turning Point*, p. 49), whereas Richards presents a detailed list of 193 *awlād al-nās* amirs for the entire fourteenth century (Richards, "Mamluk amirs", pp. 39, 40–54). My own scrutinising of the sources identified no less than 283 *awlād al-nās* amirs and sultans for the timeframe 1341–1382, against a total of 825 mamluk amirs.

[15] Ibn Duqmāq, *al-Jawhar al-Thamīn*, pp. 404–405; for similar remarks, see al-ʿAynī, *ʿIqd al-Jumān*, pp. 124–125; al-Maqrīzī, *Sulūk*, III/1, p. 63; Ibn Taghrī Birdī, *Nujūm*, X, pp. 309–310, 317). See also Holt, *The Age of the Crusades*, p. 124; Irwin, *The Middle East in the Middle Ages*, p. 143; Haarmann, "Joseph's Law", pp. 67–68; Haarmann, "The Sons of Mamluks as Fief-holders", pp. 145, 162.

[16] Al-Ṣafadī, *Aʿyān*, V, p. 447.

[17] Information on 211 amirs of this third group was recovered for the period between 1341 and 1382. See also Richards, "Mamluk amirs", p. 39.

notables, Mongol refugees, immigrants, and eunuchs, who all managed at some point in their careers to obtain military rank and income. There were for instance the quite successful amirs Badr al-Dīn Masʿūd b. Awḥad b. Masʿūd b. al-Khaṭīr (1285–1353) and his brother Sharaf al-Dīn Maḥmūd (d. 1349), both natives of Damascus,[18] or the high-ranking amir Najm al-Dīn Maḥmūd b. ʿAlī b. Sharwīn al-Baghdādī (d. 1347), who had first served at the Ilkhanid court in Baghdad before fleeing to Mamluk territory and embarking upon a second career.[19]

In short, apart from the majority of mamluks that manned the regime's military ranks and made up its socio-political elite, many others in the period between 1341 and 1382 managed to infiltrate smoothly into those ranks and to acquire equal social and political privileges. This was largely the result of a relative demilitarisation of those ranks, which turned the amirs primarily into a body politic. Because of that unique political status and potential of theirs, and because of the socio-political interaction it engendered, it is the socio-political conduct of this layer of Mamluk society—especially of the high-ranking elite among them—which will be the subject of analysis of this study. But to begin with, after this body politic's stratification, their politico-military institutional framework between 1341 and 1382 will also have to be defined, for throughout this timeframe it not only continued to identify them as a distinct social group but, as will be demonstrated in the next chapter, it equally had a key role to play in the strategies that generated socio-political conduct.

The Sultanate

As the first representative of the regime, its institutional framework, and its power and authority, the Mamluk sultanate had started off as a first-among-equals military institution in the thirteenth century. But very soon, it started to demilitarise—as the amirate did several decades later—, enabling especially non-mamluk scions of sultans to acquire it.[20] More than anything, it therefore came to be a political

[18] For their biographies, see al-Ṣafadī, *Aʿyān*, V, pp. 417–427; al-Ṣafadī, *Wāfī*, XXV, pp. 532–537, 369–370; Ibn Ḥajar, *Durar*, IV, pp. 323, 348.

[19] Al-Ṣafadī, *Aʿyān*, V, pp. 399; al-Ṣafadī, *Wāfī*, XXV, pp. 368–369; Ibn Ḥajar, *Durar*, IV, pp. 331–332.

[20] See e.g. Holt, "Succession in the early Mamluk Sultanate", pp. 144–147; Holt, *The Age of the Crusades*, pp. 114–115.

institution, incarnating authority, government, and the regime, and enabling that regime's justification, legitimisation, and control of society at large by the fact that the indispensable caliphal delegation of power to the Mamluk sultan authorised, as Linda Northrup put it, "the amalgamation of what was perceived to be an Islamic political structure with a military structure whose organisation was not, perhaps, inherently Islamic".[21] The entire institutional framework that was the backbone of the Mamluk regime was, as it were, derived from this legitimate authority of the sultan at its apex. As explained in the introduction, the power and authority generated by this framework is therefore termed 'Legitimate Power', to be distinguished in its institutional character from the divergent power that was generated by socio-political conduct and that will be discussed in the next chapter.

Accession

Throughout the Mamluk regime's existence, succession in this highly politicised and crucial institution remained void of any ordained regulation or custom, and seemed to result in a continuously disturbing tension between principles of heredity among a sultan's kin and usurpation by mamluk amirs.[22] All through the thirteenth and fourteenth centuries, from Barka Khān in 1277 to Faraj in 1399, sheer numbers (irrespective of a general lack of political success) indicate that relatives of a sultan more often succeeded to the throne than so-called usurpers.[23] The years between 1341 and 1382 were a case in point, with the uninterrupted succession of twelve of al-Nāṣir Muḥammad's descendants. While on the one hand this again reflected the demilitarisation of the institution, it is, on the other hand, only on the surface that this could look like the hereditary principle superseding the usurpatory. Despite the fact that designation by a kinsman occurred—as in the case of al-Manṣūr Abū Bakr's accession in

[21] See L.S. Northrup, *From Slave to Sultan: the career of al-Manṣūr Qalāwūn and the consolidation of Mamluk rule in Egypt and Syria (678–689 A.H./1279–1290 A.D.)*, (*Freiburger Islamstudien* 18), Stuttgart 1998, p. 167.

[22] For an overview of academic opinions on the issue, see A. Levanoni, "The Mamluk Conception of the Sultanate", *IJMES* 26 (1994), pp. 373–374.

[23] While no less than twenty of this era's succession cases concerned the accession of a former sultan's kin (involving two sons of Baybars, no less than fourteen scions of Qalāwūn—one of which became sultan three times, and another twice—, and one son of Barqūq), only six unrelated mamluks became sultan (Baybars in 1260, Qalāwūn in 1279, Kitbughā in 1294, Lājīn in 1296, and Baybars II in 1309, and then only seventy years later again Barqūq in 1382).

1341, ordained by his dying father, or of al-Kāmil Shaʿbān's in 1345, designated by his fatally ill brother, and reportedly even of al-Manṣūr ʿAlī's, who was made the heir apparent in 1377 when his father went on pilgrimage—it was not the standard practice, and even then, consent of the socio-political elite remained imperative.[24] That is, accession to the throne was not so much the result of heredity or usurpation, but rather of winning the approval and consent of the socio-political elite of high-ranking amirs.

There actually were quite a few formal accession observances and ceremonials, mainly aimed at public confirmation of the accession, and including the Abbasid caliph's delegation of divine authority, which legitimatised the new sultan's power and authority from a legal-religious and a social point of view.[25] However, a Mamluk sultan's succession was primarily only realised by the army's oath of allegiance, the *bayʿa*, reminiscent of the regime's origins and indicative of the military's key political involvement. Equally indicative of the socio-political elite's central position in this military accession process is the fact that this public oath occasionally came to be reinforced by another, more private and mutual oath between the new sultan and each of the most senior amirs, the *ḥilf*, in which this elite would pledge its support while the sultan had to promise never to harm its interests.[26]

---

[24] For al-Manṣūr Abū Bakr, see Kortantamer, *Mufaḍḍal b. Abī al-Faḍā'il*, pp. 105–106; al-Shujāʿī, *Tārīkh*, pp. 104–105; Zettersteen, *Beiträge*, pp. 222–223; for al-Kāmil Shaʿbān, see Ibn Kathīr, *al-Bidāya*, XIV, p. 216; al-Maqrīzī, *Sulūk*, II/3, p. 680; for al-Manṣūr ʿAlī, see Ibn Khaldūn, *Kitāb al-ʿIbar*, V, p. 463; al-Maqrīzī, *Sulūk*, III/1, p. 274 (though this equally may have been a *hindsight* addition by Ibn Khaldūn and al-Maqrīzī, who are the only chroniclers to refer to this designation).

[25] See P.M. Holt, "The Structure of Government in the Mamluk Sultanate", in P.M. Holt (ed.), *Eastern Mediterranean Lands in the Period of the Crusades*, p. 46; P.M. Holt, "The Position and Power of the Mamluk Sultanate", *BSOAS* 38 (1975), pp. 241–245; Northrup, *From Slave to Sultan*, pp. 166–167; Brinner, "The Struggle for Power in the Mamluk State", p. 231.

[26] Holt, "Position and Power", pp. 238, 241–242; Holt, "The Structure of Government", p. 46; Irwin, *The Middle East*, pp. 86, 129; Chapoutot—Remadi, *Liens et Relations*, pp. 87; E. Tyan, "Bayʿa", *EI*², I, pp. 1113–1114; E. Tyan, "Ḥilf", *EI*², III, pp. 388–389. An example of a *bayʿa* from the 14th century may be found in al-ʿUmarī's manual (see al-ʿUmarī. *at-Taʿrīf*, pp. 186–190; also al-Qalqashandī, *Ṣubḥ*, XIII, pp. 216–220): its text runs very parallel with an incomplete copy of such a *bayʿa*, sworn to al-Nāṣir Aḥmad in February 1342 and mentioned by al-Shujāʿī (al-Shujāʿī, *Tārīkh*, pp. 197–199). For references to mutual oaths with sultans, most notably in the case of the accession of al-Ṣāliḥ Ismāʿīl in 1342, of al-Kāmil Shaʿbān in 1345, of al-Muẓaffar Ḥājjī in 1346 and of al-Ṣāliḥ Ṣāliḥ in 1351, see al-Shujāʿī, *Tārīkh*, p. 229; al-Maqrīzī, *Sulūk*, II/3, pp. 619, 681, 714, 843.

As stated, sheer numbers clearly indicate that up to the end of the fourteenth century, this consent was more likely to favour the preceding sultan's kin than any usurper. Undoubtedly, such an attitude resulted first and foremost from a genuine conservative hope for stability, continuity and the upkeep of a favourable *status-quo* among the majority of those high-ranking amirs. Between 1341 and 1382, at first eight of al-Nāṣir Muḥammad's sons succeeded him on the Mamluk throne. Though they were all quite young adolescents upon enthronement, it is actually faintly indicative of the involvement of some sort of respect for al-Nāṣir Muḥammad's and his father's posthumous authority and for the longevity of their legacy that—apart from the infant al-Ashraf Kujuk in 1341—time and again the most serious candidate for succession, that is, one of the eldest available of those sons, seems to have been the object of that consent.[27] But after twenty years, in 1361, with the accession of the next generation in the person of al-Manṣūr Muḥammad b. Ḥājjī b. Muḥammad b. Qalāwūn, this line of practice was finally abandoned. Though the following account of the deliberations after al-Nāṣir Ḥasan's murder in 1361 is of a doubtful veracity, it remains insightful by highlighting the change that thus took place:

> [The high-ranking amirs] discussed who should be appointed in the office of sultan; some of them mentioned the amir Ḥusayn b. Muḥammad b. Qalāwūn, the last remaining of al-Malik al-Nāṣir Muḥammad's sons. But they did not agree on him out of fear that he might take the rule in his own hands, without them. Then, none of them was left. The amir Aḥmad, son of sultan Ḥasan, was mentioned. Nevertheless, they thought that proposing him—after what had happened to his father—would be wrong, since the situation urged him to take revenge for his father. So they discarded him, and agreement was reached on Muḥammad, the son of the [belated] sultan al-Muẓaffar Ḥājjī.[28]

Unlike their politically far more active predecessors, these later Qalawunids—two grandsons and two great-grandsons of al-Nāṣir Muḥammad, all mere infants upon accession apart from the young adolescent al-Manṣūr Muḥammad (ca. 1347–1398)—only came to be tolerated as a mute façade of Legitimate Power. If it were not for the rather unexpected success of al-Ashraf Shaʿbān's reign, from 1363 to 1377, their end would arguably already have been anticipated in

---

[27] See Appendix 1 for details of their age.
[28] Al-Maqrīzī, *Sulūk*, III/1, p. 64.

1361. As it happened, however, it only came in 1382, after the final degeneration of the protracted Qalawunid sultanate in the reign of two infant puppets, when al-ʿAynī quite tellingly could make Barqūq announce that

> our time is in need of a mature sultan, who can speak and reply, who can handle both the tongue and the sword, and [who is able] to understand and to be understood.[29]

In short, between 1341 and 1382, a combination of factors, like a genuine conservatism and concern for established interests—to be elaborated in the next chapter—, Qalawunid reverence, and, especially after 1361, custom and the lapse of many decades since the installation of a non-Qalawunid, all meant that the Mamluk military's sworn consent time and again came to rest with the descendants of al-Nāṣir Muḥammad b. Qalāwūn.

Prerogatives

In theory, the sultan's Legitimate Power was to ensure the overall maintenance of the law and order that guaranteed his subjects' security, welfare and wellbeing.[30] For the execution of that vast responsibility, albeit under a more realistic disguise of the realm's daily government, an institutional framework was attached to the sultan's person. This elaborate framework of supporters had responsibilities and authorities that emanated from the sultan's prerogatives and therefore derived its legitimacy from the sultan's. Since these prerogatives were both of a military and a governmental character—well-captured by Barqūq's reference above to a sultan's handling of 'both the tongue and the sword'—the institutional framework emanating from them similarly consisted of the army, including the military ranks populated by the social layer of amirs, which had to secure law, order and security, and of a military, civil and legal administration that managed the sultan's household, administered his government, handled his and

[29] Al-ʿAynī, *ʿIqd al-Jumān*, pp. 278–279.

[30] Some sultanic memoranda and the text of the *bayʿa* hint at this perception—at least in theory—of the sultanate, see e.g. L. Fernandes, "On Conducting the Affairs of the State: a Guideline of the Fourteenth Century", *AI* 24 (1988), pp. 81–91; Cl. Cahen & I. Chabbouh, "Le testament d'al-Malik as-Ṣāliḥ Ayyūb", *Bulletin d'Études Orientales* 29 (1977), pp. 97–114; al-ʿUmarī, *al-Taʿrīf*, pp. 186–190; al-Qalqashandī, *Ṣubḥ*, XIII, pp. 216–220.

his army's finances, and coordinated legal-religious life throughout Mamluk society.

As noted above, the sultan's military prerogative as chief-commander of his army—at the core of which were his personal mamluks and his amirs—was hardly ever put into practice in the period between 1341 and 1382, through the lack of any external threats worthy of any large-scale military operations ever since the last failed Ilkhanid invasion of Syria in 1312.[31] Similarly, regarding internal affairs, the sultan himself only had to perform twice as chief-in-command, in 1352 and in 1361, and lead the Egyptian Mamluk army when it marched against a rebellious amir in Damascus. On both occasions, the military force thus displayed proved sufficient to abort the rebellion and prevented a major confrontation.[32] So, though the military aspect of the sultan's prerogatives continued to be important, it did not constitute the essence of his, nor of his army's function anymore. Therefore, the socio-political facet that was built into the military institution which had always defined the Mamluk sultanate, became far more essential: the sultan's absolute control of the access to the amirate. Since the army belonged to the sultan, his was the only authority to decide on its organisation, and the bestowal of military rank and income within his army—primarily to the amirs—could only be achieved through his personal authorisation.[33] As a military commander-in-chief, the sultan's main prerogative had come to be the promotion rather than the mobilisation of his amirs.

---

[31] On this invasion and the subsequent regional calm, see e.g. Irwin, *The Middle East in the Middle Ages*, pp. 118–121.

[32] For the major source material on these episodes of Mamluk military history, see Ibn al-Wardī, *Tatimmat al-Mukhtaṣar*, pp. 500, 512; al-Shujāʿī, *Tārīkh*, p. 226, 239, 245–247, 248, 254, 258–259, 264–265, 269; al-Ḥusaynī, *Dhayl al-ʿIbar*, pp. 128–134, 159, 185, 189–191; al-Kutubī, *ʿUyūn al-Tawārīkh*, fol. 57v, 63, 69v, 83v–84126v–130, 136v–137, 171–171v; Ibn Kathīr, *al-Bidāya*, XIV, pp. 201, 203, 204, 205, 207–208, 209, 212–213, 222–223, 243–246, 266–267, 271, 272, 280–287, 314, 319; Ibn Ḥabīb, *Tadkhirat al-Nabīh*, III, pp. 158–164, 230–231, 241, 294; Ibn Duqmāq, *Nuzhat al-Anām*, fol. 87–87v; Ibn al-Shihna, *Rawḍat al-Manāẓir*, p. 131v, 133, 134; Ibn al-ʿIrāqī, *Dhayl al-ʿIbar*, I, p. 191; II, p. 133; al-ʿAynī, *ʿIqd al-Jumān*, pp. 71, 95–97, 100–101, 118–119, 123, 137–138, 139, 181–182, 238–239, 240–242; al-Maqrīzī, *Sulūk*, II/3, pp. 624–625, 628, 632, 634, 638, 645, 646, 648, 650, 652, 654, 657, 660, 661, 709–710, 711, 732, 748–750, 752, 867–872, 896–902, 907–915; III/1, pp. 50, 66–68, 104–105, 107, 110–112, 113, 120, 237–238, 335–336, 347–348; Ibn Ḥajar, *Inbāʾ al-Ghumr*, I, pp. 97–98, 268, 273, 275–276, 287.

[33] Holt, "The Structure of Government", pp. 47–48; Holt, "Position and Power", pp. 246–247.

As for his governmental prerogatives, by which he ruled and managed his business, including policing the urban centres, managing the provinces and districts, safeguarding his regime's economic welfare, and redressing social, legal and administrative wrongs, the sultan again was at the apex of an elaborate army of executive and administrative assistants. And the main prerogative which he himself retained within this governmental framework and which ensured its continued centralisation around his person, was the fact that all governmental decisions of some value had to be authorised by him personally. After any governmental decision was taken, it had to pass through an administrative process that eventually resulted in the production of a diploma in the sultan's chancery, on which the sultan's signature was an indispensable legitimating factor. Hence, the involvement of the sultan's Legitimate Power remained essential for the administrative confirmation of promotions to military rank, for the authorisation of appointments of amirs in that governmental framework, and for the assignment of financial rewards for military and administrative services subsequently rendered anywhere in the realm.[34]

Illustrative of this central importance of the sultan's signature in Mamluk governmental practice is the oft-quoted case of the infant sultan al-Ashraf Kujuk (1337–1345), who was enthroned in August 1341. Despite the fact that this sultan was a minor and therefore strictly speaking legally incompetent, the following rather artificial but insightful situation is supposed to have solved the primarily practical problem of the sultan's young age:

> when the signature was needed, Qawṣūn gave al-Ashraf Kujuk a pen in his hand and the tutor, who would read the Qur'an to him, would come to write the signature, while the pen was in the hand of al-Ashraf Kujuk.[35]

Whoever the sultan, his institutional position was a crucial cog in the Mamluk government machinery.

---

[34] See al-ʿUmarī, *Masālik*, pp. 59–61; al-Qalqashandī, *Ṣubḥ*, IV, pp. 30–31, 190, 220; XI, p. 321; al-Ẓāhirī, *Zubda*, pp. 102–103. See also Gaudefroy-Demombynes, *La Syrie*, pp. 155–156; Björkman, *Beiträge zur Geschichte der Staatskanzlei*, pp. 49–51; Holt, 'The Structure of Government", pp. 48, 57–58; Holt, "Position and Power", p. 247; Nielsen, *Secular Justice*, p. 80; Chapoutot-Remadi, *Liens et Relations*, pp. 79–83, 115–117; Levanoni, "The Mamluk Conception", pp. 374–377; Northrup, *From Slave to Sultan*, p. 172; Fernandes, "On Conducting the Affairs of the State", pp. 81–91.

[35] Ibn Taghrī Birdī, *Nujūm*, X, p. 49; similar in al-Maqrīzī, *Sulūk*, II/3, p. 593; also mentioned in Holt, "The Structure of Government", p. 48.

Nevertheless, this crucial governmental prerogative, which meant that no major decision could be taken without the sultan's written consent, was no absolute guarantee for unchallenged authority, especially not in the years between 1341 and 1382. Very often, the sociopolitical elite's involvement in the enthronement of the Qalawunids did not end with the registration of their consent, but continued in their dominance over the new sultan and in the curtailment of his prerogatives, as Qawṣūn did to the little Kujuk in the above example. In fact, the period has become known for this feature both in modern historiography and in the contemporary sources. Al-ʿAynī, for instance, declared at the beginning of al-Ṣāliḥ Ṣāliḥ's reign, in August 1351, that "the authority came to the amir Sayf al-Dīn Ṭāz, while the name was for al-Malik al-Ṣāliḥ Ṣāliḥ".[36] And Ibn Taghrī Birdī characterised the reign of al-Manṣūr ʿAlī, between 1377 and 1381, in a very similar vein:

> During his sultanate, he only had the name; the authority over the realm during his sultanate first came to Qaraṭāy, and eventually to Barqūq; he was as a tool to them, because of his minority and because of their dominance of the sovereignty.'[37]

There are a few more source references like these to a Qalawunid sultan who has nominal, that is, titular, authority only, especially for the reign of the aforementioned little al-Ashraf Kujuk in 1341, as well as for those of al-Muẓaffar Ḥājjī and al-Nāṣir Ḥasan between 1347 and 1351, and for the sultanate of al-Manṣūr Muḥammad between 1361 and 1363.[38] And while some, the youngsters in particular, bore the elite's yoke without a grudge worthy of recording, others were more reluctant to accept that practical subordination. As a result and—parallel to the period's accession practices—between 1341 and 1361 in particular, sultans like al-Manṣūr Abū Bakr, al-Nāṣir Aḥmad, al-Kāmil Shaʿbān, al-Muẓaffar Ḥājjī and al-Nāṣir

[36] Al-ʿAynī, *ʿIqd al-Jumān*, p. 93; similar comment in Ibn Taghrī Birdī, *Nujūm*, X, p. 287. In this vein, Brinner concludes that "during much of the 90-year period of the house of Qala'un (*sic*) the sultan was as much of a shadow ruler or puppet figure as was the caliph." (Brinner, "The Struggle for Power in the Mamluk State", p. 232).

[37] Ibn Taghrī Birdī, *Nujūm*, XI, p. 188; similar comments in al-Maqrīzī, *Khiṭaṭ*, III, p. 391; Ibn Ḥajar, *Inbāʾ al-Ghumr*, II, p. 45; Ibn Qāḍī Shuhba, *Tārīkh*, I, p. 74.

[38] See Ibn Khaldūn, *Kitāb al-ʿIbar*, V, p. 450, 471; al-Maqrīzī, *Sulūk*, II/3, p. 842; III/1, p. 65; Ibn Taghrī Birdī, *Nujūm*, X, pp. 232–233; Ibn Qāḍī Shuhba, *Tārīkh*, II, p. 280.

Ḥasan tried to escape that dependency, but, instead, they lost the elite's consent and, eventually, even their nominal authority. After 1361, when the Qalawunid sultanate's end was near, such deliberate attempts were no longer repeated. Only al-Ashraf Shaʿbān managed to defeat his destiny in 1366, but this was rather the pleasant but unexpected result of an act of self-defence against the destructive behaviour of unruly mamluks than the getaway of a frustrated ruler.[39] The sultan's independent performance of his Legitimate Power was especially not guaranteed in the face of a strong elite, even in spite of the very powerful potential a Mamluk sultan was offered through his position's military and governmental prerogatives.

Finances

To provide for his wide-ranging personal, military and governmental needs, the Mamluk sultan had financial means at his disposal that originated mainly from rents and taxes that were levied on his realm's cultivable lands and that were systematically divided—under his constant close administrative supervision—between himself and the amirs. The majority of the land was involved in this fiscal division, and since the last cadastral reforms of 1313 to 1325 no less than five twelfths of that land had been assigned to the sultan's financial administration, the fisc or *khāṣṣ*, to cover the necessary expenses of maintaining his household and administration, of his personal mamluks, and of his public relations.[40]

Information on the actual income that came into the sultan's fisc was extremely rare. For the year 1344, sources present the not unproblematic figure of 15 million *dirhams* as that year's income for the fisc, revealing an anguishing shortage in the expenditure, since this would have suspiciously totalled the exact double of that amount.[41]

[39] See Appendix 3, nos. 3, 9, 17–19, 23, 32, 41, 47–49, 55–56.

[40] See e.g. H. Rabie, *The Financial System of Egypt, A.H. 564–741/A.D. 1169–1341*, pp. 47–49; H. Halm, *Ägypten nach den mamlukischen Lehensregistern. I: Oberägypten und das Fayyum*, (*Beiheft zum Tübinger Atlas des Vorderen Orients, Reihe B (Geisteswissenschaften)* 38/1), Wiesbaden 1979, pp. 8, 37–42, 43–54; Sato, "The Evolution of the *Iqṭāʿ* System", p. 123; Sato, *State and Rural Society*, pp. 135–161, 234–239. For details on monthly payments to the sultanic mamluks and—in cash and kind—on very specific occasions to the army and the administration, to confirm the position and legitimacy of the sultan, as an act of public relations, as it were, see D. Ayalon, "The System of Payment in Mamluk Military Society", *JESHO* 1 (1958), pp. 37–65, 257–296.

[41] Al-Shujāʿī, *Tārīkh*, p. 272; al-Maqrīzī, *Sulūk*, II/3, p. 665.

More reliable and informative is the only other surviving piece of information: a fifteenth-century survey of Egypt, the *Tuḥfa al-Saniya*, which includes a large amount of data from official tax registers for the fiscal year 1375–1376.[42] According to this register, most of the tax income that the fisc and the sultan al-Ashraf Shaʿbān personally acquired during this specific year came to about six-hundred thousand *dīnār jayshī*.[43] Moreover, the register also mentions an undefined group of the sultan's mamluks as the direct recipients of about two hundred thousand *dīnār jayshī*, suggesting that, though otherwise stipulated in the reforms of 1313–1325, by the 1370s not all of these mamluks were paid from the fisc anymore.[44] And finally, the register mentions many of Shaʿbān's sons and brothers as the direct beneficiaries of fiscal income, mostly remarkably unlinked to any clear military rank or service, and amounting to the astonishing amount of more than seven hundred thousand *dīnār jayshī* for that particular fiscal year.[45] As a result, al-Ashraf Shaʿbān obviously had managed to lay his hands on a little more than sixteen percent of the regime's fiscal income, in a puzzling combination with his direct family.[46] Lack of comparative material makes it impossible to put these figures in a

---

[42] Ibn al-Jīʿān, *Kitāb al-Tuḥfa al-Saniya bi-asmāʾ al-bilād al-Miṣrīya*, B. Moritz (ed.), (*Publications de la Bibliothèque Khèdiviale* 10), Cairo 1898; for a detailed study of the work and its data, see H. Halm, *Ägypten nach den mamlukischen Lehensregistern. I: Oberägypten und das Fayyum*, (*Beiheft zum Tübinger Atlas des Vorderen Orients, Reihe B (Geisteswissenschaften)* 38/1), Wiesbaden 1979; H. Halm, *Ägypten nach den mamlukischen Lehensregistern. II: Das Delta*, (*Beiheft zum Tübinger Atlas des Vorderen Orients, Reihe B (Geisteswissenschaften)* 38/2), Wiesbaden 1982.

[43] The exact amount was 616,075 *dīnār jayshī* (Ibn al-Jīʿān, *al-Tuḥfa al-Saniya*, pp. 6, 7, 8, 9, 10, 12, 31, 35, 47, 54, 70, 73, 81, 92, 99, 114, 117, 124, 136, 138, 139, 140, 141, 142, 143, 144, 146, 147, 151, 152, 153, 154, 155, 156, 157, 158, 160, 164, 166, 168, 173, 176, 177, 180 181, 182, 186, 187, 190, 191, 193, 195. On the *dīnār jayshī*, a unit of account to calculate and express the fiscal value of an estate, see Sato, "The Evolution of the *Iqṭāʿ* System", pp. 119–120; Sato, *State and Rural Society*, pp. 152–155; St.J. Borsch, *The Black Death in Egypt and England. A Comparative Study*, Austin 2005, pp. 69–73.

[44] The exact amount was 210,120 *dīnār jayshī* (Ibn al-Jīʿān, *al-Tuḥfa al-Saniya*, pp. 8, 9, 10, 11, 12, 13, 14, 15, 16, 37; U. Haarmann, "The Sons of Mamluks", pp. 148–150). On the payment of the sultan's mamluks from the sultan's fisc, see Sato, "The Evolution of the *Iqṭāʿ* System", pp. 111, 114; Sato, *State and Rural Society*, p. 143.

[45] The exact amount was 708,320 *dīnār jayshī* (Ibn al-Jīʿān, *al-Tuḥfa al-Saniya*, pp. 7, 13–14, 25, 30, 35, 59, 69, 70, 75, 76, 79, 81, 90, 96, 103, 107, 112, 113, 117, 139, 147, 148, 150, 151, 157, 159, 163, 166, 171, 173, 176, 178, 179, 181, 187, 191, 194; U. Haarmann, "The Sons of Mamluks", pp. 152–158, 163).

[46] The total revenue would have been 9,584,264 *dīnār jayshī* (Ibn al-Jīʿān, *al-Tuḥfa al-Saniya*, p. 3), whereas the sultan's environment's added-up share was 1,534,515 *dīnār jayshī*.

correct historical perspective. However, at least one interesting insight is obtained when it is realised that sixteen percent hardly represents two twelfths of Egypt's annual tax revenue, whereas sixty years earlier al-Nāṣir Muḥammad had been entitled to more than double that amount. This modest share in the regime's welfare, therefore, and the fact that Shaʿbān—politically undoubtedly the most successful of all later Qalawunids—still needed quite awkward constructions to acquire it, seem to indicate that, since 1341, not just the sultan but also his finances had gone through troubled times.[47]

This is actually confirmed from information in the chronicles on the fisc's institutional history between 1341 and 1382. As with his accession and prerogatives, the sultan's fisc and finances are also portrayed as becoming an area of fierce combat in his relations with the socio-political elite. Though in principle, the fisc's bureau, the *dīwān al-khāṣṣ*, like all other governmental matters, should be under the sultan's direct control, bad financial management and political weakness had made this difficult to maintain. Successive sultans still managed to retain their control until 1347, but with increasing difficulty. Especially when the inflationary demands of the harems of al-Ṣāliḥ Ismāʿīl, al-Kāmil Shaʿbān and al-Muẓaffar Ḥājjī combined with the bad harvests of the mid-1340s, these sultans' unsuccessful attempts to overcome the subsequent financial problems—through short-lived cuts in the household's expenses, the implementation of new taxes, and the institutionalisation of corruption by the establishment of a venalities' bureau, the *dīwān al-badhl*, designed to gain profit from the sale of offices—resulted, in December 1347, in Ḥājjī's successor's loss of any direct control of the fisc.[48] This preadolescent boy Ḥasan had to forsake the actual performance of his prerogatives, including the management of his own finances, and instead he was

[47] For a more positive view, see Haarmann, "The Sons of Mamluks", pp. 154, 163 ('The Bahri state, even in its frail last decade [. . .], had been solidly built on a disproportionate share of the house of Qalāwūn in the wealth of Egypt'). Reservations need to be made on any too foregone conclusion, though, since Ibn al-Jīʿān's lists did not include the fisc's revenue from the Giza district and presented information on Egypt alone (Ibn al-Jīʿān, *al-Tuḥfa al-Saniya*, p. 3).

[48] See e.g. al-Shujāʿī, *Tārīkh*, p. 272; al-Kutubī, *ʿUyūn al-Tawārīkh*, fol. 81v; al-Ṣafadī, *Aʿyān*, I, p. 543; al-Maqrīzī, *Sulūk*, II/3, pp. 626, 665, 667, 671, 672, 678–680, 684, 685, 687, 689, 690, 693–694, 695–696, 701, 703–704, 713, 715, 720–721, 722, 724, 725–726, 738, 739–741, 745, 746. See also Ayalon, "Studies", pp. 453–454, 475.

only granted a minimal daily stipend, the *nafaqat al-sulṭān*. Henceforth, the fisc was to remain in the hands of the socio-political elite, the amir Shaykhū in particular, until the latter's murder ten years later, in 1357, when Ḥasan finally managed to take financial matters into his own hand.[49] But as had happened to his brothers before, his own financial management was disastrous and his unlimited expenditure soon posed problems that were serious enough to lead to new conflicts with the elite.[50] After Ḥasan's murder in 1361, therefore, and again parallel to the degeneration of the Qalawunid sultanate, references to such conflicts disappear from the sources, suggesting these later Qalawunids' complete subordination, even financially, to the socio-political elite. And this course of events was only temporarily tempered by Shaʿbān's financial policies, since, after 1377, al-Manṣūr ʿAlī is again reported to have received a daily stipend only.[51] As with all the sultan's prerogatives that technically should provide him with a potent source for strong Legitimate Power, even his control of his financial income was not guaranteed. Especially in the decade after 1347, therefore, and after 1377, if not earlier, the fisc, like the sultanate as a whole, was left to the control of others.

The Amirate

As detailed at the beginning of this chapter, these others were mainly distinguished from the rest of Mamluk society by the fact that they held a considerable military rank, which always brought lucrative military income and relative economic welfare, if not riches, and which occasionally gave access to a military office. As with the institution of the sultanate, therefore, this aspect of Legitimate Power, this framework of identification and domination, and its development between 1341 and 1382, equally needs to be presented before any proper analysis of the conduct of those that were identified by it can be undertaken.

---

[49] See e.g. al-Maqrīzī, *Sulūk*, II/3, pp. 750–751, 842. See also Levanoni, "The Mamluk Conception", p. 383.

[50] See e.g. Ibn Kathīr, *al-Bidāya*, XIV, p. 274; al-Maqrīzī, *Sulūk*, II/3, pp. 760, 860.

[51] See al-Maqrīzī, *Sulūk*, III/1, p. 412.

Military Rank

The command structure and military organisation of the core of the Mamluk army became fully fledged only towards the end of the thirteenth century.[52] Only then did it complete its evolution towards a three-tiered hierarchy of ranks, which was geared towards the rendering of military service, and in which each rank corresponded with the command and responsibility over a specific number of mamluks. As demonstrated above, these ranks and access to them were in the hands of the sultan alone, since they all had emerged from his prerogatives of Legitimate Power. In fact, the institution of the Mamluk sultanate essentially was a military rank itself, at the apex of this military structure, because, just like every amir, the sultan had to have a corps of mamluks of his own, which, however, was to exceed by far the number of any amir's mamluks. And conversely, from that institutional perspective, it may equally be argued that each of the amirs in fact was to become a miniature sultan in his own right, with his own different categories of mamluks, who were as reliant on his authority as he himself, his colleagues and the sultan's mamluks depended on the decreeing authority of the sultanate.

The lowest military rank that was of any socio-political significance was that of an amir of ten, *amīr ʿashara*, who had ten to twenty mamluks in his service. Second in line was the amir of forty, in charge of forty to eighty mamluks and called *amīr ṭablakhānāh* because, as a symbol of social status, from this rank onwards an amir was entitled to his own orchestra, the *ṭablakhānāh*. Thirdly, there was the highest military rank of an amir of a hundred, *amīr miʾa*, entitled to a personal corps of at least a hundred mamluks, and also called *muqaddam alf*, commander of a thousand auxiliary forces, in times of military need.

---

[52] The standard study of the Mamluk's military organisation to date remains D. Ayalon, "Studies on the Structure of the Mamluk Army", *BSOAS* 15 (1953), pp. 203–228, 448–476; 16 (1954), pp. 57–90. On its early organisation, see Northrup, *From Slave to Sultan*, pp. 192–194 (where she refers to the existence of four rather than three ranks under Qalāwūn). For the source material that provides the information on what these ranks should have looked like, see al-ʿUmarī, *Taʿrīf*, pp. 102–104; al-ʿUmarī, *Masālik*, pp. 27, 28; al-Qalqashandī, *Ṣubḥ*, IV, pp. 14, 15–16, 182, 233, 237, 240, 241; VII, pp. 158, 159; XII, p. 195; al-Maqrīzī, *Khiṭaṭ*, III, pp. 350, 353–354; al-Ẓāhirī, *Zubda*, pp. 113, 115–116, 131, 133, 134; Ibn al-Shihna, *al-Durr al-Muntakhab*, p. 248.

Parallel to this crystallisation into three ranks, the evolution of Mamluk military hierarchy also created within each one of them an extra internal distinction, inherited from the corps of the sultan's mamluks from which this ranking system had originated. This was the more emotional distinction, among the sultan's mamluks and throughout the military ranks, between those that belonged to the *khāṣṣakīya*, the sultan's favourites, and those who did not, the *barrānīya* or *khārijīya*.

In fourteenth-century Egypt, the number of high-ranking amirs of a hundred was said to have been limited to a theoretical maximum of twenty-four, eight of whom were supposed to have been *khāṣṣakīya*. There are no such specific limits known for the two lower ranks, though al-Maqrīzī claims that around 1315, their number in Egypt had been fixed to two hundred and fourteen amirs of forty—including fifty-four *khāṣṣakīya* amirs—and two hundred and seven amirs of ten—including thirty *khāṣṣakīya* amirs. The later administrative manual by al-Ẓāhirī, however, claims that their respective numbers were forty and fifty only.

In each of the seven major districts that made up fourteenth-century Mamluk Syria, similar military command structures had been set up, though only under the wings of the local governors, and in far fewer numbers. In Damascus, for instance, there were supposed to have been a dozen amirs of a hundred, in Aleppo between six and eight, in each of Tripoli and Safad only one, and none at all in Hama, al-Karak and Gazza.

The administrative manual of al-Qalqashandī, written in the early fifteenth century, claims that Egypt's fixed arrangement of twenty-four high-ranking amirs remained in practice until the very end of al-Ashraf Shaʿbān's reign, only to drop below twenty after 1382.[53] Other source material makes it seem very plausible, however, to assume that this process of numerical decline actually had started well before the end of Shaʿbān's sultanate in 1377. The tax registers of Ibn al-Jīʿān, for instance, do not just mention the sultan and his fisc, but they also list the names of many others that lived off those taxes in the fiscal year between 1375–1376, and in that way, they actually offer a comprehensive insight into the composition of the military ranks towards the end of Shaʿbān's reign. In these lists, a surprising total of no more than eighty-four amirs were listed in Egypt, and only

[53] Al-Qalqashandī, *Ṣubḥ*, IV, p. 14.

seventeen of them can be identified as belonging to the elite of amirs of a hundred. Apart from the discrepancy with al-Qalqashandī's ideal numbers, these figures also indicate that by the 1370s, the amirs' numbers show such a steep decline in only sixty years time—from more than four hundred in 1315 according to al-Maqrīzī to less than a hundred in Ibn al-Jīʿān's tax register lists—that this almost seems too dramatic to have remained unnoticed by contemporary authors. Most probably, the truth was somewhere in between, and especially al-Maqrīzī's 1315 numbers should be reconsidered. What these figures do point to, though, is that by the end of the Qalawunid era, there were less amirs' ranks to be conferred than before, and that this process of decline, which affected all ranks, including the amirs of a hundred, had started well before 1377. In fact, when the entire group of amir's ranks bestowed between 1341 and 1382 is considered, it seems that standards of al-Nāṣir Muḥammad's reign for that highest rank in particular were only kept until 1347, the final year to leave a record of twenty-four amirs of a hundred. And it is tempting to link this evolution to the effects of fourteenth-century pestilence, plague and rural unrest, and their negative impacts on the rural income upon which these ranks depended, but there is, unfortunately, too little information available to corroborate such a hypothesis.[54]

It has been argued that the second half of the fourteenth century witnessed a growing tendency to discard the career pathway of gradual promotion this hierarchy of ranks had come to impose.[55] This view generally follows al-Maqrīzī's assertion that, after 1377,

> there were promotions of the lowest, that should be a warning for the wise, because the junior mamluks whom hardly anything was reported about yesterday [. . .] became rulers.[56]

When fourteenth-century amirs' careers are actually reconstructed, however, it appears that serious exceptions to a career pathway that respected the hierarchy of military ranks can only be observed for

---

[54] For a recent analysis of the devastating impact of the plague, claiming that 'the ruin of Egypt's agricultural system was [. . .] the product of an exogenous shock (plague depopulation) applied to a socioeconomic system of landholding that was disastrously unable to deal with this kind of crisis", see St.J. Bosch, *The Black Death in Egypt and England. A Comparative Study*, Austin 2005, quotation from p. 54.

[55] See e.g. Levanoni, *Turning Point*, pp. 120–124.

[56] Al-Maqrīzī, *Sulūk*, III/1, p. 289.

three different and unrelated years—1346, and especially 1366 and 1377. References to sudden and unexpected career jumps only occur for these three years, resulting in the promotion 'in one stroke' of three amirs of ten and ten rank-and-file mamluks to the highest rank of amir of a hundred.[57] Apart from these thirteen cases, no such similar aberrations among the high-ranking amirs are found. In general, therefore, conservatism was the predominant attitude also with respect to the ranking system. High ranks in particular were not lightly conferred, and this was undoubtedly as much due to their increasing military and socio-political weight as to their limited number. It was undeniably also necessitated by an amir's expensive and time-consuming obligation to provide for a proper mamluk corps of his own. Even Barqūq, who became an amir of a hundred only two months after he had entered the military ranks, did so from the rank of amir of forty.[58]

As suggested by the example of Barqūq, and in spite of that general attitude of conservatism and institutional respect, changes in the ranks, that is, promotions to higher rank and their opposite, did figure prominently in the period's sources. When they are scrutinised from that perspective, clearly identifiable moments of major military-institutional change even pop up, moments in which the socio-political scene of amirs underwent serious transformations within a limited period of time. In Egypt, for instance, between 1341 and 1343, no less than one hundred and twenty-four amirs are recorded to have started in a new military rank, including eighty-eight between 1341 and 1342. In the year between 1365 and 1366 there were sixty-six such amirs recorded, whereas the period between 1375 and 1378 is claimed to have witnessed no less than two hundred and eighteen bestowments of military rank, including ninety-four between 1375 and 1376, and ninety in the year between 1376 and 1377.[59] Undeniably, several methodological problems discredit the possibility of making firm conclusions in this respect. In particular the nature and diversity

---

[57] See e.g. Ibn Duqmāq, *Nuzhat al-Anām*, fol, 5v–6, 108v–110v, 111; al-Maqrīzī, *Sulūk*, II/3, p. 705, 721; III/1, pp. 139, 144, 287–288; Ibn Qāḍī Shuhba, *Tārīkh*, III, p. 514.

[58] See Appendix 2.

[59] Information on Syria was unfortunately too diverse and limited to allow for similar observations, though there are some indications that more than usual changes took place in the years between 1341 and 1342, in 1352, between 1360 and 1361 and between 1378 and 1379.

of the material which the sources provide for these different dates remain to be taken into consideration, including the occasionally lengthy and remarkably detailed lists of promotions that pop up in several of the sources' reports of post-1365 events.[60] Nevertheless, even despite these setbacks, the general impression remains that from time to time, the military ranks were hit by sweeping changes that will be the subject of further analysis in the next chapter.

In short, closely linked to the sultanate, which controlled the access to the amirate and to which an amir owed military service, the amirate was institutionally as dependent on the sultanate as the sultanate was on his army and elite. In the years between 1341 and 1382, this Mamluk military command structure, that gave an institutional frame to the body politic, offered on the one hand a clearly tiered and conservatively respected pathway of promotion, but was, on the other, also subject to occasionally sweeping changes, that generated substantial transformations among the regime's staff.

Military Office

The sultan and his Legitimate Power commissioned many an amir with duties and responsibilities that went beyond military service. The military offices that institutionally gave shape to these duties and responsibilities and that were the exclusive domain of the amirs—the men of the sword, *arbāb al-suyūf*, of Mamluk administrative manuals[61]—can be grouped into two different categories. On the one hand, there were those offices that were entrusted with executive authority in specific territories throughout the Mamluk realm. On the other, there were other offices that managed elements of the sultan's court and therefore remained in his proximity in the Cairo citadel.

The first category, the executive offices, primarily concern the sultan's representatives who, within certain geographical limits, enacted his Legitimate Power and were given major responsibilities with respect to their territories' political, economic, social, judicial and military welfare. They were viceroys, governors and their subordi-

[60] See for 1366, al-Maqrīzī, *Sulūk*, III/1, pp. 117–118; identical in Ibn Taghrī Birdī, *Nujūm*, XI, pp. 33–34), for 1367, Ibn Duqmāq, *Nuzhat al-Anām*, fol. 5v–6; al-ʿAynī, *ʿIqd al-Jumān*, p. 149; al-Maqrīzī, *Sulūk*, III/1, pp. 144–145; Ibn Taghrī Birdī, *Nujūm*, XI, p. 44–45; Ibn Qāḍī Shuhba, *Tārīkh*, III, pp. 296, 297.

[61] See e.g. al-Qalqashandī, *Ṣubḥ*, IV, pp. 14, 16

nates among whom the government of the extensive Syro-Egyptian Mamluk territory was divided and who were all amirs of pre-determined rank. Key offices, that were the prerogative of the highest rank, included the function of *nā'ib al-salṭana*, second to the sultan only and therefore with far-reaching responsibilities, and—more territorially circumscribed—the governors of Upper and Lower Egypt (*kāshif*, by the end of the 1370s *nā'ib*), the *nā'ib al-Iskandarīya* (newly installed since 1365), and the *nā'ib*s of the seven major Syrian provinces—the *nā'ib al-Shām* (Damascus), the *nā'ib Ḥalab* (Aleppo), the *nā'ib Ṭarābulus* (Tripoli), the *nā'ib Ḥamā*, the *nā'ib Ṣafad*, the *nā'ib al-Karak* and the *nā'ib Ghazza*.[62]

A crucial part of these key executive offices' Legitimate Power consisted of their own—to a narrowly defined limit only though—authority to appoint their own officers and to promote amirs in the sultan's name. As with their overlord, their signature was equally indispensable to validate the diploma that was needed to confirm such appointments, as it was also stipulated to be necessary in the case of any other official document issued by the sultan and relating to a governor's territory.[63] Therefore, as with the sultan in general, each of them had a substantial amount of Legitimate Power at his disposal within his territory. Like the military ranks, therefore, these key executive offices may also be considered miniature-sultans in

[62] See al-ʿUmarī, *Taʿrīf*, pp. 94–95, 97, 130, 226–227, 235–236, 237; al-ʿUmarī, *Masālik*, pp. 55–56; Ibn Nāẓir al-Jaysh, *Tathqīf*, pp. 88, 93, 95, 96, 99, 104–106, 112; Ibn Duqmāq, *al-Jawhar al-Thamīn*, p. 412; al-Qalqashandī, *Ṣubḥ*, IV, pp. 16–17, 24–25, 64–65, 184, 194–198, 217, 222–225, 233, 234, 237, 238–239, 240, 241; VII, pp. 154–155, 156–157, 168, 170, 171, 175, 176, 177, 179; VIII, pp. 359–362; X, pp. 182–183; XI, pp. 134, 148, 405, 426–427, 438–441; XII, pp. 5, 6, 280; al-ʿAynī, *ʿIqd al-Jumān*, pp. 138–139; al-Maqrīzī, *Sulūk*, III/1, pp. 114–115; 340, 394; al-Maqrīzī, *Khiṭaṭ*, III, pp. 349–350; Ibn Ḥajar, *Inbā' al-Ghumr*, I, pp. 270, 272; II, p. 9; al-Ẓāhirī, *Zubda*, pp. 112, 129–130, 131, 132, 133, 134. See equally Ayalon, "Studies", pp. 57–58; Holt, "The Structure of Government", pp. 53, 56; Ziadeh, *Urban life in Syria*, pp. 21–24; Tarawneh, *The province of Damascus*, p. 21; Garcin, *Qūs*, pp. 390–391; Chapoutot-Remadi, "Mamlakat Ḥalab", p. 85; A. ʿAbd ar-Raziq, "Les gouverneurs d'Alexandrie au temps des Mamluks", *AI* 18 (1982), p. 127; ʿAta' Allah, *Niyābat Ghazza fī al-ʿAhd al-Mamlūkī*, Beirut 1986, esp. pp. 121, 124–125; Nielsen, *Secular Justice*, pp. 54–60, 67–68; M.ʿA. al-Ashqar, *Nā'ib al-salṭana al-mamlūkīya fī Miṣr (648–923h./1250–1517m.)*, (*Tārīkh al-miṣrīyīn* 158), Cairo 1999, esp. pp. 67–70, 72–74; 78–84, 185–195; Van Steenbergen, "The office of *Nā'ib al-salṭana* of Damascus: 741–784/1341–1382, a case study", in Vermeulen & Van Steenbergen, *Egypt and Syria—III*, pp. 429–431.

[63] See al-ʿUmarī, *Taʿrīf*, pp. 94, 226–227; al-Qalqashandī, *Ṣubḥ*, IV, pp. 5, 184, 217; XII, pp. 6, 281.

their own right, but now from the perspective of the sultan's governmental prerogatives. Within the confines of their territories governors were to appoint their own executive representatives, *nā'ib*s and *wālī*s—amirs of mostly lower military rank—who were to assist them in the execution of their wide responsibilities, again, however, within the limits of assigned territories inside their superior's only.[64]

Another broad category of key Mamluk military offices that were held by amirs of a hundred involves those functions that were executed in the sultan's vicinity and that were concerned with the orderly running of his court. On the one hand, this concerned officials linked to the ceremonial performance of the sultan's Legitimate Power in the regular public sessions, the *khidma*, where subjects' petitions for the redress of wrongs were to be considered. These officials took part either in the organisation and setting of this ceremonial, or in its judicial procedures.[65] On the other hand, this category equally included officials vested with responsibilities for certain aspects of the sultan's extended personal household, from his harem, to his mamluks, to his horses.[66] And again subordinates of lesser military rank assisted them

[64] In Egypt, the cities of Cairo and Miṣr al-Fusṭāṭ each had one *wālī*, as did the citadel, while there were another seventeen *wālī*s throughout the rest of Egypt. Likewise, each larger city and each province of Syria had numerous subordinate *nā'ib*s and *wālī*s. See e.g. al-Qalqashandī, *Ṣubḥ*, IV, pp. 20, 22–23, 26–27, 66–67, 176, 184, 186, 187, 198, 199, 200–201, 202, 217, 219, 226–227, 228–229, 230, 234, 235–236, 238, 239, 240, 241, 242.

[65] They included most notably the *amīr majlis*, responsible for the *khidma*'s organisation, the *dawādār kabīr*, in charge of presenting the petitions to the sultan and ensuring the sultan's signing of documents, the *amīr jāndār kabīr*, who guarded the access to the *khidma* and equally gathered the petitions, and the *ḥājib al-ḥujjāb*, who had judicial authority over the military, complementary to the authority of the sultan and of the *nā'ib al-salṭana*. See al-ʿUmarī, *Taʿrīf*, pp. 189, 190; al-ʿUmarī, *Masālik*, pp. 56–57, 58; al-Qalqashandī, *Ṣubḥ*, IV, pp. 18, 19, 20, 59–60; V, pp. 450, 455, 461, 462; al-Maqrīzī, *Khiṭaṭ*, III, p. 356–357, 360, 361; IV, p. 290; al-Maqrīzī, *Sulūk*, III/1, p. 230; al-Ẓāhirī, *Zubda*, p. 114. See also Ayalon, "Studies", pp. 59, 60, 62, 63–64; Holt, "The Structure of Government", p. 56; Nielsen, *Secular Justice*, pp. 83–85, 92; D. Ayalon, "Amīr Madjlis", *EI*², I, p. 445; D. Ayalon, "Dawādār", *EI*², II, p. 172; B. Lewis, "Djāndār", *EI*², II, p. 444; B. Lewis, "Ḥādjib, iv. Egypt and Syria", *EI*², III, pp. 47–48; A. Saleh, "Mihmindār", *EI*², VII, p. 2.

[66] These court functions included most notably the *ra's nawba kabīr*, who was one of the supervisors of the sultan's mamluks, the *amīr ākhūr kabīr*, who was the supervisor of the sultan's stables, his horses and the grooms, the *ustādār*, who was responsible for the citadel's living quarters and kitchens, its staff and the food supply and preparation, the *amīr silāḥ*, in charge of the sultan's weaponry, the *khāzindār kabīr* who kept the sultan's treasury and storehouses, and the *wazīr*—until 1350 an amir, then mainly a non-military—who looked after the sultan's personal finances, the expenditure in particular and including the monthly payments to household staff and the sultan's mamluks. See al-Nuwayrī, *Nihāyat al-Arab*, VI, pp. 92–142; al-

in the performance of the specific tasks the sultan had assigned to them. In the case of these court offices, however, the sultan delegated no authority in the appointment procedures to any of these officials. Nevertheless, since every amir by definition had a household like the sultan's, including a harem, mamluks and stables whose needs all had to be catered for, similar functions, under the direct authority of the amir and carried out by their own personal mamluks, can be found throughout the military ranks. Hence, aspects of the sultanate's institutional organisation were not just imitated by his executive representatives when they were exercising their local authorities, but as a matter of fact by every amir within the limits of his own institutional parameters.

When the performances of these military offices between 1341 and 1382 are also scrutinised, a few observations can be added to their mere technicalities. Frequently between 1341 and 1382, the appointment of an amir to a senior executive office in Syria fitted well within strategies that were used to defeat political opponents in Cairo.[67] In fact, such a strategy was occasionally even used to eliminate those opponents altogether, when their departure from Cairo for a new office was only used as a pretext to enable their smooth removal—sometimes even liquidation—from the political scene.[68] It should also be noted, however, that a handful of high-ranking amirs are stated to have preferred such an executive office away from the centre of Mamluk politics. For instance Ibn Taghrī Birdī claims that some experienced veteran amirs 'had a predilection for the office of *nā'ib al-Shām* and its equivalents'.[69] Some impressive careers in these

---

ʿUmarī, *al-Taʿrīf*, pp. 134–136, 137–139; al-ʿUmarī, *Masālik*, pp. 54, 57–58, 59; al-Qalqashandī, *Ṣubḥ*, IV, pp. 13, 18–19, 20, 21, 28–29; V, pp. 449, 454, 455, 456, 457, 461, 462; XI, pp. 148–153, 166, 168–172; al-Maqrīzī, *Khiṭaṭ*, III, p. 361, 362; al-Ẓāhirī, *Zubda*, pp. 97–98, 105, 114, 115, 125–126; Ibn Taghrī Birdī, *Nujūm*, XI, p. 62; see also Ayalon, "Studies", pp. 60–61, 62 63, 65; Holt, "The Structure of Government", p. 56; A. 'Abd ar-Raziq, "Le vizirat", pp. 188–239; Chapoutot-Remadi, "Le vizirat", pp. 58–59, 60–61; Eddé, "Institutions militaires ayyoubides", pp. 170–172. D. Ayalon, "Amīr ākhūr", *EI*², I, p. 442; D. Ayalon, "Amīr silāḥ", *EI*², I, pp. 445–446; D.P. Little, "Khaznadār, Khāzindār", *EI*², IV, pp. 1186–1187; A. Levanoni, "Ustādār", *EI*², X, p. 925.

[67] For amirs who were sent to Syria in those circumstances, see al-Shujāʿī, *Tārīkh*, p. 264; al-Maqrīzī, *Sulūk*, II/3, pp. 654, 761; III/2, p. 447; Ibn Taghrī Birdī, *Nujūm*, X, pp. 192–193; Ibn Qāḍī Shuhba, *Tārīkh*, II, pp. 361, 545; III, p. 325; I, pp. 61, 362.

[68] See e.g. al-Shujāʿī, *Tārīkh*, pp. 130–131; Ibn Kathīr, *al-Bidāya*, XIV, pp. 191, 236; al-ʿAynī, *ʿIqd al-Jumān*, pp. 48, 66–67; al-Maqrīzī, *Khiṭaṭ*, III, p. 55; IV, pp. 109, 113; al-Maqrīzī, *Sulūk*, II/3, pp. 681–682, 734, 823.

[69] Ibn Taghrī Birdī, *Nujūm*, XI, p. 219.

executive offices can be reconstructed from the sources, revealing that several amirs are recorded as being re-appointed to the same office more than once, even despite previous arrests and imprisonments. Out of a total of six terms that the amir Baydamur al-Khwārizmī (1312–1387) for instance acted as a *nā'ib al-Shām*, no less than five ended prematurely by his arrest. And in 1377, during his fifth term as *nā'ib al-Iskandarīya*, the amir Khalīl b. ʿAlī b. ʿArrām (d. 1380) was arrested and his property was confiscated; nevertheless, he still managed to be re-appointed to a sixth and final term two years later.[70]

In all, also among the military offices, the executive offices in particular, recurrent change was prevalent and institutional stability remained very precarious. The office of *nā'ib al-Shām*, for instance, saw the arrival and departure—and occasionally returning—of twenty-seven amirs whereas between 1310 and 1341 it had only been held by three amirs, one of whom governed for no less than twenty-seven years in a row.[71] In Aleppo forty-two *nā'ib*s are recorded to have governed between 1341 and 1382, while Safad is said to have been at the mercy of an impressive number of forty-six *nā'ib*s. How all this interfered with the actual performance of the tasks assigned to these high-ranking military officials remains less obvious, but undoubtedly it is likely that such instability in staffing resulted in the equally frequent recurrence of unsettling, unstable and haphazard governments.

In fact, some parallel instability even interfered with the positioning of the offices these successions of high-ranking amirs were assigned to between 1341 and 1382. It can actually be demonstrated that an office's authority, purpose and design often depended more on the individual it was assigned to than on its mere technical outlook. The offices of *nā'ib al-Shām* and *nā'ib Ḥalab*, for instance, witnessed a telling evolution. At first, the amir Arghūn Shāh al-Nāṣiri (d. 1349) had managed to wrest his office of *nā'ib Ḥalab* from his Damascene colleague's supervision, but upon his appointment in the office of

[70] For Baydamur, see Ibn Kathīr, *al-Bidāya*, XIV, p. 256; Ibn Duqmāq, *Nuzhat al-Anām*, fol. 40v, 51; al-ʿAynī, *ʿIqd al-Jumān*, pp. 123, 238, 258; al-Maqrīzī, *Sulūk*, III/1, pp. 156, 172, 289, 336, 337, 388; Ibn Ḥajar, *Inbā' al-Ghumr*, I, p. 270; II, pp. 4–5. For Ibn ʿArram, see e.g. al-Maqrīzī, *Sulūk*, III/1, p. 319. For several other similar cases, see al-ʿAynī, *ʿIqd al-Jumān*, p. 236; al-Maqrīzī, *Sulūk*, II/3, p. 823; III/1, pp. 305, 332; Ibn Ḥajar, *Inbāʿ al-Ghumr*, I, pp. 238, 271; Ibn Qāḍī Shuhba, *Tārīkh*, III, pp. 376, 574).

[71] See e.g. Van Steenbergen, "The Office of *Nā'ib al-salṭana* in Damascus: 741–784/1341–1382, a case study", in Vermeulen & Van Steenbergen (eds.), *Egypt and Syria*, pp. 429–448.

nā'ib al-Shām in 1348 he managed to reverse this and to re-extend his authority as the new *nā'ib al-Shām* over the rest of Syria.[72] In 1366, however, upon the transfer of the amir Manklī Bughā al-Shamsī from the office of *nā'ib al-Shām* to that of *nā'ib Ḥalab*, this process was reversed once more when the latter office was even given precedence over the former, an unseen situation which resulted from the fact that this Manklī Bughā was said to have opposed anything that could have looked like a demotion.[73] But this does not seem to have lasted for long, because in 1373, during one of the six terms of the *nā'ib al-Shām* Baydamur, his titles in the official correspondence are reported to have been changed to the extent that his office now even came to equal the office of *nā'ib al-salṭana* in Cairo.[74] And similarly telling is the evolution the latter office went through within this timeframe. When the amir Qawṣūn held it in 1341, he reportedly even managed to issue decrees and assign military ranks without the sultan's legitimising interference.[75] But in 1342, the authority of one of his less auspicious successors in the office was said to have been dramatically limited, to the conferment of Syrian auxiliary ranks only.[76] Subsequently, owing to socio-political circumstances, the office was occasionally even suspended or considered of so trivial an importance that hardly any reference to it was made.[77] Only in 1374, with the appointment of the amir Manjak al-Yūsufī, were new powers supposed to have been created for the office, including again the authority to promote low-ranking Syrian amirs.[78]

As a matter of fact, this haphazard institutional evolution is reflected in particular in the apparent temporal rise to executive authority of what were in essence non-executive military offices. In 1342, for instance, the *amīr ākhūr kabīr* ʿAlā' al-Dīn Aydughmish (d. 1342), allegedly only in charge of the sultan's stable matters, is reported to

[72] See al-Maqrīzī, *Sulūk*, II/3, pp. 727, 767; identical in Ibn Taghrī Birdī, *Nujūm*, X, pp. 157, 193.

[73] See Ibn Duqmāq, *Nuzhat al-Anām*, fol. 1v; al-ʿAynī, *ʿIqd al-Jumān*, p. 143; al-Maqrīzī, *Sulūk*, III/1, p. 127; Ibn Taghrī Birdī, *Nujūm*, XI, p. 34.

[74] Ibn Nāẓir al-Jaysh, *Tathqīf*, p. 92; also in al-Qalqashandī, *Ṣubḥ*, VII, p. 168.

[75] See al-ʿAynī, *ʿIqd al-Jumān*, p. 52; Ibn Taghrī Birdī, *Nujūm*, X, p. 23.

[76] See al-Maqrīzī, *Sulūk*, II/3, pp. 621, 639; identical in Ibn Taghrī Birdī, *Nujūm*, X, pp. 80, 86–87.

[77] See e.g. al-Maqrīzī, *Sulūk*, II/3, p. 891; on its occasional suspension, see al-Kutubī, *ʿUyūn al-Tawārīkh*, fol. 143, 149, 155v, 162v; al-Maqrīzī, *Khiṭaṭ*, III, p. 360.

[78] See Ibn Duqmāq, *Nuzhat al-Anām*, fol. 83v; al-ʿAynī, *ʿIqd al-Jumān*, p. 178; al-Maqrīzī, *Sulūk*, III/1, p. 225; Ibn Ḥajar, *Inbāʾ al-Ghumr*, I, p. 75.

have presided over the public session, the *khidma*, conferring promotions, making appointments, and executing a Legitimate Power that should only be the sultan's.[79] Though this was a unique event in the case of this court office, the situation in which executive authorities were claimed irrespective of administrative technicalities was not. Between the years 1347 and 1354, for instance, the court office of *ra's nawba kabīr*, in principal in charge of mamluks of the sultan only, experienced a similar expansion of its authorities. At that time, a succession of amirs who held that office, including Shaykhū (d. 1357), managed to appropriate extensive financial—the afore-mentioned fisc—and other administrative prerogatives, which awarded to them a considerable say in the regime's Legitimate Power.[80] This only reoccurred between the years 1378 and 1380, when the amir Barka (d. 1380) became *ra's nawba kabīr* and similarly took part in the execution of the sultan's Legitimate Power, in conjunction with his peer Barqūq (d. 1399).[81] In this specific joint venture, however, Barqūq carried another administrative title, with equally extended executive authorities, which had begun to supersede the role so briefly played by the regime's *ra's nawba kabīr* ever since 1354. Originally, this office of *atābak al-ʿasākir* had only been an honorary title, given to the high-ranking amir who led the Mamluk army on the battlefield, but when the *ra's nawba kabīr* Shaykhū took it in 1354, with the additional title of 'senior amir', *amīr kabīr*, he did so while he kept his extended executive authorities and linked them now to his new title. In this way, he managed to turn the title of *atābak al-ʿasākir* into a fully fledged military office of superior ranking, a process which was continued after his death in 1357 by several of his successors and which was brought to completion after 1378, when the amir Barqūq held it.[82] Eventually, Barqūq would set an administrative example that was to become a tradition of administrative practice for many decades to come, when,

[79] See al-Shujāʿī, *Tārīkh*, p. 194.
[80] See e.g. al-Maqrīzī, *Sulūk*, II/3, pp. 824, 842, 860, 889–891.
[81] See al-Maqrīzī, *Sulūk*, III/1, p. 324.
[82] See al-ʿUmarī, *Taʿrīf*, pp. 141–142; al-Qalqashandī, *Ṣubḥ*, IV, pp. 18, 184; XI, pp. 167–168; al-Ẓāhirī, *Zubda*, pp. 112–113, 114, 132; Ibn Duqmāq, *al-Jawhar al-Thamīn*, p. 399; al-ʿAynī, *ʿIqd al-Jumān*, p. 112; al-Maqrīzī, *Sulūk*, III/1, pp. 34, 324, 390; Ibn Taghrī Birdī, *Nujūm*, X, pp. 303, 305, 325; XI, p. 208. See also Ayalon, "Studies", p. 59; D. Ayalon, "al-Amīr al-Kabīr", *EI*², I, p. 444; Holt, "The Structure of Government", p. 54; Nielsen, *Secular Justice*, p. 68; al-Ashqar, *Nā'ib al-salṭana*, pp. 239–245.

in 1382, he managed to rise smoothly from the office of *atābak al-ʿasākir* to that of sultan.[83]

In short, military offices, whether executive and distant or in the sultan's vicinity at court, offered the amirs quite a shaky framework of extra-military responsibilities. The exact nature of those responsibilities was, however, more prone to change according to an individual amir's input than to any form of bureaucratic stasis. More than anything, the military offices therefore seem to have provided the socio-political elite with a framework for wide opportunities. And between 1341 and 1382, these wide opportunities—for a part in the regime's Legitimate Power in particular—were of such an inconsistent nature themselves, that they particularly resulted in a general appearance of institutional haphazardness.

Finances

To provide for their own personal, military and administrative needs, and, in principle, in return for their military service, the amirs, just like the sultan, were guaranteed a share in the realm's agricultural revenue. Since 1315, as discussed above, five twelfths of the realm's cultivable land was supposed to have been assigned to the sultan's fisc. Therefore only seven twelfths had remained available to provide for payments to all other military elements, the amirs and their troops in the first place. The shares of mainly tax income from one or more of these parcels of cultivable land, the *iqṭāʿ*s, that were subsequently assigned to each one of these amirs, were in most cases spread over different areas of the Egyptian or Syrian territory, and the combined annual estimated tax income of these parcels, as calculated by the sultan's administration, was always to be commensurate with that specific amir's military rank and post. The higher the military rank, the higher the *iqṭāʿ* income, while an amir posted in Syria would only be assigned an *iqṭāʿ* with a value of two thirds of that of his Egyptian peer. The resultant large variety of *iqṭāʿ*s was always personal, temporal and subject—as seen above—to the sultan's authority, whose army bureau kept close records of their annual status and whose approval was needed for any changes. At the same time, the

[83] See Ayalon, "Studies", p. 58; Brinner, "The Struggle for Power in the Mamluk State", p. 234; Levanoni, "The Mamluk Conception of the Sultanate", pp. 383–384.

amirs, in their turn, had become solely responsible for a number of issues that pertained to the management of their *iqṭāʿ* districts, including the organisation of the collection of their dues. Therefore, again as with the sultan, each one of them needed a kind of financial administration of his own, manned by civilians, crucial to manage a constant flow of income, and much needed to supervise the amir's expenditure, to his own household, to his mamluks and to their military needs.[84]

Unfortunately, for the specific period between 1341 and 1382, these general technicalities of the Mamluk regime's remuneration system as it was in the early fourteenth century and as it—as seen above in the similar case of the sultan—was supposed to have remained until beyond 1382, can again only very rarely be confirmed or refined by relevant source material. In all, for the entire period of forty-one years, only a few dozen references to amirs' *iqṭāʿ*s could be retrieved from the narrative sources, mainly limited to the disappointing information that the unspecified *iqṭāʿ* of amir X had been transferred to amir Y as a result of a change in the military ranks.[85] As seen before,

[84] See al-ʿUmarī, *Masālik*, p. 29; al-Qalqashandī, *Ṣubḥ*, III, pp. 453–454; IV, pp. 50, 183; al-Maqrīzī, *Khiṭaṭ*, III, pp. 350–351; see also H. Rabie, *The Financial System of Egypt*, pp. 47–49, 53; H. Halm, *Ägypten nach den mamlukischen Lehensregistern. I*, pp. 8, 37–42, 43–54; Sato, "The Evolution of the *Iqṭāʿ* System", p. 123; Sato, *State and Rural Society*, pp. 87–90, 135–161, 197–233, 235–236; Borsch, *The Black Death*, pp. 25–39. It was stipulated that two thirds of the *iqṭāʿ* income should go to an amir's mamluks, though at least in Damascus in January 1366 this stipulation was clearly violated more often than not, when Ibn Kathīr informs us that amirs in Damascus were ordered to make sure that their troops could benefit from at least half of the *iqṭāʿ*, suggesting that even that was not guaranteed anymore (see Ibn Kathīr, *al-Bidāya*, XIV, p. 318; mentioned in Ayalon, "Studies", pp. 459–460; Ayalon, "The System of Payment", pp. 61–62; on the stipulation, see al-Maqrīzī, *Khiṭaṭ*, III, p. 350; Rabie, *The Financial System*, p. 37).

[85] For such references to Egyptian *iqṭāʿ*s, see e.g. al-Shujāʿī, *Tārīkh*, p. 207; Ibn Duqmāq, *Nuzhat al-Anām*, fol. 6; Ibn Duqmāq, *Nuzhat al-Anām*, pp. 452, 455; al-Maqrīzī, *Sulūk*, II/3, pp. 672, 704, 725, 749, 821, 859; III/1, pp. 7, 144, 268, 287, 387, 394; for Syrian *iqṭāʿ*s, see e.g. al-Shujāʿī, *Tārīkh*, pp. 144, 207; al-Ṣafadī, *Aʿyān*, I, p. 594; II, pp. 50, 577; al-Kutubī, *ʿUyūn al-Tawārīkh*, fol. 75, 137v, 144v, 168v; al-Maqrīzī, *Sulūk*, II/3, pp. 738, 823, 875; Ibn Ḥajar, *Inbāʾ al-Ghumr*, I, p. 270. Additionally, there are occasional references to the sultan's suspension of an *iqṭāʿ* (see e.g. al-Maqrīzī, *Sulūk*, II/3, p. 672; III/1, pp. 54, 394), to an *iqṭāʿ*s unspecified re-organisation in an attempt to overcome financial straits (see al-Maqrīzī, *Sulūk*, II/3, pp. 672, 724), to the extension of an *iqṭāʿ* held by an amir of ten in 1343 (see e.g. al-Shujāʿī, *Tārīkh*, p. 257), to the one district that was part of a high-ranking amir's *iqṭāʿ* in 1354 (see al-Maqrīzī, *Sulūk*, III/1, p. 7), and, finally, to a detailed break-down of the components, including halves, thirds and quarters of districts, that made up the *iqṭāʿ*s of two low-ranking local amirs in charge of the region of Beirut and that illustrate first and foremost how *iqṭāʿ*s indeed were spread over as many parcels as possible (see Ibn Buḥtur, *Tārīkh Bayrūt*, pp. 179–180.

in the context of the sultan's fisc, the only relevant detailed piece of information that actually survives is Ibn al-Jīʿān's survey for the fiscal year between 1375 and 1376. When scrutinised for a reconstruction of the financial situation of Egypt's military in the mid-1370s, therefore, some information can be gained, even despite a number of methodological drawbacks.[86]

According to the technical manuals, the value of the *iqṭāʿ* of the lowest military rank of amir of ten as determined by al-Nāṣir Muḥammad should not exceed the annual amount of seven thousand *dīnār jayshī*.[87] From the *Tuḥfa*, however, it may be inferred that the actual range seems to have become much wider. The highest amount mentioned for an amir of ten was more than six times higher than that maximum amount, while, at the same time, four amirs of ten were—according to the *Tuḥfa*—entitled to no more than two thousand *dīnār jayshī* a year.[88] And similar situations occurred for the other two ranks. Whereas an amir of forty's *iqṭāʿ* was to range between twenty-three and thirty thousand *dīnār jayshī*, the highest *iqṭāʿ* income awarded to an amir of forty in the year between 1375 and 1376 amounted to more than twice that salary cap, while no less than one

[86] The main drawback is the frequent use (in the case of almost half of the tax districts mentioned) in this list of an unspecified general term (the *iqṭāʿ*-holders, *al-muqṭaʿūn*) instead of *iqṭāʿ*-holders' names, which obstructs the identification of their ranks; it has been argued convincingly that this general term stands for low-ranking amirs, auxiliary forces and sultan's mamluks only, since they were the only ones who were supposed to share parcels (see Haarmann, "The Sons of Mamluks", p. 148), though—remarkably—out of a total number of twenty amirs of a hundred, whose high rank at that time has been attested to from other sources, four remain conspicuously absent from the *Tuḥfa*, while similarly only one out of forty-nine amirs of forty and five out of eighty-three amirs of ten are not mentioned in the *Tuḥfa* (for the identification of these amirs, see e.g. Ibn Duqmāq, *Nuzhat al-Anām*, fol. 40, 40v, 52v, 82v, 83, 84, 100, 106v, 107, 119, 123; al-ʿAynī, *ʿIqd al-Jumān*, pp. 177, 192, 200, 210; al-Maqrīzī, *Sulūk*, III/1, pp. 161, 162, 177, 221, 224, 226, 253, 267, 268, 271, 288, 290, 296, 301, 303, 391, 404). Conclusions drawn from these data should therefore only be indicative of wider trends in the financial situation of the military ranks.

[87] See al-ʿUmarī, *Masālik*, p. 29; al-Qalqashandī, *Ṣubḥ*, IV, p. 50; al-Maqrīzī, *Khiṭaṭ*, III, pp. 351.

[88] For the highest amount, about forty-six thousand *dīnār jayshī*, see Ibn al-Jīʿān, *al-Tuḥfa al-Saniya*, pp. 25, 34, 90, 91, 104, 112, 118, 130, 163.; for the lowest, two thousand *dīnār jayshī*, see Ibn al-Jīʿān, *al-Tuḥfa al-Saniya*, pp. 43, 113, 175, 185. The latter case could of course be due to the afore-mentioned flaw in the *Tuḥfa*'s information, while in the former case, this *iqṭāʿ* seems to have preceded promotion, since its amir was made an amir of forty shortly afterwards, in early 1377 (see e.g. Ibn Duqmāq, *Nuzhat al-Anām*, fol. 107).

third of those amirs were entitled to less, or even far less, than twenty-three thousand *dīnār jayshī*.[89] And interestingly enough, the amir of a hundred who was awarded the largest *iqṭāʿ* income among his peers—more than two hundred and forty thousand *dīnār jayshī* annually—was the sultan's infant son and future successor ʿAlī, which is—as demonstrated above—mainly indicative of his father's modest attempts to reclaim financial supremacy.[90] And again, this top salary exceeded the usual income range for an amir of a hundred, stated in the technical manuals as between about eighty and two hundred thousand *dīnār jayshī* annually.[91] In all, however, the *Tuḥfa* suggests that four of those high-ranking amirs of that period again remained below this range, in one case down to less than thirty thousand *dīnār jayshī*, an amir of forty's income.[92]

On the basis of this very partial information on the financial side of the amirs' institutions, one general observation can be made which is relevant for this study of power and political culture. Indeed, the three-tiered military hierarchy was an organisational legitimising framework that identified the amirs' relative status and their military obligations and, in return, guaranteed them commensurate financial prerogatives. But at the same time, this hierarchy was also far more diverse than would appear from the surface. In terms of financial remuneration, a far more elaborate economic hierarchy existed within that military one. In fact, though they were by definition intertwined—

---

[89] For the technical manuals' information, see al-ʿUmarī, *Masālik*, p. 29; al-Qalqashandī, *Ṣubḥ*, IV, p. 50; al-Maqrīzī, *Khiṭaṭ*, III, pp. 351. For the maximum amount awarded to an amir of forty, more than seventy-five thousand *dīnār jayshī*, see Ibn al-Jīʿān, *al-Tuḥfa al-Saniya*, pp. 24, 71, 100, 106, 115, 122, 150, 167, 174, 186, 190; again, however, this *iqṭāʿ* seems to have preceded promotion to the rank of amir of a hundred, which happened in early 1377 (see e.g. Ibn Duqmāq, *Nuzhat al-Anām*, fol. 107). For sixteen amirs of forty with *iqṭāʿ*s that generated less than twenty-three thousand *dīnār jayshī*—the lowest only three thousand three hundred—, see Ibn al-Jīʿān, *al-Tuḥfa Sanīya*, pp. 8, 18, 19, 26, 29, 30, 32, 35, 37, 38, 42, 44, 47, 50, 55, 65, 72, 73, 75, 79, 82, 110, 116, 118, 134, 138, 150, 152, 155, 157, 158, 162, 163, 164, 165, 168, 169, 170, 171, 174, 175, 176, 178, 182, 183, 186, 188, 189, 190, 192, 193–194.

[90] See Ibn al-Jīʿān, *al-Tuḥfa al-Saniya*, pp. 35, 117, 150, 171, 173, 176; ʿAlī had already been promoted amir of a hundred in 1372 (see e.g. Ibn Duqmāq, *Nuzhat al-Anām*, fol. 72v).

[91] See al-ʿUmarī, *Masālik*, p. 29; al-Qalqashandī, *Ṣubḥ*, IV, p. 50; al-Maqrīzī, *Khiṭaṭ*, III, pp. 350–351.

[92] See Ibn al-Jīʿān, *al-Tuḥfa al-Saniya*, pp. 11, 35, 67, 80, 89, 106, 117, 124, 150, 171, 173, 176, 191.

only an amir's military rank brought and continued to bring such income—and indeed continued to be so, encroachment upon the financial prerogatives of another rank—on both sides—did occur. More importantly, financial diversity beyond every rank's uniform surface—in existence already at the time of al-Nāṣir Muḥammad in the format of the ranks' different income ranges—seems only to have increased.

On the one hand, this economic hierarchy continued to serve quite an essential institutional purpose in enabling a certain, controllable and gradual access to the regime's huge agricultural resources, an access that guaranteed a proportionate due to those who became members of the military ranks or of the socio-political elite, while retaining a centralised form of institutional control. Its continuously widening range, on the other hand, suggests that factors decisive for the proportions of that due were not uniquely institutional nor functional in character, but derived from other practices.

Conclusion

The development of Mamluk political power between 1341 and 1382 in its institutional, legitimate capacity has been this chapter's subject of analysis. As seen, it was legitimate since it essentially equalled the sultan's god-given authority, and it was institutionalised in that it emanated, from the sultan's prerogatives, into the various institutions that enabled his rule. Prime among those institutions were the military ranks and offices, the breeding grounds for that sultanate since they hosted the socio-political elite, to which the sultan also belonged and which he largely depended upon. In fact, Legitimate Power and many crucial institutions attached to the sultan were multiplied down those military ranks. From an institutional perspective, the amirate consisted of nothing but the sultan's clones in a subservient, reduced format, with similar, but often far less demanding institutional needs and solutions. As seen, this imitation of the sultanate was at the core of Mamluk local government even in the executive centres outside Cairo. Actually, this process of emanation from the sultan's Legitimate Power into clusters of parallel institutions around amirs was aptly summarised by al-Qalqashandī, when he claimed that:

> You should know that every amir of a hundred and [every amir] of forty generally is a sultan in a concise form. Every one of them has utility rooms like the sultan's utility rooms [. . .]; and among his soldiers, he has an *ustādār*, a *ra's nawba*, a *dawādār*, an *amīr majlis*, a *jamdārīya*, an *amīr ākhūr*, an *ustādār al-ṣuḥba* and a financial supervisor [. . .].[93]

This fundamental 'imitation' of the sultanate extended to the changing nature of the elite that populated the military ranks and offices in the middle of the fourteenth century. By then, many years of absence of any serious military challenge had turned that elite from a military into first and foremost a social and political body, open to anyone capable of achieving it. However, both the sultan—long since a politician rather than a military leader—and this body politic largely continued to be defined along the same military-institutional lines of the sultanate and amirate, since only they could lay claim to the Legitimate Power that enabled government, public order and justice, as well as tax collection and redistribution.

Behind that institutional surface, though, there clearly was another practice at work. Between 1341 and 1382, the institutions that mattered most politically—the sultanate and the amirate—clearly were very often subject to socio-political conduct that went far beyond their mere alleged technicalities. On the one hand, there was a prolonged and very dependent Qalawunid sultanate, that eventually turned into a fully fledged puppet office, while, at the very same time, the opposite happened to often hard to define military positions like that of the *atābak al-ʿasākir*. And on the other hand, the amirs' primordial framework of military ranks fell victim to numerical decline and sweeping change. Nevertheless, the same conservative respect that had kept the Qalawunids on the throne also continued to loom high over the amir's institutional career-pathway. Under the surface, however, the crucial remuneration system developed in a far less conservative manner and equally hints at the existence of a diverging socio-political practice.

The institutions that gave shape to Mamluk Legitimate Power remained crucial throughout the period between 1341 and 1382 as the socio-political elite's tools of legitimate domination, social identification and contained remuneration. At the same time, however,

---

93 Al-Qalqashandī, *Ṣubḥ*, IV, p. 60.

they clearly constituted the mouldable object rather than the vital subject of the period's political culture and process. In this study's quest for that culture and process, therefore, the nature of that subject, of that alternative socio-political practice, will be the next chapter's topic of analysis.

CHAPTER TWO

EFFECTIVE POWER

Throughout the entire period from 1341 to 1382, the sultan was more often than not subordinate to one or more amirs that had not just agreed upon his enthronement, but that had equally wrested from him the authority that was legitimately his. This distinction between institutional form and content, for which the period has become so notorious and which actually characterised the entirety of its politico-military framework, precisely identifies a key feature of the alternative socio-political reality that is the subject of this chapter. Clearly, an analysis of this period's socio-political scene equally needs to consider this kind of socio-political conduct that could give someone the ability to impose his will irrespective of the Legitimate Power framework, while at the same time constituting a driving force in the allocation and evolution of this same framework's constituents. It is, therefore, this paradox of socio-political conduct, this congruence of institutional neglect and respect, which will be addressed here. In particular, this chapter will focus on those strategies of socio-political conduct that created an individual's ability to get things done, an ability that, by analogy with Legitimate Power, is captured in the convenient term 'Effective Power'.

Observations

In order to tackle this issue of this period's Effective Power, a useful starting point actually concerns the precarious situation of the sultanate. Because of its high profile, sources often very clearly identify who overpowered this sultanate, that is, who had managed to become the champion of the period's socio-political conduct and grasp ultimate Effective Power. For the beginning of the young al-Nāṣir Ḥasan's first reign (1347–1351), al-Maqrīzī gives the following telling account of the organisation of the public session (*khidma*):

> After attending the public session in the Iwan, the amirs Manklī Bughā al-Fakhrī, Baygharā, Baybughā Tatar, Ṭaybughā al-Majdī, Arlān and all [other] amirs would leave to settle their own business, except for the amirs of the council and the government (*umarāʾ al-mashūra wa al-tadbīr*). They were Baybughā Rūs, the *nāʾib*, Shaykhū al-ʿUmarī, the *wazīr* Manjak, Uljībughā al-Muẓaffarī, [the amir Ṭāz] and Ṭānyariq. They would go to the palace and settle the regime's affairs in the sultan's presence, according to their own insight and discretion. [. . .].[1]

A guardian council of six amirs had clearly managed to encroach upon prerogatives that in principle were part of the sultan's legitimate authority alone. Additionally, the previous chapter already noted the case of one of these amirs, Shaykhū (d. 1357), who during Ḥasan's second reign (1354–1361) exceeded his executive authority tremendously, first as *raʾs nawba kabīr* and then as *atābak al-ʿasākir*. When finally, in 1378, the *atābak* Barqūq (d. 1399) and the *raʾs nawba kabīr* Barka (d. 1380) managed to occupy a similarly powerful position in the regime, the need for the by then degenerate sultanate's legitimising involvement in the administration is even completely discarded when al-Maqrīzī again observes that

> when someone wants to be appointed anywhere, he needs to talk to someone close to the amir Barka, until what he wants is assigned to him. Then [Barka] will send that man to [. . .] Barqūq, informing him of what he wants, so as to get his agreement too. Only then will he be appointed in the office that was assigned to him, either in the service of the sultan or in [. . .] Barqūq's administration.[2]

Accounts like these clearly identify some of the actual rulers in the regime, like Shaykhū, Barqūq and Barka. For the entire period between 1341 and 1382, there are numerous similar or even more specific references, including a repeated terminology used by the sources to identify Effective Power holders and express their actual superiority over the institutional framework (without even the slightest comment). The range of vocabulary used is extensive, and includes amongst many others many variants of such classics as *taṣarruf* (executive authority), *al-ḥall wa al-ʿaqd* (tying and untying), *sāsa* (governing) and—most frequently encountered in this respect—*dabbara* (managing).[3]

---

[1] al-Maqrīzī, *Sulūk*, II/3, pp. 751–752; similarly in al-Maqrīzī, *Khiṭaṭ*, IV, p. 125; Ibn Taghrī Birdī, *Nujūm*, X, p. 190.

[2] al-Maqrīzī, *Sulūk*, III/1, p. 324.

[3] The following is a full list of this vocabulary and its references: for *istibdād*, see Ibn Khaldūn, *Kitāb al-ʿIbar*, V, pp. 443, 446, 451, 460, 463, 466, 469, 470, 473;

When listing all such annotations from the sources, all individuals can be identified that were reckoned to have built up a considerable amount of Effective Power at a certain point of time between 1341 and 1382. This exercise results in a list of twenty-seven amirs, most notable among whom were Qawṣūn (d. 1342) in 1341, Shaykhū (d. 1357)

al-Maqrīzī, *Khiṭaṭ*, III, p. 391; al-Maqrīzī, *Sulūk*, II/3, pp. 842, 860, 919; al-ʿAynī, *ʿIqd al-Jumān*, p. 122; Ibn Ḥajar, *Inbāʾ al-Ghumr*, I, p. 234; Ibn Taghrī Birdī, *Nujūm*, X, p. 268; Ibn Qāḍī Shuhba, *Tārīkh*, II, p. 296; for *taṣarruf*, see al-Maqrīzī, *Sulūk*, II/3, pp. 842, 860; al-ʿAynī, *ʿIqd al-Jumān*, p. 79; Ibn Taghrī Birdī, *Nujūm*, X, pp. 22, 48, 268; XI, p. 6; for *taḥadduth*, see al-Shujāʿī, *Tārīkh*, pp. 194, 205–206 [*al-mutaḥaddith fī umūr al-dawla wa tartībihā*]; Ibn Ḥabīb, *Tadhkirat al-Nabīh*, III, p. 204; Ibn Duqmāq, *al-Jawhar al-Thamīn*, pp. 386, 444; Ibn Duqmāq, *Nuzhat al-Anām*, fol. 4; al-Maqrīzī, *Sulūk*, II/3, p. 919; III/1, pp. 4, 314; al-ʿAynī, *ʿIqd al-Jumān*, p. 147; Ibn Ḥajar, *Inbāʾ al-Ghumr*, I, p. 233; Ibn Taghrī Birdī, *Nujūm*, XI, pp. 40, 159; Ibn Qāḍī Shuhba, *Tārīkh*, II, pp. 236–237; III, pp. 51, 547; for *al-mushār ilayhī*, see Ibn Ḥabīb, *Tadhkirat al-Nabīh*, III, p. 204; al-Maqrīzī, *Sulūk*, II/3, pp. 731, 890; Ibn Taghrī Birdī, *Nujūm*, X, pp. 161, 305; Ibn Qāḍī Shuhba, *Tārīkh*, II, p. 321; for *al-ḥukm*, see al-Shujāʿī, *Tārīkh*, p. 253; al-Maqrīzī, *Khiṭaṭ*, IV, p. 249; al-Maqrīzī, *Sulūk*, II/3, p. 748, 860; Ibn Ḥajar, *Inbāʾ al-Ghumr*, I, p. 234; Ibn Taghrī Birdī, *Nujūm*, X, p. 268; Ibn Qāḍī Shuhba, *Tārīkh*, II, p. 625; III, p. 548; for *al-kalām*, see Ibn Qāḍī Shuhba, *Tārīkh*, II, p. 509; Ibn Buḥtur, *Tārīkh Bayrūt*, p. 51; Ibn Taghrī Birdī, *Nujūm*, XI, p. 32; Ibn Qāḍī Shuhba, *Tārīkh*, III, p. 326; for *al-amr*, see al-Ṣafadī, *Aʿyān*, I, p. 595 [*taṣdur ʿanhum al-awāmir wa al-nawāhī*]; al-Maqrīzī, *Khiṭaṭ*, III, pp. 390, 244; IV, p. 105; al-Maqrīzī, *Sulūk*, III/1, pp. 212, 230, 324; al-ʿAynī, *ʿIqd al-Jumān*, p. 231; Ibn Taghrī Birdī, *Nujūm*, XI, p. 5 [*ṣāra al-amr jamīʿuhu lī*], 155; Ibn Qāḍī Shuhba, *Tārīkh*, II, p. 323 [*al-amr wa al-nahy wa al-ḥall wa al-ʿaqd*]; III, p. 305 [*al-umūr kulluhā lī*], 524; I, p. 144 [*al-amr wa al-nahy wa al-qaṭʿ wa al-waṣl*]); for *al-ḥall wa al-ʿaqd*, see al-Ḥusaynī, *Dhayl al-ʿIbar*, p. 157; Ibn Khaldūn, *Kitāb al-ʿIbar*, V, p. 467; al-Maqrīzī, *Khiṭaṭ*, IV, p. 125; al-ʿAynī, *ʿIqd al-Jumān*, p. 231; Ibn Taghrī Birdī, *Nujūm*, XI, p. 163; Ibn Qāḍī Shuhba, *Tārīkh*, II, p. 323; for *qāma bi-al-dawla*, see al-Maqrīzī, *Khiṭaṭ*, III, p. 391; al-Maqrīzī, *Sulūk*, II/3, p. 842; Ibn Taghrī Birdī, *Nujūm*, X, p. 232; for *sāsa*, see al-Ḥusaynī, *Dhayl al-ʿIbar*, p. 176 [*qāma bi siyāsat al-mulk wa tadbīr al-mamālik*]; al-Maqrīzī, *Khiṭaṭ*, IV, p. 113 [*ṣāra zimām al-dawla bi yadihī fa sāsahā aḥsan siyāsa*]; for *dabbara*, see for instance al-Shujāʿī, *Tārīkh*, p. 141 (*taqlīd bi-niyābat al-salṭana wa tadbīr al-mamlaka*), 225, 240 (*mudabbir al-dawla wa munfidh al-ashghāl*), 241; al-Ḥusaynī, *Dhayl al-ʿIbar*, p. 176; al-Kutubī, *ʿUyūn al-Tawārīkh*, fol. 155v°, 159; Ibn Kathīr, *al-Bidāya*, XIV, pp. 255, 257, 290, 297; Ibn Ḥabīb, *Tadhkirat al-Nabīh*, III, p. 204; Ibn Duqmāq, *al-Jawhar al-Thamīn*, p. 406; al-Maqrīzī, *Khiṭaṭ*, III, pp. 389, 390, 391; IV, pp. 118, 129; al-Maqrīzī, *Sulūk*, II/3, pp. 551, 552, 620 (*mudabbir al-dawla wa kāfil al-sulṭān*), 628, 746, 772, 919–920; III/1, pp. 5, 35, 65, 141; Ibn Ḥajar, *Durar*, II, pp. 214–215; Ibn Ḥajar, *Inbāʾ al-Ghumr*, I, p. 4; Ibn Taghrī Birdī, *Nujūm*, X, pp. 3, 48, 78, 118 (*tadbīr mamlakatihī wa al-naẓr fī umūr al-dawla*), 141 (*ilayhī tadbīr umūr al-dawla wa ʿanhū yaṣdur wilāyat arbābihā wa ʿazlahum*), 185–186, 188, 195, 233 (growing tensions in the countryside because of "discord between the rulers (*ikhtilāf kalimat mudabbirī al-mamlaka*)"), 324; XI, pp. 3, 24, 43, 46, 53, 154, 207; Ibn Qāḍī Shuhba, *Tārīkh*, II, pp. 308 (*yudabbirān al-dawla yuʿṭiyān man yakhtārā wa yamniʿān man yurīdā*), 513; III, pp. 20, 137, 138, 330, 524; I, p. 42. For the meaning of *dabbara* in this context, see Lane, *An Arabic English Lexicon*, III, p. 844: "You say, *dabbara umūr al-bilād*, and, elliptically, *dabbara al-bilād*, *He managed, conducted, ordered* or *regulated, the affairs of the provinces*, or *country* [. . .]"

after 1347, Yalbughā al-Khāṣṣakī (d. 1366) from 1361 until his death, and Barqūq (d. 1399) from 1378 until his enthronement in 1382.[4] However, no less conspicuous is the fact that this reading of the sources identifies not just twenty-seven amirs, but also five sultans as notable Effective Power holders within this timeframe, including the most successful sultans al-Nāṣir Ḥasan, in 1351 and for the period from 1357 until his deposition in 1361, and al-Ashraf Shaʿbān, from 1367 until his murder in 1377.[5] Clearly, the Qalawunids were not automatically perceived to be excluded from the period's socio-political conduct. Nor were this conduct and the identification of its results in the sources limited to this very upper level of Mamluk society only. In Syria, for instance, the *nāʾib al-Shām* Arghūn Shāh (d. 1349) is equally said to have been dominated entirely by his personal *dawādār*, the amir Sayf al-Dīn Qarābughā (d. 1349) from 1347 onwards:

> [Qarābughā] was the ruler (*al-ḥākim*) in the entire *mamlaka* of Damascus, where nothing happened unless he had ordered it; his *ustādh* used to love him dearly and [therefore, even] when [Qarābughā] went out, it looked as though he was the *nāʾib al-Shām* [and not Arghūn Shāh].[6]

[4] For these amirs, see appendix 2; for these annotations in the sources, see al-Shujāʿī, *Tārīkh*, p. 141; al-Kutubī, *ʿUyūn al-Tawārīkh*, fol. 155v, 159; Ibn Kathīr, *al-Bidāya*, XIV, pp. 255, 257, 278, 290, 297; Ibn Ḥabīb, *Tadhkirat al-Nabīh*, III, p. 204; Ibn Duqmāq, *al-Jawhar al-Thamīn*, p. 406; Ibn Khaldūn, *Kitāb al-ʿIbar*, V, pp. 443, 451, 467, 469, 470, 473, 474; al-Maqrīzī, *Khiṭaṭ*, III, pp. 244, 389, 390, 391; IV, pp. 113, 114, 207; al-Maqrīzī, *Sulūk*, II/3, pp. 551, 552, 890, 919; III/1, pp. 4, 65, 324; III/2, pp. 474–475; al-ʿAynī, *ʿIqd al-Jumān*, pp. 122, 231; Ibn Taghrī Birdī, *Nujūm*, X, pp. 3, 22, 48, 305, 324; XI, pp. 3, 5, 6, 24, 32, 163, 188; Ibn Buḥtur, *Tārīkh Bayrūt*, p. 51; Ibn Qāḍī Shuhba, *Tārīkh*, III, pp. 20, 124, 305, 330; I, p. 42. For a list of the remaining twenty-three amirs, see app. 2; for their identification through similar annotations, see al-Shujāʿī, *Tārīkh*, pp. 194, 205–206, 240; al-Ṣafadī, *Aʿyān*, I, p. 649; Ibn Khaldūn, *Kitāb al-ʿIbar*, V, pp. 465, 467, 473; al-Maqrīzī, *Khiṭaṭ*, III, p. 244; IV, p. 249; al-Maqrīzī, *Sulūk*, II/3, pp. 620, 640, 731, 772, 842; III/1, pp. 35, 141, 314, 324; al-ʿAynī, *ʿIqd al-Jumān*, pp. 79, 231; Ibn Ḥajar, *Durar*, II, pp. 214–215; Ibn Ḥajar, *Inbāʾ al-Ghumr*, I, pp. 5, 233; Ibn Taghrī Birdī, *Nujūm*, X, pp. 78, 161, 185–186, 195, 232, 307; XI, pp. 154, 155, 163; Ibn Qāḍī Shuhba, *Tārīkh*, II, pp. 323; III, pp. 524, 547; I, pp. 42, 144.

[5] For Ḥasan and Shaʿbān's identification, see Ibn Khaldūn, *Kitāb al-ʿIbar*, V, pp. 351, 460, 463; al-Maqrīzī, *Khiṭaṭ*, III, p. 391; al-Maqrīzī, *Sulūk*, II/3, pp. 822, 842; III/1, p. 324; III/2, pp. 474–475; al-ʿAynī, *ʿIqd al-Jumān*, p. 231; Ibn Taghrī Birdī, *Nujūm*, X, pp. 218–219; XI, p. 53; Ibn Qāḍī Shuhba, *Tārīkh*, III, p. 524. The other three sultans—admittedly less explicitly referenced—were their predecessors al-Ṣāliḥ Ismāʿīl (d. 1345), al-Kāmil Shaʿbān (d. 1346) and al-Muẓaffar Ḥājjī (d. 1347), see Ibn Khaldūn, *Kitāb al-ʿIbar*, V, p. 446; al-ʿAynī, *ʿIqd al-Jumān*, p. 74; Ibn Taghrī Birdī, *Nujūm*, X, p. 118.

[6] Ibn Qāḍī Shuhba, *Tārīkh*, II, p. 625; for similar comments and accounts, see al-Ṣafadī, *Aʿyān*, IV, pp. 80–82; al-Ṣafadī, *Wāfī*, XVI, p. 424; XXIV, pp. 207–208.

The paradoxical, even chaotic socio-political picture that springs from these observations, remaining institutionally inexplicable, to a large degree accounts for modern historiography's negative reception of the period between 1341 and 1382, as alluded to in the introduction. How it came to look so erratic, and yet remained in existence for so long, will be the further focus of attention of this and the next chapter's analysis. To start with, the main conclusions that can be drawn from these initial observations are threefold. First, the institutions of Legitimate Power were subordinate to practices beyond themselves. Secondly, those who were defined as the period's champions of those practices were always very specific individuals. And thirdly, these individuals' practices clearly consisted mainly of individual strategies of social and political conduct—manners of behaviour and interaction, and the unwritten rules which they abided by—that engendered Effective Power and that so far have largely remained unnoticed, especially in this specific context.

Patrons and Clients

Encountering individuals that championed strategies of socio-political conduct that also regulated the regime's institutions, immediately imposes a Weberian, patrimonial perspective upon the identification of such conduct.[7] Indeed, defined as 'an extension of the ruler's household in which the relation between the ruler and his officials remains on the basis of paternal authority and filial dependence', this patrimonial model of rule has shown itself very useful to explain many a Middle Eastern political culture.[8] Within the context of Mamluk studies, this model has been an important guide for Ira Lapidus' appreciations of Mamluk society.[9] Though some of his view-points may have become obsolete after more than thirty years, his basic assumption that it was individuals and their relationships rather

---

[7] See M. Weber, *Economy and Society: an outline of interpretive sociology*, Berkeley 1978, vol. 1, pp. 231–232.

[8] See for instance J. Bill, R. Springborg, *Politics in the Middle East*, New York 1999 (5th ed.), pp. 101–130. Quotation from R. Bendix, *Max Weber: an intellectual portrait*, Methuen 1966 (new ed.), pp. 330–331.

[9] See for instance Lapidus, *Muslim Cities*; I.M. Lapidus, "Muslim Cities as Plural Societies: the Politics of Intermediary Bodies", in *Urbanism in Islam. Proceedings of the International Conference on Urbanism in Islam*, vol. I, Tokyo 1989, pp. 134–163.

than the state and its institutions that created Mamluk society clearly still stands.[10] When power, especially Effective Power, is defined as the ability to impose one's will upon others, it follows quite logically that, as just argued, it therefore results from a relationship defined by strategies of conduct that allow one person to impose his will upon an other.

The one powerful person in this relationship is generally called a patron, the other a client. And the more individual relationships of power a patron is able to establish, the larger his Effective Power will be.[11] Thus, the aforementioned Effective Power holders all had managed to expand their relationships of power to such an extent that their Effective Power at one precise point in time came to be publicly acknowledged. A telling illustration of this can be found in al-Maqrīzī's assessment of the power the amir Shaykhū (d. 1357) wielded in the period between 1354 and 1357:

> his clique became powerful: in every *mamlaka* there came to be many amirs that were on his side and in Damascus and every [other] city his representatives became senior amirs who were in his service; eventually, it was said that daily more than two hundred thousand *dirham* cash entered his administration."[12]

---

[10] See Lapidus, *Muslim Cities*, pp. 48–50, 187. Only his student Michael Chamberlain followed in his footsteps, see Chamberlain, *Knowledge and Social Practice*, esp. pp. 2–3, 8–9, 40–43; Chamberlain, "The Crusader Era and the Ayyubid dynasty", in C.F. Petry (ed.), *The Cambridge History of Egypt, Vol. One, Islamic Egypt*, Cambridge 1998, pp. 237–240. For this assessment of the fundamental nature of Lapidus' (and Chamberlain's) work, see also W.W. Clifford, "*Ubi Sumus?* Mamluk History and Social Theory", *MSR* 1 (1997), pp. 45–62. Apart from one PhD dissertation (W.W. Clifford, " 'State Formation' and the Structure of Politics in Mamluk Syro-Egypt, 648–741 A.H./1250–1340 C.E.", unpublished PhD. thesis, University of Chicago 1995), this approach has only haphazardly been applied to the socio-political arena of any given period in Mamluk history (see e.g. L. Wiederhold, "Legal-Religious Elite, Temporal Authority, and the Caliphate in Mamluk Society: Conclusions drawn from the examination of a 'Zahiri Revolt' in Damascus in 1386", *IJMES* 31 (1999), pp. 203–235; and T. Miura, "Administrative Networks in the Mamluk Period: Taxation, Legal Execution, and Bribery", in T. Sato (ed.), *Islamic urbanism in human history: political power and social networks*, London 1997, esp. pp. 39–42).

[11] Lapidus says that "thus, political ties took the form of patronage-clientage relations, relations between two people such that one protected and sustained the other, who in turn provided his patron with certain resources or services." (Lapidus, *Muslim Cities*, p. 187); Clifford states that "the late medieval Syro-Egyptian state can be understood as a patronage, a vast clientelistic structure [. . .]." (Clifford, "State Formation", p. 6); for similar definitions, see also Lapidus, *Muslim Cities*, pp. 48–50, 187–188; Staffa, *Conquest and Fusion*, pp. 124–126; Chamberlain, *Knowledge and Social Practice*, pp. 38–40; Clifford, "State Formation", pp. 46–47, 58; Clifford, "*Ubi Sumus?*", pp. 60, 62.

[12] Al-Maqrīzī, *Khiṭaṭ*, IV, p. 114.

Other levels of socio-political interaction equally left traces in the sources that point to the fundamental nature of patron-client relationships as regards the period's socio-political conduct. Typical terms used in that context to identify a patron's clients include *atbāʿ* (followers), *alzām* (adherents) and *aṣḥāb* (fellows, companions).[13] According to Ibn Ḥajar, the amir Alākuz al-Kashlāwī (d. 1369), for instance, originally belonged to the followers of the amir Kashlā;[14] and al-Ṣafadī claims to recall that the Damascene amir of ten Jūbān (d. 1361) belonged to the adherents of the *nāʾib al-Shām* Yalbughā al-Yaḥyāwī (d. 1347).[15] And the sources mention very explicitly at least five more names of amirs as clients of the latter, which is a further illustration of the spread of relationships an ambitious patron established.[16] Moreover, perhaps more surprisingly, there are also examples of clients who are said to have had more than one patron, even at the same time. The most telling example in this respect concerns the amir ʿAlāʾ al-Dīn Alṭunbughā al-Dawādār (d. 1343), who is supposed to have served no less than five patrons, often in recurrent alternating order.[17] The eunuch Muqbil al-Rūmī al-Kabīr (d. 1393) first was in the service of the sultan al-Ṣāliḥ Ismāʿīl (d. 1345), then of several "rulers and amirs", then of Shaykhū, and finally allied with al-Nāṣir Ḥasan.[18] And the Damascene amir of ten Muḥammad b. Qibjaq (d. 1390) was not just considered the representative of the Egyptian amir Muḥammad

[13] For mere references to the existence of such a relationship between two amirs, see for instance al-Ṣafadī, *Aʿyān*, I, p. 700; II, pp. 97, 105, 173, 174, 342, 575; III, pp. 75, 83, 278; IV, p. 105; V, p. 399; al-Ṣafadī, *Wāfī*, X, pp. 387, 435; XIII, pp. 384, 398; XV, p. 368; XXIV, pp. 209, 227, 263; al-Maqrīzī, *Sulūk*, II/3, p. 627; Ibn Ḥajar, *Durar*, I, p. 482; II, p. 94; III, p. 251; Ibn Taghrī Birdī, *al-Manhal*, III, p. 362. For a discussion of that vocabulary, see also Chamberlain, *Knowledge and Social Practice*, pp. 116–119. For the translation of the Arabic term *tābiʿ*, pl. *atbāʿ*, 'follower', as 'a military client who is engaged in a patron-client relationship [. . .] with a senior personage', see Hathaway, *The Politics of Households in Ottoman Egypt*, Cambridge 1997, pp. 22–23. For the Arabic term *lāzim*, pl. *alzām*, see also D. Richards, "Mamluk Amirs", pp. 35–36.

[14] Ibn Ḥajar, *Durar*, I, p. 404.

[15] Al-Ṣafadī, *Aʿyān*, II, p. 173.

[16] They were the amirs Ayāz al-Nāṣiri (d. 1349), Ṭuqṭāy al-Nāṣiri (1319–1358), Muḥammad b. Alāqūsh, Qalāwūz al-Nāṣiri (d. 1347) and an amir called Shaʿbān (d. 1353) (al-Ṣafadī, *Aʿyān*, I, p. 639; II, pp. 520, 616–617; IV, pp. 130–131, 341; al-Ṣafadī, *Wāfī*, IX, pp. 459–461; XVI, pp. 152–153, 470–473; XXIV, p. 266; Ibn Ḥajar, *Durar*, I, p. 420; II, p. 226; Ibn Taghrī Birdī, *al-Manhal*, VI, pp. 424–425.

[17] Al-Ṣafadī, *Aʿyān*, I, pp. 610–611; al-Ṣafadī, *Wāfī*, IX, pp. 366–369; Ibn Ḥajar, *Durar*, III, pp. 407–408; Ibn Taghrī Birdī, *al-Manhal*, III, pp. 71–72.

[18] Ibn Qāḍī Shuhba, *Tārīkh*, I, p. 498.

b. Aqbughā Āṣ (d. 1386), but at the same time also the protégée of the *nā'ib al-Shām* Baydamur al-Khwārizmī (d. 1387).[19]

Finally, with respect to social structures evolving from such basic patron-client relationships, there are equally convincing indications that an ambitious client could, on another level of socio-political interaction at the very same time himself be a patron with his own clients, hence with his own commensurate amount of Effective Power. The amir Ṣarghitmish, for instance, was an important client of the amir Shaykhū, which he continued to be until the latter's murder in 1357, while simultaneously, he had been able to build his own relationships with clients that enabled him to replace Shaykhū's with his own immediately upon Shaykhū's demise, without provoking any substantial protest.[20] Clearly, one individual played different socio-political roles at the same time.

From this perspective, these general social structures that evolved from this nucleus mode of socio-political conduct are well represented by a pyramid of vertical patron-client ties that engendered commensurate amounts of Effective Power. At the bottom, there were large numbers of amirs, mamluks and others that only had very limited ranges of Effective Power, if they had any at all. At the very top, ideally, there would be the individual patron who had absolute Effective Power, with senior clients who, in their turn, were the strongest patrons of the regime.[21]

What qualified individuals for the roles of patrons and clients in that pyramid? What was the nature of the ubiquitous relationships between them that engendered those roles, in this specific timeframe in particular? As said, they were relationships of power, but how and by whom such a relationship was established and maintained remains to be answered. In this respect, an interesting and recurrent theme when identifying those thirty-two amirs and sultans who were

---

[19] Ibn Qāḍī Shuhba, *Tārīkh*, III, pp. 444, 508; I, p. 362.

[20] Cfr. Ibn Khaldūn, *Kitāb al-ʿIbar*, V, p. 451; Ibn Duqmāq, *al-Jawhar al-Thamīn*, pp. 399–400; al-ʿAynī, *ʿIqd al-Jumān*, p. 114; al-Maqrīzī, *Khiṭaṭ*, IV, pp. 119, 257–258, 259; al-Maqrīzī, *Sulūk*, II/3, pp. 825, 860, 889–890; III/1, pp. 35, 41–42; Ibn Taghrī Birdī, *Nujūm*, X, pp. 221, 268, 307–308, 310; Ibn Qāḍī Shuhba, *Tārīkh*, III, p. 117.

[21] Such a social structure is suggested to be a basic feature of Middle Eastern patrimonial societies ("chains of vertical emanation") by Bill and Springborg (*Politics in the Middle East*, pp. 153–154). Yet, it needs to be remarked that, at the same time and contrary to their model, the years between 1341 and 1382 very often did not have a "sovereign [. . .] located at the centre of the political system" (p. 153).

the period's Effective Power holders was the fact that the terminology used for that purpose in the sources, like *tadbīr* and *taṣarruf*, often was clarified by references to these individuals' ability to promote in the military ranks and appoint in the administration, irrespective of their lack of legitimate executive authority to do so.[22] This was clearly considered an important aspect of their Effective Power.

Indeed, it seems very likely that it is the area of Legitimate Power, of access to military rank and office, and importantly also to the income they generated, in which the origins of most Mamluk patron-client ties of this period—as far as retrievable from the sources—can be situated. As will be made clear, mutual profitability was an essential regulating factor or norm for the establishment of such ties. Not just the patron hoped to gain from another client's allying with him in terms of power, service and loyalty, but equally the client only engaged himself with a patron if he thought he could gain from this, especially in terms of that access to rank and office. And given such a fickle materialistic norm, there should perhaps be no surprise in the observation (made above) of calculating clients allying with more than one patron. Actually, this is exemplified in a very telling way by al-Ṣafadī's detailed biography of the amir ʿAlāʾ al-Dīn Alṭunbughā al-Dawādār (d. 1343), mentioned before as engaged with five patrons in often recurrent alternating order:

> He is a mamluk of Ibn Bākhil, and he was a *dawādār* with the amir ʿAlam al-Dīn Sanjar al-Jāwulī; [. . .] when rumours were spread about

[22] Recurrent expressions to that extent are mentioned for a number of power holders in a variety of sources: Arghūn al-ʿAlāʾī (d. 1347) and Bahādur al-Damurdāshī (d. 1343) "could give to whom they chose and take from whom they wanted" (al-Shujāʿī, *Tārīkh*, p. 241; identical in Ibn Qāḍī Shuhba, *Tārīkh*, II, p. 308); Ṣarghitmish (d. 1358) "was given the executive authority in all the regime's affairs, including appointments and dismissals [. . .]; if someone else took charge of a dismissal or an appointment, he got furious [. . .]" (al-Maqrīzī, *Sulūk*, II/3, p. 860; identical in Ibn Taghrī Birdī, *Nujūm*, X, p. 268); Yalbughā al-Khāṣṣakī (d. 1366) "[. . .] started to dismiss whom he chose to dismiss and appoint whom he preferred [. . .]" (Ibn Taghri Birid, *Nujum*, XI, p. 5), in 1366, a group of four amirs "were installed with the authority to dissolve and solve, to give and take, and to appoint and dismiss" (Ibn Duqmāq, *Nuzhat al-Anām*, fol. 4; almost identical in al-ʿAynī, *ʿIqd al-Jumān*, p. 147); al-Ashraf Shaʿbān (d. 1377) "[. . .] dismissed and appointed without the amirs' counsel" (Ibn Ibn Taghri Birid, *Nujūm*, XI, p. 53), and he "[. . .] distributed the offices and appointed [. . .]" (Ibn Khaldūn, *Kitāb al-ʿIbar*, V, p. 467); Ṭashtamur al-ʿAlāʾī (d. 1384) "got [the authority] to appoint and dismiss, to dissolve and solve" (Ibn Khaldūn, *Kitāb al-ʿIbar*, V, p. 467), and he "used to grant to the two amirs [Barqūq and Barka] everything they wanted regarding appointments, dismissals, commands, prohibitions and the like." (Ibn Ḥajar, *Inbāʾ al-Ghumr*, I, p. 236).

> al-Jāwulī that the *iqṭā*ʿs of his mamluks were twenty to thirty thousand [*dīnār jayshī*], he reassessed the fiefs and gave to the aforementioned Alṭunbughā an *iqṭā*ʿ that was worth less than the one he had before. So [Alṭunbughā] left him and went to Egypt without the consent of the amir ʿAlam al-Dīn. But people respected the opinion of [Alṭunbughā's] master and no one dared to take him in his service. [. . .] Thereupon, he left to Ṣafad, where its *nāʾib*, the *ḥājj* Ariqṭāy, welcomed him with great friendliness. He had a square decree for an *iqṭā*ʿ written for him, which he took to Egypt [for confirmation]. But it was taken from him, so he had to return [to Syria empty-handed]. [Alṭunbughā] came to Damascus, where he wrote a eulogy on the amir Sayf al-Dīn Tankiz, as well as on Nāṣir al-Dīn al-Dawādār, and Nāṣir al-Dīn al-Khāzindār. [. . .] So [the latter two] interceded for him with their own master, who then gave him an *iqṭā*ʿ in the *ḥalqa* of Damascus. [. . .] His case was one of the causes for the conflict between Tankiz and al-Jāwulī, and while Alṭunbughā stayed in Damascus, al-Jāwulī was arrested and remained in prison for a while. When he was freed, Alṭunbughā came to him and served him briefly. Then [al-Jāwulī] sent him off to Damascus in the days of [the *nāʾib al-Shām*,] the amir ʿAlāʾ al-Dīn Alṭunbughā, who made him take sides with him, as a supervisor of the Manṣūrī *waqf*.[23]

Clearly, while a lot can be said about this revealing passage, a useful starting point is the observation that the position and role any politically active individual could take up in the pyramid of Effective Power depended entirely on what he had on offer for the other players. Identifying patrons, clients and their socio-political conduct therefore reverts to identifying the deeper grounds of such an exchange relationship. As will be seen, whoever the patron and whoever the client, their relationship always concerned the exchange of patronage, that is a patron's socio-political and economic favour or in some cases also protection, for clientage, or a client's commensurate service, subordination and assistance. These two constituents have been identified before in a similar Mamluk context by Winslow Clifford, and his use of the terms *niʿma* (favour) and *khidma* (service) in this respect will be further adopted for the present purpose.[24]

[23] Al-Ṣafadī, *Aʿyān*, I, pp. 610–611; identical in al-Ṣafadī, *Wāfī*, IX, pp. 366–369. Similar stories in Ibn Ḥajar, *Durar*, III, pp. 407–408; Ibn Taghrī Birdī, *al-Manhal*, III, pp. 71–72. On the square decree (*murabbaʿ*), see D.S. Richards, "A Mamluk Emir's 'Square' Decree", *BSOAS* 54 (1991), pp. 63–67.

[24] See for instance Clifford, "State Formation", pp. 6, 47. For examples of the use of these terms in the source material of the period from 1341 to 1382, see, apart from al-Ṣafadī's biography of Alṭunbughā (where the verbs *istakhdama*, 'to take in one's service', and *khadama*, 'to serve', were used, as well as the noun *makhdūm*, 'someone who is being served, master'), also al-Qalqashandī, *Ṣubḥ*, VIII, pp. 242–243

A Patron's Niʿma: *promotion and appointment*

The favour or *niʿma* a client could expect to receive from a patron consisted first and foremost of promotions in Egypt's and Syria's military ranks, and, because of the link between military rank and the *iqṭāʿ* system, this was at the same time synonymous with promotion in the regime's economic hierarchy. Thus, the amir Qawṣūn, for instance, is portrayed on several occasions as distributing ranks of amirs of ten and forty in exchange for support for his often heavily contested cause.[25] When the amir Quṭlūbughā al-Fakhrī (d. 1342) took Damascus in the period November–December 1341 and was threatened with being outnumbered by his opponent's troops, Ibn Taghrī Birdī made him send a call through the city of Damascus that "anyone hoping for *iqṭāʿ* and military payment should join" his troops.[26] When in 1344 the amir Manjak presented the head of the executed former sultan al-Nāṣir Aḥmad to al-Ṣāliḥ Ismāʿīl, he was rewarded with a rank of amir of forty.[27] Sultan al-Muẓaffar Ḥājjī is mentioned as assigning ranks of amir of ten, forty and hundred to his personal mamluks, in order to strengthen his position after the killing of one of his foremost clients.[28] In the final days of the year 1350, the equally ambitious sultan al-Nāṣir Ḥasan conspired against a number of his most senior amirs and promised their ranks and *iqṭāʿ*s to those that conspired with him.[29] And in 1377, the amirs Barqūq and Barka were promoted to the rank of amir of forty after supporting the

---

(copy of an official letter, sent by al-Ṣāliḥ Ṣāliḥ to Syria in 1351, which details the elements that made up the *khidma* to the sultan ["to honour and praise, accept the rulings and execute the orders . . ."] and even mentions that in return the sultan should heed the "rights" *khidma* conveyed upon subordinates [*mā lahum ʿalayhī min ḥuqūq al-khidma*]—because of his failure to do so, al-Nāṣir Ḥasan was claimed to have been deposed rightfully; such "rights"—illustrative of the normative character of this relationship—are also referred to in, for instance, al-Ṣafadī, *Aʿyān*, II, p. 617: "he abided by the right of his service"; V, p. 38: "he acknowledged the rights of those that adhered to his gate"); for further explicit references to *khidma*, see al-Ṣafadī, *Aʿyān*, II, p. 538; III, p. 317; Ibn Ḥajar, *Durar*, III, p. 250; Ibn Qāḍī Shuhba, *Tārīkh*, II, p. 380. *Niʿma*, mostly occurs in the format of the verb *anʿama*, 'to grant', especially offices and ranks, see for instance al-Maqrīzī, *Sulūk*, II/3, p. 559; al-ʿAynī, *ʿIqd al-Jumān*, pp. 210–211; Ibn Taghrī Birdī, *Nujūm*, XI, p. 150.

[25] See al-Shujāʿī, *Tārīkh*, pp. 144, 174; al-Maqrīzī, *Sulūk*, II/3, pp. 572, 574, 583; al-ʿAynī, *ʿIqd al-Jumān*, p. 57; Ibn Taghrī Birdī, *Nujūm*, X, p. 23; Ibn Qāḍī Shuhba, *Tārīkh*, II, pp. 207, 222.

[26] Ibn Taghrī Birdī, *Nujūm*, X, p. 35.

[27] Al-Shujāʿī, *Tārīkh*, p. 270.

[28] Al-Maqrīzī, *Sulūk*, II/3, p. 738; identical in Ibn Taghrī Birdī, *Nujūm*, X, p. 168.

[29] Al-Maqrīzī, *Sulūk*, II/3, p. 841; identical in Ibn Taghrī Birdī, *Nujūm*, X, p. 330.

successful rebellion of the amir Aynabak against his colleague Qaraṭāy.[30]

These are but some of the most telling examples that illustrate a patron's involvement in his clients' military promotions. There are several more,[31] including often lengthy and remarkably detailed lists of promotions that pop up in the sources when a new power holder took over.[32] Though the power holder's involvement in the latter cases is less explicitly referred to, they again offer very suggestive evidence for this aspect of patron-client ties, not in the least because of their unmistakable timing; moreover, their remarkable detail hints at a direct link with the administrative registers that confirmed these promotions and makes them even more important in this respect than a chronicler's often passing reference.[33]

In the case of appointments, similar conduct emerges, for instance, from the example of the *nā'ib Ḥalab* Arghūn Shāh (d. 1349), who is said to have secretly supported the actions of sultan al-Muẓaffar Ḥājjī against his *nā'ib al-Shām* only when he was promised the latter office.[34]

---

[30] Al-Maqrīzī, *Sulūk*, III/1, p. 308; similar stories in al-ʿAynī, *'Iqd al-Jumān*, p. 224; Ibn Taghrī Birdī, *Nujūm*, XI, p. 154; Ibn Qāḍī Shuhba, *Tārīkh*, II, p. 542; I, p. 42.

[31] See for instance al-Shujāʿī, *Tārīkh*, pp. 180, 264; al-Ṣafadī, *A'yān*, II, p. 50; III, p. 317; V, p. 259; al-Kutubī, *'Uyūn al-Tawārīkh*, fol. 170; Ibn Kathīr, *al-Bidāya*, XIV, p. 265; Ibn Duqmāq, *Nuzhat al-Anām*, fol. 80v; al-ʿAynī, *'Iqd al-Jumān*, p. 56, 175; al-Maqrīzī, *Khiṭaṭ*, IV, p. 291; al-Maqrīzī, *Sulūk*, II/3, pp. 661, 718, 721, 731; III/1, pp. 117–118, 216; Ibn Ḥajar, *Inbā' al-Ghumr*, I, p. 280; Ibn Taghrī Birdī, *Nujūm*, X, pp. 152, 154, 161; XI, pp. 32, 33–34, 63; Ibn Qāḍī Shuhba, *Tārīkh*, II, p. 225; III, pp. 430, 541; I, p. 69.

[32] Among the most prominent examples are: the elimination by the amir Yalbughā al-Khāṣṣakī of a rival in early 1366, the account of which was immediately followed by a detailed list with no less than thirty eight names of amirs that were promoted on one single day (al-Maqrīzī, *Sulūk*, III/1, pp. 117–118; identical in Ibn Taghrī Birdī, *Nujūm*, XI, pp. 33–34), an event which was explicitly linked to Yalbughā's patronage by Ibn Taghrī Birdī (Ibn Taghrī Birdī, *Nujūm*, XI, p. 32); the rise of Asandamur al-Nāṣiri in June 1367, confirmed by the listed promotion of dozens of fresh recruits (Ibn Duqmāq, *Nuzhat al-Anām*, fol. 5v–6; al-ʿAynī, *'Iqd al-Jumān*, p. 149; al-Maqrīzī, *Sulūk*, III/1, pp. 144–145; Ibn Taghrī Birdī, *Nujūm*, XI, pp. 44–45; Ibn Qāḍī Shuhba, *Tārīkh*, III, pp. 296, 297); and the elimination by the amir Barqūq of his rival Barka in 1380, the acount of which is again followed in the sources by a list that informs about the promotion of nineteen amirs (Ibn Khaldūn, *Kitāb al-'Ibar*, V, pp. 471–472; al-ʿAynī, *'Iqd al-Jumān*, pp. 264–265; al-Maqrīzī, *Sulūk*, III/2, pp. 439–440; Ibn Taghrī Birdī, *Nujūm*, XI, pp. 188, 206–207).

[33] On these five cadastral registers, one of which listed the names of *iqṭāʿ* holders and the date of the *iqṭāʿ*'s conferment, see Rabie, *The Financial System of Egypt*, pp. 38, 39–40; R.S. Cooper, "The Assesment and Collection of Kharaj Tax in Medieval Egypt", *Journal of the American Oriental Society* 96 (1976), pp. 365, 367, 372–373, 375, 379. They were discussed in detail in al-Nuwayrī, *Nihāyat al-Arab fī Funūn al-Adab*, vol. VIII, Cairo 1931, pp. 200–213.

[34] Al-Maqrīzī, *Sulūk*, II/3, p. 731.

Nevertheless, the fickleness of the relationship that sprang from this normative exchange is equally exemplified by the case of two amirs, whose conspiracy against al-Ashraf Shaʿbān in 1367 was brought to light only one day after the sultan had appointed both of them jointly in the office of *atābak al-ʿasākir*.[35]

Actually, this crucial aspect of amirs' patronage, by which the military ranks and administration were populated by clients first and foremost, sheds useful light on observations made before. When chapter one concluded that between 1341 and 1382 the Mamluk military command structure was occasionally subject to sweeping changes, a reason for this can be found in the use of that institutional framework by alternating patrons to attract and reward clients. Hence, their Effective Power had subjugated Legitimate Power and now determined its outlook and development.

A Patron's Niʿma: *financial and other benefits*

A patron's *niʿma* can also be seen to have taken other, more directly beneficial formats, including first and foremost the offering of immediate financial or economic rewards, as opposed to the postponed financial benefits that promotions could engender for a client.[36]

Actually, for the entire period from 1341 to 1382, the sources more often refer to such immediate rewards by the wealthy among the amirs, than to the bestowal of any kind of institutional benefits. Indeed, a number of the politically active seem to have gathered enough wealth from their *iqṭāʿ*s, and from additional sources of income, to enable the buying of a client's *khidma*.[37] In the short term, this often proved a very efficient and rewarding policy, though its long-term effects were often less reliable, and stable patron-client relations are less likely to have resulted uniquely from this kind of interaction. A selection of examples will suffice to illustrate this.

[35] Ibn Khaldūn, *Kitāb al-ʿIbar*, V, p. 458; Ibn Duqmāq, *Nuzhat al-Anām*, fol. 38v; al-Maqrīzī, *Sulūk*, III/1, p. 153; Ibn Taghrī Birdī, *Nujūm*, XI, p. 49; Ibn Qāḍī Shuhba, *Tārīkh*, III, pp. 310–311.

[36] Promotions had to go through an administrative process before confirmation, and any financial benefit from *iqṭāʿ* largely depended on the annual cycles of agriculture.

[37] On some of the elite's fabulous wealth by the end of al-Nāṣir Muḥammad's reign, see Van Steenbergen, "Mamluk Elite", pp. 188–192; Levanoni, *Turning Point*, pp. 53–60. On the amirs' active economic involvement—even primacy—in sectors other than agriculture too, see for instance E. Ashtor, *A Social and Economic History of the Near East in the Middle Ages*, London 1976, pp. 284–285.

In the course of the conflict between the amir Qawṣūn and the sultan al-Manṣūr Abū Bakr in August 1341, Qawṣūn was informed of his imminent arrest by an amir known as one of Abū Bakr's most important supporters, but who reportedly had switched camps when he had heard about Qawṣūn's "largess to those sultanic mamluks that joined [him]."[38] In November of the same year, however, when a similar thing happened to Qawṣūn himself, he is stated to have cried out his frustration since this unreliable client of his "had been given [. . .] forty thousand *dīnār*, along with horses, clothes and gifts".[39] In April 1342, the amir Aqsunqur al-Nāṣiri showed reluctance to depart on an ill-fated military campaign, but when a donation by the sultan of ten thousand *dīnār* and five hundred camels was presented to him, al-Maqrīzī expressed the subordination such a *niʿma* required by commenting that "he had no other option than to leave".[40] In 1351, the rebellious al-Nāṣir Ḥasan offered the amir Ṭāz substantial gifts in cash and kind, most likely as a reward for his assistance during the sultan's emancipation from Ṭāz' colleagues, though this too soon turned out to be a lost case of patronage when the very same amir dethroned him.[41] In the course of the rebellion of the *nāʾib al-Shām* Baydamur al-Khwārizmī (d. 1386) in 1361, he is said to have managed to take the citadel and rally the amirs by spending lots of money on them.[42] After sultan al-Ashraf Shaʿbān gained victory over the Yalbughāwīya-mamluks in October 1367, al-Maqrīzī states that "the sultan spent one hundred *dīnār* on each one of his mamluks".[43] Ten years later, in 1377, many mamluks were persuaded to take part in the rebellion against this al-Ashraf by promises of an immediate cash reward to each of no less than five hundred *dīnār*, an unprecedented amount that afterwards was only reluctantly paid to them.[44] And the amir Īnāl (d. 1392) is recorded

---

[38] al-Maqrīzī, *Sulūk*, II/3, p. 567; identical account in Ibn Taghrī Birdī, *Nujūm*, X, p. 13.

[39] al-Maqrīzī, *Sulūk*, II/3, p. 581; identical account in Ibn Taghrī Birdī, *Nujūm*, X, p. 34. For detailed reports of Qawṣūn's offering sums of money to Quṭlūbughā, see al-Shujāʿī, *Tārīkh*, p. 156; al-Maqrīzī, *Sulūk*, II/3, pp. 578, 580; Ibn Taghrī Birdī, *Nujūm*, X, pp. 30, 33; Ibn Qāḍī Shuhba, *Tārīkh*, II, p. 212.

[40] al-Maqrīzī, *Sulūk*, II/3, p. 635.

[41] al-Maqrīzī, *Sulūk*, II/3, pp. 837, 840, 842; additional accounts in Ibn Taghrī Birdī, *Nujūm*, X, pp. 218, 229.

[42] al-Ḥusaynī, *Dhayl al-ʿIbar*, pp. 189–190; Ibn al-ʿIrāqī, *Dhayl al-ʿIbar*, I, p. 50.

[43] al-Maqrīzī, *Sulūk*, III/1, p. 154.

[44] al-Maqrīzī, *Sulūk*, III/1, pp. 275, 290, 295; al-ʿAynī, *ʿIqd al-Jumān*, p. 212; Ibn Ḥajar, *Inbāʾ al-Ghumr*, I, pp. 197–198; Ibn Taghrī Birdī, *Nujūm*, XI, p. 152; Ibn Qāḍī Shuhba, *Tārīkh*, III, p. 511.

to have made a similar, but less successful promise when he rebelled against the amir Barqūq in December 1379.[45]

These and several other examples that characterise the period between 1341 and 1382 all support the assumption that offering immediate cash or kind rewards was reckoned to be another quite efficient means to rally clients, in the short term at least and especially in times of a patron's need for manpower and immediate support.[46] Simultaneously, however, as equally noted in the context of appointments, several of these examples similarly illustrate the absence of reliability and durability such an extremely materialist kind of conduct instilled into that relationship. Clients' mere economic calculation could work in favour of a patron as much as it could work against him.

A final and more lasting type of directly beneficial *niʿma* has to do with the protection a patron could offer against all sorts of threats, including arrests, or in order to obtain release from prison. In this respect, in early 1348, the eradication of the small *iqṭāʿ*s of a great number of *ḥalqa* soldiers was avoided when amirs showed their support for many of them.[47] In 1341, the amir Maliktamur al-Ḥijāzī successfully had a colleague's imminent arrest and imprisonment transformed into his less degrading exile to Tripoli.[48] And in 1347, the amir Shaykhū brought about the release from prison of a murdered colleague's entourage, which in this case did actually reward him with loyal clients for life.[49] Protection may have created more lasting emotional bonds than any other sort of benefit.

The key to a Patron's Niʿma: Shafāʿa *and* Maqbūl al-kalima

A key issue for an ambitious amir in enabling the *niʿma* that made him a patron—promotions and appointments and other sorts of

---

[45] al-Maqrīzī, *Sulūk*, III/1, p. 365; al-ʿAynī, *ʿIqd al-Jumān*, p. 248; Ibn Ḥajar, *Inbāʾ al-Ghumr*, I, p. 310; Ibn Taghrī Birdī, *Nujūm*, XI, p. 168; Ibn Qāḍī Shuhba, *Tārīkh*, I, p. 9.

[46] For additional references, see al-Shujāʿī, *Tārīkh*, pp. 172, 174, 180, 181, 228, 261; al-Ṣafadī, *Aʿyān*, I, p. 602; Ibn Kathīr, *al-Bidāya*, XIV, p. 265; al-Maqrīzī, *Sulūk*, II/3, pp. 577, 582, 583, 586, 632, 687, 693, 695, 702, 709, 721, 731; Ibn Taghrī Birdī, *Nujūm*, X, pp. 34, 38, 61, 65, 120, 123, 127, 135, 152, 161; Ibn Qāḍī Shuhba, *Tārīkh*, II, pp. 216, 225–226, 364.

[47] al-Maqrīzī, *Sulūk*, II/3, p. 747.

[48] al-Shujāʿī, *Tārīkh*, p. 131.

[49] al-Kutubī, *ʿUyūn al-Tawārīkh*, fol. 162–162v; almost identical account in al-Ṣafadī, *Aʿyān*, II, p. 532. For one of these clients' loyalty to Shaykhū until the latter's death in 1357, see al-Ṣafadī, *Aʿyān*, II. pp. 617–619.

benefit—was his ability to acquire sufficient control over or access to this hard currency of patron-client relationships. As explained in the previous chapter, the sultan and his authorising signature largely dominated this access, for his was the only administrative authority that could legitimate both the main income a patron generated from his *iqṭāʿ*, and the promotions and appointments that were so indispensable in the set up of patron-client relationships. Nevertheless, patrons other than the sultan did manage to introduce clients into the institutions dominated by the sultan's office. What strategies were applied to cheat the sultan out of this authority?

From one perspective, such strategy can be seen to have resulted from a more extended relationship, including not just the aspiring patron and his eager client, but also another patron, with wider abilities for *niʿma*, whose client the first patron actually comes to be, mainly in return for the enablement of his own *niʿma* to that third person in this relationship. Clearly, this is only one half of the explanation, for the higher patron would need to acquire control and access in his turn with another patron, and so on. It is however an essential half, not least because it gives deeper insight into the different roles one ambitious individual can take within the pyramid of Effective Power, and hence, into the identification of the period's patrons and clients. A key-feature of this three-tiered interplay when described in the sources is the fact that this *niʿma* for one's own clients via another patron was always the result of a sort of successful mediation or intercession (*shafāʿa*) for the client with the higher patron, in return for which the mediator offered his own *khidma* to the patron. The interaction was thus beneficial to all three parties involved, not least to the central figure of the mediator. His successful mediation not only rewarded him with the service and subordination of his clients, but also with a public confirmation of his credibility as a successful patron and mediator, both towards peers and rivals and towards prospective new clients.[50]

---

[50] The more theoretic approach to the concept of Mamluk intercession (*shafāʿa*) in fourteenth-century ethical and religious texts has been surveyed and analysed by Shaun Marmon (Shaun Marmon, "The Quality of Mercy: Intercession in Mamluk Society", *SI* 87 (1998), pp. 125–139). She defines *jāh* (position)—a term occasionally used to refer to a patron's influence and ability for *niʿma*—as creating a "moral obligation to exercise that divine quality of mercy (*raḥma*) or compassion (*shafaqa*) by acting as an intercessor" (p. 136). From the point of view of the strategies of socio-political conduct as developed here, *shafāʿa* arguably often results rather from

There are several illustrations of socio-political interaction dominated by such a concept as intercession. Among the most illustrative is al-Shujāʿī's account of the senior amir Sanjar al-Jāwulī's request to Qawṣūn in 1341 to assign the military rank of a deceased amir to this amir's ten-year old son, whose guardian Sanjar was; al-Shujāʿī suggests that Qawṣūn's objections to the boy's age were brushed aside with the argument that the final beneficiary would not be the boy, but Sanjar; in the end Qawṣūn agreed because he needed the support of Sanjar and his peers to "assist him in [pursuing] his ambitions".[51] This is one of the finest examples of the triple benefit this sort of interaction engendered, to the patron Qawṣūn, the intercessor Sanjar and the client boy. But this benefit did not only concern access to promotion and appointment. There are also several examples of how intercession was used by a patron to offer protection. In the early 1370s, for instance, Yalbughā al-Khāṣṣakī's exiled mamluks—including the amir Barqūq—were allowed to return to Cairo, after the intercession of the amir Ṭashtamur al-Dawādār with the sultan al-Ashraf Shaʿbān.[52] And an amir called Alṭunbughā al-Māridānī (d. 1373), a notorious alcoholic who had been banned to Syria, "was returned to Egypt at Manklī Bughā al-Shamsī's intercession, and he was given a rank of amir of ten".[53]

---

individual calculation than from such moral obligation. Even Marmon herself states that an intercessor's aim was social promotion ("The intercessor must assume a ritualized position of humility. In doing so he stands to increase his status, to reaffirm his "place" or *jāh*. But he also runs the risk of actual humiliation and loss of 'place' " [p. 138]). Marmon also identifies *shafāʿa*'s triple benefit: "The quality of mercy, in the case of intercession [. . .] was not twice, but three times blessed, for the one who gave, for the one who received, and most of all, for the intercessor, [. . .] who depending on the stage on which he acted, reaped the greatest benefits and suffered the most perilous losses" (p. 139).

[51] al-Shujāʿī, *Tārīkh*, p. 220. For additional similar illustrations of *shafāʿa* throughout the period, in a variety of sources, see, for instance, al-Shujāʿī, *Tārīkh*, p. 134; al-Ṣafadī, *Aʿyān*, II, p. 577; al-Kutubī, *ʿUyūn al-Tawārīkh*, fol. 170; Ibn Kathīr, *al-Bidāya*, XIV, p. 265; al-Maqrīzī, *Khiṭaṭ*, III, p. 65; al-Maqrīzī, *Sulūk*, II/3, pp. 681, 884; Ibn Taghrī Birdī, *Nujūm*, X, p. 118; Ibn Qāḍī Shuhba, *Tārīkh*, III, pp. 435, 457, 490.

[52] Ibn Khaldūn, *Kitāb al-ʿIbar*, V, p. 462; Ibn Ḥajar, *Inbāʾ al-Ghumr*, I, p. 256; II, p. 23.

[53] Ibn Qāḍī Shuhba, *Tārīkh*, III, p. 418. For similar examples, again often explicitly using the term *shafāʿa*, see al-Shujāʿī, *Tārīkh*, pp. 131, 192, 237; al-Ṣafadī, *Aʿyān*, I, p. 649; Ibn Kathīr, *al-Bidāya*, XIV, p. 218; Ibn Khaldūn, *Kitāb al-ʿIbar*, V, p. 458; Ibn Duqmāq, *Nuzhat al-Anām*, fol. 37v; al-Maqrīzī, *Sulūk*, II/3, pp. 563–565, 666, 668, 710, 747, 844–848, 917, 928; III/1, pp. 152, 268; al-ʿAynī, *ʿIqd al-Jumān*, pp. 51, 61, 140, 153, 175; Ibn Taghrī Birdī, *Nujūm*, X, pp. 136, 220, 255–260; XI, pp. 32, 47–48, 62; Ibn Qāḍī Shuhba, *Tārīkh*, II, p. 301; III, p. 310.

Nevertheless, this is only one part of the explanation for the processes that enabled a patron's encroachment upon the regime's Legitimate Power. Especially with respect to access to rank and office and the income and authority they generated, the sultan's legitimisation remained unconditional. Intercession, therefore, in the very end always had to be directed towards those amirs that had both direct access to and substantial influence on the sultan and his legitimising decision-making. These were patrons whose intercession could hardly be refused by the sultan, who had—as phrased by the contemporary scholar Tāj al-Dīn al-Subkī (d. 1370)—*maqbūl al-kalima* or a 'guaranteed say'.[54] By necessity, most socio-political conduct was closely linked in its ultimate ambitions—Effective Power, income and the securing of income for clients, but also security and protection—to this circle of trustees and intimates around the sultan who had the access to make such ultimate ambitions come true.

When discussing the year 1347, al-Maqrīzī states that the amir Arghūn Shāh (d. 1349) managed to become *nā'ib Ḥalab* not just by sending gifts, but more through the extensive intercession of two senior amirs with the sultan al-Muẓaffar Ḥājjī.[55] And according to al-ʿAynī, Arghūn Shāh's predecessor in Aleppo, the amir Baydamur al-Badrī (d. 1347), had been appointed by the sultan "on the advice of" yet another amir.[56] In 1343, the amir Arghūn al-ʿAlā'ī is reported to have "directed" the sultan in the appointments of *nā'ib*s in Syria,[57] and in 1345, this Arghūn managed to keep sultan al-Kāmil Shaʿbān from promoting and appointing one of his adversaries.[58] Similar *maqbūl al-kalima* can be observed in the case of four amirs—Ṭashtamur, Quṭlūbughā (d. 1342), Aydughmish and Ṭuquzdamur (d. 1345)—who, in late 1341, managed to secure the appointments of *nā'ib*s in Egypt and Syria, even when the sultan objected to them.[59]

Thus, only those individuals could act as patrons that had or were expected to have at least some *maqbūl al-kalima* or successful intercession, the relative size of which—that is, the amount of *niʿma* the

[54] Tāj al-Dīn al-Subkī, *Muʿīd al-Niʿam wa mubīd al-niqam*, ed. M.ʿA. al-Najjār, A.Z. Shiblī and M. Abū al-ʿUyūn, Cairo 1996(3), pp. 15–16; also Marmon, "Quality of Mercy", pp. 133–134, 136.

[55] al-Maqrīzī, *Sulūk*, II/3, p. 591.

[56] al-ʿAynī, *ʿIqd al-Jumān*, p. 79.

[57] al-Maqrīzī, *Sulūk*, II/3, p. 645.

[58] al-Maqrīzī, *Sulūk*, II/3, p. 690.

[59] al-Shujāʿī, *Tārīkh*, pp. 206–207.

patron managed to secure—reflected one's success as a patron, and the position one took in the so-called pyramid of Effective Power. At the very top were those whose *maqbūl* allowed them to patronise all other players. Ideally, this would include the sultan himself, as happened in this period with the five sultans previously identified as power holders.[60] But especially when that sultan could not or would not sprinkle his own *niʿma* and develop his own Effective Power, a patron's *maqbūl* with the sultan tended to revert to a mere exercise in administrative and political theory, and in practice this patron's authority was nearly absolute. It is this situation that is reflected in the observation made before that, irrespective of the institutional framework's organisation, the sources still accredited to many of the twenty seven amirs with crucial Effective Power a firm say in the promotion and appointment policies of the regime. Their *maqbūl* with the sultan had become such that they actually controlled that framework, and in their silent consent, the sources reveal to what extent this had come to belong to the nature of their socio-political environment.

In this vein, the amir Qawṣūn (d. 1342) is pictured on several occasions as distributing ranks of amirs of ten and forty, apparently without any actual involvement of the sultan,[61] a situation which was very cynically captured when, as mentioned in the previous chapter, Ibn Taghrī Birdī pictured the elaborate procedure to obtain the infant sultan's signature and keep up institutional appearances.[62] The fifteenth-century chronicler Ibn Qāḍī Shuhba claims that in 1367, the amir Asandamur al-Nāṣiri similarly executed promotions and appointments, when he reported that Asandamur "gave [. . .] a rank of [amir of a hundred and] commander of a thousand [. . .] and made [. . .] *dawādār* of the sultan", that "Asandamur gave [. . .] a rank of amir of forty", and that "the amir Asandamur gave [. . .] a rank of [amir of a hundred and] commander of a thousand and made [. . .]

[60] For the identification of al-Nāṣir Muḥammad b. Qalāwūn as a sultan who had successfully managed to patronise his elite of high-ranking amirs through his sultanic authority, that is, the effective use of his Legitimate Power, see Van Steenbergen, "Mamluk Elite", pp. 183–188, 195; for an alternative view, picturing the role a sultan could play for most of the period 1250–1341 merely as a balancing "gatekeeper" whose steering involvement was limited by the interests of his subordinates, see Clifford, "State Formation", esp. pp. 64–65.

[61] Al-Maqrīzī, *Sulūk*, II/3, pp. 572, 574, 583; al-ʿAynī, *ʿIqd al-Jumān*, p. 57; Ibn Taghrī Birdī, *Nujūm*, X, p. 23; Ibn Qāḍī Shuhba, *Tārīkh*, II, p. 222.

[62] Ibn Taghrī Birdī, *Nujūm*, X, p. 49; identical in al-Maqrīzī, *Sulūk*, II/3, p. 593. See also Holt, "The Structure of Government", p. 48.

assistant "*ḥājib*".[63] And in 1378, the amir Barqūq (d. 1399) is explicitly reported to have "appointed [. . .] in the office of *ra's nawba kabīr*".[64]

Undoubtedly, these situations originated from the automatic *maqbūl al-kalima* these amirs had come to enjoy; hence, the sources did not even bother to mention the nominal sultanic involvement anymore. And this occurred in particular when minors were put on the throne, as happened with seven of the period's sultans: al-Ashraf Kujuk in 1341, al-Nāṣir Ḥasan in 1347, al-Ṣāliḥ Ṣāliḥ in 1351, al-Manṣūr Muḥammad in 1361, al-Ashraf Shaʿbān in 1363, al-Manṣūr ʿAlī in 1377, and his brother al-Ṣāliḥ Ḥājjī in 1381. They had all been too young and inexperienced to contradict the amirs that had put them on the throne, so that these patrons easily managed to become sultans in all but name.

A Client's khidma: *service and subordination*

Similar to *niʿma, khidma*, or a client's usefulness to a patron in exchange for that *niʿma*, was also of varied character. A client's *khidma* in the period from 1341 to 1382 can be seen to have consisted of two types of more or less distinct character. On the one hand, there are illustrations of specific services in very particular circumstances; and on the other hand, in the absence of any such direct service, there remains the intrinsic serviceability of the basic relationship to both the patron and the client.

The first type, of direct services, could consist of many practical things, from mere public pledges or acts of support for a patron, as happened frequently for financial reward, or the dedicated execution of specific jobs or even secret missions, to so-called bribery. In this vein, Qawṣūn tried to rally his peers as his clients so that they would "assist him in [pursuing] his ambitions".[65] When sultan al-Nāṣir Ḥasan took power in early 1351, he relied heavily on four amirs who were made "his boon companions at night and his counsellors during the day".[66] The amir Yūnūs al-Dawādār (d. 1389) is said to have belonged "to those who supported [Barqūq] and fought with

[63] Ibn Qāḍī Shuhba, *Tārīkh*, III, pp. 327, 438; I, p. 69.
[64] Ibn Ḥajar, *Inbā' al-Ghumr*, I, p. 237; Ibn Qāḍī Shuhba, *Tārīkh*, III, p. 555.
[65] Al-Shujāʿī, *Tārīkh*, p. 220.
[66] Al-Maqrīzī, *Sulūk*, II/3, p. 842.

him".[67] Several murders of the period were committed on a patron's orders, as with the case of al-Manṣūr Abū Bakr, assassinated in November 1341 by a local *wālī* under the orders of Qawṣūn;[68] or the case of the *nā'ib al-Shām* Yalbughā al-Yaḥyāwī, murdered in August 1347 by the amir Manjak al-Yūsufī under the orders of al-Muẓaffar Ḥājjī;[69] or in 1380 the murder of the amir Barka by the *nā'ib al-Iskandarīya*, who claimed to have been ordered to do so by the amir Barqūq.[70] Similar direct services, illustrative of their wide range, were rendered in 1357 when an amir was made responsible for feeding the mortally wounded amir Shaykhū,[71] or in 1351, when another amir offered shelter to the hunted Manjak al-Yūsufī.[72]

A final type of this direct service rendered by a client to a patron which should be mentioned here, is a very pragmatic one and concerns the effective purchase of a patron's *niʿma*. Thus, Ibn Ḥajar mentions how the amir Dāwūd b. Asad al-Qaymarī (d. 1362) "used to seek to gain favour with the senior amirs by [offering them] merchandise and crops".[73] *Khidma* was not just about serving a patron in return for his *niʿma*, but also at first instance about attracting a patron's attention, by any means possible. And especially for clients whose political usefulness was less obvious, such as a low-ranking Syrian amir like Dāwūd, offering a share in his economic interests was almost the only means they had to attract the attention that could guarantee a measure of prosperity. In its most extreme format, this type of *khidma*, occasionally even referred to as bribery (*barṭala*), devolved into payments made in return for specific appointments, a standard practice throughout this entire period which affected mostly lower executive offices like that of *wālī* in the Egyptian and Syrian districts.[74]

---

[67] Al-Maqrīzī, *Khiṭaṭ*, IV, p. 291.

[68] See for instance al-Maqrīzī, *Sulūk*, II/3, p. 579.

[69] See for instance al-Maqrīzī, *Sulūk*, II/3, pp. 733–734.

[70] Al-Maqrīzī, *Sulūk*, III/1, p. 396–397; Ibn Ḥajar, *Inbā' al-Ghumr*, II, pp. 10–11; Ibn Qāḍī Shuhba, *Tārīkh*, I, pp. 32–34.

[71] Al-Ṣafadī, *Aʿyān*, I, p. 553.

[72] Al-Maqrīzī, *Sulūk*, II/3, p. 869; Ibn Taghrī Birdī, *Nujūm*, X, p. 272.

[73] Ibn Ḥajar, *Durar*, II, p. 96.

[74] A. ʿAbd al-Raziq situates the real take off of corruption only after 1382 (A. ʿAbd al-Raziq, *al-Badhl wa al-Barṭala*, pp. 28–31; for the role bribery played in the period from 1422 to 1517, see T. Miura, "Administrative Networks"); however, there are several references to similar quite formalised practices already from 1342 onwards (see al-Shujāʿī, *Tārīkh*, pp. 209, 212; al-Maqrīzī, *Sulūk*, II/3, pp. 606, 726, 749, 750, 753; III/I, pp. 8–9, 324; al-ʿAynī, *ʿIqd al-Jumān*, p. 174; Ibn Taghrī Birdī,

As for the other, more general type of *khidma*—serviceability to the benefit of both—, this concerns the client's simple acknowledgement of the patron's ability to impose his will upon the client, as expressed by direct service, but also more commonly by a mostly silent subordination. Through a patron's *niʿma*, his clients could have come to occupy many ranks and offices, which, as part of the *khidma* they thus owed to that patron, and including these institutions' economic, military and administrative prerogatives, were virtually his and became an important element in his Effective Power. At the very least, such interdependence is suggested by the few aforementioned long lists of changes in ranks and offices that coincided in some sources' reports with a new patron's rise to power. Obviously, these lists hint at a clear physical parallel between the rise (and fall) of a patron and his clients, and therefore between his and their fate. Moreover, just as these clients benefited from his *niʿma*, so did he benefit from that subordination. The infusion of his own clients and representatives into the institutional framework, often to the detriment of his predecessor's subordinates,[75] was a public confirmation of his *maqbūl al-kalima*, as well as an effective means to secure his subsequent commensurate control of this framework and of the unchallenged access to the regime's resources they offered. For those purposes, mere subordination was an essential quality expected from one's clients, as expressed by al-Shujāʿī, when he states that in 1342, the amir Qawṣūn planned to "promote in his turn those who came to his mind, whom he trusted and did not expect any harm from, and who were known to be at his side and reluctant to rebel against him".[76]

Nujūm, X, pp. 63, 189; Ibn Qāḍī Shuhba, *Tārīkh*, II, p. 241). For rather rare, but similar practices on a higher level of socio-political activity [though the line between *niʿma* and *khidma* and who is patronising who in such cases becomes rather blurred], see the case of the amir Arghūn Shāh (d. 1349): al-Maqrīzī in particular mentions him as having enforced through all sorts of gifts, first, in 1347, his bid for appointment as *nāʾib Ḥalab*, and secondly, in June 1348, the extension of his authority as *nāʾib al-Shām* (al-Maqrīzī, *Sulūk*, II/3, pp. 727, 767; the latter case identical in Ibn Taghrī Birdī, *Nujūm*, X, pp. 193–194).

[75] See for instance Ibn Taghrī Birdī's comments that after the assassination of Shaykhū in 1357, "sultan Ḥasan could devote himself to promoting his own mamluks", and that in 1366 "Yalbughā assigned the *iqṭāʿ*s of Ṭaybughā al-Ṭawīl's fellows to a number of his own" (Ibn Taghrī Birdī, *Nujūm*, X, p. 305; XI, p. 32). Equally, after Barka's elimination in 1380, Barqūq even assigns the former's rank and *iqṭāʿ* to his own son (see e.g. al-Maqrīzī, *Sulūk*, III/1, p. 387).

[76] Al-Shujāʿī, *Tārīkh*, p. 189; similar comment on p. 181: Qawṣūn was advised to arrest some unruly senior amirs, and "to appoint in their *iqṭāʿ*s [amirs] whom he did not expect any harm from".

Clients were not, however, only chosen for the services they could render or for their expected subordination and representation. From time to time, accounts emerge of patrons favouring specific clients for very personal, often emotional reasons. In addition to their general usefulness, a client could be distinguished from others by his attendant ability to serve, as it were, the satisfaction of a patron's personal predilections.[77] Thus, as just mentioned, in 1351, four amirs did not merely assist the sultan as counsellors when he took power, but were also chosen to spend the night with him as his boon companions.[78] And the amir Urumbughā al-Kāmilī (d. 1365), a mamluk of al-Kāmil Shaʿbān, is reported to have been "extremely dear to him",[79] whereas the love of the amir Arghūn Shāh (d. 1349) for his mamluk, the amir Qarābughā (d. 1349), is said to have been "excessive", resulting in a *maqbūl al-kalima* with his patron that made the latter look like the *nāʾib al-Shām* in all but name.[80] At court, such emotional favouritism vis-à-vis specific personal mamluks had long since resulted in the set up of the specific corps of the *khāṣṣakīya*, or the sultan's favourites.[81] But also beyond the corps of one's own mamluks, personal feelings are occasionally reported to have been involved, like in the case of Ṭānyariq al-Yūsufī, catapulted to the rank of amir of a hundred by the sultan "because of his beauty and handsomeness",[82] or that of the amir Jaridamur, arousing great passion and consequent favour with the sultan; in both cases, they had not been one of their respective sultan's mamluks.[83] Clearly, though calculating interests were imperative in the set up of patron-client ties, an analysis of the socio-political conduct of the period should not exclude the involvement of more emotional interests.

---

77 See also M. Chapoutot-Remadi, "Liens propres et identités séparées chez les Mamelouks bahrides", in Chr. Décobert (ed.), *Valeur et distance. Identités et sociétés en Egypte* (*Collection de l'atelier méditerranéen*), Paris 2000, p. 179.

78 Al-Maqrīzī, *Sulūk*, II/3, p. 842.

79 See Ibn Taghrī Birdī, *Nujūm*, XI, p. 88.

80 See Ibn Qāḍī Shuhba, *Tārīkh*, II, p. 625.

81 On the personal bonds between al-Nāṣir Muḥammad (d. 1341) and his *khāṣṣakīya*, see Van Steenbergen, "Mamluk Elite", pp. 178–179.

82 See al-Maqrīzī, *Sulūk*, II/3, p. 721; similar in Ibn Taghrī Birdī, *Nujūm*, X, p. 154.

83 See al-Maqrīzī, *Sulūk*, II/3, p. 920; also Ibn Ḥajar, *Durar*, II, pp. 214–215.

Kinship

In all, these strategies of Mamluk socio-political conduct, as they occurred in the period from 1341 to 1382, and as reconstructed so far—an interplay of patrons who acquired access to the regime's resources and clients who had serviceability on offer—seem admittedly emotionless, conditional and fluid. Even when there were suggestions of a more physical involvement, the general basic code or rule governing such interaction was its continuous beneficial nature for all individuals involved. Given the fact that Mamluk political culture of the mid-fourteenth century grew out of such patriarchal predecessors as the Ayyubid consanguineous dynasty,[84] drew heavily for its manpower on resources from equally patriarchal, tribal societies,[85] and thrived in a social environment that was heavily characterised by far more emotional and social bonds,[86] narrowing this political culture down to a combination of merely individualistic and principally materialistic conduct might turn out to be an odd and inconsistent simplification.

Nevertheless, as has been shown, source material suggests that this sort of conduct did actually characterise most—if not all—of the interaction of the politically ambitious, entrenched as they were in a highly volatile political climate where power and prosperity were gained only on an insecure footing and oblivion was always looming.[87]

---

[84] See, e.g., M. Chamberlain, "The Crusader era and the Ayyubid dynasty", in C.F. Petry (ed.), *The Cambridge History of Egypt, Vol. 1, Islamic Egypt, 640–1517*, Cambridge 1998, pp. 236–241.

[85] See, e.g., Irwin, *The Middle East in the Middle Ages*, pp. 1–18.

[86] See, e.g., J.P. Berkey, *The Formation of Islam. Religion and Society in the Near East, 600–1800*, Cambridge 2003, pp. 208–209; See also B. Martel-Thoumian, *Les civils et l'administration dans l'état militaire mamluk (IXe/XVe siècle)*, (*Publicatons de l'Insitut Français de Damas* 136), Damas 1991; Martel-Thoumian, "Les élites urbaines sous les Mamlouks circassiens: quelques éléments de réflexion", in U. Vermeulen & J. Van Steenbergen (eds.), *Egypt and Syria in the Fatimid, Ayyubid and Mamluk Eras, III* (*Orientalia Lovaniensia Analecta* 102), Leuven 2001, pp. 282–288, 306.

[87] See for instance careers of amirs like that of Manjak al-Yūsufī and Baydamur al-Khwārizmī, who were appointed several times in some of the regime's highest administrative offices, occasionally swayed substantial amounts of Effective Power, but who also were repeatedly victims of prosecution, confiscation, and imprisonment. (See Appendix 2)

Additionally, such volatility speaks from the high number of violent deaths within the political ranks: of a total number of two hundred and thirty seven individuals who were amirs or mamluks in the period from 1341 to 1382 and whose cause of death is known, one hundred and twenty six or 53% died in violent circumstances, mostly by execution or murder; most (eighty eight) of the other one hundred and

It should equally be acknowledged, however, that, as with the case of physical appeal, for a number of those cold and calculating patron-client relationships, additional features may be retrieved from the sources that are more in line with that greater Middle Eastern political and social environment. These features come particularly to the forefront when such relations are under pressure and their beneficial nature is threatened. As expected from the previous analysis, in such cases the majority of such relations around a patron tended to crumble away. As will be seen, however, a small but conspicuous core of clients often retained its loyalty and remained with their patron to the bitter end, sometimes even perishing with him. Clearly, such instances hint at the possibility of additional rules of socio-political conduct that go beyond mutual benefit.

Until quite recently, in the majority of scholarship on Mamluk political and organisational history the issue of kinship was at most awarded marginal attention. Mamluks' descendants, known as the *awlād al-nās*, in particular were considered excluded from military rank and income, as they would not have been able to develop the mamluk trainees' comradeship (*khushdāshīya*) that was thought to be quintessential to knit the socio-political 'system' that brought rank, income and power.[88] On the other hand, in recent years a number of studies have appeared that have demonstrated that kinship and families actually played a larger socio-political part than at first accepted.[89] And indeed, such a reconsideration of Mamluk scenery

eleven deaths in these ranks were due to the mortal diseases that afflicted all pre-modern societies, including the Black Death of 1348–1349, which, again, must have added to this picture of physical insecurity. At the same time, prosopographical data like these are also indicative of the high number of those living in oblivion, for they represent only a fraction of the total number of the era's known mamluks and amirs (1,430), the majority of whom were indeed mentioned when they prospered during this period, but not deemed worthy of a chronicler's attention once they had left the limelight; the same may actually be concluded from the fact that only about one third (505) of this socio-political group were deemed worthy of any biographer's attention and an entry in one of the era's biographical dictionaries.

[88] See D. Ayalon, *L'Esclavage du Mamlouk*, (*Oriental Notes and Studies* 1), Jerusalem 1951; idem, "The Muslim City", pp. 321–324; idem, "Mamluk: Military Slavery in Egypt and Syria", in D. Ayalon, *Islam and the Above of War*, Aldershot 1994, II, especially pp. 16–17; idem, "Studies", pp. 210–213, 456; idem, "Mamluk Military Aristocracy, a Non-Hereditary Nobility", *JSAI* 10 (1987), pp. 205–210. Similar definitions may be found in Levanoni, *A Turning Point*, pp. 14–19; Staffa, *Conquest and Fusion*, pp. 118–119. For a review of this approach to Mamluk history, see Haarmann, "Joseph's Law", p. 60; Rabbat, "Representing the Mamluks", pp. 65–66, Chapoutot-Remadi, "Liens propres et identités séparées", p. 181.

[89] Levanoni, *A Turning Point*, pp. 49–52; Haarmann, "Joseph's Law", pp. 66–68,

seems all the more justified when one considers that, as discussed in the previous chapter, the depoliticised military ranks in the period from 1341 to 1382 were considerably populated by non-mamluks, including many a *walad al-nās*. Therefore, apart from individual benefit, the concept of kinship, or familial and pseudo-familial ties, should be taken into consideration too, as an additional rule of socio-political conduct. Kinship as a combination of true and—already more traditionally accepted—mamluk guises could govern, or could try to govern, an important part of the period's socio-political relationships too.

Kindred

As just mentioned, it is a remarkable phenomenon that in times of tension, an unfortunate patron could often retain a small core of clients, whose bonds with him, therefore, clearly went beyond the benefits *ni'ma* could offer. And in such cases, sources often offer valuable information by identifying some of these core clients as sons and other relatives of that patron. Thus, fleeing from Damascus in 1347, after a failed rebellion against the sultan, the *nā'ib al-Shām* Yalbughā al-Yaḥyāwī (d. 1347) was accompanied by only a handful of amirs, that—according to information scattered over a variety of sources—included his two sons, his father and an undefined number of relatives.[90] Accounts for the year 1341 offer similarly insightful information, when sultan al-Manṣūr Abū Bakr not only arrested the amir Aqbughā 'Abd al-Wāḥid (d. 1344), but also the latter's two sons;[91] when the amir Qawṣūn's wrath for the desertion of dozens of amirs reportedly made him take their sons' *ḥalqa iqṭā'*s;[92] and finally when the *nā'ib Ḥalab* had to flee from Aleppo, accompanied by a small group that included two of his sons, both amirs in Aleppo.[93]

83–84; idem, "The Sons of Mamluks as Fief-holders", pp. 141–145, 162–163; Richards, "Mamluk amirs", pp. 34, 35, 39; Chapoutot-Remadi, *Liens et Relations*, pp. 563–564; M. Chapoutot-Remadi, "Liens propres et identités", p. 176.

[90] See al-Ṣafadī, *A'yān*, I, p. 552; V, p. 591; al-Ṣafadī, *Wāfī*, XXXIX, pp. 49–50; al-Kutubī, *'Uyūn al-Tawārīkh*, fol. 83, 84; Ibn Kathīr, *al-Bidāya*, XIV, pp. 222–223; al-Maqrīzī, *Sulūk*, II/3, pp. 733, 734; Ibn Taghrī Birdī, *Nujūm*, X, p. 162; Ibn Qāḍī Shuhba, *Tārīkh*, II, pp. 505, 506, 538.

[91] Al-Maqrīzī, *Khiṭaṭ*, IV, p. 226; al-Maqrīzī, *Sulūk*, II/3, p. 563.

[92] Al-Maqrīzī, *Sulūk*, II/3, p. 583.

[93] Al-Shujā'ī, *Tārīkh*, p. 173; al-Maqrīzī, *Sulūk*, II/3, p. 582; Ibn Taghrī Birdī, *Nujūm*, X, p. 34.

As suggested by these references, a patron's *maqbūl al-kalima* often was equally beneficial to his family, especially his offspring, and, as such, served quite opportunistic purposes, considering the fact that ties of blood might be less easily violated in tense circumstances. Including family members among a patron's relationships of power did not just extend his subordinate clientele, but also strengthened its cohesion and subordination.

Similar references to a patron's sons among the clients that had benefited from his *niʿma* may be found. In the year 1369, a military campaign near Aleppo ended badly for both the *nāʾib Ḥalab* and his son.[94] In 1348, the son of the *nāʾib al-Shām* died of the plague at the age of ten, when he—according to Ibn Qāḍī Shuhba—surprisingly already held a Damascene rank of amir of forty.[95] The amir Ṭaybughā al-Ṭawil (d. 1368) is reported to have had two sons who were amirs of forty until their father's defeat in 1366.[96] And when an amir was appointed *nāʾib Ṣafad* in 1343, al-Shujāʿī mentions how his son simultaneously obtained a rank of amir in that city.[97] Finally, the extent to which not just patron-client exchange, but also such family ties were part of the period's socio-political conduct is exemplified by al-Maqrīzī's description of the prestige of the young *nāʾib Ḥalab* Arghūn al-Kāmilī (1329–1357) in the year 1353:

> [. . .] the status (*shaʾn*) of the amir Arghūn [. . .] grew: despite his young age, he had [. . .] a son of three who was an amir of 100 [. . .], while [another] four ranks of amir were held by his brothers—who had come from his land of origin—and his relatives.[98]

Patrons' engagement of their kindred should not just be explained from an opportunistic perspective, but also as common human behaviour that sought to safeguard the interests of one's own.[99] Even some

---

94 Ibn Ḥabīb, *Tadkhirat al-Nabīh*, III, p. 335; Ibn Khaldūn, *Kitāb al-ʿIbar*, V, p. 459; Ibn Duqmāq, *Nuzhat al-Anām*, fol. 52; al-ʿAynī, *ʿIqd al-Jumān*, p. 157; al-Maqrīzī, *Sulūk*, III/1, p. 175; Ibn Taghrī Birdī, *Nujūm*, XI, p. 54; Ibn Qāḍī Shuhba, *Tārīkh*, II, p. 451.

95 Ibn Qāḍī Shuhba, *Tārīkh*, II, p. 552.

96 Al-ʿAynī, *ʿIqd al-Jumān*, p. 139; Ibn Taghrī Birdī, *Nujūm*, XI, p. 31. For the rebellion, see Appendix 3, nr. 44.

97 Al-Shujāʿī, *Tārīkh*, p. 257.

98 Al-Maqrīzī, *Sulūk*, II/3, p. 895.

99 See also Chapoutot-Remadi, "Liens propres et identités séparées", pp. 178–179. For a most recent appreciation of such behaviour's influence on the Mamluk regime's land-owning policies, see A. Sabra, "The Rise of a New Class? Land Tenure in fifteenth-century Egypt: A Review Article", *MSR* 8/2 (2004), pp. 203–210, esp. pp. 209–210.

level of familial continuity can be retrieved from the sources, especially with respect to lower ranks in the military hierarchy. One telling illustration concerns the young amir Khalīl b. ʿAlī b. Salār, for whom his father had arranged the 'inheritance' of his rank of amir of ten when he died in October 1341.[100] When the amir Burāq b. Baldāʿī al-Ṭaṭarī died in Damascus in 1356, a rank of amir of ten was given to each of his two sons, and one of them was also given "his father's office".[101] The same happened to the amir Aḥmad b. ʿAbd Allāh b. al-Malik al-ʿĀdil Kitbughā, who received his father's rank of amir when the latter died in November 1343,[102] and to the amir Ibrāhīm b. Alṭunqush, who succeeded his deceased father in rank and office in early 1345.[103] Up to a certain level in the regime's institutional framework, some form of heredity of rank, office and *iqṭāʿ* seems to have been acceptable to all those involved, most likely due to sincere considerations for one's own offspring that might end up in the same situation.[104] This is at least also suggested by the often remarkably friendly treatment awarded to the offspring of fallen rivals, as happened with the children of the amir Uljāy al-Yūsufī, to whom the sultan assigned an income after their father's violent death in 1373,[105] or the sons of Yalbughā al-Khāṣṣakī, who were allowed to keep their ranks of amir of forty in 1366, in spite of a successful rebellion against their father.[106]

Moreover, as suggested, many of the above illustrations equally reveal that even in these specific relations of power, *niʿma-khidma* exchange continued to be a crucial regulating factor. As with the son of the

[100] Al-Shujāʿī, *Tārīkh*, p. 157, 220; Ibn Qāḍī Shuhba, *Tārīkh*, II, p. 273.

[101] Al-Kutubī, *ʿUyūn al-Tawārīkh*, fol. 154; Ibn Kathīr, *al-Bidāya*, XIV, p. 254; Ibn Qāḍī Shuhba, *Tārīkh*, III, p. 104.

[102] Al-Shujāʿī, *Tārīkh*, p. 266; Ibn Qāḍī Shuhba, *Tārīkh*, II, p. 386.

[103] Al-Shujāʿī, *Tārīkh*, p. 276.

[104] Cfr. also Chapoutot-Remadi, "Liens et relations", pp. 563–564; Clifford, "State Formation", pp. 266–267 (who notices this phenomenon for the reign of al-Nāṣir Muḥammad: "[. . .] an-Nāṣir's own *mamālīk* and *khāṣṣ* also seem to have enjoyed the privilege of heritability [. . .]"); Richards, "Mamluk Amirs", pp. 36–39 ("[. . .] the surprising stability of certain families established by *mamlūk* amirs [. . .]" [p. 37]; "[. . .] the family of the amir Manjak (d. 776/1374–5), whose descendants [. . .] continued to hold the rank of amir and enjoy their extensive *waqfs* well into the Ottoman period, until late in the seventeenth century" [p. 39]). In addition, al-Ṣafadī claims that when the amir Baybughā Rūs (d. 1353) was *nāʾib al-salṭana* at the time of the Black Death in 1348, he offered the *iqṭāʿ*s of those who had succumbed to their sons, "whether the amirs wanted that, or not" (al-Ṣafadī, *Aʿyān*, II, p. 86).

[105] Ibn Duqmāq, *Nuzhat al-Anām*, fol. 79v; Ibn Khaldūn, *Kitāb al-ʿIbar*, V, p. 460.

[106] Ibn Duqmāq, *Nuzhat al-Anām*, fol. 6.

young *nā'ib Ḥalab* Arghūn al-Kāmilī above, also the two sons of the amir Aynabak al-Badrī were amirs, in their case even of the highest rank in Egypt, conspicuously arranged by their father in June 1377, upon his elimination of a major rival.[107] Similar situations occurred with a son of the amir Ṭashtamur Ḥummuṣ Akhḍar in 1341,[108] with a son of Manjak al-Yūsufī in 1348,[109] with two sons of the sultan al-Nāṣir Ḥasan after 1355,[110] with the sons of Yalbughā al-Khāṣṣakī after 1365[111] and with the newborn son of the amir Barqūq in 1380.[112] And, as equally suggested by the case of the brothers and relatives of that young *nā'ib Ḥalab* Arghūn al-Kāmilī above, such *ni'ma* favoured not just sons, but also the larger family, including fathers, brothers and nephews, that were often directly imported by the patron from his land of origin. Already before 1341, for instance, in the days of al-Nāṣir Muḥammad, the amir Qawṣūn had strengthened his position with his brother, the amir Sūsūn (d. 1334), and his nephew, the amir Baljak, who both had come to Egypt, together with Qawṣūn's mother and an undefined number of relatives, and who came to be promoted to the rank of amir of a hundred;[113] eventually, the number of relatives among his clients is supposed to have been considerable, when al-Maqrīzī reports that in 1341, Qawṣūn had managed to "promote sixty amirs from among his dependents and relatives".[114]

---

[107] Ibn Duqmāq, *Nuzhat al-Anām*, fol. 125v; al-'Aynī, *'Iqd al-Jumān*, p. 224; al-Maqrīzī, *Sulūk*, III/1, p. 308; Ibn Taghrī Birdī, *Nujūm*, XI, p. 155; Ibn Qāḍī Shuhba, *Tārīkh*, III, p. 542.

[108] Al-Shujā'ī, *Tārīkh*, p. 207.

[109] Al-Maqrīzī, *Sulūk*, II/3, p. 769; Ibn Taghrī Birdī, *Nujūm*, X, p. 194.

[110] Al-Maqrīzī, *Sulūk*, III/1, pp. 20, 63.

[111] Ibn Duqmāq, *Nuzhat al-Anām*, fol. 6; al-Maqrīzī, *Sulūk*, III/1, p. 100; Ibn Taghrī Birdī, *Nujūm*, XI, p. 27.

[112] Ibn Duqmāq, *al-Jawhar al-Thamīn*, p. 452; al-'Aynī, *'Iqd al-Jumān*, p. 258; al-Maqrīzī, *Sulūk*, III/1, p. 387; Ibn Taghrī Birdī, *Nujūm*, XI, p. 180; Ibn Qāḍī Shuhba, *Tārīkh*, I, pp. 26, 567.

[113] Kortantamer, *Mufaḍḍal b. Abī al-Faḍā'il*, p. 167; Zettersteen, *Beiträge*, pp. 187–188, 216; al-Yūsufī, *Nuzha*, pp. 211–212, 445–446; al-Shujā'ī, *Tārīkh*, p. 222; al-Ṣafadī, *A'yān*, IV, p. 140; al-Ṣafadī, *Wāfī*, X, pp. 285–286; XXIV, p. 279; Ibn Ḥajar, *Durar*, III, p. 258; al-Maqrīzī, *Khiṭaṭ*, IV, p. 104. For Baljak's position as an important client of Qawṣūn in the events of the year 1341, see for instance al-Maqrīzī, *Sulūk*, II/3, p. 586. Other relatives mentioned in the sources, include the amir Ṭanbughū, 'a relative' (*qarāba*) of Qawṣūn and an amir of forty (al-Shujā'ī, *Tārīkh*, p. 17); the amir Ṭughunjaq (d. 1338), 'maternal uncle' (*khāl*) of Qawṣūn and an amir of forty too, and his son Duqmāq, who was given this rank after him (al-Shujā'ī, *Tārīkh*, p. 33); and finally Qawṣūn's nephew, the amir Ṭurṭaqā b. Susun, who is reported to have married the daughter of another amir in 1338 (Zettersteen, *Beiträge*, p. 199).

[114] Al-Maqrīzī, *Khiṭaṭ*, IV, p. 104.

Some forty years later, similar references to relatives of the amir Barqūq confirm the continued importance of blood ties: he equally managed to have a number of them brought over from his home land, including his father, Anaṣ al-Ghasānī (d. 1382) and his nephew, Qajmas al-Ṣāliḥi, who each similarly obtained a rank of amir of a hundred;[115] as al-Maqrīzī did in the case of Qawṣūn, Ibn Taghrī Birdī comments that Barqūq "offered giant *iqṭā*ʿs to his young and freshly imported relatives, and appointed them in precious offices".[116]

Clearly, family promotions of this sort infused these outstanding representatives of a patron into Legitimate Power's institutional framework. As such, this combination of *niʿma* and blood ties not only strengthened the cohesion of a patron's Effective Power, but also again undoubtedly confirmed in public the extent of his *maqbūl al-kalima*, and—especially since many a promoted son may well have been a minor—enlarged his control over certain areas of the regime's institutions, including the substantial income they generated.

Marriage

Already before 1341, sultan al-Nāṣir Muḥammad, gifted with numerous offspring, can be seen to have developed a particular marriage policy that incorporated a substantial part of his high-ranking military elite into his family and bound them to his rule.[117] And in the period of forty odd years after his demise, not just blood ties, but also marriages

---

[115] Anaṣ arrived in March 1381 and received a royal welcome in Cairo; Qajmas arrived together with Barqūq's sister and an unspecified number of relatives, in October 1382, just before Barqūq took the sultanate (cfr. Ibn Duqmāq, *al-Jawhar al-Thamīn*, pp. 454–455; Ibn al-ʿIraqi, *Dhayl al-ʿIbar*, II, p. 496; al-ʿAynī, *ʿIqd al-Jumān*, pp. 261, 263; al-Maqrīzī, *Sulūk*, III/1, pp. 403, 411; Ibn Ḥajar, *Inbāʾ al-Ghumr*, II, pp. 13, 42, 50, 94; Ibn Taghrī Birdī, *Nujūm*, XI, pp. 182–183; Ibn Qāḍī Shuhba, *Tārīkh*, I, pp. 38, 57, 60, 70, 84).

[116] Ibn Taghrī Birdī, *al-Manhal*, VI, p. 396.

[117] Cfr. A. ʿAbd ar-Raziq, *La femme au temps des Mamelouks en Égypte*, Cairo 1973, pp. 269–302; Irwin, "Factions", p. 242; Irwin, *The Middle East*, p. 108; Chapoutot-Remadi, "Liens et Relations", p. 604; Levanoni, *Turning Point*, pp. 48–49; Richards, "Mamluk Amirs", p. 37; P. M. Holt, "an-Nāṣir Muḥammad b. Qalāwūn (684–741/1285–1341): His Ancestry, Kindred and Affinity", in U. Vermeulen and D. De Smet, *Egypt and Syria in the Fatimid, Ayyubid and Mamluk Eras*, (*Orientalia Lovaniensia Analecta* 73), Leuven 1995, pp. 313–324, esp. pp. 319–323; Clifford, "State Formation" p. 267. For an analysis of the political background of those marriage ties, see Van Steenbergen, "Mamluk Elite", pp. 192–194. For a rather generalising evocation of Mamluk marriage practices as a tool to link amirs' offspring and their mamluks, see Chapoutot-Remadi, "Liens propres et identités séparées", p. 178.

similar to those initiated by al-Nāṣir Muḥammad can be seen to have enhanced the links between a patron and some of his clients. In general, two kinds of marriage ties emerge in this period: on the one hand, there was a continued practice of creating kinship with the sultan through marriage, and on the other, there were those nuptial arrangements that created kinship amongst the amirs.

Actually, there are recurrent explicit references to the latter kind,[118] and the common perception of a need to create such ties of kinship within the socio-political framework is illustrated by a rare documentary source: a copy of a contract for the marriage between a rather obscure amir named ʿAbd Allāh and the daughter of a well-known high-ranking amir, Baydamur al-Badrī (d. 1347). This document includes the following telling statement:

> When [ʿAbd Allāh's] father [. . .] had died [. . .], he had been obliged to go and look for a [new] father like him. He worked hard until he found and acquired a [new] father, and although he was not his true son, he still was like a son to him; this was the noble Baydamur [. . .].[119]

So, in this case, a marriage alliance was considered of vital importance to the amir ʿAbd Allāh and his future success. The reason for this should again be sought in the realm of patrons and clients, for it can be shown that, as with blood ties, the set-up of more manageable marriages often served to enhance the material ties that linked patrons and clients and to promote their mutual benefit. Thus, the amir Mughulṭāy al-Nāṣiri (d. 1354) was spared expulsion to Syria in 1342 because he was the son-in-law of the influential amir Jankalī

---

[118] Some examples: the amir Aqbughā ʿAbd al-Wāḥid (d. 1344) was the father-in-law of the amir Arghūn Shāh (d. 1349) (al-Shujāʿī, *Tārīkh*, p. 267); the amir Ṭaydamur al-Bālisī (d. 1376) was the father-in-law of the amir Khalīl b. ʿArrām (d. 1380) (al-Nuwayrī, *Kitāb al-Ilmām*, VI, p. 373); the amir Aqsunqur al-Salārī (d. 1344) was the father-in-law of the amir Bayghará al-Nāṣiri (d. 1353) (al-Shujāʿī, *Tārīkh*, p. 254; al-Maqrīzī, *Sulūk*, II/3, p. 638; Ibn Taghrī Birdī, *Nujūm*, X, p. 86; Ibn Qāḍī Shuhba, *Tārīkh*, II, p. 352); the amir Ṭāz (d. 1362) was the father-in-law of the amir Ṭuqṭāy al-Nāṣiri (1319–1358) (al-ʿAynī, *ʿIqd al-Jumān*, p. 103; al-Maqrīzī, *Sulūk*, II/3, p. 844; Ibn Taghrī Birdī, *Nujūm*, X, p. 286); the amir Manjak (d. 1375) was the father-in-law of the amir Urus al-Bashtakī (d. 1373) (Ibn Khaldūn, *Kitāb al-ʿIbar*, V, p. 461; Ibn Duqmāq, *Nuzhat al-Anām*, fol. 83v); the amir Arghūn al-ʿAlāʾī was the father-in-law of the amir Arghūn al-Kāmilī (d. 1357) (al-Maqrīzī, *Sulūk*, II/3, p. 672); the amir Baktamur al-Muʾminī (d. 1369) was the father-in-law of the amir Julban al-ʿAlāʾī (d. 1386) (Ibn Duqmāq, *Nuzhat al-Anām*, fol. 56; Ibn Qāḍī Shuhba, *Tārīkh*, I, p. 198).

[119] See al-Qalqashandi, *Subh*, XIV, pp. 311–313; quotation from p. 312.

b. al-Bābā (d. 1346).[120] Even some of the Effective Power holders are known to have tried to link rivals and clients more closely to their person through marriages. After the elimination of al-Ashraf Shaʿbān in 1377, the amir Qaraṭāy married the daughter of his most important client, Aynabak al-Badrī; this, however, did not prevent the latter from rebelling against his son-in-law.[121] A little later, the same happened to the amir Ṭashtamur al-Dawādār with his son-in-law Barqūq.[122] Much earlier, in 1351, a combination of similar alliances had given shape to a true family nucleus of power holders that revolved around the amir Mughulṭāy al-Nāṣirī and included not just his stepson, sultan al-Nāṣir Ḥasan, but also his father-in-law and his brother-in-law.[123]

Though it is very likely that many more such marriage alliances existed in the period between 1341 and 1382,[124] the information the sources provide only allows the detailed discussion of one particular type, which—from the perspective of political power—is the most interesting one. The entire period has several specific references to marriage ties between an amir like Mughulṭāy and a reigning sultan like Ḥasan. In all, such amirs had either married a future sultan's mother,[125] or they were one of the sultan's in-laws—that is, they had daughters or sisters that were married to the sultan or they themselves had married the sultan's sister. For example, the amir Arghūn al-ʿAlāʾī was married to the mother of the two successive sultans al-Ṣāliḥ Ismāʿīl and al-Kāmil Shaʿbān,[126] the amir Mughulṭāy—as just seen—was said to have been married to the mother of al-Nāṣir Ḥasan,[127] and—at least according to the Italian traveller Bertrando de Mignanelli—Barqūq had been married to the mother

[120] Al-Shujāʿī, *Tārīkh*, p. 233.

[121] Al-Maqrīzī, *Sulūk*, III/1, p. 305; Ibn Ḥajar, *Inbāʾ al-Ghumr*, I, p. 230.

[122] Al-Maqrīzī, *Sulūk*, III/1, p. 323; Ibn Ḥajar, *Inbāʾ al-Ghumr*, I, p. 236.

[123] Al-Ṣafadī, *Aʿyān*, I, p. 649. On top of that, Aytmish also was the father-in-law of Tashbughā (Ibn Kathīr, *al-Bidāya*, XIV, p. 238).

[124] See also Irwin's similar remark for fifteenth-century Mamluk socio-political history, in his "Factions", p. 242.

[125] Chapoutot-Remadi links such a practice to a nomadic tradition that was already present with the Seljuqs, i.e. marriages with the mothers of young minor princes, often even arranged by the princes' fathers to assure their offspring's continued well-being (Chapoutot-Remadi, "Liens propres et identités séparées", p. 178).

[126] al-Shujāʿī, *Tārīkh*, p. 236; al-Maqrīzī, *Sulūk*, II/3, p. 620; Ibn Qāḍī Shuhba, *Tārīkh*, II, pp. 302, 457, 486, 513).

[127] See al-ʿAynī, *ʿIqd al-Jumān*, p. 92.

of the period's last sultan, al-Ṣāliḥ Ḥājjī.[128] The amir Mankli Bughā al-Shamsī became not just a father-in-law to sultan al-Ashraf Shaʿbān, but in February 1368 he also married the sultan's sister.[129] Similarly, the latter situation—marrying a sultan's sister—occurred with the amirs Bahādur al-Damurdāshī,[130] Ṭāz,[131] Shaykhū,[132] and Bashtak al-ʿUmarī.[133] Finally, there also was the case of the amir Ṭuquzdamur al-Ḥamawī (d. 1345), who was both stepfather and father-in-law of al-Manṣūr Abū Bakr and later again became a sultan's father-in-law when al-Ṣāliḥ Ismāʿīl married another one of his daughters.[134]

Not surprisingly, simultaneously with their marriage ties to a sultan, all these amirs were politically very active and gathered substantial amounts of Effective Power. Their marriages gave them direct access to and substantial influence over the sultan, which turned them into or confirmed their status as attractive patrons for prospective clients, with an often unparalleled *maqbūl al-kalima* and a guaranteed *niʿma.* This is actually well demonstrated by the career of the amir Uljāy al-Yūsufī: undistinguished as a high-ranking amir ever since his promotion in the early 1360s, he only acquired a high profile position of Effective Power after he married al-Ashraf Shaʿbān's mother in about 1370, a position he lost again soon after her death in 1373.[135]

---

[128] See Walter J. Fischel, "*Ascensus Barcoch.* A Latin Biography of the Mamluk Sultan Barqūq of Egypt (d. 1399) written by B. de Mignanelli in 1416", *Arabica* 6 (1959), p. 73.

[129] Ibn Duqmāq, *Nuzhat al-Anām,* fol. 39; Ibn al-ʿIraqi, *Dhayl al-ʿIbar,* II, p. 361; al-Maqrīzī, *Sulūk,* III/1, pp. 157, 263; Ibn Taghrī Birdī, *Nujūm,* XI, p. 49; Ibn Qāḍī Shuhba, *Tārīkh,* III, p. 315.

[130] He was reported to have been a brother-in-law of al-Ṣāliḥ Ismāʿīl (al-Shujāʿī, *Tārīkh,* pp. 247, 252; Ibn Qāḍī Shuhba, *Tārīkh,* II, p. 323).

[131] According to al-Maqrīzī, Ṭāz married a sister of al-Nāṣir Ḥasan in Mai 1351 (al-Maqrīzī, *Sulūk,* II/3, p. 840).

[132] In his obituary of Shaykhū, Ibn Kathīr mentions his marriage to al-Nāṣir Ḥasan's sister, see Ibn Kathīr, *al-Bidāya,* XIV, p. 258.

[133] This Bashtak married another sister of al-Ashraf Shaʿbān in December 1368 (Ibn Duqmāq, *Nuzhat al-Anām,* fol. 50v; al-ʿAynī, *ʿIqd al-Jumān,* p. 158; al-Maqrīzī, *Sulūk,* III/1, p. 170; Ibn Qāḍī Shuhba, *Tārīkh,* III, p. 369, 385.

[134] Al-Shujāʿī, *Tārīkh,* pp. 131, 140, 261, 274; al-Kutubī, *ʿUyūn al-Tawārīkh,* fol. 52, 75v; al-Maqrīzī, *Sulūk,* II/3, pp. 551, 651, 672; Ibn Taghrī Birdī, *Nujūm,* X, p. 3; Ibn Qāḍī Shuhba, *Tārīkh,* II, pp. 202, 364, 465; Ibn Buḥtur, *Tārīkh Bayrūt,* p. 147.

[135] See Ibn Khaldūn, *Kitāb al-ʿIbar,* V, p. 459; al-ʿAynī, *ʿIqd al-Jumān,* p. 174; al-Maqrīzī, *Khiṭaṭ,* IV, p. 249; al-Maqrīzī, *Sulūk,* III/1, p. 212; Ibn Ḥajar, *Inbāʾ al-Ghumr,* I, pp. 48–49; Ibn Taghrī Birdī, *Nujūm,* XI, pp. 57–58; Ibn Qāḍī Shuhba, *Tārīkh,* III, p. 439; al-Zahiri, *Zubda,* p. 148.

Ukhūwa

Apart from blood and marriage ties, more specifically 'mamluk', fictitious kinship ties can also be seen to characterise some of the more lasting patron-client relationships of the period. These actually can be linked to the more well-known mamluk concept of *khushdāshīya*, the horizontal bond of loyalty between the mamluks of one master that was supposed to have been inculcated during their period of training.[136] For a long time idealised as the mainstay of Mamluk political culture, in recent years it has gradually become understood that rather than a historical reality, it was at most a moral ideal, which never actually managed to defeat individual interests.[137] Nevertheless, very occasionally, it does turn up in source accounts of the years from 1341 to 1382, yet hardly ever as a proactive rallying factor, but rather more neutrally to denote common descent from one master's corps of mamluks, or even retroactively to justify rebellion and to undermine a rival's credibility.[138] Moreover, among those core clients of a patron whose bonds with him are suggested to have gone beyond the material benefits *niʿma* could offer, this sort of *khushdāshīya* is never identified as a major factor.

However, what is occasionally identified as such a factor is a more individualised derivative thereof. It concerns a concept which refers to fictitious or created kinship between two amirs, and which is known in the sources as '*ukhūwa*' or 'brotherhood'.[139] Only once, in

[136] See especially D. Ayalon, *L'esclavage du Mamelouk*, pp. 29–31; Ayalon, "Studies", pp. 209–211; Levanoni, *Turning Point*, pp. 14–15; Levanoni, "Rank-and-file Mamluks", p. 17; Chapoutot-Remadi, "Liens propres et identités séparées", p. 177.

[137] See Irwin, *The Middle East*, pp. 6, 90; Irwin, "Factions", pp. 237–238; Chamberlain, *Knowledge and Social Practice*, p. 43; Clifford, "State Formation", pp. 6, 48–49, 51–54; and most recently Levanoni, "The Sultan's *Laqab*—A Sign of a new order in Mamluk Factionalism?", in M. Winter and A. Levanoni, *The Mamluks in Egyptian and Syrian Politics and Society* (*The Medieval Mediterranean. Peoples, Economies and Cultures, 400–1500*), Leiden-Boston 2004, p. 115.

[138] Al-Shujāʿī, *Tārīkh*, pp. 150, 151, 156, 158, 164; al-Maqrīzī, *Sulūk*, II/3, pp. 575, 577, 742; Ibn Taghrī Birdī, *Nujūm*, X, pp. 25, 26, 170, 312; XI, pp. 4, 159, 179, 214; Ibn Qāḍī Shuhba, *Tārīkh*, II, pp. 212, 215–216, 267.

[139] Illustrative references include: "he had a brother, [i.e.] one who was like a brother to him" (*kāna lahu akh muʾākhan*) (al-Shujāʿī, *Tārīkh*, p. 149); "he had to become like a brother to him" (*la budd ākhā ʿalayhi*) (al-Shujāʿī, *Tārīkh*, p. 156); "these two were like brothers since childhood" (*hāʾulāʾi al-ithnayni* [sic] *muʾākhayni min al-ṣughr*) (al-Shujāʿī, *Tārīkh*, p. 210); "between them, there was a firm brotherhood and a deep friendship" (*kāna baynahum ukhūwa akīda wa ṣadaqa ʿaẓima*) (al-ʿAynī, *ʿIqd al-Jumān*, p. 91). For the term's double meaning, see also Lane, *An Arabic-English Lexicon*, I, p. 33: '*ākhahu* [. . .] *He fraternized with him; acted with him in a brotherly manner*' & '*akh* [. . .] a well-known term of relationship [. . .], i.e. *A brother* [. . .] and *a friend*; and *a companion, an associate*, or a *fellow*'.

the very detailed accounts of al-Shujāʿī, is an edge of the veil that covers the concept of *ukhūwa* in the Mamluk sources lifted. In 1342, when the amir Quṭlūbughā al-Fakhri (d. 1342) sought refuge with a colleague in Syria, he reportedly "reminded him of the rights of brotherhood and friendship", which made him assume that "he would [not] abandon him because of the friendship and brotherhood between them".[140] Though it can be established that the term is equally used to refer to real brothers, in many occasions this biological bond is clearly absent and the concept then refers to an association of deeper friendship between two amirs, possibly formalised by mutual oaths of loyalty.[141] Clearly, '*ukhūwa*', linked with friendship, created codes of conduct that, like ties of blood and marriage, were supposed to transcend mere material benefit.

Further information on the concept itself is lacking, since all other references to '*ukhūwa*' are limited to the identification of those amirs involved in the association. However, just as with blood and marriage bonds, also '*ukhūwa*' always clearly had a more material patron-client background, at least when it was referred to in the sources. Time and again, 'brothers' are mentioned as benefiting from their associates' political success. For example, al-Maqrīzī describes how, in 1347,

> there arrived from Syria the amir Manjak al-Yūsufī al-Silāḥdār, 'brother' of the *nāʾib* Baybughā Rūs. There was assigned to him a rank of *muqaddam alf*, he was given a robe of honour and he was appointed *wazīr* and *ustādār*. [. . .] Thereupon, Egypt's rule came to the two 'brothers' Baybughā Rūs and Manjak al-Silāḥdār.[142]

Other equally illustrative cases include an amir who, in 1348, "during his 'brother's term of office as *nāʾib* became an amir of forty in Damascus",[143] and another amir, who, in 1372 "sent his 'brother' [. . .] to Damascus to inspect the troops there, whereupon he could gather enormous wealth [. . .]".[144] Further, 'brothers' can also be seen to have shared each others' fate when things went wrong, as happened

---

[140] Al-Shujāʿī, *Tārīkh*, p. 213.

[141] See also Chapoutot-Remadi, *Liens et Relations*, pp. 486–487, who links "*ukhūwa*" to a similar, nomadic, Turkic concept of brotherhood that was designed to strengthen one's social status and which resulted from a mutual oath; the concept is also briefly referred to in Chapoutot-Remadi's "Liens propres et identités séparées", p. 177, and in Richards' "Mamluk amirs", pp. 34, 37. Ayalon also mentions it, but still only in the context of *khushdāshīya*, see Ayalon, *L'esclavage du Mamelouk*, pp. 36–37.

[142] Al-Maqrīzī, *Sulūk*, II/3, p. 748; similarly in al-Maqrīzī, *Khiṭaṭ*, IV, p. 124.

[143] Ibn Qāḍī Shuhba, *Tārīkh*, II, p. 584.

[144] Ibn Ḥajar, *Inbāʾ al-Ghumr*, I, p. 38.

in 1341, when together with the amir Bashtak (d. 1341) "his two 'brothers' Ṭulūdamur and Aywān, amirs of forty, were arrested",[145] and in 1378, when an amir was removed from Cairo and "his 'brothers' [. . .] were arrested and imprisoned".[146] There clearly was an awareness of how close these ties between a fallen patron and his 'brothers' could be.

Hence, as with marriage arrangements in particular, *ukhūwa* also enabled a patron to tie carefully chosen clients more closely to his person, allowing them a greater share of his *niʿma* and getting a more reliable *khidma* in return. Such an insight is also furthered by the troubled history of the 'brothers' of the amir Ṭāz (d. 1362), who were vital to his Effective Power in the early 1350s, who were removed to Aleppo with him in 1354, and who continued to pop up in the sources as his close associates until the eventful end of his active life in 1358.[147] However, even this reliability occasionally seems to have been limited by personal interests, as in 1342, when Quṭlūbughā's demands for refuge were eventually denied by his so-called 'brother',[148] and in 1380, when the amir Barka was betrayed to his rival Barqūq by one of his own 'brothers'.[149]

Ustādhīya

In the above 1378 case of a banished amir and his arrested 'brothers', al-Maqrīzī actually also included "his senior mamluks" among those core clients that were the targets of this amir's opponents' wrath.[150] Similarly, in 1347, the disgraced *nāʾib al-Shām* Yalbughā al-Yahyāwī (d. 1347) is described as fleeing from Damascus with a core of clients that not only included his kindred, but also an unspecified number of 'his mamluks'.[151] Though *khushdāshīya* or horizontal loyalty among mamluks has been discarded as a fundamental rule of socio-political conduct in the period from 1341 to 1382, in these

[145] Al-Shujāʿī, *Tārīkh*, p. 131; identical in al-Maqrīzī, *Sulūk*, II/3, p. 562.
[146] Al-Maqrīzī, *Sulūk*, III/1, p. 322.
[147] See al-ʿAynī, *ʿIqd al-Jumān*, pp. 103–104; al-Maqrīzī, *Sulūk*, II/3, pp. 920, 929–930; III/1, pp. 1–4; Ibn Taghrī Birdī, *Nujūm*, X, pp. 286, 302; Ibn Qāḍī Shuhba, *Tārīkh*, III, p. 129; Ibn Ḥajar, *Durar*, II, pp. 214–215.
[148] See al-Shujāʿī, *Tārīkh*, p. 213.
[149] Ibn Qāḍī Shuhba, *Tārīkh*, I, p. 309; Ibn Ḥajar, *Inbāʾ al-Ghumr*, II, p. 2.
[150] Al-Maqrīzī, *Sulūk*, III/1, p. 322.
[151] Al-Maqrīzī, *Sulūk*, II/3, p. 733.

specific cases these amirs' mamluks clearly have to be considered more than mere calculating clients that would shift their loyalties accordingly. As members of a military corps that was an amir's military stronghold, resource of manpower and privileged symbol of socio-political status, mamluks and especially the particular bond that linked each individual one of them with his master, his *ustādh*, should not be equally discarded. This vertical bond between every individual mamluk and his *ustādh*, occasionally even equated with a fictitious father-son relationship,[152] will be conveniently termed '*ustādhīya*'. Admittedly, the term itself is not used in any of the period's sources, nor in any study so far published. Nevertheless, it is very useful in this context, to capture that concept that, as *ukhūwa*, created a fictitious vertical bond of kinship between patrons and some of their clients and thus enhanced their interaction's reliability and durability.

The actual socio-political importance of the concept of *ustādhīya* not only derives from the fact that most of those politically active themselves very often owed their socio-political initiation to it, but also from the fact that the military and especially the numerical strength of the resulting corps' of mamluks often were quite decisive factors in the establishment of patrons' Effective Power. As detailed in the previous chapter, in theory an amir's corps' numerical strength was to be commensurate with the military rank he took; an ambitious amir's constant need to expand and enhance his relationships of power can, however, be demonstrated to have equally affected the size of his personal military corps of mamluks, especially at the highest military rank. Thus, the amirs Qawṣūn and Shaykhū were reported to have had seven hundred personal mamluks, the amir Uljāy al-Yūsufī five to eight hundred, and the amir Yalbughā al-Khāṣṣakī at least one thousand five hundred, acquired in less than ten years.[153]

---

[152] For an analysis of the almost inevitable establishment of fictitious kinship ties between mamluks and their masters, see also P. Forand, "The Relation of the Slave and the Client to the Master or Patron in Medieval Islam", *IJMES* 2 (1977), pp. 59–66; D. Ze'evi, "My Slave, My Son, My Lord: Slavery, Family and State in the Islamic Middle East", in M. Toru & J.E. Phillips (eds.), *Slave Elites in the Middle East and Africa*, (*Islamic Area Studies*), London-New York 2000, pp. 71–80. For a similar interpretation, see also Chapoutot-Remadi, "Liens propres et identités séparées", pp. 176–177. A perfect illustration of this transformation of slavery ties into pseudo-kinship ties is to be found in Ibn Qāḍī Shuhba's biography of the amir Jariktamur al-Manjakī (d. 1375): "he was one of the mamluks of Manjak, who adopted him as a son, so that he became known as Ibn Manjak" (Ibn Qāḍī Shuhba, *Tārīkh*, III, p. 490).

[153] See al-Shujāʿī, *Tārīkh*, p. 184; Ibn Khaldūn, *Kitāb al-ʿIbar*, V, p. 458; Ibn

Though numbers are not the Mamluk sources' greatest strength, they do hint at these corps' relative size and consequent numerical preponderance, as well as to the amirs' concern for continued acquisition of mamluks.

The reason for this can be found on the one hand in an expected residue of gratitude for a master's care and manumission and for the unparalleled potentials for rank, office and income he could unlock for them,[154] and on the other hand even more in the fact that a mamluk—manumitted or not—at this initial stage of his career was bound to depend more on his master than on any one else. The combination of the substantial financial investment, which the acquisition of mamluks required, with that expected residue of loyalty, always made it more sensible for a patron to favour his own mamluks first. And this was bound to keep an ambitious young mamluk relatively close to the *ustādh* whose circle of most privileged clients he had almost naturally become part of. The maintenance and career opportunities he was destined to receive there were unlikely to be equalled by what any other patron had to offer. Again, the basic material and calculated relationship of a patron and his clients looms even behind the concept of *ustādhīya*, this time enhanced by a mamluk's (former) slave status and his concomitant beneficial dependence.

Apart from the subsistence mamluks were to receive from their *ustādh*'s *iqṭāʿ*, occasional references in the sources suggest that his *niʿma* could bring them positions in his personal administration, and additionally even the promotion into the military ranks that would pave the way for future success.[155] In this vein, al-Maqrīzī's illustration, mentioned above, of the high status of the young *nāʾib Ḥalab* Arghūn actually not only referred to his son, brothers and relatives, but also to the fact that 'despite his young age, he had four mamluks who were amir'.[156]

Duqmāq, *Nuzhat al-Anām*, fol. 37–37v; Ibn Duqmāq, *al-Jawhar al-Thamīn*, p. 427; al-Maqrīzī, *Sulūk*, III/1, pp. 150–151, 153, 213, 331; al-ʿAynī, *Iqd al-Juman*, p. 104, 265; Ibn Ḥajar, *Inbāʾ al-Ghumr*, I, pp. 74, 265; Ibn Taghrī Birdī, *Nujūm*, X, p. 286; XI, p. 60; Ibn Qāḍī Shuhba, *Tārīkh*, II, p. 280; III, pp. 305, 429, 571; Ibn Ḥajar, *Durar*, III, p. 258; al-Ẓāhirī, *Zubda*, pp. 113, 148.

[154] Chapoutot-Remadi refers to "*ḥaqq al-tarbiya*", a master's right to his mamluk's loyalty as a reward for the latter's education (Chapoutot-Remadi, "Liens propres et identités séparées", p. 177).

[155] See for instance al-Shujāʿī, *Tārīkh*, pp. 187, 237–238; al-Maqrīzī, *Sulūk*, III/1, p. 114; Ibn Ḥajar, *Inbāʾ al-Ghumr*, II, p. 109; Ibn Taghrī Birdī, *Nujūm*, X, pp. 305, 314; XI, p. 32; Ibn Qāḍī Shuhba, *Tārīkh*, I, p. 96.

[156] Al-Maqrīzī, *Sulūk*, II/3, p. 895.

The *khidma* mamluks are recorded to have offered to their masters in return actually left more explicit traces. Apart from the more general issue of representation of a patron and his *maqbūl al-kalima*, as in the above example of Arghūn's four mamluks, it clearly encompassed even more—as already suggested—the benefit of numbers, expressed in the most evocative way by al-Shujāʿī when he makes an outnumbered amir attribute his flight from the battlefield to the fact that "he realised that quantity gains the upper hand over courage and [that] shortage of men is the most miserable merchandise".[157] On top of that, mamluks were of course first and foremost military, and their military service to their *ustādh*, often to the death, is equally well recorded.[158] The enhanced loyalty to a patron that resulted from that situation of dependence, unique chances for favour and collective military serviceability at times even expressed itself in a collective attempt to rehabilitate a fallen *ustādh* (and of course their enjoying his *niʿma*), as was the acclaimed hope of the mamluks of two imprisoned amirs when they joined a rebellion in 1351.[159] This loyalty could even be manifested posthumously, as when the mamluks of the amir Barka (d. 1380) lynched their *ustādh*'s alleged murderer.[160]

Nevertheless, in spite of those unquestionably unparalleled material benefits a mamluk could gain from his sustained loyalty to his *ustādh*, even in the case of *ustādhīya* loyalty continued to be for hire throughout this period. More than one patron was brought down by his personal mamluks' betrayal. As early as 1341, for instance, the amir Qawṣūn successfully made the sultanic mamluks abandon al-Manṣūr Abū Bakr;[161] in 1366, the amir Yalbughā al-Khāṣṣakī was overthrown by a rebellion that included his own dissatisfied mamluks;[162] and from

157 Al-Shujāʿī, *Tārīkh*, p. 173.

158 See for instance al-ʿAynī, *ʿIqd al-Jumān*, pp. 82, 114; al-Maqrīzī, *Khiṭaṭ*, IV, p. 119; al-Maqrīzī, *Sulūk*, II/3, p. 74; III/1, pp. 42, 212–213; Ibn Ḥajar, *Inbāʾ al-Ghumr*, I, p. 74; Ibn Taghrī Birdī, *Nujūm*, X, p. 308; Ibn Qāḍī Shuhba, *Tārīkh*, III, p. 429.

159 Al-Maqrīzī, *Sulūk*, II/3, p. 845; Ibn Taghrī Birdī, *Nujūm*, X, p. 257.

160 See Ibn Duqmāq, *al-Jawhar al-Thamīn*, p. 453; Ibn Khaldūn, *Kitāb al-ʿIbar*, V, p. 471; Ibn al-ʿIraqi, *Dhayl al-ʿIbar*, II, pp. 10–11; al-ʿAynī, *ʿIqd al-Jumān*, p. 260; al-Maqrīzī, *Khiṭaṭ*, IV, p. 242; al-Maqrīzī, *Sulūk*, III/1, p. 398; Ibn Ḥajar, *Inbāʾ al-Ghumr*, II, pp. 10–11; Ibn Taghrī Birdī, *Nujūm*, XI, pp. 184–185; Ibn Qāḍī Shuhba, *Tārīkh*, I, pp. 33–34.

161 See al-Shujāʿī, *Tārīkh*, pp. 136–137; identical in Ibn Qāḍī Shuhba, *Tārīkh*, II, p. 205. Also in al-Maqrīzī, *Sulūk*, II/3, pp. 567–569; identical in Ibn Taghrī Birdī, *Nujūm*, X, pp. 13–14.

162 Ibn Khaldūn, *Kitāb al-ʿIbar*, V, pp. 356–357; Ibn Duqmāq, *Nuzhat al-Anām*,

1377 onwards, opportunistic mamluks are recorded to have taken part in several rebellions that were directed against their masters.[163] Again, when confronted with personal ambitions and opportunities, even bonds of *ustādhīya* could prove of secondary value only. In this respect, Ibn Taghrī Birdī summarises the second reign of al-Nāṣir Ḥasan very aptly:

> Then he thought of promoting his own mamluks, so that they would be a clique and a mainstay for him; but they were the opposite of what he had hoped them to be, for they jumped at him and [. . .] killed him [. . .].[164]

Jinsīya

It has been suggested that '*jinsīya*' or ethnicity, a wider concept derived from kinship and mostly linked to a common place of origin, had some part to play in the socio-political conduct of the fourteenth century.[165] This would have been true especially for the ascent and reign of Barqūq, explained, both by Mamluk historians like al-Maqrīzī, Ibn Ḥajar, Ibn Qāḍī Shuhba and Ibn Taghrī Birdī, and by many a modern scholar, as a result of his deliberate reliance on Circassian fellow-mamluks.[166]

Though this approach has recently been quite convincingly questioned,[167] *jinsīya* nevertheless seems to have been considered a factor

---

fol. 2v–3v; Ibn al-ʿIraqi, *Dhayl al-ʿIbar*, I, p. 216; al-Maqrīzī, *Sulūk*, III/1, pp. 130–138; al-ʿAynī, *ʿIqd al-Jumān*, pp. 144–147; Ibn Taghrī Birdī, *Nujūm*, XI, pp. 35–40; Ibn Qāḍī Shuhba, *Tārīkh*, III, pp. 293, 305; al-Zahiri, *Zubda*, pp. 113, 148.

[163] See Ibn Khaldūn, *Kitāb al-ʿIbar*, V, pp. 463, 468; Ibn Duqmāq, *Nuzhat al-Anām*, fol. 108v; Ibn Duqmāq, *al-Jawhar al-Thamīn*, pp. 448–449; al-Maqrīzī, *Sulūk*, III/1, pp. 275–276, 331, 365; III/2, p. 473; al-ʿAynī, *Iqd al-Juman*, pp. 204, 248; Ibn Ḥajar, *Inbāʾ al-Ghumr*, I, pp. 265, 310; II, p. 94; Ibn Taghrī Birdī, *Nujūm*, XI, pp. 72, 168, 212–214; Ibn Qāḍī Shuhba, *Tārīkh*, I, pp. 9, 84–85; III, pp. 511–512, 571.

[164] Ibn Taghrī Birdī, *Nujūm*, X, p. 314.

[165] See for instance Chapoutot-Remadi, "Liens propres et identités séparées", pp. 178, 182–185.

[166] See for instance al-Maqrīzī, *Sulūk*, III/1, pp. 316, 383, 385, 388; Ibn Ḥajar, *Inbāʾ al-Ghumr*, II, p. 92; Ibn Qāḍī Shuhba, *Tārīkh*, I, pp. 24, 26, 38, 154; Ibn Taghrī Birdī, *al-Manhal*, VI, p. 396. Modern historiography of that sort has been reviewed in D. Ayalon, "Bahri Mamluks, Burji Mamluks—inadequate names for the two reigns of the Mamluk Sultanate", *Tarih* 1 (1990), pp. 3–53 (repr. in his *Islam and the Abode of War*, IV); the episode of Barqūq has been dealt with in more detail in his "The Circassians in the Mamluk Kingdom", *JAOS* 69 (1949), pp. 135–147. Chapoutot-Remadi suggests an almost continuous Circassian ascent from the late thirteenth until the late fourteenth century (Chapoutot-Remadi, "Liens propres et identités séparées", p. 183).

[167] See A. Levanoni, "Transition", pp. 93–105.

of some political importance already by those contemporary historians. And about a decade ago, while David Ayalon concluded that the issue of ethnicity actually was generally absent from the Mamluk political scene, he nevertheless also identified two exceptions to that general pattern in the fourteenth century.[168] Therefore, the concept of *jinsīya* should also be included in an analysis of the strategies that moulded the socio-political conduct of the period that led up to that reign of Barqūq.

Actually, the sources mention three occasions for the period from 1341 to 1382 which involved *jinsīya*, yet again every time against the background of very specific patron-client relations. A first occasion concerns the biographer al-Ṣafadī's rather obscure report that in 1342 'the Circassians' had allied with a Damascene amir, resulting in his promotion and appointment.[169] A second occasion is less obscure, and took place during the reign of al-Muẓaffar Ḥājjī, between 1346 and 1347, when that sultan is reported to have bought, promoted and appointed many mamluks from the Caucasus region, a great number of whom were also reported to have served him in their military capacity;[170] after al-Muẓaffar's reign, despite attempts on their side to turn the tide, most of them were reportedly removed from Cairo, after which they vanished as a collective political unit worthy of the sources' attention.[171] A third occasion concerns the rise to power of the amir of Circassian origin Barqūq, especially between 1380 and 1382, which, as mentioned, was often explained as a result of Turkish-Circassian antagonism; closer scrutiny however reveals that apart from personal and not unbiased comments of the sort made by historians like al-Maqrīzī, Ibn Ḥajar, Ibn Qāḍī Shuhba and Ibn Taghrī Birdī, there is nothing comparable to the

---

[168] See D. Ayalon, "Mamluk: Military Slavery in Egypt and Syria", in D. Ayalon, *Islam and the Abode of War*, II, pp. 7–8; he deals with these episodes of Circassian activity in more detail in his "The Circassians", esp. pp. 137–139. For the period prior to 1341, Winslow Clifford excluded all together the involvement of any element of ethnicity (Clifford, "State Formation", p. 57).

[169] See al-Ṣafadī, *Aʿyān*, II, p. 477.

[170] See Ibn al-Wardī, *Tatimmat al-Mukhtaṣar*, p. 514; also al-Maqrīzī, *Khiṭaṭ*, III, p. 391, and al-Maqrīzī, *Sulūk*, II/3, pp. 747, 757, almost identical in Ibn Taghrī Birdī, *Nujūm*, X, pp. 186, 188. On their military use by al-Muẓaffar, see al-ʿAynī, *ʿIqd al-Jumān*, p. 82. See also Ayalon, "The Circassians", pp. 137–139.

[171] On these attempts and Circassians' involvement therein, see al-Maqrīzī, *Sulūk*, II/3, pp. 751, 761; Ibn Taghrī Birdī, *Nujūm*, X, p. 190, 192; Ibn Buḥtur, *Tārīkh Bayrūt*, p. 212.

information on al-Muẓaffar's reign to justify such an explanation.[172]

In all, it is only in the forties of the fourteenth century that there seems to be sufficient evidence for the socio-political involvement of the Circassians as an ethnic group. Especially during the reign of al-Muẓaffar Ḥājjī, *jinsīya* seems to have been used deliberately, like several other kinship ties, to enhance the sultan's relationship with his clients, his mamluks in particular. Considered as a distinguishable separate social group, even by the chroniclers, who said that they "distinguished themselves by the size of their turbans [. . .]",[173] and, afterwards, apparently unable to link again with another successful patron, their ethnic isolation must have served al-Muẓaffar well to deepen their dependence on his patronage, and may have been a major reason for their sudden and rapid acquisition and promotion during his short period of rule.[174] Nevertheless, it soon turned out to be an unsuccessful experiment, and, at least for the next thirty-five years, it was never tried again.

Households and Networks

When al-Shujāʿī described how a disgraced amir sought refuge with Aydughmish in May 1342, he recorded the following discussion:

> The son of Aydughmish came to his father and said to him: 'do you want to ruin your house (*baytaka*) because of this [refugee]?' He said [to his son]: 'don't do anything that would disgrace me'. [But] his son said: 'I will go and capture him'. So he went to him and said: 'We cannot let our house (*baytanā*) be ruined because of you, for a sultan's decree [demands] obeyance.' So he took his sword and enchained him.[175]

[172] For these comments, see al-Maqrīzī, *Sulūk*, III/1, pp. 316, 383, 385, 388, 474; Ibn Ḥajar, *Inbāʾ al-Ghumr*, II, p. 92; Ibn Qāḍī Shuhba, *Tārīkh*, I, pp. 24, 26, 38, 154; Ibn Taghrī Birdī, *al-Manhal*, VI, p. 396. Also Levanoni, "Transition", pp. 100–101.

[173] See al-Maqrīzī, *Sulūk*, II/3, p. 747; also in al-Maqrīzī, *Khiṭaṭ*, III, p. 391; Ibn Taghrī Birdī, *Nujūm*, X, p. 188.

[174] The direct cause is reported to have been the *shafāʿa* or intercession with al-Muẓaffar of a high-ranking amir who claimed to be a Circassian himself, undoubtedly with the same purpose of creating a distinct and less unruly corps of mamluks in mind. (See al-Maqrīzī, *Sulūk*, II/3, pp. 747, 756–757; similar reports in al-Maqrīzī, *Khiṭaṭ*, III, p. 391; Ibn Taghrī Birdī, *Nujūm*, X, pp. 186, 188).

[175] Al-Shujāʿī, *Tārīkh*, p. 213.

Though the discussion is probably fictional, it does reveal the contemporary use of the term '*bayt*' in a context similar to that of the, much later, Ottoman Egyptian '*bayt*' as identified by Jane Hathaway. Defining it as a grandee's "entourage of slaves, domestic servants, wives and concubines, bodyguards, and assorted clients who collected at his place of residence" does not seem out of place in this fourteenth-century Mamluk context either.[176] At this time, this almost sacrosanct Mamluk *bayt* or household similarly incorporated a patron's extended family: his harem, his domestic servants and, especially, the core clients that were linked to him by different bonds of kinship—from his offspring to his own mamluks.

The sultan, of course, had the most elaborate of all *bayt*s, housed in the citadel and comprising his harem and family, his personal corps of mamluks, and his *khāṣṣakīya* amirs, court officials and inlaws. Al-Ṣāliḥ Ismāʿīl's household, for instance, included a remarkable number of kinsmen for whom he had secured military rank and office: his stepfather, two brothers and two amirs who belonged to his in-laws;[177] additionally, his sister was married to another high-ranking senior amir and he himself is recorded to have married both the daughter of an amir of highly respected lineage and the daughter of his *nāʾib al-Shām*.[178] The Effective Power he thus came to wield enabled his harem in particular to get away with tapping large parts of the regime's financial income.[179] More than two decades later, al-Ashraf Shaʿbān would manage to set up a similarly strong household as the mainstay of his Effective Power, incorporating his own

---

[176] Hathaway, *The Politics of Households in Ottoman Egypt*, pp. 19–20; see also J. Hathaway, "Mamluk Households and Mamluk Factions in Ottoman Egypt: a reconsideration", in Th. Phillip & U. Haarmann (eds.), *The Mamluks in Egyptian Politics and Society*, Cambridge 1998, p. 109. Mamluk households have also been the focus of attention in D. Ayalon, "Studies in al-Jabarti I: Notes on the Transformation of Mamluk Society in Egypt under the Ottomans", part 2, *JESHO* 3 (1960), pp. 290–299; Sh. Marmon, *Eunuchs and Sacred Boundaries*, Oxford 1995, pp. 8–9, 12. For an appreciation of Ayyubid political power as emanating from 'the household (*bayt*)', see M. Chamberlain, "The crusader era and the Ayyubid dynasty", in Petry (ed.), *The Cambridge History of Egypt. Volume 1*, pp. 237–240.

[177] See al-Shujāʿī, *Tārīkh*, pp. 236, 240, 241; al-Maqrīzī, *Sulūk*, II/3, pp. 621, 628, 630.

[178] See al-Shujāʿī, *Tārīkh*, pp. 261, 264; al-Kutubī, *ʿUyūn al-Tawārīkh*, fol. 75v; al-Maqrīzī, *Sulūk*, II/3, pp. 623, 651, 672.

[179] See e.g. al-Shujāʿī, *Tārīkh*, pp. 239, 245–247, 248, 254, 258–259, 264–265, 269, 272; Ibn Kathīr, *al-Bidāya*, XIV, pp. 203, 204, 205, 207–208, 209, 212–213; al-Maqrīzī, *Sulūk*, II/3, pp. 665, 671, 678–680. Also D. Ayalon, "The Eunuchs in the Mamluk Sultanate", *Studies in Memory of Gaston Wiet*, Jerusalem 1977, pp. 282–294 (repr. in D. Ayalon, *The Mamluk Military Society*, London 1979, III).

corps of sultanic mamluks—reportedly numbering between two and three thousand by 1377—among whom especially his intimates of the *khāṣṣakīya* were important;[180] his young offspring and his brothers, with their substantial *iqṭāʿ* assets mentioned in the previous chapter, and including his eldest son and future successor ʿAlī, who was made an amir of a hundred at the age of three and who had his own substantial corps of a few hundred mamluks;[181] and finally also a number of new kinsmen from among the high-ranking amirs, linked to the sultan through marriage.[182]

And just as an amir was to be an institutional clone of the sultan—as detailed in the previous chapter—, he also managed a household that was a copy of that of the sultan's. The amir Shaykhū's, for instance, reportedly consisted of at least seven hundred mamluks,[183] as well as of a number of intimates that included his stepson, Khalīl b. Qawṣūn.[184] In October 1361, the amir Yalbughā al-Khāṣṣakī even married the former sultan al-Nāṣir Ḥasan's widow, the lady Ṭulubāy, and, consequently, took over a considerable part of that sultan's household, including the "treasuries, weapons, horses, camels and everything [the sultan] [. . .] left behind";[185] he obtained the promotion of an unknown number of his sons to the highest military rank;[186] and he acquired a corps of personal mamluks, which, in the decade it is known to have existed, came to consist of such a large number—between one thousand five hundred and three thousand five hundred—as only Mamluk sultans are known to have been able to rally.[187]

---

[180] See Ibn Qāḍī Shuhba, *Tārīkh*, III, p. 515; on his *khāṣṣakīya*, see e.g. Ibn Duqmāq, *Nuzhat al-Anām*, fol. 53; Ibn Taghrī Birdī, *Nujūm*, XI, p. 55.

[181] See Ibn Duqmāq, *Nuzhat al-Anām*, fol. 72v; al-ʿAynī, *ʿIqd al-Jumān*, p. 169; al-Maqrīzī, *Sulūk*, III/1, p. 213.

[182] See e.g. Ibn Duqmāq, *Nuzhat al-Anām*, fol. 39, 50v; al-Maqrīzī, *Khiṭaṭ*, IV, p. 249; al-Maqrīzī, *Sulūk*, III/1, pp. 157, 170, 212, 263; al-ʿAynī, *ʿIqd al-Jumān*, p. 174; al-Zahiri, *Zubda*, p. 148.

[183] See al-ʿAynī, *ʿIqd al-Jumān*, fol. 104.

[184] See e.g. al-Kutubī, *ʿUyūn al-Tawārīkh*, fol. 162.

[185] See Ibn Duqmāq, *al-Jawhar al-Thamīn*, p. 408; al-Maqrīzī, *Sulūk*, III/1, p. 73; al-ʿAynī, *ʿIqd al-Jumān*, p. 127. The take-over of sultan al-Nāṣir Ḥasan's *bayt* is suggested by Ibn Taghrī Birdī, see Ibn Taghrī Birdī, *Nujūm*, X, p. 314.

[186] Ibn Duqmāq mentions 'sons' as high-ranking amirs, al-Maqrīzī only one son, Shaʿbān, promoted in May 1365 (Ibn Duqmāq, *Nuzhat al-Anām*, fol. 6; al-Maqrīzī, *Sulūk*, II/3, p. 100; also in Ibn Taghrī Birdī, *Nujūm*, XI, p. 27).

[187] See Ibn Duqmāq, *Nuzhat al-Anām*, fol. 37–37v; al-Maqrīzī, *Sulūk*, III/1, pp. 150–151; al-Ẓāhirī, *Zubda*, pp. 113, 148.

And as in the Ottoman case, the fourteenth-century Mamluk household also had a material centre of its own, an urban residence which housed a patron's extended family, and which could become 'a place-to-be' within the city, and, hence, a potent public symbol for that patron's *maqbūl al-kalima*.[188] These residences actually were so important as poles of socio-political attraction in the city, that, more than once, a new Effective Power holder simply moved to his predecessor's city dwelling, hoping to inherit the latter's status.[189] Moreover, these palaces were all situated in the close vicinity of the most powerful pole of attraction of them all, the sultan's citadel. In fact, one amir in particular, Aynabak al-Badrī, initiated an intimidating new practice that would be copied by his successors and that became illustrative of the amirs' successful encroachment upon the degenerating sultanate. After his seizure of Effective Power in June 1377, Aynabak kept large parts of his household in the citadel buildings that had been assigned to him before, when he had been appointed in the office of *amīr ākhūr*: the sultan's stables within the citadel's lower enclosure.[190] On top of that, he lodged his mamluks, reportedly some two hundred in number, nearby, in the madrasas of the former sultans Ḥasan and Shaʿbān, opposite that lower enclosure, and two of his sons were promoted to the highest rank, and they were made to live in the dwelling of a previous power holder, again situated, according to al-Maqrīzī, 'opposite the Chain Gate', the lower enclosure's main access.[191] Thus, Aynabak's household came to dominate

---

[188] There is a considerable number of references to an amir's residential palace (*qaṣr*, *iṣṭabl*, or *dār*), in Cairo, as the center of his patronal activity in this period (see e.g. al-Shujāʿī, *Tārīkh*, p. 184; Ibn Duqmāq, *Nuzhat al-Anām*, fol. 124v; al-Maqrīzī, *Sulūk*, II/3, p. 890; III/1, pp. 8, 42, 132, 141, 306, 308, 315.) (on these amiral dwellings, see e.g. Garcin, "Habitat médiéval et histoire urbaine à Fustat et au Caire", in J.C. Garcin, B. Maury, J. Revault & M. Zakariya, *Palais et Maisons du Caire. I: Epoque mamelouke (XIIIe–XVIe siècle)*, Paris 1982, pp. 176–213; A. Raymond, "The Residential Districts of Cairo's Elite in the Mamluk and Ottoman Periods (Fourteenth to Eighteenth Centuries)", in Haarmann & Philipp, *The Mamluks in Egyptian Politics and Society*, Cambridge 1998, pp. 207–223; L.'A. Ibrahim, "Residential Architecture in Mamluk Cairo", *Muqarnas* 2 (1984), pp. 47–59; Marmon, *Eunuchs*, pp. 3–12), there are equally telling references to the practical importance of the portal (*bāb*) of a patron's dwelling in the dispense of justice and the distribution of his *niʿma*. (see, e.g., Ibn Duqmāq, *Nuzhat al-Anām*, fol. 127; Ibn Khaldūn, *Kitāb al-ʿIbar*, V, p. 467; al-Maqrīzī, *Sulūk*, III/1, p. 307, 317).

[189] See, e.g., al-Maqrīzī, *Sulūk*, III/1, p. 141.

[190] See al-Maqrīzī, *Sulūk*, III/1, pp. 308, 313.

[191] See e.g. Ibn Duqmāq, *Nuzhat al-Anām*, fol. 125v; al-Maqrīzī, *Sulūk*, III/1, p. 308; Ibn Ḥajar, *Inbāʾ al-Ghumr*, I, p. 231.

fully this area beneath the citadel's western slope, the main access to the court and the sultan, and an urban landscape of the highest ceremonial importance.[192] From this time onwards, Aynabak's successors, Barqūq in particular, continued to live with their households within that citadel's lower enclosure, as a public confirmation of these patrons' *maqbūl al-kalima* and as a potent symbol of the Qalawunid sultanate's total subordination.[193]

However, *bayt* only covers one part, though an essential one, of the conduct that engendered socio-political action and development in the period from 1341 to 1382. The period's various strategies of individual socio-political conduct gave rise to many fluctuating alliances between amirs, mamluks and others that often extended far beyond the nucleus of that cohesive household of kin and mamluks, and that were always mutual, mostly very fragile and hardly ever uniform. In any sort of combination, any number of such alliances often can be seen to have resulted from the *niʿma* of one and the same amir, acknowledged as a patron by every one of its recipients. This phenomenon of much wider 'crystallisation' of such relationships around a patron—as limited in time, reach and socio-political impact as it may have been, and always including core clients from the patron's household—will be further referred to by the term 'network', conveniently capturing that mutual, fragile and multiform character of its constituents.[194] A network therefore denotes a group of clients and the patron they had in common at a certain point in time, and it was more precisely a vehicle for that patron's Effective Power, lifting it beyond the much narrower confines of his household. A patron's Effective Power was engendered by those clients' acknowledgement of the subordination of each individual one of them to him personally, and the wider this network of vertical relations was spread over society, the larger the patron's power would be.

In the case of the amir Barka, for instance, the sources again make mention of his household, living in 'the house of Qawṣūn',

---

[192] See e.g. W. Lyster, *The Citadel of Cairo*, Cairo 1993, pp. 30–31.

[193] See for instance Ibn Duqmāq, *Nuzhat al-Anām*, fol. 124v, 126v–127; al-Maqrīzī, *Sulūk*, III/1, pp. 306, 314, 315, 317, 365.

[194] For an overview of the term and its usage, see Miura, "Administrative Networks", pp. 39–41; his definition is very useful: "Firstly, it suggests multi-directional relationships, just as the original meaning of network derives from the word 'net'. Secondly, it means flexibility, which is also implied by the word 'net'. A third feature is generality, as it could include any sort of relationship, and be applied to any type of organization." (p. 41).

opposite the citadel's lower enclosure, and including a corps of some six hundred mamluks and several 'brothers' with high rank and office.[195] At the same time, however, they mention bonds with the *nā'ib al-Shām* 'and his companions', attesting to the spread of Barka's network into Syria.[196] And upon Barka's defeat in June 1380, the sources also identify dozens of amirs that were arrested because of their association with his patronage. Thus, al-Maqrīzī gives the following list:

> The amir Khiḍr was arrested, and the amir Qarākasak, the amir Aydamur al-Khaṭā'ī, Amīr Ḥājj b. Mughulṭāy, the amir Sūdūn Bāshā, the amir Yalbughā al-Manjakī, the amir Qarābulaṭ, the amir Qarābughā al-Abūbakrī, the amir Ilyās al-Mājārī, the amir Tamurbughā al-Sayfī, the amir Yūsuf b. Shādhī, the amir Tamurbughā al-Shāmsī, the amir Quṭlūbak al-Niẓāmī, the amir Aqbughā Sīwān al-Ṣāliḥi, the amir Aḥmad b. Humuz al-Turkumānī, the amir Kizil al-Qaramī, the amir Ṭulūtamur al-Aḥmadī, the amir Tūjī al-Ḥasanī, the amir Tankiz al-ʿUthmānī, the amir Quṭlūbak al-Sayfī, the amir Ghārib al-Ashrafī, the amir Yalbughā al-Nāṣirī, and all the fellows, adherents and mamluks of Barka.[197]

In a similar vein, information on the elaborate and quite successful network of the amir Shaykhū is revealed, extending far beyond the household that was referred to above. Upon Shaykhū's release from the prison of Alexandria in 1351, al-Maqrīzī describes his welcome in Cairo as follows:

> The people had come out to welcome him [. . .]. When they saw the boat [that brought him from Alexandria], they shouted and wished him well, and the boats of his fellows came to welcome him [. . .]; when [his] boat was about to arrive, more than a thousand boats were around it. And [once ashore, all] the amirs mounted to welcome him [. . .], so Shaykhū headed for the citadel in a magnificent procession, the like of which was unseen for an amir.[198]

And the full scope of his unparalleled patronage and consequent region-wide network actually becomes apparent from the revealing appreciation shown in some of the sources. Ibn Qāḍī Shuhba, for instance, states that "his clique became stronger and his support from the amirs that linked with him grew; he got to control the cities and the assets, and

[195] See e.g. al-Maqrīzī, *Sulūk*, III/1, pp. 381–382, 384; al-ʿAynī, *ʿIqd al-Jumān*, p. 254.
[196] Ibn Khaldūn, *Kitāb al-ʿIbar*, V, p. 470.
[197] Al-Maqrīzī, *Sulūk*, III/1, p. 385.
[198] Al-Maqrīzī, *Sulūk*, II/3, p. 848.

no [document] was issued unless on his command [. . .]".[199] Similarly, the contemporary biographer al-Ṣafadī wrote down an even more lyrical analysis:

> Thus, his clique became strong and his shooting stars lit up [the realm's] remotest parts. He promoted many people and in every province, he made more than one an amir, showing him a paradise of benevolence and [bestowing upon him] robes of silk. His representatives in the cities were important and numerous, creating an unrestrained and incessant [flow of benefit] in the [different] areas of their fortunes.[200]

Networks of Effective Power between 1341 and 1382

Though relationships of power were present at every level of socio-political interaction, there is insufficient source material on them for a complete and detailed mapping out of the alternating networks they engendered. It need not, however, be essential to retrieve and explain every single individual patron-client relationship, in order to define the period's socio-political climate. Most of the time, some information on the main networks' major components and results did survive, as with the cases of Barka and Shaykhū, and this actually suffices to reconstruct that climate and define the patterns and trends that make such an exercise worthwhile.

Therefore, the analysis will again focus on those networks that were established by and gave Effective Power to the thirty-two aforementioned amirs and sultans, whose *maqbūl al-kalima* turned each of them simultaneously or successively into one of the most important patrons of their own time and the ultimate focus of any ambitious contemporary's *shafāʿa*. Their networks not only had the highest profile in the remaining source material, but also on the socio-political scene of the time, when they were most widely spread and new ambitions and prospects of success by necessity had to heed the lines that were drawn by their patrons and by the strategies of conduct that engendered their power. Thus, these networks provided—as it were—a socio-political order for the politico-military members of

---

[199] Ibn Qāḍī Shuhba, *Tārīkh*, III, p. 124.

[200] Al-Ṣafadī, *Aʿyān*, II, p. 532. A similar, but less poetic, analysis may be found in al-Maqrīzī, *Khiṭaṭ*, IV, p. 114.

Mamluk society that was not necessarily similar to any institutional arrangement.

The elements that made it into the sources and that make it possible to recreate the story of that socio-political order between 1341 and 1382—these networks' most vital components and their resulting chronology in the given timeframe in particular—will be analysed in the remainder of this study. The latter issue of those network's chronology, however, will only be discussed in detail in the next chapter, as it is deeply linked with that chapter's subject of struggle for power, which was mainly between those networks. But at first, in conclusion to the present chapter and combining the different strategies of socio-political conduct it has portrayed, different types will be defined that allow the identification of the networks that dominated the socio-political scene of the period and imposed their order upon society.

From the perspective of the origins of their patrons' *maqbūl al-kalima*, three distinct types of networks emerged between 1341 and 1382: there were sultans who tried to derive their Effective Power from the office they held, there were amirs who derived it from their privileged status as clients, and there were amirs who derived it from their patronage over the sultan.

Sultans in power

The first type of network, generated by seven of the period's sultans, actually represents a pattern that was predominant throughout Mamluk history, but became far more embattled during the period from 1341 to 1382. It concerns the situation where the sultan was not just in control of Legitimate Power, as was his inherent prerogative, but also of a very substantial amount of Effective Power, meaning that it was the regime's strong man who was sitting on the throne. This had been the case before 1341, when during his third reign al-Nāṣir Muḥammad pulled the strings on the basis of his successful usage of his sultanic prerogatives.[201] But whereas Muḥammad had fought his way back to the throne in 1310 as a tried patron, his twelve descendants time and again faced the problem of starting off as young and

[201] See Van Steenbergen, "Mamluk Elite"; Van Steenbergen, "The amir Qawṣūn", pp. 463–466; also Clifford, "State Formation", pp. 235–274.

politically inexperienced harem recruits that were given their sultanic authority by amirs more powerful than themselves. Nevertheless, no less than six of Muḥammad's sons, and one of his grandsons, with varying success, tried to overcome this predestined nominal nature of their legitimate authority, which earned most of them their identification as power holders. They were the brothers al-Manṣūr Abū Bakr, al-Nāṣir Aḥmad, al-Ṣāliḥ Ismāʿīl, al-Kāmil Shaʿbān, al-Muẓaffar Ḥājjī and, on two occasions, al-Nāṣir Ḥasan, as well as their nephew al-Ashraf Shaʿbān.[202]

Most of these sultans proved sufficiently mature at the time of their accession—at an age that ranged between fourteen and twenty-five[203]—to engage immediately in the efficient set-up of a network of their own. Only al-Nāṣir Ḥasan, in 1347, and al-Ashraf Shaʿbān, in 1363, were weak minors when they were put on the throne, and in both cases it took some years before they somehow legally 'came of age' and could enforce their own patronage.[204] Clearly, each of these sultans' personal maturity enabled him to really perform his sultanic prerogatives and to seek to apply his control over rank, office and income without the need for anyone's consent.

There are abundant examples of these sultans' intending and even succeeding to promote and appoint mamluks and amirs without anyone interfering or using his *maqbūl al-kalima* to influence the sultan's decisions.[205] The relative success of this 'sultanic' type of patronage

---

[202] Abū Bakr and Aḥmad were not identified as power holders by the sources, but the prominent political roles they played as sultans makes it necessary for them to be discussed here.

[203] See Appendix 2: Ḥājjī was about fourteen in 1346, Ismāʿīl was about sixteen in 1342, al-Kāmil Shaʿbān was eighteen in 1345, as was Ḥasan in 1354, Abu Bakr was nineteen in 1341, and Aḥmad was twenty five in 1342.

[204] In Ḥasan's case—eleven years old at the time of his accession in 1347—the process of his coming of age and assuming real sultanic authority is very explicitly detailed by al-Maqrīzī, who refers to the 'declaring of age of the sultan' in December 1350 (al-Maqrīzī, *Sulūk*, II/3, pp. 822, 842; also in Ibn Taghrī Birdī, *Nujūm*, X, pp. 218–219). At the time of his accession in 1363, Shaʿbān was about ten, and he only gradually started to become actively involved as a patron four years later; in his case, there is no similar reference to any active process of declaring him of age.

[205] See e.g. al-Shujāʿī, *Tārīkh*, pp. 236, 240, 241; al-Kutubī, *ʿUyūn al-Tawārīkh*, fol. 162; Ibn Duqmāq, *al-Jawhar al-Thamīn*, p. 400; Ibn Duqmad, *Nuzhat al-Anām*, fol. 38–39, 40, 50v, 52v, 56v–57, 80–80v, 82, 83v, 84, 100, 101, 107; Ibn Khaldūn, *Kitāb al-ʿIbar*, V, pp. 446–447, 451, 458–459, 460–461; al-ʿAynī, *ʿIqd al-Jumān*, pp. 114, 158, 160, 175, 177, 191, 201; al-Maqrīzī, *Khiṭaṭ*, IV, pp. 113, 119, 129–130; al-Maqrīzī, *Sulūk*, II/3, pp. 621, 628, 630, 665, 684, 685–686, 687, 689, 690, 704, 705, 721, 730–731, 735–737, 743, 746, 841; III/1, pp. 35, 43, 154, 155–156, 157, 161, 170, 176–177, 185, 215, 216, 217, 219–220, 224–225, 263, 270, 271; Ibn

also becomes apparent from these sultans' ability to occasionally cross other patrons' interests.[206] Thus, al-ʿAynī summarised al-Manṣūr Abū Bakr's policies in that respect as follows:

> He promised the mamluks that were dearest to him, that the ranks of those amirs he arrested would be given to those among themselves they preferred. Consequently, they lined up before him, and when he wanted to arrest someone [that appeared before him], he told them to arrest him. Thus, he arrested Bashtak [. . .] and Aqbughā ʿAbd al-Wāḥid, and confiscated their possessions [. . .].[207]

Al-Manṣūr Abū Bakr had been enthroned in early June 1341 by designation of his father and by consent of his father's elite of high-ranking amirs.[208] He soon embarked upon a personal policy of patronage, relying heavily on a couple of amirs of a hundred from his father's *khāṣṣakīya* who belonged to his own age group and who, as suggested by al-ʿAynī, were among the main recipients of his *niʿma*. Further information on his patronage remains limited.[209] Nevertheless, it is known that one of his 'kingmakers', the *nāʾib al-salṭana* Ṭuquzdamur al-Ḥamawī (d. 1345), was closely related to him by marriage.[210] And in the course of his deposition after only two months, those clients that belonged to his household are again referred to, when al-Shujāʿī reported that in the end "there only remained with the sultan those who were dear to him [. . .], and his *nāʾib*, Ṭuquzdamur, no one else."[211]

Al-Nāṣir Aḥmad's main supporters reportedly were two high-ranking amirs, one of whom was appointed *nāʾib al-salṭana* and who subsequently became the executive strongholder of this sultan's regime. Aḥmad's household included on the one hand elements he had inherited from

Ḥajar, *Inbāʾ al-Ghumr*, I, pp. 75, 78; Ibn Taghrī Birdī, *Nujūm*, X, pp. 80, 82, 132, 154, 159–161, 165–167, 168, 172, 188, 230–231, 307, 311, 314; XI, pp. 49–50, 54, 55, 62–63, 64–65, 68; Ibn Qāḍī Shuhba, *Tārīkh*, II, pp. 302, 341, 486, 683; III, pp. 117, 124, 134, 136, 310, 315, 325, 369–370, 385, 430, 432, 434, 435, 436, 437, 457, 509; al-Ṣafadī, *Aʿyān*, I, p. 662.

[206] Al-Shujāʿī, *Tārīkh*, pp. 232–233; al-ʿAynī, *ʿIqd al-Jumān*, p. 68; al-Maqrīzī, *Sulūk*, II/3, pp. 619, 620, 621.

[207] Al-ʿAynī, *ʿIqd al-Jumān*, p. 49; similar references to this sort of *niʿma* by Abū Bakr are to be found in Ibn Ḥabīb, *Tadhkirat al-Nabīh*, III, p. 25; Ibn Taghrī Birdī, *Nujūm*, X, p. 17; Ibn Qāḍī Shuhba, *Tārīkh*, II, p. 254.

[208] See, e.g., al-Shujāʿī, *Tārīkh*, p. 107.

[209] Some of his appointees and promotees are mentioned in al-Shujāʿī, *Tārīkh*, p. 126.

[210] See e.g. al-Shujāʿī, *Tārīkh*, pp. 131, 140; al-Maqrīzī, *Sulūk*, II/3, p. 551.

[211] Al-Shujāʿī, *Tārīkh*, p. 137; also Ibn Qāḍī Shuhba, *Tārīkh*, II, p. 206.

his predecessors, such as the sultan's mamluks, and, on the other, a group of outsiders at the court—known as "the Karakians". They had come to Cairo from the desert fortress of al-Karak, where Aḥmad had been living until he was acclaimed sultan, and they acted as his scorned intimates and advisors. Finally, beyond this household, Aḥmad's network allegedly incorporated many other mamluks, like the amir Qawṣūn's, that had been left leaderless upon their *ustādh*'s elimination.[212]

Al-Ṣāliḥ Ismāʿīl's *bayt* of kinsmen and harem constituents has been reconstructed above, when the period's phenomenon of socio-political households was discussed. Moreover, in the course of the accounts of his years in office, there are also recurrent references to continuous promotions of amirs and mamluks, and to other acts of patronage, that resulted in the steady infusion of his clients into the regime's institutional framework.[213] Three clients in particular, to be discussed in more detail below, assisted Ismāʿīl in this process of network building and power-acquisition. They were his brother-in-law Bahādur al-Damurdāshī, and his stepfather Arghūn al-ʿAlāʾī, as well as the *nāʾib al-salṭana* Almalik. While Arghūn in particular often acted as the sultan's sounding board and became Ismāʿīl's most senior client, Almalik was the much-needed executive strongholder of this sultan's regime. The Effective Power which Ismāʿīl thus soon came to wield, especially enhanced by an apparently very shrewd marriage policy, enabled him, for instance, to organise without too much protest no less than eight military campaigns against his brother Aḥmad in al-Karak, and it enabled his massive household, his harem in particular, to get away with tapping large shares from the regime's revenue.[214]

Al-Kāmil Shaʿbān sought to continue his brother's networking. He, for instance, again took over large parts of Ismāʿīl's household, including that demanding harem. There is also mention of a group of his own core clients, amirs and hundreds from his mamluks, that

---

[212] See al-Shujāʿī, *Tārīkh*, pp. 209, 211–212, 217, 225; al-Maqrīzī, *Sulūk*, II/3, pp. 604, 606, 607, 618; Ibn Qāḍī Shuhba, *Tārīkh*, II, p. 241, 295, 424; al-Ṣafadī, *Aʿyān*, I, p. 374.

[213] See e.g. al-Shujāʿī, *Tārīkh*, pp. 236, 237, 238, 244, 245, 257, 273; al-Maqrīzī, *Sulūk*, II/3, pp. 632, 644.

[214] See e.g. al-Shujāʿī, *Tārīkh*, pp. 239, 245–247, 248, 254, 258–259, 264–265, 269, 272; Ibn Kathīr, *al-Bidāya*, XIV, pp. 203, 204, 205, 207–208, 209, 212–213; al-Maqrīzī, *Sulūk*, II/3, pp. 665, 671, 678–680. Also D. Ayalon, "The Eunuchs in the Mamluk Sultanate", *Studies in Memory of Gaston Wiet*, Jerusalem 1977, pp. 282–294 (repr. in D. Ayalon, *The Mamluk Military Society*, London 1979, III).

would stay loyal until his very end,[215] and of several less persistent clients, who all owed promotion, appointment and favour to Shaʿbān.[216] He got, for instance, fond of one young amir, to whom he consequently

> [. . .] offered a rank of [amir of a hundred and] commander of a thousand, [. . .] to whom he granted three hundred thousand *dirham* and ten thousand *irdabb* from the granaries in one single week, and to whom he assigned the residence of Aḥmad Shādd al-Shirābkhānāh, [ordering] that next to it a palace [. . .] should be built for him.[217]

Another client, who—like Almalik before with Ismāʿīl—soon came to be the much-needed executive stronghold of Shaʿbān's regime, was the amir Aghizlū, a low-ranking administrator, whose star started rising when his financial services proved invaluable to Shaʿbān, but whose consequent promotion to the highest military rank was blocked by his rivals.[218]

Al-Muẓaffar Ḥājjī again made full use of the *niʿma* opportunities his sultanic prerogatives offered him. Despite protests, he too kept his brothers' harem. Moreover, already two weeks after his accession to the throne, he is reported to have promoted no less than eighteen amirs in one sweep.[219] And throughout his short rule, he allegedly continued this patronage. He acquired and favoured hundreds of his mamluks, including that ethnic group of Circassians, and promoted several, as he did with two of his kinsmen and with one mamluk who "was transferred from the rank-and-file to the rank of [amir of a hundred] and commander [of a thousand] because of his beauty and handsomeness".[220] Another client of his, to be discussed in more detail below, again was the amir Aghizlū, who now, at long last, managed to get promoted to high rank and office by al-Muẓaffar. In return, he not only became the much-needed executive and financial stronghold of Ḥājjī's regime, but, at the same time, he managed to become one of his patron's most favoured clients.[221]

---

[215] See Ibn Duqmāq, *al-Jawhar al-Thamīn*, pp. 381–382; al-Maqrīzī, *Sulūk*, II/3, pp. 712, 714, 715.
[216] See al-Maqrīzī, *Sulūk*, II/3, pp. 665, 684, 685–686, 687, 689, 690, 704, 705.
[217] Al-Maqrīzī, *Sulūk*, II/3, p. 687.
[218] See e.g. al-Maqrīzī, *Sulūk*, II/3, pp. 685–686, 687, 689, 690.
[219] Al-Maqrīzī, *Sulūk*, II/3, p. 718.
[220] See al-Maqrīzī, *Sulūk*, II/3, pp. 721, 730–731, 735–737, 743, 746; Ibn Taghrī Birdī, *Nujūm*, X, p. 249; Ibn Qāḍī Shuhba, *Tārīkh*, II, p. 683; III, p. 124; al-Ṣafadī, *Aʿyān*, I, p. 662; al-Ṣafadī, *Wāfī*, IX, p. 315; XXIV, p. 390; Ibn Ḥajar, *Durar*, III, p. 272.
[221] See, e.g., al-Maqrīzī, *Sulūk*, II/3, pp. 722, 729, 730–731, 734, 735; Ibn Qāḍī Shuhba, *Tārīkh*, II, p. 515.

The main characters that supported al-Nāṣir Ḥasan's rise to Effective Power in 1351, and that will be discussed in more detail below, were the amirs Mughulṭāy and Ṭāz, who came to be related to the new and young patron through a combination of enormous bestowals, high appointments, substantial *maqbūl al-kalima*, and kinship, in return for their and their pre-existing networks' continued loyalty, service, and support.[222] Ḥasan also sought to promote more docile youngsters from among his own mamluks, but this attempt to consolidate and strengthen his power through his household would only bear fruit after 1357, during his second term.[223] At that time, he continued this earlier policy of promoting his own, young mamluks with more success and he managed to have at least two of them appointed in high executive offices, including one of his unfortunate protegees from 1351, Tankizbughā al-Māridānī (d. 1358), who, meanwhile, also had been married to the sultan's sister.[224] Apart from those officials, and apart from the numbers of rank-and-file mamluks he continued to rely on, he made several of his *khāṣṣakīya* mamluks amirs, and after 1358 he even managed to promote them to the highest military rank.[225] Additionally, he is also reported to have relied on a less conventional socio-political group, the *awlād al-nās*. Thus, by 1361, not only some of his own mamluks, but also two of his own sons held the highest military rank, as well as eight more sons of predeceased amirs, while a number of the latter also held a number of executive offices in Syria.[226] And eventually, in Syria, he also found another major supporter in the person of the *nā'ib al-Shām*, a mamluk amir who had been appointed by Ḥasan in 1360 and who was credited with a 'favoured position' with the sultan.[227]

---

[222] See e.g. al-Maqrīzī, *Sulūk*, II/3, pp. 824, 826, 836–837, 838, 840; al-ʿAynī, *ʿIqd al-Jumān*, pp. 90–91; al-Ṣafadī, *Aʿyān*, I, p. 649.

[223] See e.g. al-Maqrīzī, *Sulūk*, II/3, pp. 841, 842. Al-ʿAynī gives a slightly different version: he claims that Mughulṭāy set Ḥasan against Ṭāz, whereupon the latter decided to strike first (al-ʿAynī, *ʿIqd al-Jumān*, p. 91).

[224] See al-Maqrīzī, *Sulūk*, III/1, p. 35. On the marriage link, see al-Maqrīzī, *Sulūk*, III/1, p. 45; Ibn Qāḍī Shuhba, *Tārīkh*, III, p. 136. On his involvement in Ḥasan's earlier attempt, see al-Maqrīzī, *Sulūk*, II/3, p. 841.

[225] See al-Maqrīzī, *Sulūk*, III/1, pp. 35, 43; al-ʿAynī, *ʿIqd al-Jumān*, p. 114; Ibn Qāḍī Shuhba, *Tārīkh*, III, pp. 117, 134, 330, 457.

[226] See, e.g., Ibn Duqmāq, *al-Jawhar al-Thamīn*, pp. 404–405; al-Maqrīzī, *Sulūk*, III/1, p. 63; al-ʿAynī, *ʿIqd al-Jumān*, pp. 124–125. See also Holt, *The Age of the Crusades*, p. 124; Irwin, *The Middle East in the Middle Ages*, p. 143; Haarmann, "Joseph's Law", pp. 67, 68; Haarmann, "The Sons of Mamluks as Fief-holders", pp. 145, 162.

[227] See al-Ḥusaynī, *Dhayl al-ʿIbar*, p. 189; al-Maqrīzī, *Sulūk*, III/1, p. 66; Ibn Qāḍī Shuhba, *Tārīkh*, I, p. 227.

As with Ismāʿīl's household, also the dimensions of al-Ashraf Shaʿbān's *bayt*—his *khāṣṣakīya* and relatives in particular—have been detailed before. Shaʿbān added to this hard core of kinsmen substantial numbers of clients whom he rewarded for their loyalty by infusing them into his regime's institutions. The sources list in detail the names of new amirs from a wide variety of backgrounds, ranging from his *khāṣṣakīya* to, in the end, even former opponents, that is, rehabilitated Yalbughāwīya mamluks. Especially in the fist years, between 1367 and 1369, his freshly acquired Effective Power was consolidated by the reported promotion of, in all, about one hundred amirs.[228] Moreover, he too is reported to have appointed quite experienced assistants, to be discussed below, to become the executive strongholders of his own regime.

Every one of these networks allowed these sultans to both reign and rule, and to occasionally even cross other patrons' interests. Mostly, however, crossing other patrons' interests ended in the latter's rebellion against the sultan's network, an aspect of the political process that will be discussed in detail in the next chapter. Actually, only one of these seven sultans, al-Ṣāliḥ Ismāʿīl, died in office from natural causes; all the others' networks and consequent Effective Power proved time and again insufficient to withstand such rebellions. After mere months, the networks of al-Manṣūr Abū Bakr, al-Nāṣir Aḥmad, al-Kāmil Shaʿbān, al-Muẓaffar Ḥājjī and al-Nāṣir Ḥasan—at his first attempt in 1351—crumbled under the weight of rival interests. Only al-Ṣāliḥ Ismāʿīl, al-Nāṣir Ḥasan at his second attempt and al-Ashraf Shaʿbān managed to use their sultanic authority to set up networks that lasted longer;[229] yet again, in the latter two cases these networks in the long run succumbed to rival interests. It is clear from hindsight that this type of a sultan's network, involving Qalawunids that were given the sultanate and then tried to use the access that came with their position to acquire their own networks, proved insufficient as a mechanism for lasting and stable Effective Power.

---

[228] See Ibn Duqmāq, *Nuzhat al-Anām*, fol. 40–40v, 52v, 56v–57; al-Maqrīzī, *Sulūk*, III/1, pp. 161–162, 176–177, 185. For his promotions thereafter, see also Ibn Duqmāq, *Nuzhat al-Anām*, fol. 80–80v, 82, 84, 100, 107; al-Maqrīzī, *Sulūk*, III/1, pp. 216, 219, 225–226, 255, 270.

[229] See appendix 1 & 2: the physically weak Ismāʿīl reigned and ruled between 1342 and his natural death in 1345; Ḥasan's second reign lasted from 1354 until his deposition in 1361; Shaʿbān reigned from 1363 until his execution in 1377.

Clients in power

In those sultan's networks, and among the power holders that are identified by the sources in the period from 1341 to 1382 in general, there are several whose ability for *niʿma*, and subsequent networks and Effective Power, were conspicuously derived from their interaction and *maqbūl al-kalima* with another powerful patron. Therefore, though identified as Effective Power holders, they always remained clients themselves—privileged right hands to that patron, as it were—who in return owed some sort of service. Their socio-political status was always relative to, and at times even subordinate to, other patrons—especially the just-mentioned sultans in power—who, for various reasons, accepted these power holders' *shafāʿa* or at least enabled their *niʿma*.

In one respect this type of network concerned client amirs who had been appointed, mostly by a sultan in power, and by virtue of demonstrated executive serviceability, in a highly authoritative position in the military administration, entailing the direct and indirect access to *niʿma* that allowed for successful patronage. Thus, the amir Almalik (d. 1346) was appointed in the executive office of *nāʾib al-salṭana* by al-Ṣāliḥ Ismāʿīl in June 1343, reportedly "upon the condition that the sultan turns to his servant [for advice] on what he should say, and that no one should oppose any of the things [that servant] does [. . .]."[230] He consequently embarked upon a prolonged campaign to restore public order and good administrative practice, and he became the much-needed executive strongholder of his patron's regime.[231] Almalik himself acquired substantial access to *niʿma*, though only a few kinsmen are known to have benefited from his patronage.[232]

The amir Aghizlū al-Sayfī was promoted and appointed in a high court office by al-Muẓaffar Ḥājjī, confirming his position as the sultan's most intimate adviser and enabling him to become known as "the manager of [Muẓaffar's] reign".[233] He not only became the

---

[230] Al-Shujāʿī, *Tārīkh*, p. 255; identical in Ibn Qāḍī Shuhba, *Tārīkh*, II, p. 352; similar in al-Maqrīzī, *Sulūk*, II/3, p. 640.

[231] See al-Shujāʿī, *Tārīkh*, pp. 237, 255–257; al-Maqrīzī, *Khiṭaṭ*, III, p. 305; al-Maqrīzī, *Sulūk*, II/3, pp. 640–643; 646–647; 656, 665, 667, 672. See also Appendix 2.

[232] See al-Shujāʿī, *Tārīkh*, p. 271.

[233] See al-Maqrīzī, *Sulūk*, II/3, pp. 722, 730–731, 735; also in Ibn Taghrī Birdī, *Nujūm*, X, p. 159–161, 165 (quotation from p. 165).

much-needed executive and financial stronghold of Ḥājjī's regime, but also, at the same time, he managed to become one of his patron's most favoured clients, with unparalleled *maqbūl al-kalima* and a firm say in the sultan's decisions.[234] However, apart from the fact that his intercession was responsible for the importation and promotion of Circassians during al-Muẓaffar's reign, information on his own patronage in the political circles is lacking.[235]

In the reign of al-Ashraf Shaʿbān, quite experienced assistants were similarly appointed in order to become the executive strongholders of the sultan's regime. In November 1367, the amir Manklī Bughā al-Shāmsī, soon to be Shaʿbān's in-law, originally from al-Nāṣir Ḥasan's *khāṣṣakīya,* and a *nāʾib* in Syria since 1361, was appointed *atābak al-ʿasākir,* and, on his intercession, another senior colleague, ʿAlī al-Maridānī, originally a client of Shaykhū, who equally had many years of experience as *nāʾib,* was appointed *nāʾib al-salṭana* in January 1368.[236] A few years later, in 1374, the amir Manjak al-Yūsufī, a former Effective Power holder in sultan Ḥasan's first reign, was invited by Shaʿbān to return to Cairo. He arrived in April 1374, with his household, including his sons, an in-law and his mamluks, and he was Shaʿbān's *nāʾib al-salṭana,* with substantial executive authority, until his demise in June 1375.[237]

And finally, in September 1377, the amir Ṭashtamur al-ʿAlāʾī was appointed *atābak al-ʿasākir* after the intercession of three amirs, including Barqūq, with the minor sultan.[238] This Ṭashtamur again had a long history, first employed in the *bayt* of Yalbughā al-Khāṣṣakī and promoted amir in 1363, then, in 1370, re-promoted, from the oblivious rank-and-file to the higher military ranks, "in one stroke", and

[234] See, e.g., al-Maqrīzī, *Sulūk,* II/3, pp. 722, 729, 730–731, 734, 735; Ibn Qāḍī Shuhba, *Tārīkh,* II, p. 515.

[235] Al-Maqrīzī, *Sulūk,* II/3, pp. 735, 747, 757.

[236] On their appointments, see e.g. Ibn Khaldūn, *Kitāb al-ʿIbar,* V, pp. 458, 459; Ibn Duqmāq, *Nuzhat al-Anām,* fol. 38v; al-Maqrīzī, *Sulūk,* III/1, p. 156; Ibn Ḥajar, *Inbāʾ al-Ghumr,* I, p. 5; on their identification as *mudabbir,* see Ibn Qāḍī Shuhba, *Tārīkh,* III, p. 524; also—Manklī only though—Ibn Ḥajar, *Inbāʾ al-Ghumr,* I, p. 5.

[237] See, e.g., Ibn Khaldūn, *Kitāb al-ʿIbar,* V, p. 461; Ibn Duqmāq, *Nuzhat al-Anām,* fol. 83v; al-Maqrīzī, *Sulūk,* III/1, pp. 224, 225, 230.

[238] See Ibn Khaldūn, *Kitāb al-ʿIbar,* V, p. 467; also Ibn Duqmāq, *Nuzhat al-Anām,* fol. 127; Ibn Duqmāq, *al-Jawhar al-Thamīn,* pp. 444–445; al-ʿAynī, *ʿIqd al-Jumān,* pp. 227–228; al-Maqrīzī, *Sulūk,* III/1, pp. 314–315, 316; Ibn Ḥajar, *Inbāʾ al-Ghumr,* I, pp. 233–234.

employed in Shaʿbān's *bayt*, with a *maqbūl* that eventually led to the rehabilitation of his remaining fellow-Yalbughāwīya, and, finally, in 1377, playing a crucial role in the downfall of Shaʿbān.[239] His senior status and esteem among the remains of the Yalbughāwīya corps, as well as the control he had gained over Syria in the rebellion against a previous Effective Power holder, had made him the best possible candidate for the office of *atābak* at that time.[240] Upon arrival in Egypt in September 1377, he brought with him from Syria a handful of clients, who were equally awarded high rank and office.[241] He also is reported to have tried to enhance his position's stability by marrying his daughter to one of the amirs' rising stars, Barqūq.[242]

In another respect, this type of network also concerned clients who owed their privileged *maqbūl al-kalima* with their patron—mainly again a sultan in power—to kinship, mostly through marriage. Thus, the accession of al-Ṣāliḥ Ismāʿīl in June 1342 saw the simultaneous rise to Effective Power of two of his in-laws. One of them was the long-standing amir Bahādur al-Damurdāshī, who, despite his long and uninterrupted record of service, only came to the political forefront upon the accession of his brother-in-law Ismāʿīl. Another was the amir Arghūn al-ʿAlāʾī, who had been a low-ranking amir with al-Nāṣir Muḥammad, and a guardian of his children, then was sent off to Syria, but now, upon his stepson's accession, could enter at once into the highest political circles.[243] The possible networks these positions would have enabled them to build up, remain shrouded in historical darkness, and, particularly in the case of Bahādur, who soon died, may not have been very elaborate. Bahādur and Arghūn especially seem to have acted as the "regime's managers" when the weak sultan became temporarily unfit to do so by the end of 1342.[244] After Bahādur's death soon afterwards, Arghūn's growing *maqbūl al-kalima*

---

[239] See e.g. Ibn Duqmāq, *Nuzhat al-Anām*, fol. 62v, 109; al-Maqrīzī, *Sulūk*, IIII/1, pp. 190, 279, 284–287, 310; Ibn Qāḍī Shuhba, *Tārīkh*, III, pp. 524, 563; I, pp. 42, 143–144. Also Appendix 2.

[240] See e.g. Ibn Khaldūn, *Kitāb al-ʿIbar*, V, p. 467.

[241] See e.g. Ibn Duqmāq, *Nuzhat al-Anām*, fol. 127.

[242] See al-Maqrīzī, *Sulūk*, III/1, p. 323; Ibn Ḥajar, *Inbāʾ al-Ghumr*, I, p. 236.

[243] On these amirs, see also Appendix 2; on their repeated identification as Effective Power holders, see e.g. al-Shujāʿī, *Tārīkh*, pp. 236, 240, 242–243, 247, 252–253.

[244] See al-Shujāʿī, *Tārīkh*, pp. 239–240; al-Maqrīzī, *Sulūk*, II/3, p. 628 (mentions the name of another amir instead of Bahādur!); Ibn Qāḍī Shuhba, *Tārīkh*, II, p. 486.

is shown by his continuous involvement in crucial appointments, promotions and arrests.[245]

When the amir Baybughā Rūs acquired substantial Effective Power at the accession to the throne of al-Nāṣir Ḥasan in 1347, he got his 'brother' Manjak al-Yūsūfī, just mentioned as al-Ashraf Shaʿbān's *nāʾib* almost thirty years later, promoted and appointed in several military offices that awarded considerable opportunities for *niʿma*.[246] As the head of the regime's financial administration, he held substantial control of the regime's resources, resulting in a following of his own, especially in the lower ranks of Mamluk administration and including a substantial and loyal corps of mamluks.[247] With his 'brother' and patron Baybughā Rūs, he managed to wield considerable Effective Power for three full years, until their joint arrest. And al-Nāṣir Ḥasan's first jump to effective power in 1351 awarded his stepfather, the amir Mughulṭāy al-Nāṣiri, paramount *maqbūl al-kalima* and an impressive accreditation as Effective Power holder.[248] With his own extensive network, which included his father-in-law, the *nāʾib al-Shām*, and his brother-in-law, Ḥasan's *dawādār*, he was identified by al-Ṣafadī as "the equivalent of that regime".[249]

And a final network in this type concerns that of the amir Uljāy al-Yūsufī, since, as Ibn Taghrī Birdī put it, in about 1370:

> [. . .] Uljāy's status rose because he was the husband of the mother of the sultan, and [then] he became *atābak al-ʿasākir*. Thus, he rose to paramountcy in [Shaʿbān's] reign, whereas before his marriage with the sultan's mother [. . .] he had merely been one of the amirs [of a hundred and] commanders [of a thousand].[250]

A high-ranking amir ever since Ḥasan's second reign, Uljāy's status outgrew his peers' in 1370 only, and his network came to include

---

[245] See e.g. al-Shujāʿī, *Tārīkh*, pp. 240, 252, 261; al-Maqrīzī, *Sulūk*, II/3, pp. 620, 624, 628, 634, 639, 640, 645–646, 662–665, 667–668.

[246] See al-Maqrīzī, *Khiṭaṭ*, IV, p. 124; al-Maqrīzī, *Sulūk*, II/3, p. 748; Ibn Taghrī Birdī, *Nujūm*, X, p. 189.

[247] See al-Maqrīzī, *Khiṭaṭ*, III, p. 356; IV, pp. 124, 125–126; al-Maqrīzī, *Sulūk*, II/3, pp. 748, 749, 750, 753, 759, 760, 806, 825–826, 842, 845.

[248] See al-ʿAynī, *ʿIqd al-Jumān*, p. 92.

[249] See al-Ṣafadī, *Aʿyān*, I, p. 649. For other elements of his network, including a 'brother', see al-Maqrīzī, *Sulūk*, II/3, pp. 824, 849, 851.

[250] Ibn Taghrī Birdī, *Nujūm*, XI, pp. 57–58. Also referred to in Ibn Khaldūn, *Kitāb al-ʿIbar*, V, p. 459; al-ʿAynī, *ʿIqd al-Jumān*, p. 174; al-Maqrīzī, *Khiṭaṭ*, IV, p. 249; al-Maqrīzī, *Sulūk*, III/1, p. 204, 212; Ibn Ḥajar, *Inbāʾ al-Ghumr*, I, pp. 48–49; Ibn Qāḍī Shuhba, *Tārīkh*, III, p. 439; al-Zahiri, *Zubda*, p. 148.

no less than about eight hundred mamluks, including some hundred rehabilitated Yalbughāwīya ones, as well as undefined numbers of amirs that owed their promotions to his patronage.[251] Thus, when his wife's death obstructed his relationship with his stepson and, in July 1373, he was forced into suicide, al-Maqrīzī illustrates the dimensions of his network as follows:

> The sultan had the amir Ṭuqtamur al-Ḥasanī, the amir Sarāy al-ʿAlāʾī and Sulṭān Shāh b. Qarā, the *ḥājib*, arrested and banished. He had the amir ʿAlāʾ al-Dīn ʿAlī b. Kalfat (sic) arrested and he obliged him to bring money. He had the amir Baybughā al-Qawṣūni and the amir Khalīl b. Qumārī arrested [. . .], and there was publicly announced that whoever found and reported a mamluk from the Uljāyhīya, would get a robe of honour, and whoever offered them shelter, was warned. Thus, the sultan could seize many from them.[252]

Clearly, each one of these ten power holders owed his socio-political status to another patron's *niʿma*, and—as illustrated by the unfortunate case of Uljāy in particular—they were all predestined to remain in this subordinate position as senior client, or, as it were, second-in-command.[253] As will be discussed in more detail in the next chapter, even the faintest attempt to overstep these limits of their subordinate position brought an end to their privileged *maqbūl al-kalima*, as happened to Uljāy, forced into suicide in 1373, to Aghizlū, murdered in 1347, and to Ṭashtamur, defeated in 1378.[254] Otherwise, if they did not die from natural causes during their patrons' terms,[255] these clients lost their status when their patrons disappeared. Almalik was arrested soon after the demise of Ismāʿīl, in August 1345.[256] The same hap-pened to Manjak in December 1350, when Ḥasan freed

---

[251] See e.g. Ibn Duqmāq, *Nuzhat al-Anām*, fol. 80, 80v; al-Maqrīzī, *Sulūk*, III/1, pp. 213, 215, 217, 331; Ibn Ḥajar, *Inbāʾ al-Ghumr*, I, pp. 74, 265

[252] al-Maqrīzī, *Sulūk*, III/1, p. 215; similarly in al-ʿAynī, *ʿIqd al-Jumān*, fol. 174.

[253] When Manjak al-Yūsufī (d. 1375), for instance, was appointed *nāʾib al-salṭana*, Ibn Duqmāq informs us not just that "the sultan put him in his own position for everything and delegated to him all the regime's business", but also that he only "could issue *iqṭāʿ*s up to six hundred *dīnār* [. . .] and assign ranks of amir of forty and ten in the Syrian provinces [. . .]" (Ibn Duqmāq, *Nuzhat al-Anām*, fol. 83v).

[254] See, e.g., al-Maqrīzī, *Sulūk*, II/3, pp. 736–737 (on Aghizlū, killed by peers); III/1, pp. 212–214 (on Uljāy), 322–323 (on Ṭashtamur).

[255] This happened to Bahādur in 1343, to Manklī Bughā in 1372, to ʿAlī in 1370 and to Manjak in 1375 (see appendix 2).

[256] See, for instance, al-Maqrīzī, *Khiṭaṭ*, IV, p. 109; al-Maqrīzī, *Sulūk*, II/3, pp. 681–682; al-ʿAynī, *ʿIqd al-Jumān*, p. 75.

himself of the yoke of Baybughā and his peers,[257] and to Mughulṭāy in August 1351, when Ḥasan failed and was deposed.[258] Only one, Arghūn al-ʿAlāʾī, managed to outgrow his subordinate position and to turn himself into a fully fledged patron after his stepson, al-Ṣāliḥ Ismāʿīl, died in August 1345.

Patrons in power

Indeed, in August 1345, Arghūn succeeded in establishing himself as a powerful patron, as Ismāʿīl's prolonged terminal illness gave him the time needed to rally sufficient support for his other stepson, al-Kāmil Shaʿbān.[259] In this manner, Arghūn became one of Shaʿbān's most important 'kingmakers', and as a result this second stepson of his now owed the sultanate, and therefore *khidma*, to him. And this patronage of the sultanate, and, hence, almost generic *maqbūl al-kalima*, is the common link for the Effective Power that Arghūn and many other power holders held in the period between 1341 and 1382. Because of that virtually automatic *maqbūl*, they created very wide opportunities for *niʿma*, and the consequent ability to substantially widen their households, so that their networks could truly penetrate Mamluk society at large. Though not unusual in Mamluk history, it is the prolonged life of this type of Effective Power, and its inability to grow into a more consolidated format, which characterises this period's political history first and foremost.

In 1342, Ṭashtamur Ḥummuṣ Akhḍar and Aydughmish played a crucial role in al-Nāṣir Aḥmad's accession to the throne; very soon confronted with the limits of the position he was given, the sultan—in al-Shujāʿī's version—"delegated the business to these [kingmakers], saying: manage it as you see fit; do whatever you consider best, and I will be one of you".[260] Eventually, only Ṭashtamur remained,

[257] See Ibn Kathīr, *al-Bidāya*, XIV, pp. 236, 237; al-Maqrīzī, *Khiṭaṭ*, IV, pp. 113, 119, 128; al-Maqrīzī, *Sulūk*, II/3, p. 823; al-ʿAynī, *ʿIqd al-Jumān*, pp. 90–91; Ibn Qāḍī Shuhba, *Tārīkh*, III, pp. 10, 473.

[258] See al-Kutubī, *ʿUyūn al-Tawārīkh*, fol. 122; al-Maqrīzī, *Sulūk*, II/3, pp. 845–847; al-ʿAynī, *ʿIqd al-Jumān*, p. 92; Ibn Taghrī Birdī, *Nujūm*, X, pp. 255–259; Ibn Qāḍī Shuhba, *Tārīkh*, III, pp. 20, 74.

[259] See Ibn Khaldūn, *Kitāb al-ʿIbar*, V, pp. 445–446; al-Maqrīzī, *Sulūk*, II/3, pp. 676–678, 680–681, 682; Ibn Taghrī Birdī, *Nujūm*, X, pp. 94–96, 116–117, 118, 186.

[260] Al-Shujāʿī, *Tārīkh*, pp. 205–206. On these amirs' role in the enthronement of Aḥmad, see for instance al-Shujāʿī, *Tārīkh*, p. 203; al-ʿAynī, *ʿIqd al-Jumān*, pp. 102–103; al-Maqrīzī, *Sulūk*, II/3, p. 602.

became *nā'ib* and established a fierce but brief control over the sultan, lasting thirty-five days only.[261] From his equally short-lived network, only his two sons are referred to, as well as, very explicitly, his *bayt*, which was said to have included an undetermined number of servants and mamluks.[262]

In October 1346, Aqsunqur al-Nāṣiri and Maliktamur al-Ḥijāzī similarly put al-Muẓaffar Ḥājjī on the throne. According to Ibn Qāḍī Shuhba, Aqsunqur and another of those kingmakers were Maliktamur's 'real brothers'. Apart from those kin, his network at the time is reported to have included a substantial number and a wide variety of amirs of high and low rank.[263]

In 1347, a group of amirs, Baybughā Rus and Shaykhū in particular, enthroned al-Nāṣir Ḥasan. In 1347, Baybughā took the office of *nā'ib al-salṭana*, not merely as a sultanic substitute anymore, but as the supreme executive, "who could issue *iqṭā*ʿs to the rank-and-file, and military ranks to the amirs, in Egypt and in Syria, and [who] was in charge of the *nā'ib*s in Syria as well".[264] At the time of his arrest in early 1351, the household and network that resulted from this privileged access is reported to have included unspecified numbers of "amirs and mamluks", amongst whom were his own corps, reportedly one hundred and fifty mamluks in all,[265] and his 'brothers' Fāḍil (d. 1352) and the afore-mentioned powerful client Manjak.[266]

The other senior kingmaker of Ḥasan who simultaneously came to be a dominant patron was the amir Shaykhū. In his case, his substantial *maqbūl al-kalima* and the wide dimensions of his consequent networking, which increased continuously during the many years of his successful patronage of sultans and amirs, came to span the entire Mamluk region, as detailed above when the period's phenomenon of socio-political networks was illustrated. Hence, in 1351 and in

[261] See e.g. al-Shujāʿī, *Tārīkh*, pp. 209, 211.

[262] See al-Shujāʿī, *Tārīkh*, p. 212; also in al-Maqrīzī, *Sulūk*, II/3, p. 607. On the promotion of his sons into the highest military ranks, see al-Shujāʿī, *Tārīkh*, p. 207; al-Maqrīzī, *Sulūk*, II/3, p. 606.

[263] See al-Ṣafadī, *Aʿyān*, V, p. 447; al-Maqrīzī, *Sulūk*, II/3, pp. 722, 730; al-ʿAynī, *ʿIqd al-Jumān*, p. 79; Ibn Qāḍī Shuhba, *Tārīkh*, II, pp. 515, 538.

[264] Al-Maqrīzī, *Sulūk*, II/3, p. 751; see also al-Maqrīzī, *Sulūk*, II/3, pp. 747–748, 842. Also Appendix 2.

[265] See al-Maqrīzī, *Sulūk*, II/3, p. 822; these mamluks—and their support to their *ustādh*, even after his arrest—as well as other members of Baybughā's house, are also mentioned on pp. 825–826, 845.

[266] See al-Maqrīzī, *Sulūk*, II/3, pp. 827, 836, 837. On Fāḍil's high status due to Baybughā's patronage, see also Ibn Qāḍī Shuhba, *Tārīkh*, II, p. 41.

1354, and now in conjunction with other amirs like Ṣarghitmish, he was again deeply involved in the installation of two more sultans, al-Ṣāliḥ Ṣāliḥ and, for the second time, al-Nāṣir Ḥasan respectively.[267]

The amir Ṣarghitmish himself only managed to grow out of the powerful shadow of Shaykhū after the latter's murder in 1357. As Ibn Taghrī Birdī put it, "when Shaykhū died, Ṣarghitmish alone got to manage the state, his authority grew and he became predominant in the regime, taking and giving, increasingly respected, becoming rich, and with growing assets."[268] Little is known, however, about the actual patronage and the consequent network that briefly created such status, apart, again, from those clients that were identified when they perished with Ṣarghitmish in August 1358. They included two amirs, an undefined number of mamluks, and the amir Jirjī al-Idrīsī (1322–1370), who was arrested and exiled "together with many amirs".[269]

Sooner or later, each of the three sultans that were overpowered by these patrons—Aḥmad, Ḥājjī and Ḥasan—started their own, aforementioned, sultanic networks and tried to break free from any bonds of tutelage. Consequently, the amir Ṭashtamur died at the hands of sultan Aḥmad,[270] as did Aqsunqur and Maliktamur by order of Ḥājjī.[271] Ḥasan had Baybughā Rūs and Shaykhū arrested,[272] and during his second reign, Shaykhū died in suspicious circumstances,[273] and Ṣarghitmish was murdered in the prison of Alexandria.[274] When the stakes were this high, patronage proved to be a dangerous game, especially when the sultan decided to enter it.

---

[267] See, e.g., al-Ṣafadī, *Aʿyān*, I, p. 555; al-Kutubī, *ʿUyūn al-Tawārīkh*, fol. 88; Ibn Khaldūn, *Kitāb al-ʿIbar*, V, p. 446; Ibn Duqmāq, *al-Jawhar al-Thamīn*, pp. 383–384; al-ʿAynī, *ʿIqd al-Jumān*, p. 77; al-Maqrīzī, *Sulūk*, II/3, pp. 711–712; Ibn Taghrī Birdī, *Nujūm*, X, pp. 137–139; Ibn Qāḍī Shuhba, *Tārīkh*, II, pp. 515, 520, 679; for their identification as power holders, see al-ʿAynī, *ʿIqd al-Jumān*, p. 79.

[268] Ibn Taghrī Birdī, *Nujūm*, X, p. 307; similar comments in al-Maqrīzī, *Khiṭaṭ*, IV, pp. 257–258, al-Maqrīzī, *Sulūk*, III/1, p. 35; Ibn Qāḍī Shuhba, *Tārīkh*, III, p. 138.

[269] See al-Maqrīzī, *Sulūk*, III/1, pp. 41–43; more details also in al-Kutubī, *ʿUyūn al-Tawārīkh*, fol. 167; Ibn Khaldūn, *Kitāb al-ʿIbar*, V, p. 451; al-Maqrīzī, *Khiṭaṭ*, IV, pp. 119, 259; al-ʿAynī, *ʿIqd al-Jumān*, p. 114.

[270] See, e.g., al-Shujāʿī, *Tārīkh*, pp. 211–212, 216; al-Maqrīzī, *Khiṭaṭ*, IV, p. 108; al-Maqrīzī, *Sulūk*, II/3, p. 637.

[271] See, e.g., al-Maqrīzī, *Sulūk*, II/3, pp. 729–730.

[272] See, e.g., al-Maqrīzī, *Khiṭaṭ*, IV, p. 113; al-Maqrīzī, *Sulūk*, II/3, pp. 823, 825, 827–828; al-ʿAynī, *ʿIqd al-Jumān*, p. 90.

[273] See, e.g., al-Maqrīzī, *Khiṭaṭ*, IV, p. 114; al-Maqrīzī, *Sulūk*, III/1, pp. 33–34; al-ʿAynī, *ʿIqd al-Jumān*, p. 111.

[274] See, e.g., al-Maqrīzī, *Khiṭaṭ*, IV, pp. 119, 259; al-Maqrīzī, *Sulūk*, III/1, pp. 41–42, 44; al-ʿAynī, *ʿIqd al-Jumān*, p. 114.

Nevertheless, there also were others who proved more successful in their sovereignty over the sultan. Already in 1341, the amir Qawṣūn supported the accession of the designated al-Manṣūr Abū Bakr, then put an end to it, and enthroned the infant Kujuk, who was too young to even realise he was a sultan.[275] Upon Qawṣūn's acquisition of such unparalleled Effective Power, his network would come to include a household of allegedly seven hundred mamluks and, according to al-Maqrīzī, "sixty amirs from among his retinue [of mamluks] and [from] his relatives".[276] On top of that, in the period from August to December 1341, sources mention his involvement in more than two hundred and sixty promotions, both of his own mamluks, and of mamluks and clients of others whose support he needed and whose *shafāʿa* he therefore accepted.[277] Upon his premature fall from power in January 1342, this all-encompassing network of his became particularly apparent from detailed reports on the arrest of dozens of high- and low-ranking amirs and mamluks "from Qawṣūn's alliance", and on the subsequent, almost uncontrollable, witch hunt in Cairo against anyone suspected to be a "Qawṣūnī".[278]

Several years later, in 1351, the amir Ṭāz managed to replace the maturing Ḥasan with his one-year younger brother al-Ṣāliḥ Ṣāliḥ.[279] Though he had been involved in the political process before, Ṭāz was only then able to make full use of his patronage over the new sultan and to enhance his Effective Power, to the extent that, three years later, in late 1354, it came to equal Shaykhū's. The network that enabled this was again tightly knit by kinship. Apart from his mamluk corps, surprisingly only sixty mamluks strong in late 1350,[280] his core clients included his two 'brothers' and his brother-in-law.[281]

---

[275] See e.g. al-Shujāʿī, *Tārīkh*, pp. 138–139, 140; al-Maqrīzī, *Khiṭaṭ*, III, p. 55; al-Maqrīzī, *Sulūk*, II/3, p. 570.

[276] See al-Maqrīzī, *Khiṭaṭ*, IV, p. 104; for promotion and appointment of two of his nephews, see al-Shujāʿī, *Tārīkh*, pp. 144, 148.

[277] See e.g. al-Shujāʿī, *Tārīkh*, pp. 144, 148, 154–155, 157, 175, 192, 196–197, 220, 232–233; al-ʿAynī, *ʿIqd al-Jumān*, pp. 54, 57, 60, 68; al-Maqrīzī, *Sulūk*, II/3, pp. 572, 574, 577, 583, 586, 620. check

[278] See al-Maqrīzī, *Sulūk*, II/3, pp. 592–593; similar in Ibn Taghrī Birdī, *Nujūm*, X, pp. 45–46.

[279] See e.g. al-Maqrīzī, *Sulūk*, II/3, pp. 841–842, 843–844; al-ʿAynī, *ʿIqd al-Jumān*, pp. 91–93.

[280] See al-Maqrīzī, *Sulūk*, II/3, p. 822.

[281] See al-Maqrīzī, *Sulūk*, II/3, pp. 832, 835, 844, 909; al-Ṣafadī, *Aʿyān*, II, pp. 617, 619; Ibn Ḥajar, *Durar*, II, p. 226.

Actually, one of those two brothers, the very young Jaridamur (ca. 1342–1391), was said to have been "transferred from one *iqṭāʿ* to another, to become a prime member of al-Nāṣir Ḥasan's *khāṣṣakīya*".[282] Afterwards Ḥasan's successor Ṣāliḥ's infatuation with the same Jaridamur was identified as the main reason for his continued subordination to the latter's 'brother' Ṭāz.[283]

About a decade later, in 1361, Yalbughā al-Khāṣṣakī and his peers deposed Ḥasan for al-Manṣūr Muḥammad, and, after two years, replaced the unruly latter with the ten-year old al-Ashraf Shaʿbān.[284] Core elements in Yalbughā's household, including his many mamluks, the Yalbughāwīya, have been mentioned before. Moreover, through his patronage, not just more senior clients, but also considerable numbers of those by nature generally quite young Yalbughāwīya mamluks were projected into the regime's institutional framework.[285] In March 1366, for example, the sources mention an unprecedented complete list of more than forty newly promoted high- and low-ranking amirs.[286]

In 1377, the seven-year old al-Manṣūr ʿAlī was enthroned by some of his own corps of mamluks, including the amirs Qaraṭāy and Aynabak.[287] Both of them set up very short-lived networks that would actually pave the way for the rise of the amir Barqūq. In the period March–June 1377, Qaraṭāy's patronage of the sultan, and his assumption soon afterwards of the office of *atābak al-ʿasākir* gave him every possible opportunity to outgrow his fellow-patrons, and to start establishing his own network.[288] Its dimensions are indicated in the sources

---

[282] Ibn Qāḍī Shuhba, *Tārīkh*, I, p. 397.

[283] See al-Maqrīzī, *Sulūk*, II/3, p. 920; Ibn Ḥajar, *Durar*, II, pp. 214–215.

[284] See e.g. Ibn Khaldūn, *Kitāb al-ʿIbar*, V, p. 452; al-ʿAynī, *ʿIqd al-Jumān*, pp. 122, 129–130; al-Maqrīzī, *Sulūk*, III/1, pp. 64–65, 82, 83. Additionally, in 1366, when he lost control of al-Ashraf Shaʿbān, he is reported to have tried to make Shaʿbān's brother Anūk sultan, as it were so as to renew his sultanic patronage and, thus, enable the continuation of his control over the sultan (see for instance Ibn Duqmāq, *Nuzhat al-Anām*, fol. 3; Ibn Khaldūn, *Kitāb al-ʿIbar*, V, p. 456; al-Maqrīzī, *Sulūk*, III/1, pp. 133–134).

[285] See Ibn Taghrī Birdī, *Nujūm*, XI, p. 32.

[286] See Ibn Duqmāq, *Nuzhat al-Anām*, fol. 2, 4; al-Maqrīzī, *Sulūk*, III/1, pp. 110, 114, 117–118, 127; al-ʿAynī, *ʿIqd al-Jumān*, pp. 143, 147.

[287] See al-ʿAynī, *ʿIqd al-Jumān*, pp. 205, 209–210; al-Maqrīzī, *Sulūk*, III/1, p. 287; Ibn Ḥajar, *Inbāʾ al-Ghumr*, I, pp. 193, 195, 197.

[288] On his taking of the office of *atābak*, after his colleague suddenly succumbed to the plague, see Ibn Khaldūn, *Kitāb al-ʿIbar*, V, p. 465; Ibn Duqmāq, *Nuzhat al-Anām*, fol. 123; al-Maqrīzī, *Sulūk*, IIII/1, p. 303.

at the time of his precipitate fall from power, in June 1377.[289] Al-Maqrīzī, for instance, informs us that "during the night, Aynabak had surrounded the residences of the amirs that were with Qaraṭāy, as well as of his most intimate mamluks, [. . .] [and] he went to the palace of Qaraṭāy [. . .] and arrested the amirs and all the fellows of Qaraṭāy [. . .]."[290] Moreover, Ibn Qāḍī Shuhba adds that thereupon, "all who had become amir because of Qaraṭāy' were imprisoned".[291] Upon Aynabak's victory over Qaraṭāy, in the closing days of June 1377, he took the office of *atābak al-ʿasākir* for himself, and immediately started consolidating his newly acquired status.[292] Apart from his household, which, as detailed above, guarded the main access to the sultan's citadel, Aynabak's patronage clearly also benefited others, when the sources mention a considerable list of amirs that were given entry into the highest levels of the regime's military institutions, replacing the recipients of his predecessor's patronage with his own.[293] And when his end was near and his opponents multiplied, Ibn Duqmāq, for instance, informs us how a desperate Aynabak abandoned his remaining supporters.

> [his brother] Quṭlūqujāh went out [. . .] with two hundred mamluks, but [their opponents] defeated and arrested him. When Aynabak was informed of that, he sent the amirs that were with him—Aydamur al-Shamsī, Aqtamur ʿAbd al-Ghanī, Bahādur al-Jamali and Mubārak al-Ṭāzī—to Qubbat al-Naṣr, while he himself jumped on his horse and fled [. . .].[294]

Again, all of the latter patrons—Qawṣūn, Ṭāz, Yalbughā, Qaraṭāy and Aynabak—were similarly identified as Effective Power holders at the time of their pupil's accession to the throne.[295] Nevertheless, unlike

---

[289] See Ibn Duqmāq, *Nuzhat al-Anām*, fol. 124; al-Maqrīzī, *Sulūk*, III/1, pp. 305–306; Ibn Ḥajar, *Inbaʾ*, I, p. 230.

[290] al-Maqrīzī, *Sulūk*, III/1, p. 306; also in Ibn Duqmāq, *Nuzhat al-Anām*, fol. 124; Ibn Ḥajar, *Inbāʾ al-Ghumr*, I, p. 230.

[291] Ibn Qāḍī Shuhba, *Tārīkh*, III, p. 542.

[292] See e.g. Ibn Duqmāq, *Nuzhat al-Anām*, fol. 125; al-Maqrīzī, *Sulūk*, III/1, p. 307; Ibn Qāḍī Shuhba, *Tārīkh*, III, pp. 545, 546, 564.

[293] See e.g. al-Maqrīzī, *Sulūk*, III/1, p. 307; Ibn Ḥajar, *Inbāʾ al-Ghumr*, I, p. 230.

[294] Ibn Duqmāq, *Nuzhat al-Anām*, fol. 126.

[295] See for instance al-Shujāʿī, *Tārīkh*, p. 141; Ibn Khaldūn, *Kitāb al-ʿIbar*, V, pp. 443, 465, 467, 469, 470, 473, 474; al-ʿAynī, *ʿIqd al-Jumān*, p. 122, 231; al-Maqrīzī, *Sulūk*, II/3, pp. 551, 552; III/1, pp. 35, 65, 324; Ibn Taghrī Birdī, *Nujūm*, X, pp. 3, 22, 48; XI, pp. 3, 5, 6, 24, 32, 154, 155, 163, 188; Ibn Ḥajar, *Durar*, II, pp. 214–215.

colleagues such as Ṭashtamur, Maliktamur, Baybughā and Shaykhū, they had never really been faced with 'their' sultans' rising against them; as will be detailed in the next chapter, their very often premature end was always rather due to other unstable factors within their networks. Very much as with Arghūn al-ʿAlāʾī, who was al-Kāmil Shaʿbān's stepfather and therefore had a more balanced relationship with his ambitious appointee,[296] these patrons seem to have been able to enhance their patronage over the sultan by additional means, which enabled them to incorporate him into their households. Thus, as said, the amir Ṭāz had great influence on al-Ṣāliḥ Ṣāliḥ since the latter was passionately in love with Ṭāz's 'brother'. And in June 1377, Aynabak clearly hoped to achieve the same level of control over the sultanate when he failed to enthrone his own stepson, the amir Aḥmad b. Yalbughā al-Khāṣṣakī (d. 1400), whom he claimed to be a posthumous son of al-Nāṣir Ḥasan, and therefore a rightful heir to the Qalawunid throne.[297]

In addition to the creation of kinship bonds, another successful method of incorporating the sultan into the *bayt* was the assumption of legal guardianship over the minor sultan. This is explicitly referred to by the sources for the reigns of several sultans (Ḥasan, Ṣāliḥ, Muḥammad, al-Ashraf Shaʿbān, ʿAlī and Ḥājjī), and it is not unlikely to have been involved in the reign of the infant Kujuk either.[298] As these sultans all started off as minors, if not mere infants, they were incapable of the full legal competence their office required, and were therefore—quite conveniently—in need of a guardian's supervision,

[296] A most telling illustration of this relationship between the ambitious Shaʿbān and his kingmaker Arghūn is the fact that, in 1346, though tension was growing between them, Arghūn decided to come to the aid of his stepson in the rebellion that would mean the end for both of them (see al-Maqrīzī, *Sulūk*, II/3, p. 712; also al-ʿAynī, *ʿIqd al-Jumān*, p. 77).

[297] See al-ʿAynī, *ʿIqd al-Jumān*, p. 224; al-Maqrīzī, *Sulūk*, III/1, p. 309; Ibn Ḥajar, *Inbāʾ al-Ghumr*, I, p. 231. On this incident, see also Brinner, "The Struggle for Power in the Mamluk State", pp. 231–232.

[298] See Ibn Khaldūn, *Kitāb al-ʿIbar*, V, pp. 452, 453, 471–472; al-Maqrīzī, *Khiṭaṭ*, III, p. 391; al-Maqrīzī, *Sulūk*, II/3, pp. 822, 842, 919; III/1, p. 5; Ibn Taghrī Birdī, *Nujūm*, X, pp. 218–219, 232. As for Qawṣūn, he was only reported to have been chosen *nāʾib al-salṭana* on behalf of the infant Kujuk, though in his case, this office of 'the sultan's substitute' clearly came very close to that of a legal guardian: according to al-ʿAynī, "because the sultan was an infant who was not competent to speak, nor to reply, [the amirs] preferred that Qawṣūn would be his substitute" (al-ʿAynī, *ʿIqd al-Jumān*, p. 51); on his assumption of the office of *nāʾib al-salṭana*, clearly acting as a legal guardian for the minor sultan, see also al-Shujāʿī, *Tārīkh*, pp. 138, 141; al-Maqrīzī, *Sulūk*, II/3, p. 571.

a position their kingmakers seem to have accepted quite happily. Reportedly, in December 1350, Ḥasan even had been obliged to eliminate those amirs that had been acting as his guardians, before he could even think of becoming a 'sultan in power'.[299] Nevertheless, even in the latter case legal guardianship had empowered those unfortunate patron-guardians for some period of time, as it had repeatedly enabled other patrons, such as Qawṣūn, Ṭāz, Yalbughā, Qaraṭāy and Aynabak, to successfully justify and, thus, enhance their control over the sultan and his sultanic prerogatives. Moreover, the fact that such guardianship could be transferred also assisted patrons who had not been involved in the accession procedures to acquire similar levels of control over the sultan. This is what happened briefly to Asandamur in 1366 and to the amirs Barqūq and Barka in 1378, who had not been among the minor sultan's kingmakers, but who nevertheless managed to assume the same control over the sultanate as their kingmaking colleagues before them.[300]

When Ibn Khaldun described the political set-up at the time of the fully degenerated sultanate of the infant al-Ṣāliḥ Ḥājjī—as it had been described to him by one of Barqūq's most senior associates—he stated that "the amir Barqūq was made [the sultan's] legal guardian for the government and the supervision of the Muslims, because, at the time, [Ḥājjī] was too young to perform this obligation".[301] In fact, together with his peer Barka, whose network was reconstructed above, such legal guardianship had allowed Barqūq to patronise the sultanate already long before Ḥājjī's enthronement in 1381, enabling a steady infusion of his kinsmen and many other clients into the regime's institutions.[302] As with Aynabak's *bayt* before, Barqūq's continued to be centred on the citadel's lower enclosure, in the sultanic stables, even after his take-over of the office of *atābak al-ʿasākir* in April 1378.[303] Circassian or not, Barqūq got, as al-Maqrīzī put it,

---

[299] See al-Maqrīzī, *Sulūk*, II/3, p. 822; Ibn Taghrī Birdī, *Nujūm*, X, pp. 218–219. On those guardians, see also Levanoni, "The Mamluk Conception", pp. 382, 383.

[300] See for instance Ibn Taghrī Birdī, *Nujūm*, XI, pp. 46, 188. Quite tellingly, like Yalbughā before him, this Asandamur equally tried to have his candidate enthroned when he lost control of al-Ashraf Shaʿbān (Ibn Khaldūn, *Kitāb al-ʿIbar*, V, p. 458; al-Maqrīzī, *Sulūk*, III/1, p. 152).

[301] Ibn Khaldūn, *Kitāb al-ʿIbar*, V, p. 471; also p. 473.

[302] See Ibn Khaldūn, *Kitāb al-ʿIbar*, V, pp. 471–472, 473; al-ʿAynī, *ʿIqd al-Jumān*, pp. 264–265; al-Maqrīzī, *Sulūk*, III/2, pp. 439–440; Ibn Taghrī Birdī, *Nujūm*, XI, pp. 188, 206–207.

[303] See e.g. Ibn Khaldūn, *Kitāb al-ʿIbar*, V, pp. 467, 468; Ibn Duqmāq, *Nuzhat al-Anām*, fol. 129; al-Maqrīzī, *Sulūk*, III/1, pp. 323–324.

"a large number [of mamluks], imported from [his] homeland, and he advanced them in a way as they could not have dreamt of, and he awarded to many of them ranks of amir."[304] In 1380, high military rank and *iqṭāʿ* were even bestowed upon Barqūq's newborn son Muḥammad.[305] And a few months later, Barqūq also had his old father brought over from his homeland, and he made him a high-ranking amir, in an unseen public demonstration of his Effective Power.[306] In October 1382, high military rank and income were also given to another relative, who had come with Barqūq's sister and with an unspecified number of other members of his family.[307] Thus, not only mamluks, but also several relatives joined Barqūq's forces, reflecting Ibn Taghrī Birdī's comment that Barqūq 'offered giant *iqṭāʿ*s to his young and freshly imported relatives, and appointed them in precious offices'.[308] More importantly, Barqūq's main achievement actually was the steady acquisition of the majority of military ranks and offices throughout the state for people that 'belonged to his side'. In April 1378, Aytmish al-Bajāsī (d. 1400)—Barqūq's 'friend' (*ṣāḥib*)—was appointed to high office, as was Īnāl al-Yūsufī (d. 1392)—his 'relative' (*qarāba*)—shortly afterwards.[309] In November 1379, ten amirs are reported to have been promoted, including one of his household's employees.[310] And the same happened in June 1380, when the promotion of nineteen amirs was recorded in the sources, as well as the appointment of eight amirs to the highest offices.[311] By the time of al-Manṣūr ʿAlī's demise, therefore, in May 1381, only few obstacles remained for Barqūq's usurpation of Legitimate Power. By November 1382, indeed, the end of the Qalawunid sultanate became possible when Barqūq managed 'to make all the amirs, young and old, swear to obey him'.[312] Above all, this reflects the eventual successfulness of his many years of patronage and the wide extension of his subsequent network over the body politic.

---

[304] Al-Maqrīzī, *Sulūk*, III/2, p. 474.
[305] See e.g. al-Maqrīzī, *Sulūk*, III/1, p. 387.
[306] See e.g. Ibn Khaldūn, *Kitāb al-ʿIbar*, p. 473.
[307] See Ibn Ḥajar, *Inbāʾ al-Ghumr*, II, p. 94; Ibn Qāḍī Shuhba, *Tārīkh*, I, p. 84.
[308] Ibn Taghrī Birdī, *al-Manhal*, VI, p. 396.
[309] See respectively al-Maqrīzī, *Sulūk*, III/I, p. 323, and Ibn Khaldūn, *Kitāb al-ʿIbar*, V, p. 468.
[310] See e.g. al-Maqrīzī, *Sulūk*, III/1, p. 367.
[311] See al-Maqrīzī, *Sulūk*, III/1, pp. 387–389.
[312] Al-Maqrīzī, *Sulūk*, III/2, p. 478.

By making full use of the wide range of available strategies of socio-political conduct—from material exchange to its enhancement through kinship—Barqūq created a powerful household and extended it to become a much wider network that thrived on the *maqbūl al-kalima* he had acquired through his patronage and guardianship over the Qalawunids' last two sultans, and that enabled him for the first time in many decades to create the general consensus his sultanate needed.

CHAPTER THREE

STRUGGLE FOR POWER

When illustrating aspects of patronage and networks in the previous chapter, the examples used seemed to coincide not infrequently with moments of struggle for power. To mention just one example, the impressive lists of promotions that attest to the infusion of clients into the regime's state structures by amirs like Yalbughā, Asandamur, and Barqūq, are in each case dated as following immediately upon these patrons' successful involvement in such tense moments. They occurred immediately after Yalbughā removed a rival in 1366, after Asandamur overcame a putsch against his predominance in 1367, and after Barqūq managed to eliminate Barka in 1380. Actually, this obvious link between patronage and struggle for power should come as no surprise. As demonstrated, patronage involved a client's support in exchange for *niʿma*, and there were no more suitable occasions for a patron to need support than during the intense moments of struggle for power. Such struggles clearly provoked precipitate exchange, furthered networking, deeply influenced the interaction that created Effective Power, and, therefore, constitutes another crucial element of the era's socio-political development. This chapter analyses in detail how this exactly happened, how such struggle—especially the motives it originated in, the course it took and the outcome it resulted in—was deeply intertwined with the period's strategies of socio-political conduct that defined the networks of the years between 1341 and 1382.

Observations

Tension—that is, strained relationships, even hostility, between individuals—and its occasional outburst in the shape of a conflict—that is, a confrontation or even clash between those individuals—have long been considered an essential factor in the development of any given society.[1]

[1] See e.g. W.G. Runciman, *A Treatise on Social Theory, Volume II: Substantive Social*

Ten years ago, Michael Chamberlain and Winslow Clifford similarly highlighted the constructive part they played in the social dynamics of the preceding Ayyubid and early Mamluk eras.[2] Conveniently reduced to a common denominator—struggle for power—, tension and conflict will be shown to deserve a similar socio-political constructiveness for the subsequent historical period of 1341 to 1382.

Tension and conflict, and the insecurity they brought, can be observed to have played quite a substantial part in the lives and careers of those who were politically involved. Ibn Qāḍī Shuhba claims to have read somewhere the following call of despair from the amir Barqūq:

> He said to one of his intimates: 'From the moment I became an amir [in 1377] until now [in 1382], I have not felt secure and I have not eaten well'. Thereupon, he said to [Barqūq]: 'how come?' He said: 'Because I became an amir in the days of Aynabak [al-Badrī], with whom we were in dire straits; when Aynabak disappeared, Ṭashtamur came, and when Ṭashtamur disappeared, Barka remained, and when Barka disappeared, the mamluks of the *sayyid*s (the sons of al-Ashraf Shaʿbān), remained, whom I feared much; only when they were gone, I felt secure and I found peace.'[3]

And four decades earlier, prior to the major January 1342 conflict that resulted in the amir Qawṣūn's removal from Effective Power, this patron is similarly recorded to have been deeply involved in another five conflicts in as many months.[4] Also beyond the capital, socio-political tension and conflict often tended to prevail, as was recorded in Damascus in 1359, at the arrest of the *nā'ib* and some of his core clients, and again in 1379, when an imminent rebellion of amirs and mamluks against another *nā'ib* was exposed.[5]

The fact that the sources record and describe no less than seventy-four socio-political clashes for this period of forty-one years, helps

Theory, Cambridge-New York-Melbourne 1989, pp. 3, 38, 283–284, 340; R.E. Dowse and J. Hughes, *Political Sociology*, Chicester 1986, pp. 65, 67–69; G.G. Lenski, *Power and Privilege: a Theory of Social Stratification*, New York 1966, pp. 31–32.

[2] See e.g. Chamberlain, *Knowledge and Social Practice*, pp. 8–9; Clifford, *State Formation*, pp. 3, 34–35. Of equal importance is Lutz Wiederhold's highly informative analysis of a socio-political conflict in Damascus in 1386 (Wiederhold, "Legal-Religious Elite, Temporal Authority, and the Caliphate").

[3] Ibn Qāḍī Shuhba, *Tārīkh*, I, p. 85.

[4] See Appendix 3, nos. 1, 3, 4, 5, 6.

[5] See e.g. al-Kutubī, *ʿUyūn al-Tawārīkh*, fol. 170 and Ibn Ḥajar, *Inbā' al-Ghumr*, I, p. 299.

to explain both why Barqūq lamented the insecure times he was living in, and why those times were often represented in modern historiography as a period of continuous, ubiquitous struggle for power.[6] From their mere enumeration, it may in fact be observed that these disturbances took a great variety of guises, from clashes of individuals to public street fighting and combats between substantial numbers of the regime's subjects. The former include the eliminations of opponents through arrest and imprisonment, or even murder. For instance, already in July 1341, less than a month after al-Nāṣir Muḥammad's demise, the amir Bashtak (d. 1341) was summoned to appear before the sultan without his personal retinue of mamluks, allegedly to confirm his appointment as *nāʾib al-Shām*, but in reality to facilitate his arrest.[7] And in 1368, sources suggest that the sudden death of the *nāʾib Ḥalab* Ṭaybughā al-Ṭawīl was the result of his poisoning by order of the sultan.[8] Additionally, this wide set of rather contained disturbances of public order also involved a number of quarrels that remained limited to public insinuations and altercations in which, eventually, a compromise or other peaceful solution was preferred over a more violent degeneration. Thus, in 1348 for instance, there was such an argument between the amirs Shaykhū and Manjak over the control of the sultan's fisc, resolved when the latter amir noticed his lack of support and gave in; or in 1380, there was a quarrel between the amirs Barka and Aytmish al-Bajāsī, peacefully ended after mediation of the amir Barqūq and a number of respectful *shaykh*s and *qāḍī*s.[9] Conflicts of interest like these, however, frequently evolved into the polarisation of the majority of those socio-politically active into two opposite camps, occasionally even engaging the manpower of socio-political outsiders like gangs from the common people, and resulting in displays of military power and—if necessary—violence. In 1354, for instance, the amir Ṭāz thus confronted the amirs Shaykhū and Ṣarghitmish on the battlefield, but had to surrender without a fight when he realised his troops were outnumbered.[10] And in 1380, a sequence of tension, rivalry and quarrels between the amirs Barqūq and Barka resulted in a

[6] See Appendix 3 for a descriptive chronological list.
[7] See Appendix 3, nr. 1.
[8] See Appendix 3, nr. 51.
[9] See Appendix 3, nos. 24, 72.
[10] See Appendix 3, nr. 37.

major confrontation between both their networks, during which—in al-Maqrīzī's following account—the entire city of Cairo was turned into a battlefield and Barka was infamously defeated.

> [Barka] left with his companions through a secret gate in his dwelling and headed for Bāb Zuwayla. He entered it, passed through Cairo with his companions, until he reached Bāb al-Futūḥ with an enormous army [that had rallied around him on the streets of Cairo]. [. . .] From there, he departed for Qubbat al-Naṣr. Between his and Barqūq's supporters, there was a skirmish [. . .]. [The next day], Barqūq announced among the common people that 'whoever catches one of Barka's mamluks will get his property, if we get his life'. [Then], the amir Allān al-Shaʿbānī, the amir Aytmish al-Bajāsī and the amir Quruṭ al-Turkumānī mounted [their horses], on behalf of Barqūq, to fight the amir Barka. But the amir Yalbughā al-Nāṣirī, one of Barka's supporters, headed towards them, fought them and defeated them disgracefully, killing many. They [all] spent the night in arms [. . .], and the next morning, [. . .] Barqūq had the sultan brought to him in the stable's pavilion, while the drums in the citadel's drummery beat to war. Thereupon, the sultan's mamluks came to him [. . .] as did a large crowd. Every group of them took up position on one of the tombs between the citadel and Qubbat al-Naṣr, so as to shoot arrows at Barka's supporters when they would start fighting them. [. . .] But [Barka] mounted [his horse] at the time of the midday nap—for it was summertime—, together with the amir Yalbughā al-Nāṣirī, [and they moved up] via two [different] routes. [Barka] unexpectedly [managed] to march up to the foot of the drummery, [from where] they wanted to attack the citadel. The common people took stones to throw at them, while, at the same time, those who were high up, on the citadel['s walls], shot arrows at them, while the amir Allan withstood them with about one hundred horsemen. Then, there was a very fierce battle, in which Aḥmad b. Humuz al-Turkumānī and Barka's mamluks, about six hundred horsemen, proved themselves very brave, routing Barqūq's supporters twenty times [. . .]. But when the common people's stones and the citadellers' arrows became too much for them, Barka was thrown off his horse. His supporters made him mount [his horse] again and, thus defeated, they brought him back to their encampment at Qubbat al-Naṣr. Meanwhile, Aytmish had attacked Yalbughā al-Nāṣirī with an axe, hitting him so that he almost died [. . .]. Many of them were wounded, and from them, the amir Mubārak Shāh al-Māridīnī fled with a group to the amir Barqūq. When night fell, Barka was deserted by most of his companions, while the horses of those who stayed behind were on the brink of collapse from their many wounds. [Therefore], he ordered them to try to rescue themselves. And after midnight, he left from Qubbat al-Naṣr with his *ustādār*, the amir Aqbughā Ṣiwān, [and went] to the mosque of al-Maqs, outside Cairo's Bāb al-Qanṭara, where they hid. But one of those who were there exposed them, so

> that the great amir [Barqūq] sent his *dawādār* Yūnus al-Nawrūzī to them, who took them and brought them to him [. . .]. [Then, Barqūq] [. . .] had him enchained and transported to Alexandria [. . .], where he was imprisoned.[11]

The sources use quite a few Arabic terms to denote any of these conflicts, ranging from the rather neutral *waqʿa* (incident, encounter) to more loaded terms like *intiqāḍ* (collapse) and *thawra* (eruption).[12] Most frequently used, however, irrespective of the specific type of conflict involved, is the term *fitna.* Actually, with meanings that include trial, disagreement, battle and elimination, *fitna* turns out to be as wide-ranging in its use as the period's conflicts in their guises; first and foremost, however, it indicates any sort of perceived disorder and, as such, clearly expresses the contemporary perception of these conflicts, whatever their actual nature, as a disturbance of an established public order.[13]

The period's long sequence of a variety of conflicts, and also the tension that often built up in between, undoubtedly had a profound, disturbing influence on the individuals and networks involved, and therefore on the socio-political scene of the period. Yet, as can be learned from the previous chapter, while individuals and networks perished, others appeared along the same lines of socio-political conduct, as did the public order which soon was to be disturbed again. The disturbing concept of struggle for power clearly played a part

---

[11] al-Maqrīzī, *Sulūk*, III/1, pp. 382–384. See Appendix 3, nr. 73.

[12] For *waqʿa*, see e.g. al-Shujāʿī, *Tārīkh*, p. 157; Ibn Kathīr, *al-Bidāya*, XIV, p. 318; Ibn Taghrī Birdī, *Nujūm*, XI, p. 167; for *intiqāḍ* and *thawra*, see e.g. Ibn Khaldūn, *Kitāb al-ʿIbar*, V, pp. 453, 455, 460, 468. Other occasional terms, often in varying forms, include *mukhāmara* (plot, conspiracy) (see e.g. Ibn Duqmāq, *Nuzhat al-Anām*, fol. 125v; Ibn Duqmāq, *al-Jawhar al-Thamīn*, p. 441; al-Maqrīzī, *Khiṭaṭ*, IV, p. 129; al-Maqrīzī, *Sulūk*, II/3, p. 635; Ibn Ḥajar, *Inbāʾ al-Ghumr*, I, p. 232), *waḥsha* (estrangement) (al-Maqrīzī, *Sulūk*, II/3, p. 815; Ibn Taghrī Birdī, *Nujūm*, X, p. 217; XI, p. 153), *khurūj ʿan al-ṭāʿa* (disobedience) (al-ʿAynī, *ʿIqd al-Jumān*, pp. 123, 154; al-Maqrīzī, *Sulūk*, III/1, p. 66, 310; Ibn Taghrī Birdī, *Nujūm*, XI, pp. 4, 102; Ibn Qāḍī Shuhba, *Tārīkh*, III, p. 384), *ʿiṣyān* (insubordination) (Ibn Taghrī Birdī, *Nujūm*, XI, p. 156) and *khulf* (discord) (Ibn Ḥajar, *Inbāʾ al-Ghumr*, I, p. 310).

[13] For the use of the term *fitna*, see al-Shujāʿī, *Tārīkh*, pp. 149, 191, 263; Ibn Kathīr, *al-Bidāya*, XIV, p. 259; Ibn Ḥabīb, *Tadhkirat al-Nabīh*, III, p. 292; al-ʿAynī, *ʿIqd al-Jumān*, pp. 154–155, 233; al-Maqrīzī, *Khiṭaṭ*, III, pp. 117, 118; al-Maqrīzī, *Sulūk*, II/3, pp. 574, 579, 655, 729, 761, 803, 816, 845, 862; III/1, pp. 115, 152, 279, 315, 321, 322, 331, 382; Ibn Qāḍī Shuhba, *Tārīkh*, III, pp. 309, 350. For a definition of *fitna*, see Chamberlain, *Knowledge and Social Practice*, p. 8; Wiederhold, "Legal-Religious Elite, Temporal Authority, and the Caliphate", p. 225; Ibn Manẓūr, *Lisān al-ʿArab*, s.e., 20 vols., Cairo 1303 h., vol. XVII, pp. 193–198.

in the era's socio-political development, but this part was not necessarily a destructive one.

Motives

A first aspect to be dealt with in order to decipher the rather constructive part struggle for power played in the development of the period's networks and Effective Power concerns the motives from which tension and conflict evolved. It is generally acknowledged that a discrepancy between individuals' ambitions and opportunities can be detrimental to any socio-political interaction.[14] And the Mamluk socio-political scene of the period from 1341 to 1382 was no different in this respect.

To begin with, also in the case of those many conflicts that afflicted the period from 1341 to 1382, every single one of them may be observed to evolve first and foremost around individuals. Even in many of the conflicts of 1366 and thereafter, occasionally ascribed to the collective empowerment of rank-and-file mamluks,[15] the sources clearly identify individuals—amirs and, sometimes, the odd mamluk—as the leading characters and the prime beneficiaries of success and failure. In 1366, at least six amirs are defined the leaders of Yalbughā al-Khāṣṣakī's rebellious mamluks, including Asandamur al-Nāṣiri, who continued to be awarded a leading role in those unruly mamluks' subversive actions until his own downfall as a patron in 1367.[16] A decade later, in 1377, the two simultaneous rebellions that

[14] See e.g. Runciman, *A Treatise on Social Theory, Volume II: Substantive Social Theory*, Cambridge 1989, p. 3 ("resources being limited and their distribution unequal, all persons are thereby in either actual or potential competition with one another"); Dowse and Hughes, *Political Sociology*, Chicester 1986, p. 65 ("Men prefer higher levels of satisfaction to lower levels and will act so as to maximize their satisfactions and will be prepared to incur costs"); Lenski, *Power and Privilege: A Theory of Social Stratification*, New York 1966, pp. 31–32 ("[. . .] if man is a social being [. . .] if most of his important actions are motivated by self interest or partisan group interest, and if many or most objects of his striving are in short supply, then it follows logically that a struggle for rewards will be present in every human society [. . .]").

[15] This point of view was especially formulated in Levanoni, *Turning Point*, pp. 118–132; Levanoni, "Rank-and-file Mamluks vs. amirs", pp. 17–32.

[16] See appendix 3, nos. 45, 46, 47, 48, 49; see also, e.g., Ibn Duqmāq, *Nuzhat al-Anām*, fol. 2v–3v, 5–5v, 37–38v; al-Maqrīzī, *Sulūk*, III/1, pp. 130–138, 141, 142–143, 150–154.

were fatal to al-Ashraf Shaʿbān, on the road to the Hijaz and in Cairo, were reportedly led by four amirs and by two amirs and two mamluks respectively.[17] And in reports of the two other cases of socio-political conflict that directly involved mamluks after 1377, in 1378 and 1382, again it was a variety of amirs, and only one mamluk, that attracted most of the attention in the sources.[18] Now, it should not be entirely ruled out that the latter element stemmed from a distorting narrative technique used in those sources, resulting in the apparent involvement of individuals rather than collectives. Especially in the period 1366–1367, the collective part played by the leaderless swarms of Yalbughāwīya mamluks in the creation of tension and conflict is undeniable. Generally, however, and even in the latter case, it was individuals that emerged from those conflicts, and, as shown in the previous chapter, reaped fruits like *niʿma, maqbūl* and Effective Power. The period's ubiquitous tension and conflicts, in whatever guises, were between individuals: ambitious patrons who generally hoped to find backing in the support their clients owed them.

Despite a few major drawbacks, such as a general lack of information on the deeper grounds of those Mamluk individuals' true motives or objectives, as well as the sources' not infrequent lack of distinction between conflicts' motives, causes and consequences, it will be shown below that it can be safely assumed that, as in any other society, in the case of the Mamluk socio-political scene of this period the detrimental nature of that discrepancy between ambition and opportunity was a crucial element. When opportunities for *niʿma* could no longer match individual ambitions—and this was very likely to be the case between 1341 and 1382, in view of the numerical decline in military ranks as suggested in chapter one—, competition was the only option, and, by lack of any alternative solution, the subsequent tension between competitors often rose until the eruption of conflict, in one of its many guises, and a consequent reshuffle brought a temporary outcome.[19] Therefore, even despite

---

[17] See appendix 3, nos. 55, 56, 57; see also, e.g., Ibn Duqmāq, *Nuzhat al-Anām*, fol. 108v–109; al-Maqrīzī, *Sulūk*, III/1, pp. 275–278, 279–280.

[18] See appendix 3, nos. 69, 74; see also, e.g., Ibn Duqmāq, *al-Jawhar al-Thamīn*, pp. 446–447; al-Maqrīzī, *Sulūk*, III/1, pp. 331–332; III/2, pp. 473–474; Ibn Ḥajar, *Inbāʾ al-Ghumr*, I, p. 265; II, p. 94.

[19] For a similar analysis of the issue of competition in Ayyubid and early Mamluk Damascus, see Chamberlain, *Knowledge and Social Practice*, pp. 91–107.

those historiographical drawbacks, the origins of each of the period's extraordinary number of seventy-four conflicts can be roughly traced back to one generalising motive: a clear and common appreciation of *maqbūl al-kalima* as a valuable and indispensable tool to realise one's ambitions. And within the ubiquitous ensuing competition for that *maqbūl*, two motifs pop up that allow for a typology of those processes of conflict and enable an illustration of the similarity in motives. For tension over *maqbūl* ensued either between ambitious unequals, that is clients and their patrons, or between ambitious equals.

Struggle between patrons and clients

On the one hand, struggle for power arose when an ambitious client tried to extend his *maqbūl* at the expense of his patron, or vice versa. In no less than forty-two of the era's cases of internal socio-political conflict, motives can be traced back to this competition for *maqbūl al-kalima* between a client, or a small group of clients, and a patron.

Twenty-eight times, discredited or jeopardised *maqbūl al-kalima* is recorded to have been the very direct occasion for a client to revolt in frustration. Before al-Nāṣir Muḥammad's death in 1341, his son and successor al-Manṣūr Abū Bakr was on bad terms with one of his later kingmakers, according to al-Maqrīzī because that amir had refused the future sultan's intercession for a mamluk, a quarrel which ended with the amir's disgraceful arrest in 1341.[20] In 1341, the sultan's mamluks' dissatisfaction with Qawṣūn's patronage over them came to a violent confrontation with the amirs, in which at least one was killed.[21] When sultan al-Nāṣir Aḥmad, after his departure for al-Karak, refused to return to Cairo in 1342, all the amirs' *maqbūl al-kalima* was threatened by the inaccessibility of Aḥmad's legitimate power, whereupon they eliminated his supporters and deposed him.[22] Shortly before, in May 1342, the *nāʾib al-salṭana* Ṭashtamur had been cunningly arrested by this al-Nāṣir Aḥmad when his personal ambi-

[20] See al-Maqrīzī, *Sulūk*, II/3, p. 564; al-Maqrīzī, *Khiṭaṭ*, IV, p. 226; also Apppendix 3, nr. 2. Marmon equally uses this insult of Abū Bakr as an illustration of the social value of 'the themes of authority, intercession, mercy and anger' (Marmon, "The Quality of Mercy", pp. 136–138).

[21] See e.g. al-Shujāʿī, *Tārīkh*, pp. 149–154. See also Appendix 3, nr. 4.

[22] See e.g. al-Shujāʿī, *Tārīkh*, pp. 225, 228–229. See also Appendix 3, nr. 9.

tions faced obstruction by Ṭashtamur.[23] And a similar situation resulted in the arrest of the amirs Baybughā Rūs, Shaykhū and Manjak by their client al-Nāṣir Ḥasan in 1350.[24] In 1357, Shaykhū was fatally wounded by a mamluk whose request for higher income he had refused.[25] In 1366, when Yalbughā al-Khāṣṣakī denied *maqbūl al-kalima* and disregarded the intercession of six amirs for the improvement of his mamluks' situation, this public humiliation made them take the lead in the latter's revolt against their patron.[26] This situation reoccurred in 1377, when al-Ashraf Shaʿbān discarded the intercession of the amir Ṭashtamur al-Dawādār for the financial whims of several groups of his mamluks and consequently had to face a rebellion led by this Ṭashtamur.[27] Frustrated *maqbūl* also made a number of amirs reportedly plan a rebellion—prematurely exposed and prevented by their arrest—against their patron Asandamur in 1367, as happened, in the same year, to another two amirs with their patron al-Ashraf Shaʿbān.[28] And shortly before, a first, unsuccessful, rebellion against Asandamur by al-Ashraf Shaʿbān and a group of amirs originated from similar frustrations over Asandamur's overbearing attitude towards Yalbughāwīya mamluks.[29] And some years later, in 1373, the amir Uljāy al-Yūsufī had actually revolted when he was faced with the quick evaporation of his *maqbūl* after the death of his wife, the sultan's mother.[30]

On the other hand, fourteen reported cases all began when patrons acted, or were about to act, against clients or would-be clients that were considered suspicious or deficient in their *khidma*. In 1358, for

---

[23] For Aḥmad's despair with Ṭashtamur, see e.g. al-Shujāʿī, *Tārīkh*, pp. 211, 215.

[24] For Ḥasan's arrests, see e.g. al-Maqrīzī, *Sulūk*, II/3, p. 823; also Appendix 3, nos. 7, 29.

[25] See e.g. al-Maqrīzī, *Sulūk*, III/1, p. 34; also Appendix 3, nr. 38.

[26] See al-Maqrīzī, *Sulūk*, III/1, pp. 130–131; also Appendix 3, nr. 45.

[27] See e.g. al-Maqrīzī, *Sulūk*, III/1, p. 279; also Appendix 3, nr. 55.

[28] For the rebellion against Asandamur, see al-Maqrīzī, *Sulūk*, III/1, p. 141; for the one against Shaʿbān, see e.g. Ibn Duqmāq, *Nuzhat al-Anām*, fol. 38v; also Appendix 3, nos.46, 50; for four more such prematurely exposed rebellions by frustrated clients in this period, see nos. 43, 64, 69, 74.

[29] See e.g. Ibn Khaldūn, *Kitāb al-ʿIbar*, V, p. 457; Ibn Duqmāq, *Nuzhat al-Anām*, fol. 5; al-ʿAynī, *ʿIqd al-Jumān*, p. 148; al-Maqrīzī, *Sulūk*, III/1, p. 142. See also Appendix 3, nr. 47. Additionally, similar violent situations upon clients' rebellions occurred in nos. 5, 6, 70.

[30] See e.g. al-Maqrīzī, *Sulūk*, III/1, p. 212; also Appendix 3, nr. 53. Additionally, 9 more cases of such polarisations upon a client's revolt occurred, see nos. 10, 43, 49, 52, 56, 58, 60, 61, 62.

instance, the amir Ṣarghitmish moved to have the *nā'ib Ḥalab*, his former peer Ṭāz, arrested and his still dangerously impressive network carefully dismantled, and in 1377, the amir Aynabak al-Badrī had the Abbasid caliph banished to Upper Egypt, after his refusal to acknowledge Aynabak's candidate's rights to the Mamluk throne.[31] Very often a sultan aspiring to Effective Power was involved. In 1368, e.g., the *nā'ib Ḥalab* Ṭaybughā al-Ṭawil was murdered on suspicion of his involvement in subversive activities against al-Ashraf Shaʿbān.[32] In 1347, as part of a shrewd operation to create a more docile elite, the notorious al-Malik al-Muẓaffar had his *nā'ib al-Shām* decapitated, three senior amirs in Egypt eliminated, and many more amirs threatened, whereupon they moved to depose him.[33] And the same situation occurred two more times in the period: one year earlier al-Kāmil Shaʿbān had to face two simultaneous rebellions, when he tried to dispose of his *nā'ib al-Shām* and two senior amirs in Egypt, and in 1361, al-Nāṣir Ḥasan was deposed after he had failed to arrest his most senior client, Yalbughā al-Khāṣṣakī.[34] Conversely, when the power holder Asandamur similarly threatened the young but unruly sultan al-Ashraf Shaʿbān in 1367, the latter—almost to his own surprise—managed to overcome his patron and to start his independent rule.[35]

Struggle between patrons

Quite a few of the era's conflicts, however, involved the clash of two equals, bound to struggle for power when one aspired to higher *maqbūl al-kalima* and his network's expansion, but was impeded by the positions the other occupied. Thirty-two conflicts throughout the timeframe started from this premise, leading again to the different

[31] For Ṭāz' arrest, see e.g. al-Maqrīzī, *Sulūk*, III/1, p. 40; for the caliph's banishment, see al-Maqrīzī, *Sulūk*, III/1, p. 309; also Appendix 3, nos. 39, 59.

[32] See e.g. Ibn al-Shihna, *Rawḍat al-Manāẓir*, fol. 132v; al-ʿAynī, *ʿIqd al-Jumān*, pp. 154–155; also Appendix 3, nr. 51.

[33] See e.g. al-Maqrīzī, *Sulūk*, II/3, pp. 732–733, 734, 740–744; also Appendix 3, nos. 20, 21, 23.

[34] For Shaʿbān's unfortunate actions, see e.g. al-Maqrīzī, *Sulūk*, II/3, pp. 708, 709, 710–711; for Ḥasan's, see e.g. al-Maqrīzī, *Sulūk*, III/1, pp. 60–61; also Appendix 3, nos. 17, 18, 41. Additionally, similar situations, though not always fatal to the patron, occurred in nos. 8, 15, 30, 31.

[35] See e.g. Ibn Duqmāq, *Nuzhat al-Anām*, fol. 37–37v; also Appendix 3, nr. 48.

guises the era's conflicts took. Thus, for instance, already in July 1341, Qawṣūn's conniving against his peer Bashtak triggered the latter's arrest, and in August 1377, when consensus and a new balance failed to re-appear after Aynabak's removal, the amirs Yalbughā al-Nāṣiri, Barqūq and Barka had their victorious peers arrested and sent to the prison of Alexandria.[36]

Not unexpectedly, most of the era's quarrels also fell in this category, like that in 1348 between the amirs Shaykhū and Manjak over the control of the sultan's fisc; in 1352 between the amirs Ṭāz and Ṣarghitmish and in 1380 between the amirs Barka and Aytmish al-Bajāsī, the latter two both caused by a mixture of mutual suspicions.[37] And many conflicts of interest that evolved into polarisation and confrontation of networks similarly found their origin in such disputes between equals over *maqbūl al-kalima*. The major turmoil and infighting of 1351, after al-Nāṣir Ḥasan's deposition, reportedly resulted from the fact that the decision to allow the amir Shaykhū to return from prison appeared as a threat to two amirs' assets and positions, since they had taken them from him upon his arrest.[38] In 1354, Shaykhū and Ṣarghitmish confronted Ṭāz' troops after they had been informed of his plans to have them arrested.[39] In 1361, after al-Nāṣir Ḥasan's final deposition, his Syrian representative, the *nā'ib al-Shām* Baydamur al-Khwārizmī, felt threatened by Yalbughā al-Khāṣṣakī and staged an unsuccessful rebellion.[40] A final illustration of rivalling patrons concerns the year 1380, when the exposure of Barka's plan to arrest Barqūq brought the aforementioned violent end to a long series of quarrels between them.[41]

In all, through this matrix of struggle between unequals and between equals, the generalising motive mentioned before clearly appears as an important factor in this period's conflicts. Every time ambitions

---

[36] See e.g. al-Maqrīzī, *Sulūk*, II/3, pp. 560, 561–562; III/1, pp. 313–314; also Appendix 3, nos. 1, 63; for similar arrests, or even direct eliminations, of one patron at the initiative of another, see nos. 12, 13, 19, 22, 25, 26, 40, 54, 66, 68.

[37] See e.g. al-Maqrīzī, *Sulūk*, II/3, p. 760, 862; III/1, p. 379; see also Appendix 3, nos. 24, 34, 72; for the other quarrels, see nos. 16, 27, 28, 36, 65.

[38] See al-Maqrīzī, *Sulūk*, II/3, pp. 844–845; also Appendix 3, nr. 33.

[39] See al-Maqrīzī, *Sulūk*, II/3, pp. 929–930; III/1, pp. 1–4; also Appendix 3, nr. 37.

[40] See Ibn Kathīr, *al-Bidāya*, XIV, p. 280; also Appendix 3, nr. 42.

[41] See e.g. Ibn Khaldūn, *Kitāb al-'Ibar*, V, p. 469; also Appendix 3, nr. 73; for the period's remaining polarisations and confrontations between patron's networks, see nrs 3, 11, 14, 32, 44, 57, 67, 71.

for self-improvement and more Effective Power—by necessity via expanding patronage and furthering *maqbūl al-kalima*—were confronted with the limits of that patronage and collided with another's sphere of influence, tension ensued and conflict in its different guises had to unlock the resulting stalemate. In this period between 1341 and 1382, the ambitious clearly were numerous, the stalemates often high profile, and reports of socio-political conflicts, therefore, rife.

Ambitions

Due to the nature of the socio-political game, and the central importance of the sultan's legitimate authority, it could be expected that many an ambitious individual of the period would not just seek to enhance or safeguard his *maqbūl al-kalima*, and thus his Effective Power, but that he also would strive to eliminate all shreds of insecurity, as Barqūq lamented above, and to acquire the ultimate key to all *maqbūl*, the sultanate. Surprisingly, however, the formal acquisition of legitimate power is only reported to have been involved in a few conflicts throughout the period. And even these generally continued to be more concerned with the acquisition of *maqbūl al-kalima* than with aspirations for the sultanate.

In the year 1341, al-Maqrīzī recounts how rumours about the amir Bashtak's ambitions for the sultanate made him lose his peers' support against Qawṣūn's conniving; some months later, al-Maqrīzī again cited such rumours to have had some responsibility for the revolt that brought down Qawṣūn, and a similar situation is reported to have caused the downfall of the amir Aghizlū in 1347.[42] Moreover, as will be detailed below, more than thirty years later, in 1381, Barqūq had to dispel similarly destructive rumours about his sultanic ambitions.[43] In all four cases—and no more have been recorded—it remains uncertain to what extent these rumours and their allegations were true, but the fact remains that amirs with such ambitions clearly were deemed unwelcome throughout the period of forty odd years.

[42] For Bashtak, see al-Maqrīzī, *Sulūk*, II/3, p. 561; repeated in Ibn Taghrī Birdī, *Nujūm*, X, pp. 6–7; for Qawṣūn, see al-Maqrīzī, *Sulūk*, II/3, p. 586; repeated in Ibn Taghrī Birdī, *Nujūm*, X, p. 38; for Aghizlū, see al-Maqrīzī, *Sulūk*, II/3, p. 736; repeated in Ibn Taghrī Birdī, *Nujūm*, X, p. 166. See also Appendix 3, nos. 1, 6, 22.

[43] Ibn Taghrī Birdī, *Nujūm*, XI, p. 207.

As for the Qalawunids, however, the story is quite the opposite. In 1342, the amir Ramaḍān, another son of al-Nāṣir Muḥammad b. Qalawun, is reported to have started an unsuccessful conflict aimed at his own enthronement, and in 1361, his last remaining brother, the amir Ḥusayn, debarred from succession so many times, was convinced by members of the former sultan's '*bayt*' to engage in a similar conflict.[44] Considering Ramaḍān and Ḥusayn's family background, these two failed conflicts that aimed at the enthronement of a specific Qalawunid were not unusual, and were actually repeated regularly. Some were successful, like the ones that made Kujuk sultan in 1341, Aḥmad in 1342, al-Kāmil Shaʿbān in 1345, and ʿAlī in 1377.[45] Several others, indeed, were not: such as, in addition to Ramaḍān and Ḥusayn's failed attempts, in 1366, when a hunted Yalbughā al-Khāṣṣakī enthroned another Qalawunid rival sultan; in 1367, when Asandamur al-Nāṣiri failed to have an amir with faint Qalawunid references enthroned; and in 1377, when the amirs Ṭashtamur al-Dawādār and Aynabak al-Badrī in turn similarly failed to have their candidates accepted for the sultanate.[46] In fact, every conflict that hoped to end a sultan's reign may be deemed guilty of some ambition for legitimate power. What most of them have in common, though, is the fact that those for whom the sultanate was sought were passive objects, linked to the house of Qalāwūn, but firmly patronised by others, rather than ambitious proactive subjects. In fact, only the aforementioned Ramaḍān, and al-Kāmil Shaʿbān in 1345, are recorded as taking a leading part in the campaigns that aimed for their enthronement. And even then, the enhancement of others' *maqbūl al-kalima* and Effective Power can be shown to be the motive that enabled much of the conflict. For, after Ramaḍān's failed attempt, the one who was most severely punished was an amir of middle rank, whereas the one who had most to gain from Shaʿbān's succession in 1345 was his stepfather Arghūn al-ʿAlāʾī.[47]

---

[44] For Ramaḍān, see al-Shujāʿī, *Tārīkh*, p. 241; al-Maqrīzī, *Sulūk*, II/3, p. 630;. See also Appendix 3, nos. 10, 43.

[45] See Appendix 3, nos. 3, 5, 14, 56.

[46] On 1366, see e.g. Ibn Duqmāq, *Nuzhat al-Anām*, fol. 3; al-Maqrīzī, *Sulūk*, III/1, pp. 133–134; on 1367, see e.g. al-Maqrīzī, *Sulūk*, III/1, p. 152; on 1377, see e.g. Ibn Duqmāq, *Nuzhat al-Anām*, fol. 109v–110; al-Maqrīzī, *Sulūk*, III/1, pp. 285, 309; see also Appendix 3, nos. 45, 49, 57, 59.

[47] The amir Bukā al-Khidrī was executed (al-Shujāʿī, *Tārīkh*, p. 252).

Apart from Barqūq in the 1380s, therefore, the only non-Qalawunid amir that can be shown to have made attested, serious claims for the sultanate, was the amir Baybughā Rūs. In 1352, when he had been outmanoeuvred and removed to remote Aleppo, he "made his ambition to obtain the reign for himself public", and acclaimed himself sultan, with the honorific al-Malik al-ʿĀdil.[48] However, his attempt, born from isolation rather than opportunism, only briefly posed a threat, since his troops dissolved when they heard about the Egyptian army's approach. In all, therefore, and in accordance with the conservatism and opportunism that lay, as identified in chapter one, at the origin of the prolonged Qalawunid sultanate, personal ambitions beyond the enhancement of Effective Power seem to have been unheard-of, something a non-Qalawunid amir could not, or should not—considering the damage of rumours to that extent—aspire to.

Even Barqūq is reported to have taken no risks prior to his enthronement in 1382. As Ibn Taghrī Birdī observed for the year 1381:

> When [al-Ṣāliḥ Ḥājjī's] brother al-Malik al-Manṣūr ʿAlī passed away, people discussed [the possibility of] the sultanate of the *atābak* Barqūq al-ʿUthmānī, and rumours to that extent were spread. However, such talking worried the regime's most senior amirs, saying: 'we will not accept that a mamluk of Yalbughā [al-Khāṣṣakī] will reign as a sultan over us', and similar things. That was told to Barqūq, so that he feared that that would not come true for him. [Therefore], he gathered the amirs, the *qāḍī*s and the caliph [...] in the citadel of the mountain, and discussed with them the sultanate of one of the sons of al-Ashraf Shaʿbān. They told him: 'that would be the best', and they summoned them from the sultan's apartments. This Amīr Ḥājj came, with some of his brothers. But they discovered that one of them was weakened by smallpox, and that the other was an infant. Therefore, the choice was made to make this Amīr Ḥājj sultan.[49]

Even in its degenerated final years, a manageable Qalawunid sultanate continued to be preferred, for various reasons, but especially, at this time, so as not to discredit the *maqbūl al-kalima* of patrons other than Barqūq. Tellingly, it would take another year and a half, a lot of *niʿma*, and only one conflict, before Barqūq finally managed to make overt his covert ambitions for the sultanate.

---

[48] See e.g. Ibn Ḥabīb, *Tadhkirat al-Nabīh*, III, p. 158; al-Maqrīzī, *Sulūk*, II/3, p. 868.

[49] Ibn Taghrī Birdī, *Nujūm*, XI, p. 207.

Strategies

As suggested at the very beginning of this chapter, strategies of socio-political conduct were often deeply rooted in conflict. Actually, it will be argued that they defined these conflicts just as they defined the period's networks. Thus, they set the rules of the game, not just in terms of its *maqbūl*-linked motives, but also of its course and outcome, enabling, on the one hand, those who managed best to play by these rules to be victorious, and, on the other hand, ensuring that competition never got out of hand and threatened the collective social status of all those involved.

Exchange

When networks collided and the extent and cohesion of a competitor's support was tested, the limits of network expansion had to be explored and clients' opportunities to publicly sell their services to the highest bidder were maximised. Patrons, therefore, are reported to rally all the support they could get, using every instrument of patronage they could dispose of. In August 1341, for instance, in the course of his conflict with al-Manṣūr Abū Bakr, the amir Qawṣūn is reported to have acquired several of the sultan's mamluks' support "because of his largesse".[50] And during and after the Syrian revolt against him, in December 1341, he tried to acquire support in similar ways, bestowing an almost uninterrupted flow of promotions and gifts upon amirs and mamluks in Cairo.[51] In 1344, in the course of one of the many campaigns against the former sultan al-Nāṣir Aḥmad in al-Karak, a final breakthrough was only achieved after military rank and income had been bestowed upon some of Aḥmad's local trustees.[52] Equally telling is the fact that it is reported that one year later, in 1345, al-Kāmil Shaʿbān was enthroned only after his stepson Arghūn al-ʿAlāʾī had established a consensus to that extent in exchange for "a lot of money"; and in 1367, al-Ashraf Shaʿbān's

---

[50] See al-Maqrīzī, *Sulūk*, II/3, pp. 567, 568.
[51] See e.g. al-Shujāʿī, *Tārīkh*, pp. 174–175; al-Maqrīzī, *Sulūk*, II/3, pp. 586, 587.
[52] See e.g. al-Shujāʿī, *Tārīkh*, p. 264; al-Maqrīzī, *Sulūk*, II/3, pp. 654, 657, 661. For the official documents that confirmed this patronage, see F. Bauden, "The Recovery of Mamluk Chancery Documents in an Unsuspected Place", in M. Winter and A. Levanoni (eds.), *The Mamluks in Egyptian and Syrian Politics and Society*, (*The Medieval Mediterranean* vol. 51), Leiden 2004, pp. 59–76.

victory over the Yalbughāwīya mamluks was celebrated with an unprecedented gift of "one hundred *dīnār* to each one of his own mamluks".[53]

Perhaps more surprisingly, however, is the fact that such instruments of patronage equally involved the postponed prospect of benefit. Support was equally gained by promising such *niʿma* in the event of victory, without any immediate reward. In the example of August 1341, for instance, the amir Qawṣūn acquired some of the sultan's mamluks' support, not just because of his 'largesse', but also because of "the many promises he made them".[54] And in November 1341, the *nāʾib al-Shām* is reported to have managed to set amirs and other local troopers in Aleppo against his opponent, the *nāʾib Ḥalab*, when "he made them promises, caused them to side against him and told them: [his] money will be yours when his life is ours".[55] In 1361, in the course of the revolt that would be fatal to al-Nāṣir Ḥasan, Yalbughā al-Khāṣṣakī reportedly only managed to turn one of Ḥasan's supporters when he overloaded him with promises.[56] In September 1367, a defeated Asandamur al-Nāṣiri unexpectedly managed to revolt a second time when he promised the sultanate to the amir that guarded him and "offered money to [the Yalbughāwīya], made them promises and raised their hopes".[57] In June 1373, when al-Ashraf Shaʿbān had to face a revolting amir, he is reported to have contacted the amir Aynabak al-Badrī, promising him military rank if he could make a group of Yalbughāwīya desert their rebelling patron.[58] In 1377, this same Aynabak made similar promises to Barqūq and Barka for support against his patron Qaraṭāy.[59] And a final illustration concerns the year 1379, when the revolting amir Īnāl al-Yūsufī won over his patron's mamluks to his side when he promised them money and *iqṭāʿ*s in return.[60]

Clearly, *niʿma* not only could take the shape of direct reward, but also of postponed, future gain. In that case, afterwards, promises had to be fulfilled if the victorious patron wished to enjoy his success

[53] On 1345, see e.g. al-Maqrīzī, *Sulūk*, II/3, p. 677; on 1367, see al-Maqrīzī, *Sulūk*, III/1, p. 154.
[54] See al-Maqrīzī, *Sulūk*, II/3, pp. 567, 568.
[55] See al-Shujāʿī, *Tārīkh*, p. 172.
[56] See Ibn Taghrī Birdī, *Nujūm*, X, p. 313.
[57] See al-Maqrīzī, *Sulūk*, III/1, p. 152.
[58] See al-Maqrīzī, *Sulūk*, III/1, p. 213.
[59] See e.g. Ibn Ḥajar, *Inbāʾ al-Ghumr*, I, p. 230.
[60] See e.g. al-ʿAynī, *ʿIqd al-Jumān*, p. 248.

and avoid frustrated ambitions and grounds for renewed tension. Hence the long lists of promotions upon Yalbughā's, Asandamur's and Barqūq's victories, which were both consolidations of their newly acquired *maqbūl* and indispensable rewards for their supporters. This need for reward actually became painfully clear in 1377: when Qaraṭāy and his companions got the support of sultanic mamluks in their revolt against al-Ashraf Shaʿbān, they promised them a cash reward of no less than five hundred *dīnār*; upon their success, therefore, payment was demanded, and eventually received, but, as al-Maqrīzī informed, not without problems:

> [The amirs only] awarded them one hundred *dīnār* per mamluk. But they renounced [that] and flocked together [. . .]. They captured the amir Ṭashtamur al-Laffāf and threatened to decapitate him. But then the amir Qaraṭāy came and guaranteed them the payment of what they had been promised. He continued to try to win their favour, until they released al-Laffāf. Then, the amirs gave all their attention to the payment of the mamluks.[61]

Maqbūl al-Kalima

So, not just physical strength and martial prowess were decisive factors in times of socio-political conflict, but also, perhaps even more, the ability to gain and retain support and successfully bestow patronage, before, during, and after the conflict. For it was not just a conflict's motives, but also the course it took that concerned the opponents' *maqbūl*, and their consequent ability to generate successful support. Especially in terms of the many promises that were made to potential clients, the latter had to be convinced that their support would not be idle, that the fulfilment of such promises was to be expected. Moreover, those clients that had already been the recipients of the same patron's *niʿma* needed to be equally convinced that their support would continue to be beneficial.

As a result, in a substantial number of the period's conflicts, especially in the case of polarisations and confrontations, a final solution was reached when the majority of a patron's supporters were no

---

[61] See e.g. al-Maqrīzī, *Sulūk*, III/1, pp. 290–291, 295. This patronage and its exceptional character is again referred to by Ibn Qāḍī Shuhba, when he reports that in 1382, upon his enthronement, Barqūq would have reprimanded the surviving beneficiaries for betraying their *ustādh* for money (Ibn Qāḍī Shuhba, *Tārīkh*, I, p. 88).

longer convinced of such benefit, and decided to swap loyalties.[62] Quite illustrative for such opportunistic behaviour and its social acceptance is the following anecdote, mentioned by Ibn Kathīr in his account of Quṭlūbughā al-Fakhrī's successful revolt against the *nā'ib al-Shām* Alṭunbughā in 1341:

> Al-Fakhrī had become very angry with several amirs, among them the amir Ḥusām al-Dīn al-Bashmaqdār [. . .], because of [the following:] He was a supporter of ʿAlā' al-Dīn Alṭunbughā, and after what had happened, he fled with those that fled [from Alṭunbughā]. However, [unlike the rest] he did not come to al-Fakhrī, but entered the city [of Damascus] and remained undecided: he did not go with that one, and did not join this one. Then, he realised what was slipping from his hands and [. . .] resorted to al-Fakhrī—it was said that he was rather put in detention when he came—while he was very worried. But then, he was given the kerchief of safe-conduct.[63]

In line with the period's strategies of conduct, in the face of victory or defeat, clearly self-interest and saving one's skin came first.[64] Therefore, in the course of competition, the portrayal of a patron as potentially successful and capable of acquiring the *maqbūl al-kalima* he sought was as crucial as his actual patronage. Hence, especially when a patron's victory seemed inevitable, this was reflected in the explosive increase of his appeal as a patron, and vice versa. Perception and opportunism were the keys to socio-political success, pending the realisation of their prospects within certain limits of time.

Very often, it was a patron's network's inferior numbers that eventually turned that situation to his disadvantage. In December 1342, for instance, the revolting amir Ramaḍān b. al-Nāṣir Muḥammad was reported to have rallied "soldiers from al-Ḥusaynīya, mamluks of [the amir] Bukā al-Khidrī and the common people", but when his opponents, as a precautionary measure, disabled further support by locking up all amirs in the citadel and then threatened to attack his troops, his supporters all dispersed.[65] In 1346, fleeing was all that was left for al-Kāmil Shaʿbān too, when only four hundred remained

---

[62] See Appendix 3, nos. 3, 5, 6, 8, 9, 10, 18, 21, 23, 35, 37, 39, 41, 42, 45, 47, 53, 55, 56, 61, 62, 71, 73.

[63] Ibn Kathīr, *al-Bidāya*, XIV, p. 197.

[64] For similar observations on other Mamluk periods, see Clifford, "State Formation" pp. 4–8, 34–40, 63, 66; Irwin, "Factions", p. 238; Irwin, *The Middle East*, pp. 155–156.

[65] See e.g. al-Shujāʿī, *Tārīkh*, p. 243; al-Maqrīzī, *Sulūk*, II/3, p. 631.

of the one thousand horsemen that were reported to have supported him at first.[66] When the amir Ṭāz was outnumbered in 1353, even his own mamluks deserted him.[67] And in the course of the defeat of the amir Barka, as quoted above, his abandonment by most of his supporters after they had been defeated in the clashes with Barqūq's made him even send away the small number that had maintained its loyalty, to save them from further bloodshed.[68]

Sometimes, however, not so much numbers, but rather more specific circumstances influenced a patron's credibility and determined his network's strength. When Qawṣūn, for instance, revolted against al-Manṣūr Abū Bakr in 1341, he gained every possible support, even from those amirs that had decided to stay aloof at first, when the sultan refrained from any credible reaction.[69] Or in December 1341, the aforementioned amir Alṭunbughā was deserted by his troops outside Damascus, though they were said to have outnumbered al-Fakhrī's at least three to one; some sources say this was due to the hardship they endured as a result of al-Fakhrī's blockade of the access to Damascus and its commodities, while others claim that al-Fakhrī had managed to make them secret promises, whereupon the desertion of a small group convinced the rest to follow.[70] In 1361, when the *nā'ib al-Shām* Baydamur al-Khwārizmī revolted against Yalbughā al-Khāṣṣakī, he too quickly lost all support when a number of amirs decided to turn against him, in anticipation of the arrival of Yalbughā, the sultan and the entire Egyptian army.[71] In 1366, the same Yalbughā lost all credibility and support himself upon the sultan's success in crossing the Nile, with his troops, without having to relinquish his authority, and despite Yalbughā's attempts to prevent this and keep the sultan isolated on the Nile's West bank.[72]

The calculation and the anticipation of a patron's *maqbūl al-kalima* were generally accepted and expected strategies of socio-political conduct, especially in tense times. This is allusively illustrated in Ibn

---

[66] See al-Maqrīzī, *Sulūk*, II/3, p. 712.
[67] See al-Maqrīzī, *Sulūk*, III/1, p. 3.
[68] See Ibn Ḥajar, *Inbā' al-Ghumr*, II, p. 4.
[69] See al-Shujāʿī, *Tārīkh*, p. 137.
[70] See e.g. al-Kutubī, *ʿUyūn al-Tawārīkh*, fol. 55v; al-ʿAynī, *ʿIqd al-Jumān*, pp. 54–55.
[71] See e.g. al-Ḥusayni, *Dhayl al-ʿIbar*, p. 190; Ibn Kathīr, *al-Bidāya*, XIV, pp. 283–284.
[72] See e.g. Ibn Duqmāq, *Nuzhat al-Anām*, fol. 3v.

Khaldūn's comment on how, in his view, al-Ashraf Shaʿbān had miscalculated his own credibility during his fatal pilgrimage of 1377, and, in vain, had "thought that [his opponents] would show some respect, or that [at least] some of them would side with him".[73] Upon his deposition *in absentio* by Qaraṭāy and his companions, however, even the senior amirs that had remained in Cairo "pretended to be unaware of [the rebels] out of fear for themselves", showing no intention whatsoever to side with a sultan in dire straits.[74] And the same awareness of the era's volatile political culture speaks from the following contemplation, quoted in al-Shujāʿī's chronicle:

> [Qawṣūn] had always thought that his mamluks and scions would defend him, and that some of the amirs and his retinue would help him. But when he witnessed his mamluks fleeing and all the amirs hoping for his downfall, his determination was broken, the loss of his zeal was ascertained, his energy melted away and he was deprived of his strength.[75]

Communication: Intimidation and Manipulation

As demonstrated, in this volatile political culture, a patron's portrayal as reliable and successful was often imperative for his survival and that of his network. Direct interference, therefore, in that portrayal could be a powerful tool, in particular to destabilise a patron. The spread of rumours in the build-up of tension and conflict has been mentioned before, and, indeed, verbal and non-verbal techniques of communication can be shown to have played a crucial part as such interfering and destabilising factors, not just at the start, but also in the course of conflicts. During negotiations, and in the format of rumours, patrons are quite often recorded in remarkable detail to intimidate opponents, or even to manipulate their environment. This is of course due to such techniques' usefulness for narrative purposes, and the historical value of many a story's details may be rightly questioned. Nevertheless, at the very least, their occurrence confirms the socio-political appreciation of a patron's portrayal, and their ubiquitous and frequently axial character, often far beyond

[73] Ibn Khaldūn, *Kitāb al-ʿIbar*, V, p. 463.
[74] al-Maqrīzī, *Sulūk*, IIII/1, p. 277.
[75] al-Shujāʿī, *Tārīkh*, p. 186.

the anecdotal, seems to imply that they were more than the mere result of historical imagination.

In no less than half of the era's recorded cases of socio-political conflict, attempts to intimidate, to fill patrons and clients with fear, are described.[76] Techniques used for this purpose included boasting about the unmatchable size and strength of one's network, and the public threatening of an opponent's personal integrity. Clearly, the main intention of such techniques was to discredit the credibility of an opponent's *maqbūl*, and, as such, to make his network forsake his patronage. In times of negotiations, prior to possible violent confrontations, these techniques were rife. In December 1341, for instance, in the build-up to the conflict between al-Fakhrī and Alṭunbughā, the former sent a letter to Alṭunbughā, which, for such undermining purposes, was to be handed over at the most public of all moments of Mamluk ceremonial, the weekly session or *khidma*; according to al-Shujāʿī, this was al-Fakhrī's disturbing message read out at that occasion:

> All of us [Syrian amirs] have agreed on the enthronement of al-Malik al-Nāṣir Aḥmad, son of our *ustādh*, and together with us, all the amirs in the Egyptian territories have agreed to be obedient. You are on your own, with this tiny, little troop of yours: when you will need them, they will be of no avail to you; they will forsake [you] and come to us. [Therefore], it would [only] be for your own good to come and accept the installation of this sultan. [. . .][77]

As already mentioned, despite their superior numbers, Alṭunbughā's clients would eventually indeed relinquish their patron. Correspondence is recorded to have been similarly successful in the conflict between the *nā'ib al-Shām* and the *nā'ib Ḥalab* Ṭāz in the year 1358: Ibn Kathīr reports to have been told that the latter surrendered when the *nā'ib al-Shām* publicly announced to him that he was outnumbered.[78] And similar intimidation dominated the correspondence that was recorded between al-Ashraf Shaʿbān and the amir Uljāy in 1373, and between the amirs Barqūq and Barka in 1380: in the thick of the fighting, a rather humiliating settlement was proposed to both Uljāy and Barka, implying that their defeat was inevitable, their

---

[76] See Appendix 3, nos. 3, 5, 6, 8, 9, 11, 17, 18, 21, 23, 24, 27, 30, 33, 34, 37, 39, 40, 41, 42, 44, 45, 46, 47, 48, 49, 50, 51, 53, 55, 61, 64, 66, 69, 72, 73, 74.

[77] al-Shujāʿī, *Tārīkh*, p. 176.

[78] Ibn Kathīr, *al-Bidāya*, XIV, p. 259.

maqbūl vaporising and supporting them useless.[79] And each time, indeed, it only took a few hours before they were defeated.

Additionally, destabilising intimidation was also the purpose of many rumours that were spread, especially when they concerned the allegedly imminent threat of a patron's arrest.[80] As seen before, the eruption of many a conflict resulted from such intimidating rumours, as did its outcome. In 1341, for instance, Qawṣūn managed to rally many amirs against al-Manṣūr Abū Bakr when he intimated to them the sultan's intentions to arrest them.[81] The *nā'ib al-Shām* Yalbughā al-Yaḥyāwī (d. 1347) rose in revolt twice in as many years when rumours reached him that the sultan had sent someone to arrest him.[82] In 1361, quite an intimidating failed attempt to verify rumours of a murder plot eventually triggered Yalbughā al-Khāṣṣakī's deposition of al-Nāṣir Ḥasan.[83] In 1373, it is reported that rumours of Uljāy al-Yūsufī's imminent arrest triggered his unsuccessful revolt, and in 1377, part of the revolt against al-Ashraf Shaʿbān is ascribed to a similar, but more direct scaring of the amir Ṭashtamur al-Dawādār.[84] Finally, the year 1380 saw the recorded spread of quite a few intimidating rumours, on the amir Barka's alleged arrest by Aytmish al-Bajāsī, on Barka's plans to arrest some of Barqūq's clients, and even on his plan to arrest Barqūq himself, eventually culminating in the violent confrontation of both networks.[85]

Apart from such boasting and threatening with arrest, additional communicative techniques to destabilise an opponent's position involved manipulation, exerting a shrewd or even devious influence on the sultan, a patron or a peer, often in order to depreciate an amir's *maqbūl* both in perception and in practice. Insinuating opponents' involvement in subversive activities was the message that did the trick, and again, the technique most often used to this end was the spreading of rumours. In June 1341, the amir Qawṣūn, for instance,

---

[79] For 1373, see e.g. al-Maqrīzī, *Sulūk*, III/1, p. 213; for 1380, see e.g. Ibn Ḥajar, *Inbā' al-Ghumr*, II, pp. 3–4.

[80] Apart from the examples below, see also al-Maqrīzī, *Sulūk*, II/3, pp. 561–562, 567, 579, 625, 710–711, 742–743, 805, 826, 827–828, 846, 862, 929; III/1, pp. 40, 131, 141, 150, 312, 315, 321.

[81] See e.g. al-Shujāʿī, *Tārīkh*, pp. 135, 136.

[82] See e.g. al-Kutubī, *ʿUyūn al-Tawārīkh*, fol. 78v, 82v–83.

[83] See e.g. al-Maqrīzī, *Sulūk*, III/1, pp. 60–61.

[84] See Ibn Ḥajar, *Inba al-Ghumr*, I, p. 74; al-Maqrīzī, *Sulūk*, III/1, pp. 212, 279.

[85] See Ibn Khaldūn, *Kitāb al-ʿIbar*, V, p. 467; Ibn Taghrī Birdī, *Nujūm*, XI, pp. 174–175.

manipulated a fellow amir so that the arrest of the amir Bashtak became inevitable: he spread the rumour that the latter planned that amir's arrest, whereupon he and his incensed colleagues happily agreed to capture Bashtak.[86] Similarly, the arrest of the *nāʾib al-salṭana* Aqsunqur al-Salārī in June 1343 is reported to have been the result of another amir's manipulation, since he "had slandered him with the fact that he secretly sided with [the former sultan] al-Nāṣir Aḥmad and corresponded with him".[87] Other such examples concern the removal from Syria of the amir Ṭurghāy al-Nāṣiri in 1342, accused of secret participation in the revolt of Ramaḍān; the arrests of the amirs Shaykhū, Manjak and Baybughā Rūs, in al-ʿAynī's version "by Mughulṭāy al-Nāṣiri's manipulation of al-Nāṣir Ḥasan"; the banishment in 1376 of the amir Muḥammad b. Aqbughā Āṣ by a rival's intriguing; and finally the arrest of the amir Yalbughā al-Nāṣiri in 1378, conveniently accused of siding with the embattled amir Ṭashtamur al-Dawādār.[88] As can be seen, these and many other accusations against rivals for Effective Power, uttered either directly or indirectly, all found inspiration in the same trove of conspiracy theories. They occasionally concerned the aforementioned unwelcome sultanic ambitions that were attributed to Bashtak, Qawṣūn, Aghizlū and Barqūq, or the sympathising with known subversive elements, like in the cases of Aqsunqur, Ṭurghāy and Yalbughā above. Additionally, such accusations could concern active participation in such conspiracies, as in 1348, when three amirs were conveniently eliminated after being accused of plotting the overthrow of the amir Baybughā Rūs, or even participation in murderous plans, like Bashtak in 1341, who allegedly was also accused of having poisoned al-Nāṣir Muḥammad, or Qawṣūn in the same year, accused of having that Bashtak and al-Manṣūr Abū Bakr assassinated, or sultan al-Kāmil Shaʿbān in 1346, accused of similar actions against two of his brothers.[89] Finally, with respect to revolts against several sultans of the era's first decade, such actions often found grateful justification in

[86] See e.g. al-Maqrīzī, *Sulūk*, II/3, pp. 561–562.

[87] See e.g. al-Maqrīzī, *Sulūk*, II/3, p. 639.

[88] For 1342, see e.g. al-Shujāʿī, *Tārīkh*, p. 244; for 1351, see al-ʿAynī, *ʿIqd al-Jumān*, p. 90; for 1376, see e.g. Ibn Khaldūn, *Kitāb al-ʿIbar*, V, p. 462; for 1378, see Ibn Qāḍī Shuhba, *Tārīkh*, I, p. 417.

[89] On 1348, see e.g. al-Maqrīzī, *Sulūk*, II/3, p. 761; on 1341, see al-Shujāʿī, *Tārīkh*, p. 130; al-Maqrīzī, *Sulūk*, II/3, pp. 586–587; on 1346, see al-Maqrīzī, *Sulūk*, II/3, pp. 688, 706.

allegations of the beleaguered sultan's unfit, even illicit behaviour.[90]

Actually, from all these, and many more similar cases that concern the interference with a patron's portrayal, the main impression that remains indeed is a resultant atmosphere of continuous insecurity and lack of safety, as Barqūq lamented at the beginning of this chapter. Words could be very dangerous, even for the *maqbūl al-kalima* of the most powerful Effective Power holder, and their potentially destabilising effect was continuously omnipresent.

Therefore, not just a conflict's motives, but also the course it took and even the outcome that resulted were deeply embedded in such strategies of conduct that evolved against a background of individual survival and benefit. Whatever their format and whatever the amount of violence involved, reliable patronage was crucial to rally and retain sufficient support beyond the confines of one's household, and any interference with that picture of reliability, due to the course of events, opponents' deliberate communicative actions, or both, was lethal.

Order out of Chaos: 1341–1382

Not surprisingly, the struggle for power, ubiquitous, dissimilar and opportunistic as it was, was as decisive in the era's history of networks and power holders as patronage was. More surprising, however, is the fact that it may even be concluded from the preceding that, to a large degree, conflicts themselves evolved around nothing but moments of intense, even extreme patronage in a competitive format. For, they involved the same characters as patronage did, their causes were alike, and they abided, in a more intemperate, at times even devious, way, by the same unwritten rules of conduct. And actually, they even had similar outcomes: the creation (but also the simultaneous annihilation) of networks and Effective Power. Conflict was therefore not necessarily about disturbing, but rather about preserving, furthering, or even creating patronage, and, as such, socio-political order along the lines of the resultant networks.

[90] See e.g. Ibn al-Wardī, *Tatimmat al-Mukhtaṣar*, p. 496; al-Shujāʿī, *Tārīkh*, pp. 135, 141, 143, 146–148, 163; Ibn Kathīr, *al-Bidāya*, XIV, pp. 192, 201, 219; al-Maqrīzī, *Sulūk*, II/3, pp. 567, 568, 709, 710.

Indeed, as will be discussed in the remainder of this chapter, all the era's predominant networks that brought their patrons Effective Power were deeply involved in most of the period's conflicts. The inevitable competition for *niʿma* and *maqbūl al-kalima* involved their patrons, whose factual patronage and portrayal as patrons bore heavily on the resultant conflicts' outcome, and whose success or failure either enabled the network's confirmation and enhancement, or caused its vaporisation. Every network, therefore, entered the public arena going through a moment of conflict, and, apart from Barqūq's, almost every network was also forced to leave that arena as a consequence of conflict.

From the perspective of such a succession of networks, the socio-political history of the period between 1341 and 1382 can be divided into six distinguishable episodes. In general, each of these episodes can be observed to have started when some sense of chaos loomed, that is when no dominant network was capable of rising from a conflict that brought an end to the former dominant network.

Episode 1: 1341–1342

The first episode is quite a brief one, and runs from the death of al-Nāṣir Muḥammad in June 1341 to the accession of al-Ṣāliḥ Ismāʿīl in June 1342. Its eventful history makes up for its briefness, when it is realised that this episode witnessed the coming and going of three sultans and was disrupted by nine moments of severe conflict within twelve months. In fact, it was al-Nāṣir Muḥammad's eldest surviving sons al-Manṣūr Abū Bakr and al-Nāṣir Aḥmad and his senior amirs Qawṣūn and Ṭashtamur who engaged in the set-up of no less than four networks that dominated the episode and that were deeply involved in its conflicts.

Al-Malik al-Manṣūr Abū Bakr was enthroned in early June 1341 by designation of his father and, most importantly, by the consent of his father's elite of high-ranking amirs, thus avoiding the turmoil and conflict that may have been anticipated.[91] He soon managed to deploy his own patronage, providing an alternative to his kingmakers', Qawṣūn's in particular. The resulting tension equally quickly, in August 1341, developed into conflict and a trial of patrons' strength.

[91] See e.g. al-Shujāʿī, *Tārīkh*, p. 107.

As a result of Abū Bakr's inertia and lack of immediate reaction, however, almost all those involved in the conflict eventually joined Qawṣūn, whereupon al-Shujāʿī reported that in the end "there only remained with the sultan his favorites [. . .] and his *nāʾib*, Ṭuquz-damur, no one else".[92]

Upon Qawṣūn's release from any patron's rivalry, he came to dominate society at large, enthroning the infant Kujuk and extending his patronage to all those who had supported him, and beyond, until his downfall five months later, in January 1342.[93] The two rebellions that ended Qawṣūn's dominance—one in Syria and another in Egypt, indicative of the wide spread of Qawṣūn's patronage—as well as the subsequent enthronement of al-Nāṣir Aḥmad were orchestrated by three amirs who were also veterans from al-Nāṣir Muḥammad's reign: Quṭlūbughā al-Fakhrī and Ṭashtamur Ḥummuṣ Akhḍar in Syria, and Aydughmish in Egypt.[94] At first, Quṭlūbughā al-Fakhrī was the amir who stepped in Qawṣūn's footsteps in January 1342 as the acting power holder.[95] But—for unspecified reasons—he, Aydughmish and many other senior amirs are soon afterwards reported to have decided to leave Egypt for Syria, effectuating a remarkable sweep in the political scene's outlook, since "a group of 'Syrian' amirs was established in Egypt, and a group of the amirs of Egypt left for Syria".[96] Eventually, therefore, only Ṭashtamur remained, became *nāʾib* and established a fierce control over the new sultan.[97] But unlike Qawṣūn before him, he failed to set up a network to

[92] al-Shujāʿī, *Tārīkh*, p. 137; also Ibn Qāḍī Shuhba, *Tārīkh*, II, p. 206. See Appendix 3, nr. 3.

[93] On the arrested amirs, see al-Shujāʿī, *Tārīkh*, pp. 192, 232–233; Ibn Duqmāq, *al-Jawhar al-Thamīn*, p. 372; al-ʿAynī, *ʿIqd al-Jumān*, pp. 60, 68; for this witch hunt, see e.g. al-Maqrīzī, *Sulūk*, II/3, pp. 592–593; Ibn Taghrī Birdī, *Nujūm*, X, pp. 45–46.

[94] On the lively debates between those three that allegedly accompanied Aḥmad's enthronement, see e.g. al-Shujāʿī, *Tārīkh*, pp. 203–204; al-Maqrīzī, *Sulūk*, II/3, p. 602; Ibn Qāḍī Shuhba, *Tārīkh*, II, pp. 234–235.

[95] When Aydughmish and the Egyptian amirs swore allegiance to Aḥmad, already in February 1342, Quṭlūbughā name was explicitly included in the oath "every time the sultan was mentioned" (See al-Shujāʿī, *Tārīkh*, pp. 198–199; al-Maqrīzī, *Sulūk*, II/3, p. 599). For Quṭlūbughā days as ruler over and *nāʾib* of Aḥmad, see al-Shujāʿī, *Tārīkh*, p. 205.

[96] al-Shujāʿī, *Tārīkh*, pp. 206–207, also p. 211. Whereas in al-Shujāʿī's account this switch is the amirs' own decision, al-ʿAynī identifies the sultan as its direct cause (see al-ʿAynī, *ʿIqd al-Jumān*, pp. 62–63).

[97] See e.g. al-Shujāʿī, *Tārīkh*, pp. 209, 211 ("when he took the office of *nāʾib*, he

consolidate the power that the sword and his colleagues had left him with, and the sultan managed to have him arrested fairly easily, after only thirty-five days in power.[98] That sultan, al-Nāṣir Aḥmad, had succeeded in enhancing and creating—despite Ṭashtamur's obstruction—a network of his own, that made it possible for him to arrest the latter amir and to establish his authority. Despite this initial success, however, Aḥmad preferred his isolation from a majority of amirs he did not trust—a situation his patronage could not or would not change—and soon disappeared from the political scene when he decided to return to his beloved city of al-Karak, taking with him the regalia, his harem, and his treasures, and leaving behind the bulk of his supporters.[99] When he thus abandoned his freshly acquired Effective Power, and became inaccessible for any interaction, let alone for any intercession—so vital to the socio-political process—, "the situation corrupted, every amir feared the other", and something like a power vacuum arose.[100]

Eventually, this socio-political deadlock was resolved through consensus. Aḥmad's departure was equally detrimental to all amirs, who were all bereft of their access to *niʿma*, so that, weak as they were individually, they could not but join forces, in Egypt and in Syria. Confronted with this new situation, Aḥmad's remnant of supporters in Cairo wisely forsook him, and, consequently, unanimous agreement was reached to replace Aḥmad with his younger brother, al-Ṣāliḥ Ismāʿīl, who was enthroned at the end of June 1342.[101] And to avoid unruly behaviour like his brother's, the elite of high-ranking amirs did not just swear allegiance to this new sultan, but equally demanded him to swear allegiance to them.[102] The main short-term

placed the sultan under his guardianship and did not leave him to deal independently with any of the affairs of government; he did not allow any amir to enter with the sultan or to meet with him [...]. [As a result], no one could talk to the sultan anymore. Every time the sultan wanted to give someone something, Ṭashtamur disagreed [...] and whatever the sultan wished someone to acquire, was taken and was prevented by Ṭashtamur. [...] [Hence], the sultan had no say in any of the regime's affairs."); al-Maqrīzī, *Sulūk*, II/3, pp. 606–607.

[98] See Appendix 3, nr. 7.

[99] al-Shujāʿī, *Tārīkh*, p. 218; for his departure's detailed story, see al-Shujāʿī, *Tārīkh*, pp. 215–218; also in al-Maqrīzī, *Sulūk*, II/3, pp. 608–609; al-ʿAynī, *ʿIqd al-Jumān*, p. 63.

[100] See al-Shujāʿī, *Tārīkh*, p. 224.

[101] See Appendix 3, nr. 9.

[102] See e.g. al-Shujāʿī, *Tārīkh*, pp. 229–230, 231; Ibn Kathīr, *al-Bidāya*, XIV, p. 202. See also Holt, "The Structure of Government', pp. 46–47.

consequence of the entire situation, however, was that all the candidates for renewed dominant patronage had disappeared, and from the diversity of amirs whose weakness rather than strength had triggered the enthronement of Ismāʿīl, a new regulating focus for socio-political conduct was not likely to re-appear soon.

In short, this first episode of the period's socio-political history saw the final rise and precipitous fall of the patron Qawṣūn and his wide network. At first, it rose in competition with the network of Abū Bakr, but soon after the latter's elimination it became paramount in an absolutist manner. As a result, Qawṣūn's network proved irreplaceable in the short term after his fall, and it left no one who was capable or even willing to fill the gap left by Qawṣūn. Indeed, one year after al-Nāṣir Muḥammad's death, socio-political chaos finally was about to prevail.

Episode 2: 1342–1347

The accession to the throne of al-Ṣāliḥ Ismāʿīl in June 1342 initiated an episode of modest opportunities for new networks to arise, and, thus, for some socio-political order to return. Nevertheless, the political scene would remain quite unstable for another decade at least, and was destined to relapse into a state of chaos, in which it was unclear what networks, if any, prevailed or would come to prevail. In this second episode, from the accession of Ismāʿīl to the deposition of his brother al-Muẓaffar Ḥājjī in the closing days of 1347, three networks of sultans—Ismāʿīl's and Ḥājjī's, and that of their brother al-Kāmil Shaʿbān—would succeed each other with varying degrees of success. Eventually, however, they would again be equalled by the successive networks of at least two kingmakers, Arghūn al-ʿAlāʾī's and Maliktamur al-Ḥijāzī's. The recurrent prevalence of socio-political instability and tension that resulted from such variety of networks speaks from the fact that the episode witnessed no less than fourteen conflicts, though chaos, that is the absence of any dominant network, only ensued by the end of 1347.

But at first, and with no individual amir capable of patronising him, Ismāʿīl started his rule with a potent message of his political intentions. Much against his amirs' advice, he decided to release all amirs and mamluks that had been captured in the course of the events of episode one, and even returned a handful to their former ranks.[103] Making this conciliatory policy the basis of his rule, his inclusive rather than exclusive patronage enabled him to acquire a firm amount of Effective Power, disturbed only by the prolonged campaigning against his brother Aḥmad in al-Karak.[104] Ismāʿīl's potentials to actually succeed his father and to recreate his reign's stability and longevity were, however, cut short in August 1345, when Ismāʿīl finally succumbed to an illness that had weakened him for many years.

But there were others ready to take his place: two of his senior supporters and his full brother Shaʿbān in particular. Fairly quickly, Ismāʿīl's stepfather Arghūn al-ʿAlāʾī managed to rise above the tension that resulted from the sultan's demise and he created sufficient support for his candidate for the throne, his other stepson Shaʿbān. In that way, Arghūn became the new sultan's most important kingmaker and got an even firmer say in the regime.[105]

Nevertheless, it seems that from the start al-Kāmil Shaʿbān was quite eager to step into his deceased brother's footsteps.[106] The circumstances of Shaʿbān's accession were quite different, however, and his ability to play the game by its proper rules turned out to be insufficient. Tension was rife throughout his short-lived reign, since he had to face ambitious kingmakers like Arghūn, an empty treasury, and quite a demanding household. In the end, by October 1346, his harem's inflationary demands, the subsequent discontent of senior amirs, in Egypt and in Syria, and his own inability to defuse that deadlock, turned against him, as well as against the patron deemed responsible for his deficient regime, his stepfather Arghūn. And in the subsequent confrontation, both their networks proved too small to offer any serious resistance and soon left their patrons for better prospects.[107]

---

[103] See al-Shujāʿī, *Tārīkh*, pp. 232–233; al-ʿAynī, *ʿIqd al-Jumān*, p. 68; al-Maqrīzī, *Sulūk*, II/3, pp. 619, 620, 621, 623.

[104] See Appendix 3, nr. 11.

[105] See al-Maqrīzī, *Sulūk*, II/3, pp. 677–678, 681–683. See Appendix 3, nr. 14.

[106] See, e.g., his own partaking in the political manoeuvring that preceded his accession (al-Maqrīzī, *Sulūk*, II/3, pp. 677–678). His ambitions also speak from the fact that he tried to eliminate as many rivals for the sultanate, that is, brothers, as he could, through murder and arrest (Ibn Ḥabīb, *Tadhkirat al-Nabīh*, III, p. 87; al-Maqrīzī, *Sulūk*, II/3, pp. 688, 710–711).

[107] See al-Maqrīzī, *Sulūk*, II/3, pp. 707–708; 711–712. See Appendix 3, nr. 18.

Foremost among those who triggered the downfall of Arghūn and his stepson was the amir Maliktamur al-Ḥijāzī. He was yet another veteran of al-Nāṣir Muḥammad's high-ranking elite, who had been continuously involved in the political theatre of both episodes, until now, in October 1346, when he became its lead actor and the primary kingmaker of the new sultan, al-Muẓaffar Ḥājjī.[108] From the conflict he initiated, he therefore immediately emerged as the realm's new power holder.[109] Yet again, as had happened in the case of Arghūn al-ʿAlāʾī and Shaʿbān before, Ḥājjī proved reluctant to accede to Maliktamur's patronage. He even developed a policy of his own that enabled him to confront and eradicate Maliktamur and his network in July 1347.[110]

The latter conflict, however, was not only the direct result of growing tension between two patrons, but also of a more general, ambitious and deliberate policy. This policy was made overt in early September 1347, when, in al-Maqrīzī's words, Ḥājjī's supporters "gathered all the Nāṣirīya, Ṣāliḥīya and Kāmilīya mamluks, and won them over to make a new start for Muẓaffar's regime".[111] The latter sultan's ultimate goal, indeed, seems to have been "a new start" for his regime, when he proceeded to eliminate those that had put him on the throne—in an impressive sequence of quite daunting lethal operations—in order to make room for an entirely new, more docile, elite, that would enable their patron Ḥājjī to indulge carefreely in his household of doubtful repute.[112] In retrospect, al-Maqrīzī reported that "in a period of forty days, he killed thirty-one amirs, among whom were eleven amirs of [a hundred] [. . .]".[113] However,

[108] See al-Kutubī, *ʿUyūn al-Tawārīkh*, fol. 88; al-Maqrīzī, *Sulūk*, II/3, p. 712.

[109] The appointment of the new *nāʾib al-salṭana* is for instance accredited to Maliktamur's direct interference (al-Maqrīzī, *Sulūk*, II/3, p. 718).

[110] See al-Maqrīzī, *Sulūk*, II/3, pp. 729–730. See Appendix 3, nr. 19.

[111] al-Maqrīzī, *Sulūk*, II/3, p. 735.

[112] Al-Maqrīzī explicitly states that one of Ḥājjī's closest supporters, the amir Aghizlū (d. 1347) "had decided with the sultan to delegate the matters of rule to him [= Aghizlū], to manage them without [bothering] him [= Ḥājjī], so that the sultan could indulge in his pleasures" (al-Maqrīzī, *Sulūk*, II/3, p. 735); on the dismantling of Shaʿbān's household, and its gradual, much contested, reinstatement by Ḥājjī, see al-Maqrīzī, *Sulūk*, II/3, pp. 715, 720–721, 722, 725–726, 739–740, 741–742.

[113] al-Maqrīzī, *Sulūk*, II/3, p. 757. On the elimination of Maliktamur, Aqsunqur and the rest of their network, see al-Maqrīzī, *Sulūk*, II/3, pp. 729–730. On the elimination of other amirs, both in Egypt and in Syria, see Ibn Kathīr, *al-Bidāya*, XIV, pp. 222–223; al-Kutubī, *ʿUyūn al-Tawārīkh*, fol. 82v–84v, 88; al-Maqrīzī, *Sulūk*, II/3, p. 734.

as had happened to his brother before him, he overplayed his hand. When he finally also turned against some of his own most senior supporters, the greater part of his own network soon disbanded and, in December 1347, deposed him.[114] Again according to al-Maqrīzī, one senior amir would have explained this to the sultan as follows:

> Your own mamluk, whom you have raised, mounted against you and informed us about your bad intentions; you have killed the mamluks of your father, you have taken their property, and you have disgraced their harems, without a cause; and you intended to slay [all those] who remained, though you had been the first to swear not to harm the amirs and not to destroy anyone's *bayt.*[115]

Al-Muẓaffar Ḥājjī's brutal policy of elimination again left the regime with a sort of power vacuum, since, after his deposition, there was no major patron left whose network enabled any substantial amount of Effective Power. As al-Ṣafadī put it, "the amirs al-Muẓaffar had killed were the remainder of the seniors of al-Nāṣir's regime".[116]

Upon this extinction of al-Nāṣir Muḥammad's elite and the subsequent end of al-Muẓaffar's patronage, the era's second episode came to an end. Very similar to episode one, this had been an eventful era, dominated largely by the successful patronage of sultan al-Ṣāliḥ Ismāʿīl. After his untimely demise, however, his socio-political achievement remained largely unmatched, due to the inability of any one kingmaker, and the incapability of any other sultan, to carefully build similarly inclusive and balanced networks.

Episode 3: 1347–1361

Despite the fact that al-Muẓaffar Ḥājjī's policy of elimination had largely left the regime in a state of socio-political chaos, it also allowed for a crucial development to take place: the steady rise of a new generation of patrons. In the next decade, the junior mamluks of al-Nāṣir Muḥammad's regime, who had only been promoted amir after 1342, became the new focus of all socio-political attention.[117] In this

---

[114] See al-Maqrīzī, *Sulūk*, II/3, pp. 740–743. See Appendix 3, nos. 19, 20, 21, 23.

[115] al-Maqrīzī, *Sulūk*, II/3, p. 743; identical in Ibn Taghrī Birdī, *Nujūm*, X, p. 172.

[116] al-Ṣafadī, *Aʿyān*, II, p. 178; similar in al-Kutubī, *ʿUyūn al-Tawārīkh*, fol. 88; Ibn Taghrī Birdī, *Manhal*, V, p. 53.

[117] For a similar observation, dating this change however slightly earlier, to 1345–6, see also Irwin, *The Middle East in the Middle Ages*, p. 125.

longest of all episodes, from the first accession of al-Nāṣir Ḥasan in December 1347 until his second deposition in 1361, a few of these junior amirs—most importantly the amirs Baybughā Rūs, Shaykhū al-ʿUmari, Ṭāz, and, after 1351, Ṣarghitmish—set up several simultaneous networks as patrons, some of which would prove more successful than others. Moreover, in due time, yet another network of a sultan, of al-Nāṣir Ḥasan, would raise its head on the socio-political scene and interfere deeply in its development. This development—from a rather chaotic diversity of networks to a larger degree of socio-political unity after 1354—not surprisingly found a parallel in the conflicts in which all these networks got involved, to the extent that up to 1354, the tension between divergent networks is reflected in the occurrence of no less than fourteen conflicts, whereas the resultant increasing unity of socio-political interests during the remaining eight years resulted in only four more conflicts after 1354.

Ḥasan's accession to the Mamluk throne in December 1347 was again the result of consensus, now among those junior amirs that had brought down his brother Ḥājjī. Unlike his brother Ismāʿīl five years before, however, the eleven-year old Ḥasan proved too young to rule in any effective fashion. He acquiescently remained under the tutelage of those kingmakers who ensured that shared sovereignty by the set up of a very strict regime under a sort of guardian council in which very soon two amirs—Baybughā Rūs and Shaykhū—became predominant.[118]

Despite the fact that the times were generally dire—especially when the plague hit the region and caused ruin and despair—and tension between the members of this guardian council was continuously high and frequently found an outlet in all kinds of conflicts, these two leading characters never seem to have clashed and the overall stability of the arrangement was only shattered in December 1350, as a result of another patron's unexpected engagement. At that time, Baybughā Rūs and Shaykhū were away from Cairo, which offered al-Nāṣir Ḥasan himself the perfect opportunity to be declared of age by the remaining amirs, to have those absentees arrested, and to embark upon his own campaign of patronage.[119] Soon, however, the

---

[118] See al-Maqrīzī, *Sulūk*, II/3, p. 746. See also Levanoni, "The Mamluk Conception of the Sultanate", p. 383.

[119] See e.g. Ibn Kathīr, *al-Bidāya*, XIV, pp. 236, 237; al-Maqrīzī, *Sulūk*, II/3, pp. 823, 824, 827–828. See Appendix 3, nr. 29.

ambitious Ḥasan seems to have made the same capital error some of his unfortunate brothers had made before, when he decided to turn against his most senior supporters, including the amir Ṭāz, and tried to promote more docile junior amirs in their stead.[120] As was written down in a copy of an official letter to Syrian officials, which served to justify Ḥasan's smooth deposition and the arrest of his intimates in August 1351:

> [Ḥasan] had agreed with the youngsters to arrest, imprison and destroy the amirs, in particular the respected senior amirs. When this had been confirmed to the amirs, they had gathered and agreed to depose him from the august rule [. . .][121]

Both the patron who had been most deeply involved in Ḥasan's short-lived rule, the amir Ṭāz, and Shaykhū's former client Ṣarghitmish, who stood by Ṭāz in the subsequent violent confrontation among the remaining amirs, emerged victoriously from all these conflicts, which boosted their patronage to an unprecedented level and turned them into the new sultan al-Ṣāliḥ Ṣāliḥ's prime kingmakers.[122] They were not the only ones, however, since the arrested Shaykhū surprisingly managed to be returned to his former status shortly after Ṣāliḥ's accession. And actually, throughout the period from 1351 to 1354, Shaykhū's shadow continued to loom large over both Ṭāz and Ṣarghitmish.[123] In fact, his successful return in 1351 had been due to both their combined efforts.[124] In the case of Ṭāz, this rather surprising support for another, fallen patron at a time when his own patronage was about to assume wider dimensions, was explained by al-ʿAynī as a result of their "firm brotherhood and strong friendship".[125] Clearly, there was a relationship between them, and all elements suggest that between 1351 and 1354 this relationship evolved from Ṭāz' subordination as a client and an equal to Ṣarghitmish, to his competition as a patron with Shaykhū, resulting

---

[120] See e.g. al-Maqrīzī, *Sulūk*, II/3, pp. 841, 842. Al-ʿAynī gives a slightly different version: he claims that one of Ḥasan's supporters set him against the amir Ṭāz, whereupon the latter decided to strike first (al-ʿAynī, *ʿIqd al-Jumān*, p. 91).

[121] See al-Qalqashandī, *Subh*, VIII, pp. 242–243. See also Appendix 3, nr. 32.

[122] See e.g. al-Maqrīzī, *Sulūk*, II/3, pp. 841–842, 843. See Appendix 3, nr. 33.

[123] See e.g. al-Maqrīzī, *Sulūk*, II/3, p. 862: Shaykhū reconciles the competing peers Ṭāz and Ṣarghitmish.

[124] See e.g. al-Maqrīzī, *Sulūk*, II/3, pp. 844–848.

[125] al-ʿAynī, *ʿIqd al-Jumān*, p. 91.

from his own successful networking.[126] In the course of this process, socio-political tension continued to prevail, and even moved far beyond Cairo, when, in the period August-November 1352, Baybughā Rūs—unlike Shaykhū ousted to remote Aleppo—desperately attempted to reclaim his former status too, and started a futile rebellion from Syria.[127] In October 1354, this tension eventually resulted in a failed attempt by Ṭāz and his supporters to eliminate their competitors for absolute control over the sultan, Shaykhū and his client Ṣarghitmish, causing, instead, their own downfall.[128]

Hence, Ṭāz' attempt to impose his patronage on the whole of the episode's socio-political scene failed, and actually enabled Shaykhū to confirm his authority. After this elimination of Ṭāz and his network in October 1354, Shaykhū had Ḥasan put on the throne again, and—as the sole kingmaker worthy of that name—finally managed to establish his absolute Effective Power. It is indicative of the socio-political stability his unrivalled patronage now managed to create that the three ensuing years remained free from any noteworthy disturbance, competition or conflict on the regime's socio-political scene.[129] In July 1357, however, Shaykhū, at the height of his power, was lethally wounded in a failed attempt to kill him—allegedly by a frustrated mamluk whose request for an *iqṭāʿ* he had rejected—and he died a few months later, in November 1357.[130]

Upon Shaykhū's untimely elimination in 1357, and after the quick subsequent dissolution of his long-lived network, two new individuals finally saw an opportunity to rise from the shadow of their patron: Ṣarghitmish and al-Nāṣir Ḥasan. In the course of their competition for manoeuvring their patronage into the vacuum left by Shaykhū, sultan Ḥasan cunningly managed to arrest Ṣarghitmish and to reinstate a clear-cut socio-political order less than a year after Shaykhū's

[126] When Ṭāz arrived in Damascus, "in a group of his supporters", on his way to Aleppo to become *nā'ib* there, in November 1354, Ibn Kathīr for instance comments that, by that time, "he had been the equal of the amir Shaykhūn [*sic*], but [the latter] had overcome him and sent him to the city of Aleppo" (Ibn Kathīr, *al-Bidāya*, XIV, p. 251).

[127] See Appendix 3, nr. 35.

[128] See Ibn Duqmāq, *al-Jawhar al-Thamīn*, p. 170; al-Maqrīzī, *Sulūk*, II/3, pp. 929–930; III/1, pp. 1–4; al-ʿAynī, *ʿIqd al-Jumān*, pp. 102–104.

[129] On Shaykhū's leading role in the enthronement of Ḥasan, see e.g. al-Maqrīzī, *Sulūk*, III/1, p. 1; al-ʿAynī, *ʿIqd al-Jumān*, pp. 102–103.

[130] See al-Maqrīzī, *Khiṭaṭ*, IV, p. 114; al-Maqrīzī, *Sulūk*, III/1, p. 33. See also Appendix 3, nr. 38.

demise, in August 1358. And upon his further victory over Ṣarghitmish' household, Ḥasan is reported to have rewarded his own supporters and to have filled the institutional vacancies which Ṣarghitmish's discarded clients had left, with his own fresh mamluks in particular.[131] As a consequence, for another three years, the socio-political scene was dominated by one single focus for patronage only. And this predominance resulted again in relative stability and absence of tension or conflict. In the end, however, as had happened to some of his brothers before him, Ḥasan's growing indulgence in his private household, away from the political scene, and his increasing financial demands,[132] soon made him too weak a patron, and his relationships too fragile, to continue to check the frustrations and ambitions of some of his own clients. As Ibn Taghrī Birdī put it,

> he had thought of raising his mamluks, so that they would become a clique and support for him, but they became the opposite of what he had hoped for, since they jumped on him [. . .][133]

Hence, in March 1361, Ḥasan's mamluks took over, ended his patronage and announced another phase of socio-political chaos in which no-one truly managed to immediately impose his unrivalled authority. This is the point at which, therefore, this period's long third episode came to an end, an episode in which political order had become prevalent for such a relatively long span of time. This episode had witnessed the very slow return of some socio-political order to the ranks of the politically active, with the rise of a new, younger, group of patrons in the wake of Ḥasan's accession in 1347. In hindsight, only one of these patrons, Shaykhū, and his growing network and power actually turn out to have emerged victoriously from this episode's many conflicts between the various networks that had started it. And after Shaykhū's murder in 1357, this order continued to prevail, as this process was repeated to some extent by his two protégées, enabling sultan Ḥasan to emerge fairly quickly as the single patron to whom one could turn for any benefit, and, at long last, putting him in charge of his own regime. In this way, in the period

---

[131] See al-Maqrīzī, *Sulūk*, III/1, pp. 35, 43; al-ʿAynī, *ʿIqd al-Jumān*, p. 114; Ibn Qāḍī Shuhba, *Tārīkh*, III, pp. 117, 134, 330, 457. See also Appendix 3, nr. 40.
[132] See e.g. al-Ḥusayni, *Dhayl al-ʿIbar*, p. 188; al-ʿAynī, *ʿIqd al-Jumān*, pp. 124, 126–127.
[133] Ibn Taghrī Birdī, *Nujūm*, X, p. 314.

between 1347 and 1361, the still rather diffuse socio-political order of this episode's first half evolved into a fully fledged, reasonably balanced and generally lucid harmony. After 1354, for the first time since Ismāʿīl's death in 1345, it became quite straightforward again for the ambitious individual to decide how to interact within his social environment in order to ensure success.

Episode 4: 1361–1366

This shorter episode, which lasted from Ḥasan's deposition in March 1361 until the death of his mamluk Yalbughā al-Khāṣṣakī in 1366, was actually quite similar to the preceding one, in that, again, it eventually saw the rise, supremacy, and—admittedly more precipitate—fall of one man's patronage, and, therefore, a general prevalence of increasing socio-political order. From another perspective, it was also quite different, since, by 1361, after the extinction of al-Nāṣir Muḥammad's amirs in 1347, time and Ḥasan's patronage policies had similarly brought an end to the socio-political predominance of Muḥammad's mamluks, and new opportunities arose for a variety of others, Ḥasan's own amirs and mamluks in the first place.[134] In this episode of five years, two of Ḥasan's most senior amirs—the unfortunate Yalbughā and Ṭaybughā al-Ṭawīl—managed to create their own networks in a far more stable socio-political environment than before. For, illustrative of their—especially Yalbughā's—success to again patronise Mamluk society, only four conflicts ensued, two of which, however, ended their own patronage, in the case of Yalbughā even in an especially dramatic way.

Actually, it has to be admitted that in the case of 1361, not so much the criterion of recurrent chaos in the political ranks justifies periodisation, but rather the radical change of identity that affected those who populated those ranks. The year 1361 witnessed the extinction, as it were, of the long tentacles of al-Nāṣir Muḥammad's regime, not just through the final elimination of his sons, but also because of the disappearance of his amirs and mamluks. Chaos did not reoccur as it had before, since among the handful of amirs responsible for Ḥasan's deposition in March 1361 there was one dominant

[134] This new swap in the Mamluk elite's composition was also noticed by Ibn Taghrī Birdī, see Ibn Taghrī Birdī, *Nujūm*, X, pp. 313–314.

character indeed who could rely on his already substantial network of personal mamluks and fellow amirs.[135] A *khāṣṣakī* mamluk of Ḥasan, this Yalbughā al-Khāṣṣakī had been promoted amir in 1357, and now, in 1361, in conjunction with his peers, he became one of the kingmakers of the new sultan, al-Manṣūr Muḥammad, and, in 1363, of that unfit sultan's cousin, the ten-year old al-Malik al-Ashraf Shaʿbān.[136] And together with that other patron that emerged from the ruins of Ḥasan's regime, Ṭaybughā al-Ṭawil, Yalbughā patronised these sultans and was their guardian. Hence, he found himself ideally placed to embark upon an ambitious networking campaign.

Already in the middle of 1361, this campaign had been reinforced as a result of two conflicts that were rooted in the previous episode: in June, another peer from Ḥasan's reign, the *nāʾib al-Shām*, felt threatened by Yalbughā's quick rise and tried to set up a counter-network in Syria, which obliged Yalbughā to organise a military campaign against Syria; and in July, during Yalbughā's absence from Cairo, members of the sultan's household attempted to enforce the enthronement of yet another son of al-Nāṣir Muḥammad. Both attempts by the former sultan's frustrated supporters failed miserably, ending any further threat or tension from that side and actually boosting Yalbughā's portrayal as a patron.[137] Subsequently, both Yalbughā and Ṭaybughā wielded unrivalled power, free from any noteworthy socio-political conflicts and contenders until February 1366.[138] By then, however, tension between the period's two patrons had reached the boiling point and erupted into conflict. Ṭaybughā and his supporters were defeated and the victorious patron Yalbughā could "grant the *iqṭāʿ*s of the fellows of Ṭaybughā al-Ṭawil to a number of his own fellows".[139]

---

[135] See e.g. al-Maqrīzī, *Sulūk*, III/1, pp. 60–62; al-ʿAynī, *ʿIqd al-Jumān*, p. 121.

[136] On Muḥammad's installation, see e.g. al-Maqrīzī, *Sulūk*, III/1, p. 64. On the promotion of Yalbughā and some of his peers, see al-Maqrīzī, *Sulūk*, III/1, pp. 35, 42. On Shaʿbān's installation, see e.g. al-Maqrīzī, *Sulūk*, III/1, pp. 82, 83; al-ʿAynī, *ʿIqd al-Jumān*, pp. 129–130.

[137] See e.g. al-Ḥusayni, *Dhayl al-ʿIbar*, pp. 189–191; Ibn Kathīr, *al-Bidāya*, XIV, pp. 280–281, 282–284. See also Appendix 3, nr. 42, 43. In October 1361, Yalbughā would even completely incorporate the remains of that household into his own (see Ibn Duqmāq, *al-Jawhar al-Thamīn*, p. 408; al-Maqrīzī, *Sulūk*, III/1, p. 73; al-ʿAynī, *ʿIqd al-Jumān*, p. 127; Ibn Taghrī Birdī, *Nujūm*, X, p. 314).

[138] On Yalbughā and Ṭaybughā's joint rule, see e.g. al-ʿAynī, *ʿIqd al-Jumān*, p. 122; Ibn Taghrī Birdī, *Nujūm*, XI, p. 4; Ibn Qāḍī Shuhba, *Tārīkh*, III, p. 220.

[139] See Appendix 3, nr. 44; for the quotation, see Ibn Taghrī Birdī, *Nujūm*, XI, p. 32.

As a result, again one patron only, Yalbughā, got to dominate society and managed to impose the order of his patronage. His order was, however, only a short-lived one. Very soon, in December 1366, his widening network and absolute Effective Power still proved to be resting on insecure footing, and on inept patronage, when, of all people, frustrated amirs from among his own mamluks ushered in his and his household's and network's precipitate downfall. They managed to incite a substantial number of his infamously numerous mamluks to turn against their *ustādh*, so that, eventually, no more than one amir and some one hundred mamluks are reported to have remained loyal to the very end.[140] And Yalbughā's end was unprecedented and gruesome, when some of those vindictive mamluks avenged their earlier mistreatments and lynched their *ustādh*.[141] In his case, especially, success and power proved very volatile.

Thus, in December 1366, this episode ended, when the socio-political scene was left to the large and diffuse group of amirs that had obstructed Yalbughā's Effective Power. From the ashes of al-Nāṣir Ḥasan's network, it had witnessed the quick and simultaneous rise to prominence of two patrons, of whom Yalbughā in particular had managed to impose his patronage and to recreate the order he and his peers had smashed before. In the longer run, however, he equally failed to maintain it, and a confusing chaos returned when his clients decided to bite—or rather eat—the hand that fed them.

Episode 5: 1366–1377

Episode 5 ran from the fall of Yalbughā al-Khāṣṣakī in December 1366 until the deposition and consequent murder of sultan al-Ashraf Shaʿbān, some ten years later, in March 1377. As noted above, in December 1366 a new power vacuum ensued, since, in the short term, among those victorious clients of Yalbughā there were no patrons left with sufficient resources to become another factor of socio-political stability. During this chaotic phase, the maturing sultan

---

140 See Ibn Duqmāq, *Nuzhat al-Anām*, fol. 2v–3v; al-Maqrīzī, *Sulūk*, III/1, pp. 131–138 (quote p. 136); al-ʿAynī, *ʿIqd al-Jumān*, pp. 144–146, 147. His maltreatment of his mamluks, and some amirs' denied *shafāʿa*, are said to have been at the basis of this conflict (see al-Maqrīzī, *Sulūk*, III/1, pp. 130–131). See also Appendix 3, nr. 45.

141 See al-Maqrīzī, *Sulūk*, III/1, pp. 136–137.

Shaʿbān seems to have realised his own—quite unexpected—potentials, and slowly started acting accordingly, eventually resulting in a sultan's type of network that would soon become dominant again. But, first, during a brief interlude that lasted from the closing days of 1366 to October 1367, weaker figures tried to fill the vacuum left by their patron Yalbughā, reviving parts of his network in the absence of any substantial power base of their own. In this process, eventually one such heir of Yalbughā, Asandamur al-Nāṣiri, gained the upper hand, stepped in his former patron's footsteps and for a brief period of time managed to create a quite unstable network of his own. The fickle and chaotic character of this interlude of ten months is again perfectly illustrated by the occurrence of no less than five socio-political conflicts, five attempts to overcome that instability and to realise the opportunities it offered to many. The resultant successful dominance by Shaʿbān's patronage of the next decade's socio-political scene is equally tellingly characterised by the fact that no more than six further conflicts ensued, two of which actually only occurred in March 1377 and ended Shaʿbān's rule.

As was the case with so many of the Yalbughāwīya mamluks, Asandamur al-Nāṣiri had entered Yalbughā's gigantic corps from another *ustādh*'s service, sultan Ḥasan's in his case, and he had been promoted amir by Yalbughā, attaining the highest military rank in the course of March 1366.[142] In December 1366, this Asandamur had been one of the highest-ranking among the six amirs that reportedly rose against their patron, and, subsequently, by March 1367, he "took the status of his *ustādh* Yalbughā, managed the regime's business, issued the promotion and dismissal of its officials, and lived in Yalbughā's residence at al-Kabsh".[143] Following a precedent Yalbughā had set before upon al-Nāṣir Ḥasan's deposition, this boost of Asandamur's status, which incorporated important elements of his fallen patron's household, ensued from his victorious emergence from a major military encounter with former peers and mamluks from Yalbughā's network.[144] Moreover, in June 1367, upon another victorious

[142] See al-Maqrīzī, *Sulūk*, III/1, p. 117; Ibn Qāḍī Shuhba, *Tārīkh*, III, pp. 275, 326; also Appendix 2.

[143] al-Maqrīzī, *Sulūk*, III/1, p. 141; for his involvement in the rebellion against Yalbughā, see e.g. Ibn Duqmāq, *Nuzhat al-Anām*, fol. 2v; al-Maqrīzī, *Sulūk*, III/1, pp. 130–131.

[144] See e.g. Ibn Duqmāq, *Nuzhat al-Anām*, fol. 5; al-Maqrīzī, *Sulūk*, III/1, p. 141. See also Appendix 3, nr. 46.

military confrontation—now with the maturing sultan and his growing entourage—, Asandamur equally managed to extend his network and project dozens of his own clients, in one stroke, into the regime's institutional structures, favouring both amirs, and a variety of mamluks.[145] Nevertheless, as had happened to his patron before him too, all this was done to no avail. By October 1367, Yalbughā's mamluks' infamous unruliness finally also turned against their new patron Asandamur, who, too, proved incapable of patronising them any longer, after which they both perished.[146] And they actually perished at the hands of their sultan, al-Ashraf Shaʿbān. Threatened in his very existence by Asandamur and his unruly clients, Shaʿbān was almost forced to establish his own network as a sultan, which, at first, seemed rather successful by lack of any remaining serious alternative to Asandamur's and—especially—due to the unruliness of Yalbughā's mamluks, that threatened all amirs. In October 1367, after he had overcome Asandamur and those mamluks repeatedly in no less than three conflicts in one month's time, al-Ashraf wisely decided to eliminate the remainder of that disturbing corps: he allegedly executed several hundreds of Yalbughāwīya mamluks, and he deported the rest to Syria and Aswan.[147]

Liberated from any further interference, al-Ashraf Shaʿbān's turn had come to establish his patronage. By a rather calculated use of his prerogatives as a sultan, and a wise choice of experienced senior supporters to assist him, he ushered in a decade of renewed socio-political order along the lines of his patronage. In July 1373, this widely extended network of his was even further strengthened, when he received its full support in a confrontation with a frustrated senior amir, whose outnumbered forces very typically changed sides in the heat of the conflict.[148] Thereupon, at the height of his power, four more undisturbed years ensued, during which the absence of any serious socio-political tension made him feel so safe and secure that he decided to leave Cairo for the pilgrimage to Mecca, as the first

[145] See al-Maqrīzī, *Sulūk*, III/1, p. 144; also Ibn Duqmāq, *Nuzhat al-Anām*, fol. 5v–6. See also Appendix 3, nr. 47.

[146] See Ibn Duqmāq, *Nuzhat al-Anām*, fol. 37–37v; al-Maqrīzī, *Sulūk*, III/1, pp. 150–152. See also Appendix 3, nos. 48, 49.

[147] See Ibn Taghrī Birdī, *Nujūm*, XI, p. 48; Ibn Qāḍī Shuhba, *Tārīkh*, III, pp. 311–312.

[148] See e.g. al-Maqrīzī, *Sulūk*, III/1, pp. 212–214. See also Appendix 3, nr. 53.

sultan to do so since his grandfather in 1332.[149] Upon his departure in March 1377, however, Shaʿbān was entirely taken by surprise when no other than his own and, especially, his son ʿAlī's mamluks rose in rebellion. En route to Mecca, tensions arose on the awarding of benefits, which eventually made Shaʿbān lose both his mamluks' and his amirs' support and which forced him to flee back to Cairo.[150] Meanwhile, however, former Yalbughāwīya mamluks, that had been allowed to return to Cairo a few years before and to enter the corps of Shaʿbān's eldest son, had engaged in an unchallenged rebellion in Cairo aimed at the enthronement of their new *ustādh*, so that, upon Shaʿbān's precipitate return to Cairo, he failed to find the support he had hoped for, and met his destiny instead.[151] Within a few days only, the results of a decade of successful patronage vaporised and the socio-political order which Shaʿbān had carefully managed to maintain was fully disintegrated, when the diverging socio-political interests of a variety of individual amirs replaced their former patron's socio-political guidance.

In short, a renewed and successful process towards uniform socio-political order again dominated this episode of eleven years. Bereft of any guarantee for sustained future benefit by their own actions against their *ustādh*, Yalbughā al-Khāṣṣakī's leaderless mamluk corps of unparalleled size—and every one, high and low, with them—were at first forced to drift along in an extremely fragmented socio-political environment. Only when the maturing sultan managed to eliminate them, did order return and Shaʿbān increasingly came to dominate his own regime during the ten years of his uniting patronage. To a great extent, he thus succeeded where his own patrons, and many before them, had failed. Nevertheless, as had happened to Yalbughā before, the hunger of those he had been feeding so generously could not be satisfied.

[149] On Shaʿbān's preparations to maintain public and socio-political order during his absence, see e.g. Ibn Duqmāq, *Nuzhat al-Anām*, fol. 106v–107, 108; al-Maqrīzī, *Sulūk*, III/1, pp. 272, 274.

[150] See e.g. Ibn Duqmāq, *Nuzhat al-Anām*, fol. 109; al-Maqrīzī, *Sulūk*, III/1, pp. 279–280. See also Appendix 3, nr. 55.

[151] See e.g. Ibn Duqmāq, *Nuzhat al-Anām*, fol. 108v–109v; al-Maqrīzī, *Sulūk*, III/1, pp. 275–279; Ibn Ḥajar, *Inbāʾ al-Ghumr*, I, pp. 193–194. See also Appendix 3, nr. 56. Their hopes and ambitions may have been awakened by Shaʿbān's designation of ʿAlī as heir apparent shortly before the departure to the Hijaz, in combination with reports of the sultan's illness (see e.g. Ibn Duqmāq, *Nuzhat al-Anām*, fol. 106v; al-Maqrīzī, *Sulūk*, III/1, pp. 272, 274).

Episode 6: 1377–1382

This era's ultimate episode ran from the accession to the throne of Shaʿbān's infant son ʿAlī in February-March 1377 until the end of his brother's sultanate in November 1382, and it did not just witness the final degeneration of the Qalawunid sultanate, but also the rise to power of the amir Barqūq. Socio-political darkness prevailed anew, when a confusing number of amirs and would-be amirs put their own *ustādh* ʿAlī on the throne and when each of them tried his own socio-political luck. As had happened before, in 1347 and in 1361, the general identity of those fortune hunters changed entirely. This time, the group of amirs that came to dominance in this final episode actually consisted of those that had been prevented from doing so by Shaʿbān when he took over in 1367. Though from a variety of mamluk backgrounds and belonging to different generations, they all shared former membership of Yalbughā's corps in the 1360s, isolation or exile after 1367, and a return to some prominence in the service of al-Ashraf Shaʿbān's clients, his son ʿAlī in particular, in the early 1370s. Al-Maqrīzī put it as follows in a comment that identified the change in identity of those who occupied the Mamluk institutional framework after March 1377:

> the junior mamluks whom hardly anything was reported about yesterday, but [who] then pursued [practices of] murder, banishment and [all] sorts of torture, became rulers whom the fruits of all things are levied for and who speak judgement in the provinces, at their own discretion; from then onwards, the region's situation transformed because of its people's transformation.[152]

Additionally, as had equally happened before, in 1342, in 1347, and, particularly, in 1366, it took some time until new patrons were capable of overcoming that confusing socio-political darkness. This episode equally started with a chaotic interlude in 1377, when several tried their luck, but chaos continued to prevail. Two patrons in particular, Qaraṭāy al-Ṭāzi and Aynabak al-Badrī, would, in alternating order, attempt to impose their patronage. Their ultimate failure, however, speaks from the fact that each of them perished in the course of the six conflicts they each fell into in as many months. In their case, order did not automatically follow out of conflict. Only

[152] al-Maqrīzī, *Sulūk*, III/1, p. 289.

gradually was this chaotic interlude defeated again, when new patrons—the amirs Yalbughā al-Nāṣiri, Barka and, especially, Barqūq—came to prominence, more successfully than ever, in the course of the twelve conflicts that ensued.

By March 1377, a small band of low-ranking amirs and mamluks had emerged who had been most successful in their intriguing against al-Ashraf Shaʿbān, and the amirs Qaraṭāy and, thereafter, Aynabak soon were to become predominant among them.[153] The former, Qaraṭāy, stemmed from the mamluk corps of the afore-mentioned amir Ṭāz; he had moved to the corps of Yalbughā al-Khāṣṣakī and had shared its fate in 1367, and he had been allowed to return from his place of exile in Syria together with his fellow mamluks in the early 1370s; he then became a senior mamluk—according to Ibn Khaldūn even a legal guardian—of Shaʿbān's infant son, the amir ʿAlī.[154] When he and his peers managed to have their young new master's enthronement confirmed in March 1377, they all transferred themselves to commensurate positions in his new, sultan's '*bayt*', taking all the high ranks and offices of Shaʿbān's murdered associates to themselves.[155] Thus, al-Maqrīzī informs us how

> Qaraṭāy was established as *ra's nawba kabīr*, in the rank of [amir of a hundred and] commander [of a thousand] and in the *iqṭāʿ* of the amir Ṣarghitmish, and he was granted what [the latter] left behind [. . .], and there was ordered to him [. . .] to sit at the [sultan's] right-hand side in the audience hall.[156]

Because of this unparalleled *maqbūl* with al-Manṣūr ʿAlī, this Qaraṭāy thereupon managed to demonstrate equally unparalleled patronage, but only until June 1377. By then, the cunning intriguing of his most senior, but fatally ambitious, client, his father-in-law Aynabak al-Badrī, was successful enough to discredit that *maqbūl* and to cause Qaraṭāy's precipitate fall from power.[157]

---

[153] For these amirs and mamluks, ten of whom were identified by name, see Ibn Duqmāq, *Nuzhat al-Anām*, fol. 109v.

[154] See Ibn Khaldūn, *Kitāb al-ʿIbar*, V, p. 463; Ibn Ḥajar, *Inbāʾ al-Ghumr*, I, p. 256; Ibn Qāḍī Shuhba, *Tārīkh*, III, p. 564.

[155] See e.g. Ibn Khaldūn, *Kitāb al-ʿIbar*, V, p. 465; Ibn Duqmāq, *Nuzhat al-Anām*, fol. 110v, 111; al-Maqrīzī, *Sulūk*, IIII/1, pp. 287–288. For the confirmation of ʿAlī's reign, see also Appendix 3, nr. 57.

[156] al-Maqrīzī, *Sulūk*, III/1, p. 287.

[157] See Ibn Duqmāq, *Nuzhat al-Anām*, fol. 124; al-Maqrīzī, *Sulūk*, III/1, pp. 305–306; Ibn Ḥajar, *Inbāʾ*, I, p. 230. See also Appendix 3, nr. 58.

Like Qaraṭāy, Aynabak had been among the kingmakers of al-Manṣūr ʿAlī in March 1377, upon whose accession he "had taken the rank of [amir of a hundred and] commander [of a thousand] of Baybughā al-Sābiqī", and he took charge of the sultanic stables as *amīr ākhūr*.[158] And upon his victory over Qaraṭāy, in the closing days of June 1377, he in his turn was obliged to try and consolidate his newly acquired status, by rewarding his supporters and furthering his patronage.[159] Already in early August 1377, however, his failure to do so became apparent when especially the Syrian *nāʾib*s refused to accept his sovereignty, which typically caused a very swift increase of opponents on all fronts and initiated his own precipitate fall from power.[160]

Upon the downfall of Aynabak, which came as a result of the consensus of all the amirs rather than another patron's competition, the absence of yet another strong man to offer a new, single focus for patronage again created a power vacuum, a confusing divergence of interests and relationships, and continued the interlude of socio-political chaos. This deadlock, especially in terms of guardianship of the infant sultan, government and patronage, was temporarily resolved in an unprecedented manner. This time, not a new nominal sultan, but a nominal power holder was installed with the high-ranking amirs' consensus, whose sole function similarly was to be an executive stronghold that safeguarded the interests of the amirs that had empowered him. The choice fell on the *nāʾib al-Shām* Ṭashtamur al-Dawādār, who was summoned to Egypt and made *atābak al-ʿasākir* in early September 1377, by the amirs Yalbughā al-Nāṣiri, Barqūq and Barka in particular.[161]

By April 1378, however, it had become clear that his was not the network that would gain new predominance, and his end was soon to come when increasingly frustrated members of his household tried

[158] al-Maqrīzī, *Sulūk*, III/1, pp. 278, 288; also in Ibn Duqmāq, *Nuzhat al-Anām*, fol. 111; Ibn Ḥajar, *Inbāʾ al-Ghumr*, I, p. 196.

[159] See e.g. Ibn Duqmāq, *Nuzhat al-Anām*, fol. 125; al-Maqrīzī, *Sulūk*, III/1, p. 307.

[160] See e.g. Ibn Duqmāq, *Nuzhat al-Anām*, fol. 125v–126; al-Maqrīzī, *Sulūk*, III/1, pp. 310–313; Ibn Ḥajar, *Inbāʾ al-Ghumr*, I, pp. 231–232. See also Appendix 3, nos. 60, 61, 62.

[161] See e.g. Ibn Khaldūn, *Kitāb al-ʿIbar*, p. 467; Ibn Ḥajar, *Inbāʾ al-Ghumr*, I, p. 233.

to revert that situation.[162] The main person responsible for Ṭashtamur's end actually was the amir Barqūq, who, like his fellow-amir Barka, had managed to substantially further his patronage in the wake of several conflicts that preceded the clash with Ṭashtamur's supporters and the most important victim of which had been Barqūq and Barka's senior, Yalbughā al-Nāṣiri.[163] After Ṭashtamur's arrest in April 1378, Barqūq and Barka continued to live cheek by jowl, managing the regime in a joint fashion and each spreading his own patronage.[164] By June 1380, however, increasing tension between the two equally exploded in a major confrontation in Cairo's streets, in which, finally, Barqūq gained the upper hand.[165]

As the regime's sole remaining most senior patron from among the many candidates this episode had started with, Barqūq managed now to make his patronage the focus for any socio-political ambition, and, more importantly, to maintain that socio-political status he built up after 1378. Unlike such patrons as Qawṣūn, Shaykhū and Yalbughā before him, he continued to succeed in overcoming the frustrations of several of his subordinates and, consequently, in using the rallying force of conflict to maintain and further that position. Thus, for instance, after Barka's elimination in June 1380, unemancipated, young mamluks from Barka's and from Yalbughā al-Nāṣiri's corps are recorded to have been transferred to that of Barqūq.[166] In an equal fashion, it was his achievement to have acquired the majority of crucial institutions throughout the realm for people that "belonged to his side", very often in the wake of conflict, when he frequently succeeded to replace his defeated opponents' with his own supporters. The widening tentacles and success of this network have been discussed in detail in the preceding chapter. Indicative of that success of Barqūq's patronage in avoiding tension and preventing the rise of any competitor is the fact that only one more conflict ensued upon Barka's elimination.[167]

---

[162] See e.g. Ibn Duqmāq, *Nuzhat al-Anām*, fol. 128v–129. See also Appendix 3, nr. 67.

[163] See e.g. Ibn Qāḍī Shuhba, *Tārīkh*, p. 417. For those preceding conflicts, see Appendix 3, nos. 64, 65, 66.

[164] See e.g. al-Maqrīzī, *Sulūk*, III/1, p. 335; Ibn Ḥajar, *Inbā' al-Ghumr*, I, pp. 236–237, 265.

[165] See e.g. al-Maqrīzī, *Sulūk*, III/1, pp. 382–384. See Appendix 3, nos. 72, 73.

[166] See al-ʿAynī, *ʿIqd al-Jumān*, p. 257.

[167] See Appendix 3, nr. 74.

By the time of sultan al-Manṣūr ʿAlī's demise, therefore, in May 1381, only a few obstacles remained for Barqūq's usurpation of Legitimate Power and the final fulfilment of his socio-political ambitions: the unification of his network with the realm's institutional framework. Surprisingly, according to Ibn Taghrī Birdī at least, a major final obstacle for Barqūq's enthronement was his respect for two aged relics of al-Nāṣir Muḥammad's awe-inspiring regime, who allegedly continued to hold high rank and public esteem until their death a few months later.[168] Barqūq's enthronement and the long anticipated end of the degenerated Qalawunid phantom sultanate of the infants ʿAlī and Ḥājjī only became possible by November 1382. And the sheer fact that, by then, that transition went so smoothly and that Barqūq managed "to make all the amirs, young and old, swear to obey him" reflects the eventual successfulness of his many years of extending patronage, and the sufficient width of his subsequent network.[169] Very symbolically, Barqūq immediately moved his '*bayt*' up, from the sultanic stables to the apartments in the citadel's southern enclosure, and, once again, rewarded the staunchest of his supporters with new ranks and offices.[170] As Ibn Ḥajar put it, "Aytmish was made *atābak al-ʿasākir*, al-Jūbānī *amīr majlis*, Jarkas al-Khalīlī *amīr ākhūr*, Sūdūn al-Shaykhūnī *nāʾib al-salṭana*, Qazdamur al-Ḥasanī *raʾs nawba* and Yūnus [was appointed] in the office of *dawādār*".[171]

In short, in 1377, this sixth and final episode started with an interlude of chaos, a socio-political quagmire, which, despite several short-lived attempts to drain it, remained impossible to escape from. Nevertheless, at long last, the ban that seemed to have doomed the majority of the socio-political initiatives over the entire period between 1341 and 1382 was lifted. After many years of socio-political ups and downs, the odds were finally in an amir's favour, when an amir's successful patronage, cultivated during four years towards increasing paramountcy, coincided with the Qalawunid sultanate's long-anticipated ultimate phase of degeneration, and an amir again usurped the throne, ready to further the socio-political order he had managed to create, but now tapping directly from its major source, the sultanate.

---

[168] Ibn Taghrī Birdī, *Nujūm*, XI, pp. 214–215.
[169] Quoted from al-Maqrīzī, *Sulūk*, III/2, p. 478.
[170] See al-Maqrīzī, *Sulūk*, III/2, pp. 477, 478; al-ʿAynī, *ʿIqd al-Jumān*, pp. 280–281.
[171] Ibn Ḥajar, *Inbāʾ al-Ghumr*, II, p. 93.

CONCLUSION

To ambitious individuals who were trying to make a living in Egypt or Syria, the years between 1341 and 1382 undoubtedly must have seemed confusing and at times even chaotic. On the one hand, they had to face the inescapable factor of a social and economic environment that was collapsing under the unpredictable onslaughts of pestilence, plague and famine. On the other, they lived in a volatile political climate that never fully managed to regain the stability it had known before 1341, during the reign of al-Nāṣir Muḥammad. As a result of this instability, political loyalties were by nature hazardous, and even the bulwark of the Mamluk regime, the institutional framework that represented the legitimacy of Mamluk power and government, was liable to many changes. Very short-term perspectives on any individual's social, economic and political future were the maximum sort of stability and security one could hope for, and feelings of chaos and confusion undoubtedly prevailed.

It is the Mamluk historian's privilege, however, not to have to endure the hardship of the times he studies, and to have the benefit of hindsight, as fragmentary as this may be. Beyond the limits of such an individual's perspective, a more general reconstruction of those factors that created that perception of insecurity and confusion makes it possible to gain insight into the period's political culture, into the presence of certain wider rationales, patterns or processes in its volatile political climate.

The sheer number of socio-political conflicts which this period witnessed is of course to be credited for much of that insecurity and confusion which those years came to be known for, both to contemporary individuals and in later historiography. Upon closer analysis, however, it becomes obvious that these conflicts should not only be considered numerous, multiform, and confusing, but also—even more importantly—as being deeply rooted in the same constructive strategies that shaped Mamluk socio-political society at large. These strategies of exchange were always initiated in the interaction between an amir and his immediate environment: his extended family or his *bayt*, consisting of his kin, servants and assorted privileged clients, and centred in a dedicated urban residence. Beyond the emotional, or moral, confines of that *bayt*, however, any prospects' short-term perspective and the prevalent insecurity made all loyalties available for hire. Some temporary measure of security and order was therefore only achieved when an amir managed to hire some of these loyalties and to extend his patronage beyond his household into Mamluk political society at large. The wider this subsequent network could be extended and the more subservient households and networks could be incorporated, the more socio-political order and stability could prevail. Between 1341 and 1382, three distinct types of such networks had become a very intrinsic part of the period's political culture, either generating Effective Power for a sultan, for a client, or for a patron. The recurrent pre-dominance in Mamluk society of these types of networks and of the specific strategies of social bondage employed resulted in the repeated creation of moments of some more general public order and stability. At times like these, an individual's pathway to success was neither hazardous nor confused, as long as he managed to engage in the predominant networks' strategies. This may not have been all that clear to every individual involved, but everyone's search for some level of security and future prospects—and eventually for Effective Power—did tend to enhance the rise of one or more wide networks of related interests and, hence, to forestall tension and discord in those individuals' interaction.

Nevertheless, the period's dynamics of socio-political development generally did find their origin in such tension and discord, which were never entirely prevented and which caused the instability and changes that created confusion. In fact, the many conflicts that occurred between 1341 and 1382 were very often moments of extreme patronage beyond the household's limits, that sought to solve that tension, and in particular the competition for *maqbūl al-kalima*, by ending the patronage of some, and enabling or enhancing the patronage of others. Conflicts were the catalyst of the socio-political reality of households and networks that defined the nature of the socio-political elite and of their volatile institutional framework. Conflicts, therefore, had a creative influence on that society at least as much as that they caused confusion, and they were as much responsible for Mamluk political society's adoption of public order as they were for the destruction of that order and for the occasional predominance of chaos.

At the same time, tension and conflict may also be deemed largely responsible for the conservatism and the conditionality that were prevalent in the strategies that engendered that socio-political order. Since these strategies were driven by the ambition for individual survival and benefit, or for the widest possible extension of the individual's short-term perspective, all wished to engage in the most beneficial of possible relationships with a patron, whoever he was and as long as he seemed to be in a winning mood, that is, portraying a guaranteed *maqbūl*. Ultimately, ambitions always aimed at the patronage of one or a handful of interchangeable individuals whose *maqbūl al-kalima* was successfully portrayed. Moreover, no one wished to give grounds for breaking one's own fragile portrayal as a successful patron, unless there was no other option left but the insecurity of conflict, and even then, the ambition was to bend those rules to improve one self, not to break them. While the players changed frequently, the game was bound to continue, and so were its rules. Both patronage and conflict were therefore part of a political culture that often tended to create a rather lucid social environment of pervasive simultaneous and subsequent socio-political networks. Only occasionally—in 1342, 1347, 1366–1367 and in 1377–1378—was this social environment left in chaos, but never for too long, since the general need for socio-political benefit meant that order was bound to emerge eventually.

The cyclical nature of the period's socio-political development as suggested by that alternation of order and chaos is actually most clearly epitomised by the cycles of rise and fall of the period's four 'generations' that populated the upper echelons of the regime's politicised military, the socio-political elite. Each of these generations emerged from the conflicts that had ended their predecessors' elite-status. At first, they had been senior amirs of al-Nāṣir Muḥammad's regime, but after 1347 they were replaced by their junior counterparts; then after 1361 a mixture of mamluks originating from the post-al-Nāṣir Muḥammad era, around a nucleus of former clients of al-Nāṣir Ḥasan, emerged, and, finally, after 1377, there came a similarly mixed group, who all, however, had the *ustādh* Yalbughā and years of expulsion in common.

As said, struggle for power—in its creative and destructive capacities—was responsible for cycles of socio-political chaos and order that were similar to those characterising the elite's composition.

Throughout the entire period, no one seemed to be able to end those cycles indefinitely and to finally overcome continuously resurging ambitions for social and political self-improvement, progress and Effective Power. Some managed to impose their order on society for limited periods of time—one occasionally longer than the other. But only after 1380, when the amir Barqūq managed to maintain the order he had created out of the 1377 chaos, was the pattern somehow broken, when he made his network of Effective Power coincide with the regime's Legitimate Power and prospects for longer stability became very real.

This was most likely as much due to his successful patronage, including the containment of any further struggle for power, as to the 'degenerative' longevity of Qalawunid reign and—considering the respect which allegedly had prevented Barqūq from usurping the throne before—the extinction of the final representatives of al-Nāṣir Muḥammad's regime. The combination of a general conservatism and esteem for Qalawunid descent with the need to create a consensus among the elite that ensured the interests of all those involved had actually been responsible for the repeated enthronement of Qalawunids during such a prolonged period. Until 1354 and the second accession of al-Nāṣir Ḥasan, patronage, networks and those interests had remained too fragmented to allow for any alternative. Only after 1354 did wider networks that incorporated most of the elite and that joined most of their interests reoccur. They, however, never managed to consolidate that predominance due to conflicts with too ambitious subordinates. When chaos, fragmentation and discord consequently re-appeared, after 1361 and after 1377, a conservative consensus was again the only option and yet another Qalawunid was called on to enact the sultanate. Only Barqūq managed to change this pattern, to overcome rivalries and to consolidate his power. Not surprisingly perhaps, upon his enthronement, Barqūq took the title of 'al-Malik al-Ẓāhir', portraying himself in the vein of the regime's very first sultan Baybars (1260–1277) and avoiding any link with the Qalawunids. Another political era was to begin, though it was perhaps not entirely Garcin's "restoration of the Mamluk state."[1] In fact, those Qalawunid cycles of extending and collapsing

[1] See J.-Cl. Garcin, "The Regime of the Circassian Mamluks", in C.F. Petry, *The Cambridge History of Egypt. Vol. 1. Islamic Egypt, 640–1517*, Cambridge 1998, p. 290.

networks proved very hard to remove—a last convulsion appeared when Ḥājjī was returned to the throne in the period 1389–1390—and similar cycles were bound to return throughout the fifteenth century, when time and again sons succeeded their mamluk fathers on the throne. But their containment would never again be as problematic as it had been between 1341 and 1382. Some more permanent order had emerged from chaos after all.

APPENDIX ONE

THE QALAWUNID SULTANATE, 1279–1382

Qalawunid sultans:	reigns:
– al-Manṣūr Qalāwūn (d. 1290)	1279–1290
– al-Ashraf Khalīl b. Qalāwūn (d. 1294)	1290–1293
– al-Nāṣir Muḥammad b. Qalāwūn (ca. 1283–1341)	1293–1294 1299–1309 1310–1341
– al-Manṣūr Abū Bakr b. Muḥammad b. Qalāwūn (1322–1342)	1341
– al-Ashraf Kujuk b. Muḥammad b. Qalāwūn (1337–1345)	1341–1342
– al-Nāṣir Aḥmad b. Muḥammad b. Qalāwūn (1316–1344)	1342
– al-Ṣāliḥ Ismāʿīl b. Muḥammad b. Qalāwūn (1326–1345)	1342–1345
– al-Kāmil Shaʿbān b. Muḥammad b. Qalāwūn (1327–1346)	1345–1346
– al-Muẓaffar Ḥājjī b. Muḥammad b. Qalāwūn (1332–1347)	1346–1347
– al-Nāṣir Ḥasan b. Muḥammad b. Qalāwūn (1335–1361)	1347–1351
– al-Ṣāliḥ Ṣāliḥ b. Muḥammad b. Qalāwūn (1337–1360)	1351–1354
– al-Nāṣir Ḥasan b. Muḥammad b. Qalāwūn [2]	1354–1361
– al-Manṣūr Muḥammad b. Ḥājjī b. Muḥammad b. Qalāwūn (1347–1398)	1361–1363
– al-Ashraf Shaʿbān b. Ḥusayn b. Muḥammad b. Qalāwūn (1352–1377)	1363–1377
– al-Manṣūr ʿAlī b. Shaʿbān b. Ḥusayn b. Muḥammad b. Qalāwūn (1369–1381)	1377–1381
– al-Ṣāliḥ Ḥājjī b. Shaʿbān b. Ḥusayn b. Muḥammad b. Qalāwūn (1373–1412)	1381–1382 1389–1390

APPENDIX TWO

EFFECTIVE POWER HOLDERS BETWEEN 1341 AND 1382

This appendix consists of a concise alphabetical list of the thirty-four Effective Power Holders—twenty-seven amirs and seven sultans—that were identified in this study for the years between 1341 and 1382. In addition to the final section of chapter two, where their households and networks were detailed, this appendix presents what military ranks and offices these power holders held and when, it indicates their involvement in the period's many conflicts, which are listed in Appendix 3 and analysed in the final section of chapter three, and it identifies the major biographical source material on them, in chronicle obituaries and in biographical dictionaries.

1. Abū Bakr b. al-Malik al-Nāṣir Muḥammad b. Qalāwūn, al-Malik al-Manṣūr Sayf al-Dīn (1322–1342)

military rank:	amir of forty	?–2/1341
	amir of a hundred:	2/1341–5/1341
sultan:		5/1341–7/1341

conflicts nos. 2, 3

sources: al-Qalqashandī, *Subḥ*, VIII, pp. 380–382; al-Kutubī, *ʿUyūn al-Tawārīkh*, fol. 58v; al-ʿAynī, *ʿIqd al-Jumān*, p. 65; Ibn Taghrī Birdī, *Nujūm*, X, pp. 17–18; Ibn Qāḍī Shuhba, *Tārīkh*, II, pp. 254–255 al-Ṣafadī, *Aʿyān*, I, pp. 720–723, nr. 416; al-Ṣafadī, *Wāfī*, X,
pp. 250–252, nr. 4747; Ibn Ḥajar, *Durar*, I, pp. 462–464, nr. 1244

2. Aghizlū al-Sayfī, Shujāʿ al-Dīn (d. 1347)

military rank:	amir of a hundred	(10/1345)
	amir of a hundred	7/1347–9/1347
military office:	*wālī*	?–9/1344
	shādd (financial supervisor)	9/1344–1346
	wazīr	(10/1345)
	amīr silāḥ	7/1347–9/1347
	nāʾib Ghazza	(9/1347)

conflicts nos. 16, 20, 22

sources: al-Shujāʿī, *Tārīkh*, p. 239; al-Maqrīzī, *Khiṭaṭ*, III, p. 391; al-Maqrīzī, *Sulūk*, II/3, pp. 756–757; Ibn Taghrī Birdī, *Nujūm*, X, pp. 167–168, 186; Ibn Qāḍī Shuhba, *Tārīkh*, II, pp. 513–515 al-Ṣafadī, *Aʿyān*, I, pp. 543–545, nr. 288; al-Ṣafadī, *Wāfī*, IX, pp. 294–296, nr. 4225; Ibn Ḥajar, *Durar*, I, p. 390, nr. 997; Ibn Taghrī Birdī, *Manhal*, II, pp. 460–462, nr. 475.

3. Aḥmad b. al-Malik al-Nāṣir Muḥammad b. Qalāwūn, al-Malik al-Nāṣir Shihāb al-Dīn (1316–1344)

sultan: 3/1342-7/1342
conflicts nos. 7, 8, 9, 11
bronnen: al-Kutubī, *ʿUyūn al-Tawārīkh*, fol. 71–71v; Ibn Qāḍī Shuhba, *Tārīḥ*, II, pp. 421–423; al-ʿAynī, *ʿIqd al-Jumān*, p. 73; Ibn Taghrī Birdī, *Nujūm*, X, pp. 50, 72.
al-Ṣafadī, *Aʿyān*, I, pp. 370–375, nr. 189; al-Ṣafadī, *Wāfī*, VIII, pp. 86–90, nr. 3513; Ibn Ḥajar, *Durar*, I, pp. 294–296, nr. 745; Ibn Taghrī Birdī, *Manhal*, II, pp. 158–164, nr. 295.

4. ʿAlī al-Māridānī al-Nāṣirī, ʿAlāʾ al-Dīn (ca. 1310–1370)

military rank:	amir of forty	1345–1/1351
	amir of a hundred	9/1351–12/1352
	amir of a hundred	(Damascus) 6/1363–10/1366
military office:	*nāʾib al-Shām*	12/1352–5/1358
	nāʾib Ḥalab	5/1358–11/1358
	nāʾib al-Shām	11/1358–6/1359
	nāʾib Ṣafad	6/1359–12/1359
	nāʾib Ḥamā	1/1360–12/1360
	nāʾib al-Shām	8/1361–6/1362
	nāʾib al-salṭana	15/1/1368–8/1370

conflicts no. 39
sources: Ibn Duqmāq, *Nuzhat al-Anām*, fol. 62v–63; Ibn al-ʿIrāqī, *Dhayl al-ʿibar*, II, p. 309; al-ʿAynī, *ʿIqd al-Jumān*, p. 163; al-Maqrīzī, *Sulūk*, III/1, p. 192; Ibn Taghrī Birdī, *Nujūm*, XI, p. 116; Ibn Qāḍī Shuhba, *Tārīkh*, III, pp. 391–392.
al-Ṣafadī, *Wāfī*, XXII, p. 367, nr. 260; Ibn Ḥajar, *Durar*, III, pp. 77–78, nr. 160.

5. Almalik al-Jūkandār, al-Ḥājj, Sayf al-Dīn (1277–1346)

military rank:	amir of a hundred	?–4/1342
	amir of a hundred	8/1342–8/1345
	amir of a hundred	(4/1346)
military office:	*nāʾib Ḥamā*	4/1342–7/1342
	nāʾib al-salṭana	6/1343–8/1345
	nāʾib al-Shām	(8/1345)
	nāʾib Ṣafad	8/1345–4/1346

conflicts nos. 14, 17

sources: al-Kutubī, *ʿUyūn al-Tawārīkh*, fol. 75v; Ibn Ḥabīb, *Tadhkirat al-Nabīh*, III, pp. 82–83; al-Maqrīzī, *Khiṭaṭ*, IV, p. 108; al-Maqrīzī, *Sulūk*, II/3, p. 723; Ibn Taghrī Birdī, *Nujūm*, X, pp. 175–176; Ibn Qāḍī Shuhba, *Tārīkh*, II, pp. 487–489.
al-Ṣafadī, *Aʿyān*, I, pp. 618–620, nr. 335; al-Ṣafadī, *Wāfī*, IX, pp. 372–373, nr. 4297; Ibn Ḥajar, *Durar*, I, p. 411, nr. 1064; Ibn Taghrī Birdī, *Manhal*, III, pp. 85–88, nr. 547.

6. Aqsunqur al-Nāṣirī, Shams al-Dīn (d. 6/8/1347)

military rank:	amir of a hundred	1337–5/1342
	amir of a hundred	7/1342–2/1344
	amir of a hundred	8/1345–8/1347
military rank:	*nāʾib Ghazza*:	4/1342–7/1342
	amīr ākhūr kabīr	7/1342–2/1344
	nāʾib Ṭarābulus	2/1344–8/1345
	nāʾib al-salṭana	(8/1345)

conflicts nos. 12, 18, 19
sources: Ibn Ḥabīb, *Tadhkirat al-Nabīh*, III, pp. 98–99; al-Maqrīzī, *Sulūk*, II/3, p. 754; Ibn Taghrī Birdī, *Nujūm*, X, pp. 178–180; Ibn Qāḍī Shuhba, *Tārīkh*, II, p. 515.
al-Ṣafadī, *Aʿyān*, I, pp. 554–556, nr. 298; al-Ṣafadī, *Wāfī*, IX, pp. 311–313, nr. 4246; Ibn Ḥajar, *Durar*, I, p. 394, nr. 1015; Ibn Taghrī Birdī, *Manhal*, II, pp. 496–499, nr. 501.

7. Arghūn al-ʿAlāʾī al-Nāṣirī, Sayf al-Dīn (d. 1347)

military rank:	amir of ten	(1332)–9/1341
	amir of forty (Safad)	9/1341–1342
	amir of a hundred	10/1342–1346
military office:	*raʾs nawba kabīr*	6/1342–10/1346

conflicts nos. 10, 13, 14, 16, 18
sources: al-Shujāʿī, *Tārīkh*, p. 274; Ibn Ḥabīb, *Tadhkirat al-Nabīh*, III, p. 92; al-ʿAynī, *ʿIqd al-Jumān*, p. 79; al-Maqrīzī, *Khiṭaṭ*, IV, p. 390; al-Maqrīzī, *Sulūk*, II/3, p. 756; Ibn Taghrī Birdī, *Nujūm*, X, pp. 185–186; Ibn Qāḍī Shuhba, *Tārīkh*, II, pp. 486, 513.
al-Ṣafadī, *Aʿyān*, I, pp. 456–457, nr. 233; al-Ṣafadī, *Wāfī*, VIII, p. 355, nr. 3788; Ibn Ḥajar, *Durar*, I, p. 353, nr. 875.

8. Asandamur al-Sharafī al-Nāṣirī, al-Dawādār, Sayf al-Dīn (d. 1368)

military rank:	amir of forty	?–3/1366
	amir of a hundred	3/1366–10/1367
military office:	*atābak al-ʿasākir*	6/1367–10/1367

conflicts nos. 45, 46, 47, 48, 49

sources: Ibn Duqmāq, *Nuzhat al-Anām*, fol. 42; al-Maqrīzī, *Sulūk*, III/1, p. 164; Ibn Taghrī Birdī, *Nujūm*, XI, p. 103
Ibn Ḥajar, *Durar*, I, p. 386, nr. 982; Ibn Taghrī Birdī, *Manhal*, II, pp. 440–443, nr. 464.

9. Aydughmish al-Nāṣirī al-Ṭabbākhī, ʿAlāʾ al-Dīn (d. 1342)

military office:	*amīr ākhūr kabīr*	1310–4/1342
	nāʾib al-salṭana	(8/1341)
	nāʾib Ḥalab	4/1342–7/1342
	nāʾib al-Shām	7/1342–11/1342

conflicts nos. 6
sources: al-Shujāʿī, *Tārīkh*, p. 251; Ibn Ḥabīb, *Tadhkirat al-Nabīh*, p. 40; Ibn Taghrī Birdī, *Nujūm*, X, pp. 99–100; Ibn Qāḍī Shuhba, *Tārīkh*, II, pp. 320–322.
al-Ṣafadī, *Aʿyān*, I, pp. 652–654, nr. 367; al-Ṣafadī, *Wāfī*, IX, pp. 488–489, nr. 4452; Ibn Ḥajar, *Durar*, I, pp. 426–428, nr. 1120; Ibn Taghrī Birdī, *Manhal*, III, pp. 165–168, nr. 598.

10. Aynabak al-ʿIzzī al-Badrī, ʿIzz al-Dīn (d. 1378)

military rank:	amir of forty	3/1366–12/1366
	amir of ten	?–7/1373
	amir of forty	7/1373–3/1377
	amir of a hundred	3/1377–8/1377
military office:	*amīr ākhūr kabīr*	3/1377–7/1377
	atābak al-ʿasākir	7/1377–8/1377

conflicts nos. 56, 57, 58, 59, 60, 61, 62
sources: al-Maqrīzī, *Sulūk*, III/1, pp. 308, 327; Ibn Ḥajar, *Inbāʾ*, I, p. 262; Ibn Taġrī Birdī, *Nujūm*, XI, p. 32; Ibn Qāḍī Shuhba, *Tārīkh*, III, p. 558.
Ibn Taghrī Birdī, *Manhal*, III, pp. 221–224, nr. 629.

11. Bahādur al-Damurdāshī al-Nāṣirī, Sayf al-Dīn (d. 1343)

military rank:	amir of a hundred	ca. 1330–3/1343
military office:	*raʾs nawba kabīr*	?–3/1343

conflict no. 10
sources: al-Shujāʿī, *Tārīkh*, p. 252; Ibn Taghrī Birdī, *Nujūm*, X, p. 104; Ibn Qāḍī Shuhba, *Tārīkh*, II, pp. 322–323.
al-Ṣafadī, *Aʿyān*, II, pp. 62–63, nr. 480; al-Ṣafadī, *Wāfī*, X, pp. 299–300, nr. 4812; Ibn Ḥajar, *Durar*, I, p. 498, nr. 1362; Ibn Taghrī Birdī, *Manhal*, III, pp. 431–432, nr. 370.

12. Barka al-Jūbānī al-Yalbughāwī, Zayn al-Dīn (d. 1380)
military rank: amir of ten 1377–6/1377
amir of forty 6/1377–8/1377
amir of a hundred 8/1377–6/1380
military office: *amīr majlis* 9/1377–4/1378
ra᾿s nawba kabīr 4/1378–6/1380
conflicts nos. 64, 67, 68, 69, 72, 73.
sources: al-ʿAynī, *ʿIqd al-Jumān*, p. 263; Ibn Ḥajar, *Inbā᾿*, II, p. 23; Ibn Taghrī Birdī, *Nujūm*, XI, p. 204; Ibn Qāḍī Shuhba, *Tārīkh*, I, pp. 42–43.
Ibn Taghrī Birdī, *Manhal*, III, pp. 351–355, nr. 661.

13. Barqūq al-ʿUthmānī al-Yalbughāwī al-Jarkasī, Sayf al-Dīn (ca. 1341–1399)
military rank: amir of forty 6/1377–8/1377
amir of a hundred 8/1377–12/1382
military office: *amīr ākhūr kabīr* 9/1377–4/1378
atābak al-ʿasākir 4/1378–12/1382
sultan: 12/1382–6/1389
2/1390–6/1399
conflicts nos. 64, 65, 66, 67, 68, 69, 71, 73, 74.
sources: Ibn Khaldūn, *Kitāb al-ʿIbar*, V, p. 472; al-Maqrīzī, *Sulūk*, III/1, p. 316, III/2, p. 476; Ibn Hajar, *Inbā᾿*, II, pp. 72–73; Ibn Taghrī Birdī, *Nujūm*, XI, p. 223–334; Ibn Qāḍī Shuhba, *Tārīkh*, I, p. 73.
Ibn Taghrī Birdī, *Manhal*, III, pp. 285–342, nr. 657; al-Sakhāwī, *Ḍaw᾿*, III, pp. 10–12, nr. 48.

14. Baybughā Rūs al-Qāsimī al-Nāṣirī, Sayf al-Dīn (d. 1353)
military rank: amir of forty 12/1344–?
amir of a hundred 1345–1/1351
military office: *amīr majlis* ?–1/1348
nā᾿ib as-salṭana 1/1348–1/1351
nā᾿ib Ḥalab 9/1351–11/1352
conflicts nos. 23, 24, 25, 27, 28, 29, 35
sources: Ibn Ḥabīb, *Tadhkirat al-Nabīh*, III, p. 164; al-Maqrīzī, *Sulūk*, II/3, p. 905; Ibn Taghrī Birdī, *Nujūm*, X, pp. 293–294; Ibn Qāḍī Shuhba, *Tārīkh*, III, p. 51.
al-Ṣafadī, *Aʿyān*, II, pp. 86–95, nr. 504; al-Ṣafadī, *Wāfī*, X, pp. 356–358, nr. 4851; Ibn Ḥajar, *Durar*, I, pp. 511–512, nr. 1387; Ibn Taghrī Birdī, *Manhal*, III, pp. 486–489, nr. 731.

15. Ḥājjī b. al-Malik al-Nāṣir Muḥammad b. Qalāwūn, al-Malik al-Muẓaffar Zayn al-Dīn (Sayf al-Dīn) (1332–1347)

military rank:	amir of forty	12/1342–?
sultan:		9/1346–12/1347

conflicts nos. 19, 20, 21, 23

sources: Ibn Ḥabīb, *Tadhkirat al-Nabīh*, III, pp. 100–101; Ibn Taghrī Birdī, *Nujūm*, X, p. 186; Ibn Qāḍī Shuhba, *Tārīkh*, II, pp. 519–521.
al-Ṣafadī, *Aʿyān*, II, pp. 176–180, nr. 552; al-Ṣafadī, *Wāfī*, XI, p. 238–240, nr. 341; Ibn Ḥajar, *Durar*, II, pp. 3–5, nr. 1476; Ibn Taghrī Birdī, *Manhal*, V, pp. 50–55, nr. 879.

16. Ḥasan Qumārī b. al-Malik al-Nāṣir Muḥammad b. Qalāwūn, al-Malik al-Nāṣir Nāṣir al-Dīn Abū al-Maʿālī (1335–1361)

sultan:		12/1347–8/1351
		10/1354–3/1361

conflicts nos. 29, 30, 32, 40, 41

sources: Ibn Ḥabīb, *Tadhkirat al-Nabīh*, III, p. 240; al-ʿAynī, *ʿIqd al-Jumān*, pp. 124–127; al-Maqrīzī, *Khiṭaṭ*, IV, pp. 118–120; Ibn Qāḍī Shuhba, *Tārīkh*, III, p. 191.
al-Ṣafadī, *Aʿyān*, II, pp. 247–252, nr. 587; al-Ṣafadī, *Wāfī*, XII, pp. 266–267, nr. 238: Ibn Ḥajar, *Durar*, II, pp. 38–40, nr. 1560; Ibn Taghrī Birdī, *Manhal*, V, pp. 125–132, nr. 927.

17. Ismāʿīl b. al-Malik al-Nāṣir Muḥammad b. Qalāwūn al-Malik al-Ṣāliḥ ʿImād al-Dīn Abū al-Fidāʾ (1326–1345)

military rank:	amir of forty	6/1341–?
sultan:		6/1342–8/1345

conflict no. 11

sources: al-Qalqashandī, *Ṣubḥ*, VII, pp. 360–363; al-Kutubī, *ʿUyūn al-Tawārīkh*, fol. 75 v.–76; Ibn Ḥabīb, *Tadhkirat al-Nabīh*, III, p. 79; Ibn Taghrī Birdī, *Nujūm*, X, pp. 98, 142; Ibn Qāḍī Shuhba, *Tārīkh*, II, pp. 456–457.
al-Ṣafadī, *Aʿyān*, I, pp. 524–525, nr. 271; al-Ṣafadī, *Wāfī*, IX, pp. 219–220, nr. 4123; Ibn Ḥajar, *Durar*, I, p. 380, nr. 960; Ibn Taghrī Birdī, *Manhal*, II, pp. 425–427, nr. 452.

18. Maliktamur al-Ḥijāzī al-Nāṣirī, Sayf al-Dīn (ca. 1310–8/1347)

military rank:	amir of a hundred	?–8/1341
	amir of a hundred	1341–8/1347
military office:	*amīr majlis*	7/1341–8/1341

conflict nos. 18, 19

sources: Ibn Ḥabīb, *Tadhkirat al-Nabīh*, III, pp. 98–99; al-Maqrīzī, *Sulūk*, II/3, p. 755; Ibn Taghrī Birdī, *Nujūm*, X, p. 184; Ibn Qāḍī Shuhba, *Tārīkh*, II, pp. 537–538.

al-Ṣafadī, *Aʿyān*, V, pp. 444–447, nr. 1869; Ibn Ḥajar, *Durar*, IV, pp. 358–359, nr. 977.

19. Manjak al-Yūsufī al-Nāṣirī al-Turkī al-Silāḥdār, Sayf al-Dīn (ca. 1315–1375)

military rank:	amir of forty	8/1344–?
	amir of a hundred	?–10/1347
	amir of a hundred	1/1348–12/1350
	amir of forty (Damascus)	1/1360–?
military office:	*ḥājib al-ḥujjāb* (Damascus)	10/1347–1/1348
	wazīr	1/1348–6/1348
	wazīr	7/1348–12/1350
	ustādār	1/1348–12/1350
	nāʾib Ṣafad	(10/1351)
	nāʾib Ṭarābulus	11/1354–1/1358
	nāʾib Ḥalab	1/1358–4/1358
	nāʾib al-Shām	4/1358–10/1358
	nāʾib Ṣafad	10/1358–1/1359
	nāʾib Ṭarābulus	9/1367–2/1368
	nāʾib al-Shām	2/1368–3/1374
	nāʾib as-salṭana	5/1374–6/1375
	atābak al-ʿasākir	5/1374–6/1375

conflicts nos. 24, 27, 28, 29

sources: Ibn Duqmāq, *Nuzhat al-Anām*, fol. 90v; Ibn al-ʿIrāqī, *Dhayl al-ʿIbar*, II, pp. 385–386; al-ʿAynī, *ʿIqd al-Jumān*, p. 187; al-Maqrīzī, *Sulūk*, III/1, p. 247; Ibn Ḥajar, *Inbāʾ*, I, pp. 148, 190; Ibn Taghrī Birdī, *Nujūm*, XI, pp. 56, 133–134; Ibn Qāḍī Shuhba, *Tārīkh*, III, pp. 473–475.
Ibn Ḥağar, *Durar*, IV, pp. 360–361, nr. 985.

20. Manklī Bughā al-Shamsī al-Nāṣirī, Sayf al-Dīn (ca. 1320–1372)

military rank:	amir of forty	11/1357–8/1358
	amir of a hundred	8/1358–7/1361
military office:	*nāʾib Ṣafad*	7/1361–7/1362
	nāʾib Ṭarābulus	7/1362–8/1362
	nāʾib Ḥalab	8/1362–7/1363
	nāʾib al-Shām	7/1363–11/1366
	nāʾib Ḥalab	11/1366–10/1367
	nāʾib al-salṭana	(11/1367)
	atābak al-ʿasākir	11/1367–11/1372

not involved in conflicts

sources: Ibn Duqmāq, *Nuzhat al-Anām*, fol. 72v, 73v; Ibn al-ʿIrāqī, *Dhayl al-ʿIbar*, II, p. 361; al-ʿAynī, *ʿIqd al-Jumān*, p. 169; al-Maqrīzī, *Sulūk*, III/1, p. 210; Ibn Ḥajar, *Inbāʾ*, I, pp. 70–71, 190; Ibn Taghrī Birdī, *Nujūm*, XI, pp. 124–125; Ibn Qāḍī

Shuhba, *Tārīkh*, III, pp. 426–427.
Ibn Ḥajar, *Durar*, IV, p. 367, nr. 998.

21. Mughulṭāy b. Sūsūn al-Nāṣirī, ʿAlāʾ al-Dīn (d. 1354)

military rank:	amir of ten	6/1341–9/1341
	amir of forty	9/1341–1/1342
	amir of forty	7/1342–?
	amir of a hundred	?–8/1351
military office:	*amīr ākhūr kabīr*	12/1347–8/1351
	raʾs nawba kabīr	1/1351–8/1351

conflicts nos. 32, 33
sources: al-Ḥusaynī, *Dhayl al-ʿIbar*, p. 161; al-Maqrīzī, *Sulūk*, III/1, p. 14; Ibn Taghrī Birdī, *Nujūm*, X, p. 300; Ibn Qāḍī Shuhba, *Tārīkh*, III, p. 74.
Ibn Ḥajar, *Durar*, IV, pp. 355–356, nr. 970.

22. Qaraṭāy al-Ṭāzī, Shihāb al-Dīn (d. 1378)

military rank:	amir of a hundred	3/1377–7/1379
military office:	*raʾs nawba kabīr*	3/1377–5/1377
	atābak al-ʿasākir	5/1377–7/1377

conflicts nos. 56, 57, 58
sources: al-Maqrīzī, *Sulūk*, III/1, p. 326; Ibn Ḥajar, *Inbāʾ*, I, p. 256; Ibn Taghrī Birdī, *Nujūm*, XI, p. 191; Ibn Qāḍī Shuhba, *Tārīkh*, III, pp. 563–564

23. Qawṣūn al-Nāṣirī al-Sāqī, Sayf al-Dīn (ca. 1300–1342)

military rank:	amir of forty	?–ca. 1326
	amir of a hundred	ca. 1326–1/1342
military office:	*nāʾib al-salṭana*	8/1341–1/1342

conflicts nos. 1, 3, 4, 5, 6
sources: Ibn Ḥabīb, *Tadhlkirat al-Nabīh*, III, pp. 31–34; al-ʿAynī, *ʿIqd al-Jumān*, pp. 65–66; al-Maqrīzī, *Khiṭaṭ*, IV, p. 104; al-Maqrīzī, *Sulūk*, II/3, p. 615; Ibn Taghrī Birdī, *Nujūm*, X, pp. 46, 75; Ibn Qāḍī Shuhba, *Tārīkh*, II, pp. 278–281.
al-Ṣafadī, *Aʿyān*, IV, pp. 136–141, nr. 1389; al-Ṣafadī, *Wāfī*, XXIV, pp. 277–279, nr. 287; Ibn Ḥajar, *Durar*, III, pp. 257–258, nr. 662.

24. Quṭluqtamur al-ʿAlāʾī, al-Ṭawīl al-Jāshankīr, Sayf al-Dīn (d. 1377)

military rank	amir of a hundred	6/1362–5/1365
	amir of a hundred	6/1367–3/1377
	amir of forty	5/1377–6/1377
	amir of a hundred	6/1377–7/1377
military rank	*amīr jāndār*	?–5/1365
	nāʾib Ṣafad	5/1365–6/1365
	amīr jāndār	6/1367–?

conflict no. 63
sources: Ibn Duqmāq, *Nuzhat al-Anām*, fol. 5v, 103v, 127v; al-ʿAynī, *ʿIqd al-Jumān*, p. 233; al-Maqrīzī, *Sulūk*, III/1, pp. 75, 99, 100, 318; Ibn Taghrī Birdī, *Nujūm*, XI, p. 190; Ibn Qāḍī Shuhba, *Tārīkh*, III, pp. 564–565

25. Ṣarghitmish al-Nāṣirī, Sayf al-Dīn (d. 1358)

military rank:	amir of forty	?–1348
	amir of a hundred	1348–9/1358
military office:	*raʾs nawba kabīr*	3/1351–3/1353
	atābak al-ʿasākir	11/1357–9/1358

conflicts nos. 4, 33, 34, 35, 36, 37, 39, 40.
sources: Ibn Ḥabīb, *Tadhkirat al-Nabīh*, III, p. 213; al-ʿAynī, *ʿIqd al-Jumān*, p. 115; al-Maqrīzī, *Khiṭaṭ*, IV, p. 257; al-Maqrīzī, *Sulūk*, II/3, p. 536; III/1, p. 44; Ibn Taghrī Birdī, *Nujūm*, X, pp. 30, 328; Ibn Qāḍī Shuhba, *Tārīkh*, III, pp. 137–138.
al-Ṣafadī, *Aʿyān*, II, pp. 555–560, nr. 795; Ibn Ḥajar, *Durar*, II, pp. 206–207, nr. 1978; Ibn Taghrī Birdī, *Manhal*, VI, pp. 342–344, nr. 1217.

26. Shaʿbān b. al-Malik al-Nāṣir Muḥammad b. Qalāwūn, al-Malik al-Kāmil Sayf al-Dīn Abū l-Futūḥ (ca. 1327–1346)

military rank:	amir of ten	6/1341–?
	amir of forty	6/1342–?
sultan:		8/1345–9/1346

conflicts nos. 17, 18
sources: Ibn Ḥabīb, *Tadhkirat al-Nabīh*, III, p. 90; Ibn Qāḍī Shuhba, *Tārīkh*, II, pp. 489–490.
al-Ṣafadī, *Aʿyān*, II, pp. 521–524, nr. 772; al-Ṣafadī, *Wāfī*, XVI, pp. 153–155, nr. 178; Ibn Ḥajar, *Durar*, II, pp. 191–192, nr. 1938; Ibn Taghrī Birdī, *Manhal*, VI, pp. 250–253, nr. 1188.

27. Shaʿbān b. Ḥusayn b. Muḥammad b. Qalāwūn, al-Malik al-Ashraf Zayn al-Dīn Abū al-Maʿālī (1352–1377)

sultan: 6/1363–3/1377

conflicts nos. 47, 48, 49, 50, 51, 52, 53, 55, 56.
sources: Ibn Duqmāq, *Nuzhat al-Anām*, fol. 112v–114v; Ibn al-ʿIrāqī, *Dhayl al-ʿIbar*, II, pp. 448–449; al-ʿAynī, *ʿIqd al-Jumān*, pp. 214–216; al-Maqrīzī, *Sulūk*, II/3, p. 903; III/1, p. 282; Ibn Ḥajar, *Inbāʾ*, I, p. 210; Ibn Taghrī Birdī, *Nujūm*, XI, pp. 81–83; Ibn Qāḍī Shuhba, *Tārīkh*, III, p. 524–525.
Ibn Ḥajar, *Durar*, II, p. 190, nr. 1936; Ibn Taghrī Birdī, *Manhal*, VI, pp. 233–248, nr. 1186.

28. Shaykhū al-ʿUmarī al-Nāṣirī, al-Atābak, Sayf al-Dīn (ca. 1303–1357)

military rank:	amir of forty	12/1341–1/1342
	amir of ten	1342–?
	amir of a hundred	1346–1/1351
	amir of a hundred (Damascus)	1/1351–1/1351
	amir of a hundred	9/1351–8/1357
military office:	ra'ʾs nawba kabīr	12/1347–1/1351
	nāʾib Ṭarābulus	(1/1351)
	atābak al-ʿasākir	9/1351–?
	raʾs nawba kabīr	8/1352–1354
	atābak al-ʿasākir	1354–8/1357

conflicts nos. 4, 24, 28, 29, 35, 36, 37, 38

Sources: al-Kutubī, *ʿUyūn al-Tawārīʾ*, fol. 162–162v; Ibn Ḥabīb, *Tadhkirat al-Nabīh*, III, p. 204; al-ʿAynī, *ʿIqd al-Jumān*, pp. 111–112; al-Maqrīzī, *Sulūk*, II/3, p. 865; Ibn Taghrī Birdī, *Nujūm*, X, pp. 30, 324–325; Ibn Qāḍī Shuhba, *Tārīkh*, III, pp. 124–125.

al-Ṣafadī, *Aʿyān*, II, pp. 531–536, nr. 778; al-Ṣafadī, *Wāfī*, XVI, pp. 211–212, nr. 240; Ibn Ḥajar, *Durar*, II, pp. 196–197, nr. 1950; Ibn Taghrī Birdī, *Manhal*, VI, pp. 257–262, nr. 1192.

29. Ṭashtamur al-Badrī an-Nāṣirī al-Sāqī Ḥummuṣ Akhḍar, Sayf al-Dīn (d. 1342)

military rank:	amir of forty	ca. 1312–?
	amir of a hundred	?–8/1336
	amir of a hundred	3/1342–5/1342
military office:	*nāʾib Ṣafad*	8/1336–7/1340
	nāʾib Ḥalab	7/1340–11/1341
	nāʾib al-salṭana	4/1342–5/1342

conflicts nos. 5, 7

sources: al-Shujāʿī, *Tārīkh*, pp. 249–250; Ibn Ḥabīb, *Tadhkirat al-Nabīh*, III, p. 49; al-Maqrīzī, *Sulūk*, II/3, p. 637; Ibn Taghrī Birdī, Nujūm, X, pp. 101–102; Ibn Qāḍī Shuhba, *Tārīkh*, II, pp. 268–271.

al-Ṣafadī, *Aʿyān*, II, pp. 586–591, nr. 811; al-Ṣafadī, *Wāfī*, XVI, p. 437–442, nr. 474; Ibn Ḥajar, *Durar*, II, pp. 219–220, nr. 2017; Ibn Taghrī Birdī, *Manhal*, VI, pp. 392–394, nr. 1245.

30. Ṭashtamur al-ʿAlāʾī al-Dawādār, Sayf ad-Dīn (d. 1384)

military rank:	amir of ten	11/1363–?
	amir of forty	12/1370–?
	amir of a hundred	?–3/1377
military rank:	*dawādār kabīr*	12/1370–3/1377
	nāʾib al-Shām	3/1377–4/1377

	atābak al-ʿasākir	9/1377–4/1378
	nāʾib Ṣafad	10/1380–11/1382
	nāʾib Ḥamā	11/1382–?

conflict no. 67

sources: Ibn Duqmāq, *Nuzhat al-Anām*, fol. 62v; Ibn Taghrī Birdī, *Nujūm*, XI, p. 304; Ibn Qāḍī Shuhba, *Tārīkh*, I, pp. 143–144.
Ibn Ḥajar, *Durar*, II, p. 220, nr. 2018; Ibn Taghrī Birdī, *Manhal*, VI, pp. 395–396, nr. 1247.

31. Ṭāz b. Quṭghāj al-Nāṣirī, Amīr Majlis, Sayf al-Dīn (d. 1362)

military rank:	amir of forty	12/1342–8/1347
	amir of a hundred	8/1347–11/1354
	amir of forty (Damascus)	1361–10/1362
military rank:	*amīr majlis*	9/1351–11/1354
	nāʾib Ḥalab	11/1354–1/1358

conflicts nos. 4, 27, 32, 33, 34, 35, 37, 39

sources: Ibn Ḥabīb, *Tadhkirat al-Nabīh*, III, p. 255; al-ʿAynī, *ʿIqd al-Jumān*, p. 129; al-Maqrīzī, *Khiṭaṭ*, III, p. 119; al-Maqrīzī, *Sulūk*, III/1, p. 78; Ibn Taghrī Birdī, *Nujūm*, XI, p. 15; Ibn Qāḍī Shuhba, *Tārīkh*, III, p. 208.
al-Ṣafadī, *Aʿyān*, II, pp. 567–571, nr. 799; al-Ṣafadī, *Wāfī*, XVI, pp. 383–384, nr. 418; Ibn Ḥajar, *Durar*, II, pp. 214–215, nr. 1998; Ibn Taghrī Birdī, *Manhal*, VI, pp. 362–365, nr. 1228.

32. Uljāy al-Yūsufī al-Nāṣirī, Sayf al-Dīn (d. 1373)

military rank:	amir of a hundred	8/1358–7/1360
	amir of a hundred	10/1360–5/1367
	amir of a hundred	10/1367–7/1373
military office:	*ḥājib al-ḥujjāb*	8/1358–?
	ḥājib al-ḥujjāb (Damascus)	8/1360–10/1360
	amīr jāndār kabīr	10/1360–?
	ḥājib al-ḥujjāb	4/1361–5/1362
	amīr jāndār kabīr	5/1362–?
	amīr jāndār kabīr	4/1365–5/1367
	amīr silāḥ	10/1367–1/1373
	atābak al-ʿasākir	1/1373–7/1373

conflicts nos. 52, 53

sources Ibn Duqmāq, *Nuzhat al-Anām*, fol. 79–80; al-ʿAynī, *ʿIqd al-Jumān*, p. 174; al-Maqrīzī, *Khiṭaṭ*, IV, p. 249; al-Maqrīzī, *Sulūk*, III/1, p. 230; Ibn Ḥajar, *Inbāʾ*, I, p. 73; Ibn Taghrī Birdī, *Nujūm*, XI, p. 129; Ibn Qāḍī Shuhba, *Tārīkh*, III, pp. 439–440.
Ibn Ḥajar, *Durar*, I, p. 405, nr. 1045; Ibn Taghrī Birdī, *Manhal*, III, p. 40–44, nr. 527.

33. Yalbughā al-ʿUmarī al-Nāṣirī al-Khāṣṣakī, Sayf al-Dīn (d. 1366)

military rank:	amir of forty	11/1357–9/1358
	amir of a hundred	9/1358–12/1366
military office:	*amīr majlis*	9/1358–3/1361
	atābak al-ʿasākir	3/1361–12/1366

conflicts nos. 41, 42, 43, 44, 45.

sources: Ibn Ḥabīb, *Tadhkirat al-Nabīh*, III, p. 301; Ibn Qāḍī Shuhba, *Tārīkh*, III, p. 305–306.
Ibn Ḥajar, *Durar*, IV, pp. 348–350, nr. 1218.

34. Yalbughā al-Nāṣirī al-Yūsufī al-Yalbughāwī, Sayf al-Dīn (d. 1391)

military rank:	amir of forty	8/1373–3/1377
	amir of forty (Damascus)	6/1377
	amir of forty	6/1377
	amir of a hundred	7/1377–4/1378
	amir of a hundred (Damascus)	5/1378–7/1378
	amir of a hundred	12/1379–6/1380
	amir of a hundred (Damascus)	1/1380–11/1381
	amir of a hundred	11/1381–12/1381
military office:	*amīr ākhūr kabīr*	8/1377–8/1377
	amīr silāḥ	3/1378–4/1378
	nāʾib Ṭarābulus	7/1378–12/1379
	amīr silāḥ	12/1379–6/1380
	nāʾib Ḥalab	12/1381–8/1385
	nāʾib Ḥalab	11/1387–2/1389
	nāʾib al-Shām	8/1390–11/1391

conflicts nos. 61, 63, 65, 68

sources: Ibn Khaldūn, *Kitāb al-ʿIbar*, V, p. 457; Ibn Taghrī Birdī, *Nujūm*, XI, pp. 126–127; Ibn Qāḍī Shuhba, *Tārīkh*, I, pp. 417–419.
Ibn Ḥajar, *Durar*, IV, pp. 440–442, nr. 1219.

APPENDIX THREE

STRUGGLE FOR POWER BETWEEN 1341 AND 1382

This appendix consists of a concise chronological, descriptive list of the seventy-four socio-political conflicts, which the years between June 1341 and November 1382 witnessed, and which were analysed in Chapter Three. It identifies dates, key participants from among the period's Effective Power Holders, the nature of the conflict, and its direct outcome.

1341

1. June 1341: A senior amir was arrested, imprisoned, and later assassinated, as a result of the spread of damaging rumours, the origins of which were attributed to the amir Qawṣūn.

2. June 1341: A senior amir was arrested by order of al-Manṣūr Abū Bakr, allegedly in revenge for the public humiliation of the latter sultan (his refusal to accept Abū Bakr's *shafāʿa*) several years earlier.

3. August 1341: Al-Manṣūr Abū Bakr was forced to abdicate as a result of a staged rebellion, orchestrated by the amir Qawṣūn, which had resulted in his confrontation with a large majority of amirs in Cairo.

4. September 1341: Qawṣūn defeated a rebellion by the sultan's mamluks after a fight outside the citadel.

5. October-December 1341: The *nāʾib Ḥalab* Ṭashtamur rallied support against Qawṣūn and in favour of the enthronement of al-Nāṣir Aḥmad, and in a number of subsequent, mostly non-violent, confrontations, Qawṣūn's supporters in Syria eventually all forsook their patron.

1342

6. November 1341–January 1342: In Egypt, the amir Aydughmish turned growing opposition against Qawṣūn into a rebellion, which managed to fight off Qawṣūn's supporters and to make him surrender; Qawṣūn and his supporters were imprisoned and, in the end, Qawṣūn was murdered.

7. April-May 1342: The amir Ṭashtamur and a fellow amir were arrested by order of al-Nāṣir Aḥmad, who had them decapitated after his return to al-Karak.

8. April-May 1342: The *nāʾib Ṣafad* rose in rebellion against al-Nāṣir Aḥmad when he received rumours of his imminent arrest, and he managed to gain the support of all amirs in Syria.

9. June 1341: After al-Nāṣir Aḥmad's departure for al-Karak, the amirs in Egypt joined their Syrian colleagues, convinced Ahmad's remaining supporters to forsake him, and enthroned al-Ṣāliḥ Ismāʿīl.

10. December 1342: One of Ismāʿīl's brothers staged a rebellion on behalf of the sultanate, but supporters were prevented from joining his forces; after their defection, Ismāʿīl's brother was arrested, imprisoned, and later killed.

11. August 1342–June 1344: The eventful siege of al-Nāṣir Aḥmad's desert fortress in al-Karak, by order of al-Ṣāliḥ Ismāʿīl, lasted for two years.

1343

12. June 1343: Rumours, allegedly spread by Aqsunqur al-Nāṣirī, resulted in the arrest of the *nāʾib al-salṭana* on charges of contacts with Aḥmad in al-Karak.

1344

13. July 1344: Arghūn al-ʿAlāʾī slandered an unruly financial officer, who was consequently arrested, tortured and killed.

1345

14. August 1345: After a quarrel between the amir Arghūn al-ʿAlāʾī and the *nāʾib al-salṭana* Almalik, al-Kāmil Shaʿbān was enthroned and Almalik was sent off to Syria.

15. September 1345: A quarrel between al-Kāmil Shaʿbān and hundreds of his mamluks on a financial rearrangement resulted in the punishment of many mamluks and their expulsion from the citadel.

1346

16. February 1346: The amirs Aghizlū en Arghūn al-ʿAlāʾī quarrelled about a financial office, and Aghizlū was reprimanded by the sultan for overstepping his bounds.

17. September 1346: The *nāʾib al-Shām* Yalbughā al-Yaḥyāwī rose in rebellion against al-Kāmil Shaʿbān upon rumours of his imminent arrest; this rebellion would spread to Egypt and end the sultan's rule.

18. September 1346: Upon escaping their arrest, the amirs Maliktamur al-Ḥijāzī, Arghūn Shāh (d. 1349) and Aqsunqur al-Nāṣirī successfully rallied support against al-Kāmil Shaʿbān, outnumbered his troops and forced him to abdicate in favour of his brother al-Muẓaffar Ḥājjī.

1347

19. July-August 1347: The amirs Maliktamur al-Ḥijāzī en Aqsunqur al-Nāṣirī were accused of engaging in subversive activities, and they were consequently arrested and killed by order of al-Muẓaffar Ḥājjī.

20. September 1347: The senior amirs Ṭughāytamur al-Najmī, Maḥmūd b. Sharwīn en Baydamur al-Badrī were accused of treason, sent off to executive offices in Syria, but killed on the road, by order of al-Muẓaffar Ḥājjī and Aghizlū.

21. September 1347: The *nā'ib al-Shām* Yalbughā al-Yaḥyāwī rose a second time in rebellion, for similar reasons, but this time, the amirs of Damascus retained their loyalty to al-Muẓaffar Ḥājjī and Yalbughā was arrested and killed.

22. September 1347: Some senior amirs managed to convince al-Muẓaffar Ḥājjī to arrest Aghizlū, and they took the opportunity to kill Aghizlū.

23. November 1347: Led by the amir Baybughā Rūs, the amirs confronted the destructive al-Muẓaffar Ḥājjī and his supporters in combat, outnumbered the latter and killed the sultan; he was replaced by his brother al-Nāṣir Ḥasan.

1348

24. June 1348: The amirs Manjak and Shaykhū quarrelled about the control over the sultan's fisc, which was retained by Shaykhū after the spread of rumours, which discredited Manjak and his patron Baybughā Rūs.

25. June 1348: Several senior amirs, suspected of plotting, were arrested by order of the amir Baybughā Rūs.

1349

26. July 1349: The *nā'ib al-Shām* Arghūn Shāh was murdered by his colleague, the *nā'ib Ṭarābulus* as a result of the former's public humiliation of the latter.

27. July 1349: Mutual suspicions and accusations were spread by the amirs Baybughā Rūs and Manjak on the one hand, and by the amirs Ṭāz and Mughulṭāy on the other; eventually, the situation calmed down without any major disruptions.

1350

28. March-June 1350: A quarrel similar to the former ensued between the amir Manjak on the one hand and the amirs Shaykhū and Mughulṭāy on the other.

29. December 1350: The amirs Baybughā Rūs, Manjak and Shaykhū were arrested by order of the maturing al-Nāṣir Ḥasan, and they were imprisoned in Alexandria.

1351

30. February 1351: When he was informed of his imminent arrest, the *nā'ib Ṣafad* rose in rebellion against al-Nāṣir Ḥasan, but gave up when he heard of the arrest of his patron Baybughā Rūs.

31. February-March 1351: The amirs of Aleppo rebelled against the *nā'ib Ḥalab*, who fled to Egypt.

32. August 1351: When the news reached them that the sultan planned their arrest, the senior amirs Ṭāz and Mughulṭāy acted first, arrested al-Nāṣir Ḥasan's major supporters and, consequently, forced the sultan to abdicate in favour of al-Ṣāliḥ Ṣāliḥ.

33. September 1351: The decision to release Shaykhū from prison created so much tension in Cairo, that a harsh fight ensued between the amirs Ṭāz and Ṣarghitmish on the one hand, and the amir Mughulṭāy and his supporters on the other, which was won by the former two.

1352

34. April-May 1352: Rumours triggered a quarrel between the amirs Ṣarghitmish and Ṭāz, which was resolved through the mediation of the amir Shaykhū.

35. August-November 1352: The *nā'ib Ḥalab* Baybughā Rūs staged a rebellion from Syria against the amirs Shaykhū, Ṣarghitmish and Ṭāz, proclaimed himself sultan in Damascus, but had to relinquish this when news arrived that the entire Egyptian army was coming, with the sultan, causing panic and the defection of his supporters; subsequently, Baybughā Rūs and his supporters were arrested and executed.

36. December 1352–February 1353: The amirs Shaykhū and Ṣarghitmish had a long argument over the *wazīr*, a client of the former who had offended the latter.

1353

1354

37. October 1354: Threatened by rumours of their imminent arrests, the amirs Shaykhū and Ṣarghitmish staged a rebellion against the sultan and the amir Ṭāz, outnumbered their supporters and returned al-Nāṣir Ḥasan to the throne, while Ṭaz was sent off to remote Aleppo.

1355

1356

1357

38. July 1357: The attempted murder of the amir Shaykhū failed, but Shaykhū was lethally wounded and died soon afterwards.

1358

39. January 1358: A confrontation between the *nā'ib Ḥalab* Ṭāz and the *nā'ib al-Shām* ʿAlī al-Māridānī, instructed by the amir Ṣarghitmish to escort the former to Egypt, was avoided when, ultimately, Ṭāz gave in, and was arrested without further problems.

40. August 1358: Al-Nāṣir Ḥasan managed to arrest Ṣarghitmish and to send him to Alexandria, where he was murdered; his clients who consequently rose in rebellion, were defeated.

1359

1360

1361

41. March 1361: After mutual intimidations and threats, al-Nāṣir Ḥasan failed to arrest the amir Yalbughā al-Khāṣṣakī and was defeated in an ensuing fight.

42. June-August 1361: The *nā'ib al-Shām* Baydamur al-Khwārizmī staged a rebellion against Yalbughā al-Khāṣṣakī, but lost all support when the sultan and the Egyptian armies approached Damascus.

43. July 1361: During the sultan's and Yalbughā al-Khāṣṣakī's absence, the last remaining son of al-Nāṣir Muḥammad, Ḥusayn, was prompted to rebel and to usurp the sultanate, but he failed and was arrested.

1362

1363

1364

1365

1366

44. February 1366: Yalbughā al-Khāṣṣakī fought off his last remaining rival for Effective Power, the amir Ṭaybughā al-Ṭawīl, and his troops, and sent him to the prison of Alexandria.

45. December 1366: After a prolonged build-up of tension, Yalbughā al-Khāṣṣakī was left by most of his remaining supporters when the sultan and Yalbughā's own mamluks, who had turned against him, managed to return to Cairo; Yalbughā was arrested and subsequently lynched by those mamluks.

1367

46. March 1367: When the arrest of several amirs was imminent, they rose, but failed to overcome the amir Asandamur al-Nāṣirī and his supporters.

47. June 1367: A violent confrontation, won by the amir Asandamur al-Nāṣirī and the Yalbughāwīya mamluks, ensued when the sultan al-Ashraf Shaʿbān and the senior amirs felt threatened; after the fight, which left several casualties, many amirs were arrested and sent to Alexandria.

48. October 1367: When al-Ashraf Shaʿbān was told that Asandamur planned his deposition, he rallied support among the amirs and finally managed to defeat Asandamur; after the intercession of several amirs, Asandamur was given house arrest only.

49. October 1367: The next day, Asandamur managed to rise again, was defeated for the second time, and was arrested and sent to Alexandria, where he soon died.

50. October 1367: Two former supporters of Asandamur, who were made the new *atābak al-ʿasākir* by al-Ashraf Shaʿbān, used their new post to plan the sultan's murder, whereupon they were arrested and sent to Alexandria.

1368

51. June 1368: The *nāʾib Ḥalab* Ṭaybughā al-Ṭawīl was murdered, allegedly by order of al-Ashraf Shaʿbān, as a result of rumours of his imminent rebellion.

1369

1370

1371

52. June 1371: The amir Uljāy al-Yūsufī staged a rebellion against al-Ashraf Shaʿbān, failed, but was pardoned and rehabilitated.

1372

1373

53. July 1373: Upon the demise of his wife, the mother of al-Ashraf Shaʿbān, Uljāy sought to safeguard his position by staging another rebellion against the sultan, but he was, again, outwitted by the latter, and he had to flee and he drowned in the Nile.

1374

1375

54. October 1375: Ṭashtamur al-Dawādār's careful spreading of rumours resulted in the expulsion of a fellow competitor for the sultan's favour.

1376

1377

55. March 1377: On the road to the Hijaz, Ṭashtamur al-Dawādār orchestrated a rebellion of the sultan's mamluks, which obliged al-Ashraf Sha'bān to flee.

56. March 1377: Meanwhile, in Cairo, the sultan's absence was used by the mamluks of his son ʿAlī to spread the false news of al-Ashraf Shaʿbān's death and to proclaim ʿAlī the new sultan; when the hunted al-Ashraf Shaʿbān, therefore, returned, he found no refuge and was killed by his son's supporters.

57. March 1377: When Ṭashtamur al-Dawādār and the sultan's mamluks returned to Cairo and found out what had happened, they fought Qaraṭāy al-Ṭāzī and the others who had enthroned al-Manṣūr ʿAlī, but they were defeated, and Ṭashtamur was sent to Damascus to become *nāʾib al-Shām.*

58. June 1377: The amir Aynabak al-Badrī drugged his patron Qaraṭāy al-Ṭāzī, incapacitated his major supporters and sent them all off to Syria.

59. July 1377: A quarrel ensued between the amir Aynabak al-Badrī and the caliph al-Mutawakkil when the former tried to impose his new candidate for the sultanate, and the latter caliph refused to comply; consequently, al-Mutawakkil was banished and replaced by another, but no new sultan was installed.

60. July 1377: Uncertified rumours of a Syrian rebellion, led by the *nāʾib al-Shām* Ṭashtamur al-Dawādār forced Aynabak al-Badrī to dispatch troops to Syria; they never arrived, because of mutiny and Aynabak's swift fall from power.

61. July 1377: Threatening rumours caused the vanguard of Aynabak's army, the amir Yalbughā al-Nāṣirī in particular, to rise in rebellion against their own commander, so that Aynabak was forced to leave his troops and flee back to Egypt.

62. July 1377: Back in Egypt, several amirs rose against the discredited patron Aynabak, who was soon outnumbered, who thereupon abandoned his supporters, and who then was arrested and sent to the prison of Alexandria.

63. July 1377: When the amir Yalbughā al-Nāṣirī returned from Syria, he managed to arrest the amirs who had defeated Aynabak, and he equally sent them to the prison of Alexandria.

64. August 1377: The amirs Barqūq and Barka arrested a number of amirs, charged with subversive activities.

65. August 1377: After a quarrel between Yalbughā al-Nāṣirī and Barqūq, the latter chased the former amir from his residence in the sultan's stables.

1378

66. February 1378: Barqūq forced a senior amir to step down from his office and to accept a transfer to Syria, but after his departure from Cairo, the latter amir was dismissed and banished.

67. April 1378: The amirs Barqūq en Barka forced Ṭashtamur al-Dawādār into a fight, defeated him and sent him to the prison of Alexandria.

68. April 1378: The amir Yalbughā al-Nāṣirī was cunningly arrested by Barqūq and Barka and sent to Alexandria.

69. July 1378: A senior amir, and large numbers of low-ranking amirs and mamluks were arrested by Barqūq and Barka upon rumours of their plotting, and they were all sent to Alexandria.

1379

70. July 1379: An amir in Aleppo rose in rebellion against the *nā'ib Ḥalab*, but was defeated and forced to flee.

71. November 1379: A rebellion by the amir Īnāl al-Yūsufī against Barqūq resulted in a fight and in the siege of the residence of Barqūq, which ended with the victory of the latter and the arrest of Īnāl, who was sent to the prison of Alexandria.

1380

72. May 1380: Rumours and mutual suspicions caused a quarrel between one of Barqūq's senior clients and the amir Barka, which was only resolved after mediation.

73. June 1380: Growing competition and mutual suspicion erupted in a sequence of fights between the networks of the amirs Barqūq en Barka, in which, eventually, Barka was defeated, arrested and sent to Alexandria, where he was soon murdered.

1381

1382

74. October 1382: One month prior to his enthronement, Barqūq had several low-ranking amirs and dozens of his and of others' mamluks arrested and sent to Alexandria, after he had been informed of their plotting against him.

BIBLIOGRAPHY

Primary Sources

ʿAynī, Badr al-Dīn Maḥmūd al-, *ʿIqd al-Jumān fī Tārīkh Ahl al-Zamān*, Ms. Cairo Dār al-Kutub 1584 *tārīkh*.

Ḥusaynī, Shams al-Dīn Muḥammad b. Ḥamza al-, *Dhayl al-ʿIbar fī Khabar man Ghabar*, ed. M.S. b. Basyūnī Zaghlūl, Beirut 1985.

Ibn Buḥtur, Ṣāliḥ b. Yaḥyā, *Taʾrīkh Bayrūt*, ed. L. Cheikho, *Récits des anciens de la famille de Buḥtur b. ʿAlī, Emir du Gharb de Beyrouth*, (*al-Mashriq* 1, 2), Beirut 1898 ff.—printed Beirut 1902, 1915, 1927.

Ibn Duqmāq, Ṣārim al-Dīn Ibrāhīm b. Muḥammad b. Aydamur, *al-Jawhar al-Thamīn fī siyar al-Khulafāʾ wa al-Mulūk wa al-Salāṭīn*, ed. S.ʿA. ʿĀshūr, Mecca 1982.

——, *Nuzhat al-Anām fī Tārīkh al-Islām*, Oxford Bodleian Ms. Marshall 36.

Ibn al-Jīʿān, Sharaf al-Dīn Yaḥyā, *Kitāb al-Tuḥfa al-saniya bi-asmāʾ al-bilād al-Miṣrīya*, ed. B. Moritz, Cairo 1898 (1974).

Ibn Ḥabīb, al-Ḥasan b. ʿUmar b. al-Ḥasan b. ʿUmar, *Tadhkirat al-Nabīh fī Ayyām al-Manṣūr wa Banīh*, ed. M.M. Amīn, 3 vols., Cairo 1976–1986.

Ibn Ḥajar al-ʿAsqalānī, Shihāb al-Dīn Aḥmad, *al-Durar al-Kāmina fī aʿyān al-miʾa al-thāmina*, ed. H. an-Nadawī, 4 vols., Beirut 1993.

——, *Inbāʾ al-Ghumr bi Abnāʾ al-ʿUmr*, 9 vols., ed. M. ʿAbd al-Muʿīd Khān, Beirut 1986(3).

Ibn al-ʿIrāqī, Walī al-Dīn Aḥmad b. ʿAbd al-Raḥīm b. al-Ḥusayn, *al-Dhayl ʿalā al-ʿIbar fī Khabar man ʿAbar*, 3 vols., ed. S.M. ʿAbbās, Beirut 1989.

Ibn Kathīr, ʿImād al-Dīn ʾIsmāʿīl b. ʿUmar, *al-Bidāya wa al-Nihāya*, 14 vols., Beirut 1990(2).

Ibn Khaldūn, ʿAbd al-Raḥmān, *Kitāb al-ʿIbar wa Dīwān al-Mubtadā wa al-Khabar fī ayyām al-ʿArab wa al-ʿAjam wa al-Barbar wa man ʿāṣarahum min dhawī al-sulṭān al-akbar*, ed. N. al-Hārūnī, 7 vols., Cairo 1867–1868.

Ibn Nāẓir al-Jaysh, Taqī al-Dīn ʿAbd al-Raḥmān b. Muḥammad, *Kitāb Tathqīf al-Taʿrīf bi-al-Muṣṭalaḥ al-Sharīf*, ed. R. Vesely, (*Textes arabes et études islamiques* 27), Cairo 1987.

Ibn Qāḍī Shuhba, Taqī al-Dīn Abū Bakr b. Aḥmad, *Tārīkh Ibn Qāḍī Shuhba*, 3 vols., ed. A. Darwich, (*Publications de l'Institut Français de Damas* 101, 145, 146), Damascus 1977–1994.

Ibn al-Shihna, Zayn al-Dīn, *Rawḍat al-Manāẓir fī ʿIlm al-Awāʾil wa al-Awākhir*, Ms. London British Library Oriental and India Office Collection or. 1618.

Ibn al-Shihna, Muḥibb al-Dīn, *Al-Durr al-Muntakhab fī Tārīkh mamlakat Ḥalab*, ed. K. Ohta, *The History of Aleppo, known as ad-Durr al-Muntakhab by Ibn ash-Shiḥna*, (*Studiae Culturae Islamicae* 40), Tokyo 1990.

Ibn Taghrī Birdī, Jamāl al-Dīn Abū al-Maḥāsin Yūsuf, *al-Manhal al-Ṣāfī wa al-Mustawfī baʿda al-Wāfī*, ed. M.M. Amīn, vol. I–(X), Cairo 1986–(2002).

——, *al-Nujūm al-Ẓāhira fī Mulūk Miṣr wa al-Qāhira*, ed. I.ʿA. Ṭarkhān, 16 vols., Cairo 1963–1972.

Ibn al-Wardī, Zayn al-Dīn ʿUmar, *Tatimmat al-Mukhtaṣar fī Akhbār al-Bashar*, in al-Malik al-Muʾayyad ʿImād al-Dīn Abū al-Fidāʾ, *Tārīkh Abū al-Fidāʾ al-musammā al-Mukhtaṣar fī ʾAkhbār al-Bashar*, ed. M. Dayyūb, Beirut 1997, vol. 2, pp. 449–522.

Kutubī, Ṣalāḥ al-Dīn Muḥammad b. Shākir b. ʾAḥmad al-, *ʿUyūn al-Tawārīḫ*, Cambridge University Library Ms. Add. 2923 (9).
Maqrīzī, Aḥmad b. ʿAlī al-, *al-Mawāʿiẓ wa al-Iʿtibār bi dhikr al-Khiṭaṭ wa* l-Āthār, 4 vols., Cairo 1996.
——, *Kitāb al-Sulūk li Maʿrifat Duwal al-Mulūk*, vols. I–II, ed. M. M. Ziyāda, Cairo 1956–1958; vols. III–IV, ed. S.A.F. ʿĀshūr, Cairo 1970–1973.
Mufaḍḍal Ibn ʾAbī al-Faḍāʾil, *Kitāb al-Nahj al-sadīd wa al-durr al-farīd fīmā baʿda taʾrīkh Ibn al-ʿAmīd*, ed. S. Kortantamer, *Ägypten und Syrien zwischen 1317 und 1341 in der Chronik des Mufaddal b. Abi l-Fadāʾil*, (*Islamkundliche Untersuchungen* 23), Freiburg i. Br. 1973.
Nuwayrī, Shihāb al-Dīn al-, *Nihāyat al-Arab fī Funūn al-Adab*, 33 vols., Cairo 1931–1998.
Nuwayrī, Muḥammad al-Iskandarānī al-, *al-Ilmām bimā jarat bihi al-Aḥkām wa al-Umūr al-maqḍiya fī Waqʿat al-Iskandirīya sana 767 h.*, ed. A.S. Atiya, 7 vols., Hyderabad 1968–1973.
Qalqashandī, Shihāb al-Dīn Aḥmad al-, *Ṣubḥ al-Aʿshā fī Ṣināʿat al-Inshāʾ*, 14 vols., Cairo 1913–1919.
Ṣafadī, Ṣalāḥ ad-Dīn Khalīl b. Aybak al-, *Kitāb al-Wāfī bi-al-Wafayāt*, vol. I–(XXIX), (*Bibliotheca Islamica* 6), Istanbul-Damaskus-Wiesbaden-Beirut-Stuttgart-Berlin 1949–(1999).
——, *Aʿyān al-ʿAṣr wa Aʿwān al-Naṣr*, eds. ʿA. Abū Zayd, N. Abū ʿUmsha, M. Muwʿad & M. Sālim Muḥammad, 6 vols., Beirut-Damascus 1998.
Shujāʿī, Shams al-Dīn al-, *Taʾrīkh al-Malik al-Nāṣir Muḥammad ibn Qalāwūn al-Ṣāliḥī wa Awlādihi*, ed. B. Schäfer, vol. 1, Wiesbaden 1977.
ʿUmarī, Shihāb al-Dīn Aḥmad b. Yaḥyā b. Faḍl Allāh al-, *al-Taʿrīf bi-al-Muṣṭalaḥ al-Sharīf*, ed. M.Á. Shams al-Dīn, Beirut 1988.
——, *Masālik al-Abṣār fī Mamālik al-Amṣār*, ed. A.F. Sayyid, (*Textes arabes et études islamiques* 23), Cairo 1985.
Ẓāhirī, Ghars al-Dīn Khalīl Ibn Shāhīn al-, *Kitāb Zubdat Kashf al-Mamālik fī Bayān al-Ṭuruq wa al-Masālik*, ed. Paul Ravaisse, Paris 1894.
Zettersteen, K., *Beiträge zur Geschichte der Mamlūkensultane in den Jahre 690–741 der Higga nach arabischen Handschriften herausgegeben*, Leiden 1919.

Secondary Sources

Amitai-Preiss, *Mongols and Mamluks. The Mamluk-Ilkhanid war, 1260–1281*, (*Cambridge Studies in Islamic Civilization*), Cambridge 1995.
Ashqar, M.ʿA., al-, *Nāʾib al-salṭana al-mamlūkīya fī Miṣr (648–923 h./1250–1517 m.)*, (*tārīkh al-miṣrīyīn* 158), Cairo 1999.
ʿAṭāʾ Allāh, M., *Niyābat Ghazza fī al-ʿAhd al-Mamlūkī*, Beirut 1986.
Ayalon, D., "The Circassians in the Mamlūk Kingdom", *Journal of the American Oriental Society* 69/3 (1949), pp. 135–147.
——, *L'Esclavage du Mamelouk*, (*Oriental Notes and Studies* 1), Jerusalem 1951.
——, "Studies on the Structure of the Mamluk Army", *BSOAS* 15 (1953), pp. 203–228, 448–476; 16 (1954), pp. 57–90.
——, "The System of Payment in Mamluk Military Society", *JESHO* 1 (1958), pp. 37–65, 257–296.
——, "The Muslim City and the Mamluk Military Aristocracy", *Proceedings of the Israel Academy of Sciences and Humanities* 2 (1968), pp. 311–329.
——, "Mamluk: Military Slavery in Egypt and Syria", in D. Ayalon, *Islam and the Abode of War*, Aldershot 1994, II.

——, "Mamluk Military Aristocracy, a Non-Hereditary Nobility", *Jerusalem Studies of Arabic and Islam* 10 (1987), pp. 205–210.
——, "Bahri Mamluks, Burji Mamluks—inadequate names for the two reigns of the Mamluk Sultanate", *Tārīkh* 1 (1990), pp. 3–53.
Björkman, W., *Beiträge zur Geschichte der Staatskanzlei im Islamischen Ägypten*, Hamburg 1928.
Brinner, W.M., "The Struggle for Power in the Mamluk State: Some Reflections on the Transition from Bahri to Burji Rule", *Proceedings of the 26th International Congress of Orientalists, New Delhi, 4–10 January 1964*, New Delhi 1970, pp. 231–234.
Borsch, St.J., *The Black Death in Egypt and England. A Comparative Study*, Austin 2005.
Chamberlain, M., *Knowledge and Social Practice in Medieval Damascus, 1190–1350*, (Cambridge Studies in Islamic Civilization), Cambridge 1995.
Chapoutot-Remadi, M., "Liens propres et identités séparées chez les Mamelouks bahrides", in Chr. Décobert (ed.), *Valeur et distance. Identités et sociétés en Egypte*, (*Collection de l'atelier méditerranéen*), Paris 2000, pp. 175–188.
Chapoutot-Remadi, R., "Liens et Relations au sein de l'Élite Mamluke sous les Premiers Sultans Bahrides, 648/1250–741/1341", unpublished Ph.D. thesis, Université de Provence. Aix-Marseille I 1993.
Clifford, W.W., "State Formation and the Structure of Politics in Mamluk Syro-Egypt, 648–741 AH/1250–1340 CE", unpublished Ph.D. thesis, University of Chicago 1995.
——, "Ubi Sumus? Mamluk History and Social Theory", *MSR* 1 (1997), pp. 45–62.
Duhmān, M.A., *Wulāt Dimashq fi ʿahd al-mamālīk*, Damascus 1963 (1984).
Eddé, A., "Quelques institutions militaires ayyoubides", in U. Vermeulen & D. De Smet (eds.), *Egypt and Syria in the Fatimid, Ayyubid and Mamluk Eras*, (*Orientalia Lovaniensia Analecta* 73), Leuven 1995, pp. 163–174.
Fernandes, L., "On conducting the affairs of the state: a guideline of the fourteenth century", *AI* 24 (1988), pp. 81–91.
Forand, P., "The Relation of the Slave and the Client to the Master or Patron in Medieval Islam", *IJMES* 2 (1977), pp. 59–66.
Garcin, J.-Cl., *Un centre musulman de la haute Égypte médiévale: Qūs*, Cairo 1976.
——, "Habitat médiéval et histoire urbaine à Fusṭāṭ et au Caire", in J.-C. Garcin, B. Maury, J. Revault & M. Zakariya (eds.), *Palais et maisons du Caire, I: Époque mamelouke (XIIIe–XVIe siècles)*, Paris 1982, pp. 145–216.
Gaudefroy-Demombynes, M., *La Syrie à l'Époque des Mamelouks*, (*Bibliothèque Archéologique et Historique* 3), Paris 1923 (Frankfurt 1993).
Haarmann, U., "Arabic in speech, Turkish in lineage: Mamluks and their sons in the intellecual life of fourteenth century Egypt and Syria", *JSS* 33 (1988), pp. 81–114.
——, "The sons of Mamluks as Fief-Holders in Late Medieval Egypt", in T. Khalidi (ed.), *Land Tenure and Social Transformation in the Middle East*, Beirut 1984, pp. 141–168.
——, "Joseph's Law—the careers and activities of mamluk descendants before the Ottoman conquest of Egypt" in Th. Philipp & U. Haarmann (eds.), *The Mamluks in Egyptian Politics and Society*, (*Cambridge Studies in Islamic Civilization*), Cambridge 1998, pp. 55–84.
——, al-, "al-Aḥwāl al-Dākhilīya fi salṭanat al-Ashraf Shaʿbān b. Ḥusayn b. Muḥammad b. Qalāwūn. 764–778 h./1362–1376 m.", *ʿĀlam al-Fikr* 3/3 (1983), pp. 761–822.
——, "al-Amīr Qawṣūn: ṣūra ḥayya li-niẓām al-ḥukm fi salṭanat al-mamālīk", *al-majalla al-ʿarabīya li-al-ʿulūm al-insānīya* 8/32 (1988), pp. 6–55.
Halm, H., *Ägypten nach den mamlukischen Lehensregistern*, (*Beihäfte zum Tübinger Atlas des Vorderen Orients, Reihe B: Geisteswissenschaften* 382), 2 vols., Wiesbaden 1979–1982.

Hathaway, J., *The Politics of Households in Ottoman Egypt. The Rise of the Qazdaglis*, Cambridge 1997.

——, "Mamluk Households and Mamluk Factions in Ottoman Egypt: a reconsideration", in Th. Phillip & U. Haarmann (eds.), *The Mamluks in Egyptian Politics and Society*, (*Cambridge Studies in Islamic Civilisation*), Cambridge 1998, pp. 107–117.

Holt, P.M., "The position and power of the Mamlūk Sultan", *BSOAS* 38/2 (1975), pp. 237–249.

——, "The Structure of government in the Mamluk sultanate", in P.M. Holt (ed.), *Eastern Mediterranean Lands in the Period of the Crusades*, Warminster 1977, pp. 44–61.

——, *The Age of the Crusades: The Near East from the Eleventh Century to 1517*, (*A History of the Near East*), London 1986.

——, "an-Nāṣir Muḥammad b. Qalāwūn (684–741/1258–1341) : his Ancestry, Kindred and Affinity", in U. Vermeulen & D. De Smet (eds.), *Egypt and Syria in the Fatimid, Ayyubid and Mamluk Eras*, (*Orientalia Lovaniensia Analecta* 73), Leuven 1995, pp. 313–324.

Humphreys, R.St., "Egypt in the world system of the later Middle Ages", in C.F. Petry (ed.), *The Cambridge History of Egypt, Volume 1, Islamic Egypt, 640–1517*, Cambridge 1998, pp. 453–454.

——, "The Politics of the Mamluk Sultanate: A Review Essay", *MSR* 9/1 (2005), pp. 221–231.

Ibrahim, L.A., "The great Ḫanqah of the Emir Qawṣūn in Cairo", *Mitteilungen des Deutschen Archäologischen Instituts Abteilung Kairo* 30/1 (1974), pp. 37–64.

Irwin, R., *The Middle East in the Middle Ages: The Early Mamluk Sultanate 1250–1382*, London 1986.

——, "Factions in medieval Islam", *JRAS* (1986), pp. 228–246.

Krebs, W., "Innen- und Außenpolitik Ägyptens 741–784/1341–1382", unpublished Ph.D. thesis, University of Hamburg, 1980.

Lapidus, I.M., *Muslim Cities in the Later Middle Ages*, Cambridge (Mass.) 1967.

Levanoni, A., "The Mamluks' Ascent to Power in Egypt', *SI* 72 (1990), pp. 121–144

——, "The Mamluk Conception of the Sultanate", *IJMES* 26 (1994), pp. 373–392

——, *A Turning Point in Mamluk History: The third reign of al-Nāsir Muḥammad ibn Qalāwūn (1310–1341)*, (*Islamic History and Civilization: Studies and Texts* 10), Leiden 1995.

——, "Rank-and-file Mamluks versus amirs: new norms in the Mamluk military institution", in Th. Philipp & U. Haarmann (eds.), *The Mamluks in Egyptian Politics and Society*, Cambridge 1998, pp. 17–31.

——, "Al-Maqrīzī's account of the Transition from Turkish to Circassian Mamluk Sultanate: History in the Service of Faith", in H. Kennedy (ed.), *The Historiography of Islamic Egypt (C. 950–1800)*, (*The Medieval Mediterranean. Peoples, Economies and Cultures, 400–1453* 31), Leiden-Boston-Köln 2001, pp. 93–105.

——, "The Sultan's Laqab—A Sign of a New Order in Mamluk Factionalism?", in A. Levanoni & M. Winter (eds.), *The Mamluks in Egyptian and Syrian Politics and Society*, (*The Medieval Mediterranean. Peoples, Economies and Cultures, 400–1453* 51), Leiden-Boston-Köln 2004, pp. 143–161.

Little, D.P., "An analysis of the Relationship between Four Mamluk Chronicles for 737–745", *JSS* 19 (1974), pp. 252–268.

——, "Historiography of the Ayyubid and Mamluk epochs", in C.F. Petry (ed.), *The Cambridge History of Egypt, Volume 1, Islamic Egypt, 640–1517*, Cambridge 1998, pp. 412–444.

Lopez, M., H. Miskinin & A. Udovitch, "England to Egypt, 1350–1500: Long-term Trends and Long-distance Trade", in M. Cook (ed.), *Studies in the Economic History of the Middle East*, London 1970, pp. 93–128.

Marmon, Sh.E., "The quality of mercy: intercession in mamluk society", *SI* 87/2 (1998), pp. 125–139.

Martel-Thoumian, B., *Les Civils et l'Administration dans l'État Mamluk (IX/XVe siècle)*, Damas 1991.
——, "Les élites urbaines sous les Mamlouks circassiens: quelques éléments de réflexion", in U. Vermeulen & J. Van Steenbergen (eds.), *Egypt and Syria in the Fatimid, Ayyubid and Mamluk Eras III*, (*Orientalia Lovaniensia Analecta* 102), Leuven 2001, pp. 271–308.
Miura, T., "Administrative Networks in the Mamluk Period: Taxation, Legal Execution, and Bribery", in S. Tsugitaka (ed.), *Islamic urbanism in human history: political power and social networks*, London 1997, p. 39–76.
Nielsen, J.S., *Secular Justice in an Islamic State: Maẓālim under the Bahri Mamluks*, Istanbul 1985.
Northrup, L.S., *From Slave to Sultan: the career of al-Manṣūr Qalāwūn and the consolidation of Mamluk rule in Egypt and Syria (678–689 AH/ 1279–1290 AD)*, (*Freiburger Islamstudien* 18), Stuttgart 1998.
——, "The Bahri Mamluk Sultanate, 1250–1390", in Carl F. Petry (ed.), *The Cambridge History of Egypt, Volume 1, Islamic Egypt, 640–1517*, Cambridge 1998, pp. 242–289.
Petry, C.F., *The civilian elite of Cairo in the Later Middle Ages*, Princeton 1981.
——, *Protectors or Praetorians? The Last Mamluk Sultans and Egypt's Waning as a great Power*, New York 1994.
Rabbat, N.O., "Representing the Mamluks in Mamluk Historical Writing", in H. Kennedy (ed.), *The Historiography of Islamic Egypt (C. 950–1800)*, (*The Medieval Mediterranean. Peoples, Economies and Cultures, 400–1453* 31), Leiden-Boston-Köln 2001, pp. 59–75.
Rabie, H., *The Financial System of Egypt (1169–1341)*, London 1972.
Richards, D.S., "Mamluk amirs and their families and households", in Th. Philipp & U. Haarmann (eds.), *The Mamluks in Egyptian Politics and Society*, Cambridge 1998, pp. 32–54.
Sato, T., "The evolution of the *iqṭāʿ* system under the Mamluks—an analysis of ar-Rawk al-Ḥusāmī and ar-Rawk an-Nāṣirī", *Memoirs Research Dept. Toyo Bunko* 37 (1979), pp. 99–131.
——, *State and Rural Society in Medieval Islam. Sultans, Muqtaʿs and Fallahun*, (*Islamic History and Civilization. Studies and Texts* 17), Leiden 1997.
Shoshan, B., "Grain Riots and Moral Economy: Cairo 1350–1517", *Journal of Interdisciplinary History* 10/3 (1980), pp. 459–478.
——, "The Politics of Notables in Medieval Islam", *Asian and African Studies: Journal of the Israel Oriental Society* 20 (1986), pp. 179–215.
Surūr, M.J., *Dawlat Banī Qalāwūn fī Miṣr. al-ḥāla al-siyāsiya wa al-iqtiṣādīya fī ʿahdihā bi wajh khāṣṣ*, Cairo 1947
Tarawneh, T.Th., *The Province of Damascus during the Second Mamluk Period (748/ 1382–922/1516)*, Indiana 1987.
Van Steenbergen, J., "The Amir Qawṣūn, Statesman or Courtier? (720–741 AH/1320–1340 AD), in U. Vermeulen & J. Van Steenbergen (eds.), *Egypt and Syria in the Fatimid, Ayyubid and Mamluk Eras III*, (*Orientalia Lovaniensia Analecta* 102), Leuven 2001, pp. 449–466.
——, "The office of *Nā'ib as-salṭana* of Damascus: 741–784/1341–1382, A Case Study", in U. Vermeulen & J. Van Steenbergen (eds.), *Egypt and Syria in the Fatimid, Ayyubid and Mamluk Eras III*, (*Orientalia Lovaniensia Analecta* 102), Leuven 2001, pp. 429–448.
——, "Mamluk Elite on the Eve of al-Nāṣir Muḥammad's death (1341): A Look Behind the Scenes of Mamluk Politics", *MSR* 9/2 (2005), pp. 173–199.
Wiederhold, Lutz, "Legal-Religious Elite, Temporal Authority, and the Caliphate in Mamluk Society: Conclusions drawn from the examination of a Ẓāhirī Revolt in Damascus in 1386", *IJMES* 31 (1999), pp. 203–235.

Ze'evi, D., "My Slave, My Son, My Lord: Slavery, Family and State in the Islamic Middle East", in M. Toru & J.E. Phillips (eds.), *Slave Elites in the Middle East and Africa*, (*Islamic Area Studies*), London-New York 2000, pp. 71–80.

Ziadeh, N.A., *Urban Life in Syria under the Early Mamlūks*, Westport (Connecticut) 1970.

INDEX

Abbasid 24, 132
ʿAbd Allāh 83
ʿabīd 17
Abū Bakr b. Muḥammad b. Qalāwūn, al-Manṣūr 23, 24, 29, 66, 73, 78, 85, 91, 102, 103, 107, 116, 130, 137, 141, 144, 145, 147, 148, 150, 175, 177
Aghizlū al-Sayfī 105, 108, 112, 134, 145, 152, 177, 189, 190, 191
Aḥmad b. ʿAbd Allāh b. al-Malik al-ʿĀdil Kitbughā 80
Aḥmad b. Ḥasan b. Muḥammad b. Qalāwūn 25
Aḥmad b. Humuz al-Turkumānī 99, 126
Aḥmad b. Muḥammad b. Qalāwūn, al-Nāṣir 19, 24, 29, 102, 103, 104, 107, 113, 115, 130, 131, 135, 137, 143, 145, 147, 148, 149, 151, 175, 178, 189, 190
Aḥmad b. Yalbughā al-Khāṣṣakī 119
Aḥmad Shādd al-Shirābkhānāh 105
Alākuz al-Kashlāwī 59
Aleppo 35, 39, 42, 78, 79, 136, 138, 156, 192, 196
Alexandria 99, 115, 127, 133, 191, 193, 194, 195, 196
ʿAlī al-Anṣārī, *see raʾs nawba*
ʿAlī b. Kalfat, ʿAlāʾ al-Dīn 112
ʿAlī b. Shaʿbān b. Ḥusayn b. Muḥammad b. Qalāwūn, al-Manṣūr 29, 33, 48, 72, 96, 117, 119, 121, 135, 136, 163, 164, 165, 166, 168, 175, 195
ʿAlī al-Māridānī 109, 112, 178, 193
Allān al-Shaʿbānī 126
Almalik al-Jūkandār 104, 105, 108, 112, 178, 190
Alṭunbughā al-Dawādār, ʿAlāʾ al-Dīn 59, 61–62
Alṭunbughā al-Māridānī 69
Alṭunbughā al-Nāṣirī, ʿAlāʾ al-Dīn 62, 140, 141, 143
alzām (adherents) 59
amirate 15, 20, 27, 33, 38, 49, 50
amīr ākhūr 40, 43, 50, 97, 166, 168, 179, 180, 181, 184, 188
amīr ʿashara (amir of ten) 34, 46, 47, 59, 63, 69, 71, 80, 112, 179, 180, 181, 184, 185, 186
Amīr Ḥājj, *see* Ḥājjī b. Shaʿbān b. Ḥusayn b. Muḥammad b. Qalāwūn, al-Ṣāliḥ
Amīr Ḥājj b. Mughulṭāy 99
amīr jāndār 40, 184, 187
amīr majlis 40, 50, 168, 181, 182, 187, 188
amīr miʾa (amir of a hundred) 34, 48, 50, 63, 71, 75, 79, 81, 87, 96, 103, 105, 111, 152, 165, 166, 177, 178, 179, 180, 181, 182, 183, 184, 185, 186, 187, 188
amir of a hundred, *see amīr miʾa*
amir of forty, *see amīr ṭablakhānāh*
amir of ten, *see amīr ʿashara*
amīr silāḥ 40, 177, 187, 188
amīr ṭablakhānāh (amir of forty) 34, 47, 50, 63, 71, 79, 80, 81, 87, 88, 112, 177, 178, 179, 180, 181, 182, 183, 184, 185, 186, 187, 188
Anaṣ al-Ghasānī 82
Angus, *see amīr ākhūr*
Anna, *see* Ṭulubāy
Anūk b. Ḥusayn b. Muḥammad b. Qalāwūn, al-Manṣūr 117
appointment (to appoint) 28, 39, 41, 42, 44, 61, 63, 64, 67, 68, 69, 70, 71, 93, 102, 103, 105, 106, 107, 111, 116, 119, 121, 125, 152, 168
Aqbughā ʿAbd al-Wāḥid 78, 83, 103
Aqbughā Sīwān al-Ṣāliḥī 99, 126
Aqsunqur al-Nāṣirī 66, 114, 115, 179, 190, 191
Aqsunqur al-Salārī 83, 145
Aqtamur ʿAbd al-Ghanī 118
arbāb al-suyūf (men of the sword) 38
Arghūn al-ʿAlāʾī 61, 70, 83, 84, 104, 110, 113, 119, 135, 137, 150, 151, 152, 179, 190
Arghūn al-Kāmilī 79, 81, 83
Arghūn Shāh al-Nāṣirī 42, 56, 64, 70, 74, 75, 83, 90, 91, 190, 191
Ariqṭāy 62
Arlān 54
Armenia 20

Asandamur al-Nāṣirī 64, 71, 120, 123, 128, 131, 132, 135, 138, 139, 161, 162, 179, 194
aṣḥāb (fellows, companions) 59
al-Ashraf Kujuk b. Muḥammad b. Qalāwūn, *see* Kujuk b. Muḥammad b. Qalāwūn, al-Ashraf
al-Ashraf Shaʿbān b. Ḥusayn b. Muḥammad b. Qalāwūn, *see* Shaʿbān b. Ḥusayn b. Muḥammad b. Qalāwūn, al-Ashraf
Aswan 162
atābak al-ʿasākir 44, 45, 50, 54, 65, 109, 110, 111, 117, 118, 120, 136, 166, 168, 179, 180, 181, 183, 184, 185, 186, 187, 188, 194
atbāʿ (followers) 59
awlād al-nās 20, 21, 77, 78, 106
Ayalon, David 93
Ayāz al-Nāṣirī 59
Aydamur al-Khaṭāʾī 99
Aydamur al-Shamsī 118
Aydughmish al-Nāṣirī, ʿAlāʾ al-Dīn 43, 70, 94, 113, 148, 180, 189
Aynabak al-Badrī 64, 81, 84, 97, 98, 117, 118, 119, 120, 124, 132, 133, 135, 138, 164, 165, 166, 180, 195
al-ʿAynī 12, 13, 25, 29, 70, 103, 106, 119, 145, 148, 155
Aytmish al-Bajāsī 121, 125, 126, 133, 144, 168
Aywān 88
Ayyūb, al-Ṣāliḥ 6
Ayyubid 6, 76, 95, 124, 129
bāb (portal) 97

Bāb al-Futūḥ 126
Bāb al-Qanṭara 126
Bāb Zuwayla 126
Bahādur al-Damurdāshī 61, 85, 104, 110, 112, 180
Bahādur al-Jamālī 118
Baktamur al-Muʾminī 83
Baljak 81
Barka al-Jūbānī 44, 54, 61, 63, 64, 73, 74, 88, 91, 98, 99, 100, 120, 123, 124, 125, 126, 133, 138, 141, 143, 144, 165, 166, 167, 181, 195, 196
Barka Khan, al-Saʿīd 23
Barqūq al-ʿUthmānī 1, 4, 8, 17, 23, 26, 29, 37, 44, 54, 56, 61, 63, 64, 67, 69, 72, 73, 74, 81, 82, 84, 88, 92, 93, 98, 109, 110, 117, 120, 121, 122, 123, 124, 125, 126, 127, 133, 134, 136, 138, 139, 141, 143, 144, 145, 146, 147, 164, 165, 166, 167, 168, 172, 181, 195, 196
barrānīya, see khārijīya
Bashtak 88, 103, 125, 133, 145
Bashtak al-ʿUmarī 85, 145
bayʿa (oath of allegiance) 24, 26
Baybars, al-Ẓāhir 23, 172
Baybars al-Jāshnikīr, al-Muẓaffar 23
Baybughā al-Qawṣūnī 112
Baybughā Rūs 54, 80, 87, 111, 113, 114, 115, 119, 131, 136, 145, 154, 156, 181, 191, 192
Baybughā al-Sābiqī 166
Baybughā Tatar 54
Baydamur al-Badrī 70, 83, 191
Baydamur al-Khwārizmī 42, 43, 60, 66, 76, 133, 141, 193
Baygharā al-Nāṣirī 54, 83
bayt (household) 7, 8, 26, 30, 32, 40, 41, 46, 94, 95, 96, 97, 98, 103, 104, 106, 107, 109, 113, 114, 116, 117, 118, 119, 120, 122, 135, 146, 151, 152, 153, 157, 159, 160, 161, 165, 166, 168, 169, 170, 177
benefit, *see niʿma*
Black Death 77, 80
bribery (*barṭala*) 73
brother 22, 24, 31, 33, 72, 79, 81, 84, 85, 86, 87, 88, 90, 95, 99, 102, 104, 105, 110, 111, 114, 116, 117, 118, 119, 135, 136, 145, 149, 150, 151, 153, 154, 155, 157, 164, 190, 191
brotherhood, *see ukhūwa*
Bukā al-Khiḍrī 135, 140
Burāq b. Baldāʿī al-Ṭaṭarī 80

Cairo 18, 21, 38, 40, 41, 43, 49, 69, 88, 99, 104, 116, 126, 129, 130, 137, 149, 154, 156, 159, 162, 163, 167, 189, 192, 193, 195, 196
caliphate (caliph, caliphal) 15, 23, 24, 132, 136, 195
Chain Gate (Bāb al-Silsila) 97
Chamberlain, Michael 124
Circassian 92, 93, 94, 105, 109, 120
citadel (of Cairo) 17, 38, 40, 95, 97, 98, 118, 120, 126, 136, 140, 168, 189, 190
client 57, 58, 59, 60, 61, 62, 63, 64, 65, 66, 67, 68, 70, 72, 73, 74, 75, 76, 77, 78, 79, 83, 84, 85, 86, 87,

88, 89, 93, 94, 95, 98, 100, 101, 103, 104, 105, 108, 109, 110, 112, 116, 117, 120, 123, 129, 130, 137, 139, 143, 144, 155, 156, 157, 160, 162, 164, 165, 169, 170, 171, 192, 193, 196
Clifford, Winslow 62, 124
common people 16, 17, 125, 126, 140
communication 142
compete, competition, competitive 8, 129, 130, 137, 140, 146, 147, 155, 156, 166, 167, 170, 194, 196
conflict (conflicts) 6, 8, 16, 17, 18, 19, 66, 123, 124, 125, 127, 128, 129, 130, 132, 133, 134, 135, 136, 137, 139, 142, 143, 144, 146, 147, 148, 150, 152, 154, 155, 157, 158, 159, 161, 162, 164, 165, 167, 169, 170, 171, 172, 177, 189–196
conservatism, conservative 25, 26, 37, 38, 50, 136, 171, 172
credibility 68, 86, 141, 142, 143
Crusaders 19

dabbara (*tadbīr*) 54, 61
Damascus 27, 35, 39, 46, 56, 62, 63, 78, 87, 124, 129, 140, 141, 156, 191, 192, 193, 195
dawādār 40, 50, 56, 61, 71, 111, 127, 168, 186
Dāwūd b. Asad al-Qaymarī 73
de Mignanelli, Bertrando 84
demilitarisation 6, 20, 21, 22, 23
al-Dhahabī 11
dīwān al-badhl (venalities' bureau) 32
dīnār jayshī (currency of account) 31, 47, 48, 62
dīwān al-khāṣṣ (fisc's bureau) 32
Duqmāq 81

Effective Power 7, 8, 53, 54, 55, 56, 58, 60, 61, 62, 65, 68, 70, 71, 74, 76, 82, 84, 85, 88, 89, 95, 97, 98, 100, 101, 104, 106, 107, 108, 109, 110, 111, 113, 116, 118, 121, 123, 124, 128, 129, 132, 134, 135, 136, 145, 146, 147, 149, 151, 153, 156, 160, 170, 172, 177, 189, 193
ethnicity, *see jinsīya*
eunuchs 20, 22, 59
exchange 62, 65, 72, 79, 80, 122, 123, 137, 169

Fāḍil 114
al-Fakhrī, *see* Quṭlūbughā al-Fakhrī
Faraj (b. Barqūq) 23
favour, *see niʿma*
fisc, *see khāṣṣ*
fitna (disorder) 127

Gazza 35
Ghārib al-Ashrafī 99
governor, *see nāʾib*
guardian, guardianship 54, 69, 119, 120, 122, 149, 154, 159, 165, 166

ḥājib 72, 112
ḥājib al-ḥujjāb 40, 183, 187
Ḥājjī b. Muḥammad b. Qalāwūn, al-Muẓaffar 24, 29, 32, 56, 63, 64, 70, 73, 93, 94, 102, 105, 107, 108, 109, 114, 115, 132, 150, 152, 153, 154, 173, 175, 182, 190, 191
Ḥājjī b. Shaʿbān b. Ḥusayn b. Muḥammad b. Qalāwūn, al-Ṣāliḥ 72, 85, 119, 120, 136, 168, 175
al-ḥall wa al-ʿaqd 54
ḥalqa 17, 62, 67, 78
Hama 35
ḥarāfish 17
Ḥasan b. Muḥammad b. Qalāwūn, al-Nāṣir 18, 21, 25, 29, 30, 32, 33, 53, 54, 56, 59, 63, 66, 72, 74, 81, 84, 85, 92, 96, 97, 102, 106, 107, 109, 111, 112, 113, 114, 115, 116, 117, 119, 120, 131, 132, 133, 138, 144, 145, 154, 155, 156, 157, 158, 159, 160, 161, 171, 172, 175, 182, 191, 192, 193
Hathaway, Jane 95
heredity 23, 24, 80
Hijaz 129, 163, 195
ḥilf (mutual oath) 24
household, *see bayt*
Hugh, *see atābak al-ʿasākir*
Ḥusām al-Dīn al-Bashmaqdār 140
Ḥusayn b. Muḥammad b. Qalāwūn, al-Amjad 25, 135, 193
al-Ḥusaynīya 140

Ibn Bahādur al-Muʾminī 13
Ibn Bākhil 61
Ibn Duqmāq 12, 13, 20, 112, 118
Ibn al-Furāt 13
Ibn Ḥajar al-ʿAsqalānī 10, 13, 59, 73, 92, 93, 168

Ibn al-Jīʿān, *see Tuḥfa al-Saniya*
Ibn Kathīr 11, 46, 85, 140, 143, 156
Ibn Khaldūn 13, 120, 141–142, 165
Ibn Qāḍī Shuhba 71, 79, 89, 92, 93, 99, 114, 118, 124, 139
Ibn Taghrī Birdī 11, 29, 41, 63, 71, 74, 82, 92, 93, 111, 115, 121, 136, 157, 168
Ibrāhīm b. Alṭunqush 80
Ilkhans, Ilkhanid 19, 22, 27
Ilyās al-Mājārī 99
Īnāl al-Yūsufī 66, 121, 138, 196
individual (individuals) 6, 7, 8, 15, 55, 57, 58, 60, 62, 68, 70, 76, 100, 123, 127, 128, 134, 158, 169, 170, 171
institution (institutions, institutional) 5, 6, 7, 15, 16, 22, 23, 26, 33, 37, 38, 41, 45, 48, 49, 50, 53, 54, 57, 58, 65, 68, 71, 74, 80, 82, 96, 101, 104, 107, 117, 118, 120, 162, 164, 167, 169, 170
intercession, *see shafāʿa*
intimidation 142, 143, 144
intiqāḍ (collapse) 127
iqṭāʿ 20, 45, 46, 47, 48, 62, 63, 64, 65, 67, 68, 74, 78, 80, 82, 90, 96, 112, 114, 117, 121, 138, 156, 159, 165
Ismāʿīl b. Muḥammad b. Qalāwūn, al-Ṣāliḥ 20, 24, 32, 56, 59, 63, 84, 85, 95, 102, 104, 105, 107, 108, 110, 112, 113, 147, 149, 150, 151, 153, 154, 158, 175, 182, 190
Ittifāq 152

jamdārīya 50
Jankalī b. al-Bābā 83–84
Jaridamur 75, 117
Jariktamur al-Manjakī 89
Jarkas al-Khalīlī 168
jinsīya (ethnicity) 92, 93, 94
Jirjī al-Idrīsī 115
Jonas, *see* Yūnus
Jūbān 59
al-Jūbānī 168
Julbān al-ʿAlāʾī 83

al-Kabsh 161
Kāmilīya (mamluks of al-Kāmil Shaʿbān) 152
al-Kāmil Shaʿbān b. Muḥammad b. Qalāwūn, *see* Shaʿbān b. Muḥammad b. Qalāwūn, al-Kāmil
al-Karak 19, 35, 104, 130, 137, 149, 151, 189, 190
Karakians 104
kāshif (governor of Upper or Lower Egypt) 39
Kashlā 59
Khalīl b. ʿAlī b. ʿArrām 42, 83
Khalīl b. ʿAlī b. Salār 80
Khalīl b. Qawṣūn 96
Khalīl b. Qumārī 112
khārijīya 35
khāṣṣ (sultan's fisc) 30, 31, 32, 33, 35, 44, 45, 47, 125, 133, 191
khāṣṣakīya 20, 35, 75, 95, 96, 103, 106, 107, 109, 117, 159
khāzindār 40
khidma (public session) 40, 44, 53, 143
khidma (service) 62, 63, 65, 68, 72, 73, 74, 80, 88, 91, 108, 113, 131
Khiḍr 99
Khiḍr b. ʿUmar b. Aḥmad b. Baktamur al-Sāqī 20
khushdāshīya (comradeship) 77, 86, 87, 88, 95
kin, kinsmen 23, 25, 95, 96, 98, 104, 105, 107, 108, 114, 120, 169
kindred 78, 79, 88
kinship 76, 77, 78, 83, 86, 89, 92, 94, 95, 106, 110, 116, 119, 122
Kitbughā, al-ʿĀdil 23
Kizil al-Qaramī 99
Kujuk b. Muḥammad b. Qalāwūn, al-Ashraf 25, 28, 29, 72, 116, 119, 135, 148, 175
kuttāb 18
al-Kutubī, Muḥammad b. Shākir 11

Lājīn, al-Manṣūr Ḥusām al-Dīn 23
Lapidus, Ira 57
legitimacy, legitimisation 6, 7, 23, 26, 28, 48, 49, 68, 70, 169
Legitimate Power 7, 15, 23, 26, 28, 33, 34, 38, 39, 40, 44, 49, 50, 53, 57, 61, 65, 70, 71, 82, 101, 121, 130, 134, 135, 168, 172

madrasa 97
Maḥmūd, Sharaf al-Dīn 22
Maḥmūd b. ʿAlī b. Sharwīn al-Baghdādī, Najm al-Dīn 22, 191
Maliktamur al-Ḥijāzī 21, 67, 114, 115, 119, 150, 152, 182, 190, 191
mamluk (mamluks) 6, 17, 19, 20, 21, 22, 23, 27, 30, 31, 34, 35, 37, 40,

41, 44, 46, 47, 60, 61, 62, 63, 66, 69, 75, 76, 77, 78, 82, 86, 88, 89, 90, 91, 92, 93, 94, 95, 96, 97, 98, 99, 102, 103, 104, 106, 107, 109, 111, 112, 114, 115, 116, 117, 118, 121, 124, 125, 126, 128, 129, 130, 131, 137, 138, 139, 140, 141, 142, 150, 153, 156, 157, 158, 159, 160, 161, 162, 163, 164, 165, 167, 171, 173, 189, 190, 193, 194, 195, 196
manipulation 142, 144, 145
Manjak al-Yūsufī 43, 54, 63, 73, 76, 80, 81, 83, 87, 89, 109, 111, 112, 114, 125, 131, 133, 136, 145, 183, 191
Manklī Bughā al-Fakhrī 54
Manklī Bughā al-Shamsī 43, 69, 85, 109, 112, 183
al-Manṣūr Abū Bakr b. Muḥammad b. Qalāwūn, *see* Abū Bakr b. Muḥammad b. Qalāwūn, al-Manṣūr
al-Manṣūr ʿAlī b. Shaʿbān b. Muḥammad b. Qalāwūn, *see* ʿAlī b. Shaʿbān b. Muḥammad b. Qalāwūn, al-Manṣūr
al-Manṣūr Muḥammad b. Ḥājjī b. Muḥammad b. Qalāwūn, *see* Muḥammad b. Ḥājjī b. Muḥammad b. Qalāwūn, al-Manṣūr
maqbūl al-kalima (guaranteed say) 67, 70, 71, 72, 74, 75, 79, 82, 85, 91, 97, 98, 100, 101, 102, 106, 108, 109, 110, 111, 112, 113, 114, 122, 129, 130, 131, 132, 133, 134, 135, 136, 137, 139, 140, 141, 143, 144, 146, 147, 165, 170, 171
al-Maqrīzī 12, 13, 20, 35, 36, 53, 58, 66, 70, 74, 79, 81, 82, 85, 87, 88, 90, 92, 93, 97, 99, 102, 112, 116, 118, 120, 126, 130, 134, 139, 152, 153, 164, 165
al-Maqs 126
Marie, *see* Ittifāq
Marmon, Shaun 68, 69, 130
marriage 82, 83, 84, 85, 86, 88, 95, 96, 103, 104, 106, 110, 111
Masʿūd b. Awḥad b. Masʿūd b. al-Khaṭīr, Badr al-Dīn 22
Maya 1–202
Mecca 162, 163
Mongols 19, 22
Mubārak Shāh al-Māridānī 126
Mubārak al-Ṭāzī 118
Mughulṭāy al-Nāṣirī 83, 84, 106, 111, 112, 145, 184, 191, 192
Muḥammad b. Alāqūsh 59
Muḥammad b. ʿAlī b. al-Naqqāsh, Shams al-Dīn 18
Muḥammad b. Aqbughā Āṣ 59–60, 145
Muḥammad b. Barqūq 121
Muḥammad b. Ḥājjī b. Muḥammad b. Qalāwūn, al-Manṣūr 25, 29, 72, 117, 119, 159, 175
Muḥammad b. Qalāwūn, al-Nāṣir 1, 2, 3, 4, 5, 6, 7, 12, 20, 23, 25, 26, 32, 36, 47, 49, 65, 71, 75, 80, 81, 82, 83, 101, 110, 125, 130, 135, 145, 147, 148, 150, 152, 153, 158, 159, 168, 169, 171, 172, 175, 193
Muḥammad b. Qibjaq 59
muqaddam alf, *see amīr miʾa*
Muqbil al-Rūmī al-Kabīr 59
al-Mutawakkil 195
al-Muẓaffar, Ḥājjī b. Muḥammad b. Qalāwūn, *see* Ḥājjī b. Muḥammad b. Qalāwūn, al-Muẓaffar

nafaqat al-sulṭān 33
nāʾib 19, 20, 38, 39, 40, 42, 54, 62, 70, 87, 109, 111, 114, 124, 148, 156, 166
nāʾib Ghazza (governor of Gazza) 39, 177, 179
nāʾib Ḥalab (governor of Aleppo) 39, 42, 43, 64, 70, 74, 78, 79, 81, 90, 125, 132, 138, 143, 178, 180, 181, 183, 186, 187, 188, 189, 192, 193, 194, 196
nāʾib Ḥamā (governor of Hama) 39, 178, 187
nāʾib al-Iskandarīya (governor of Alexandria) 39, 42, 73
nāʾib al-Karak (governor of al-Karak) 39
nāʾib Ṣafad (governor of Safad) 39, 79, 178, 183, 184, 186, 187, 189, 192
nāʾib al-salṭana (viceroy) 38, 39, 40, 43, 80, 103, 104, 108, 109, 112, 114, 119, 130, 145, 152, 168, 178, 179, 180, 181, 183, 184, 186, 190
nāʾib al-Shām (governor of Damascus) 39, 41, 42, 43, 56, 59, 60, 62, 64, 66, 73, 74, 75, 78, 79, 88, 95, 99, 106, 111, 125, 132, 133, 138, 140, 141, 143, 144, 159, 166, 178, 180, 183, 186, 188, 190, 191, 193, 195
nāʾib Ṭarābulus (governor of Tripoli) 39, 179, 183, 186, 188, 191

al-Nāṣir Aḥmad b. Muḥammad b. Qalāwūn, *see* Aḥmad b. Muḥammad b. Qalāwūn, al-Nāṣir
Nāṣir al-Dīn al-Dawādār 62
Nāṣir al-Dīn al-Khāzindār 62
al-Nāṣir Ḥasan b. Muḥammad b. Qalāwūn, *see* Ḥasan b. Muḥammad b. Qalāwūn, al-Nāṣir
Nāṣirīya (mamluks of al-Nāṣir Muḥammad) 152
al-Nāṣir Muḥammad b. Qalāwūn, *see* Muḥammad b. Qalāwūn, al-Nāṣir
negotiations 142, 143
network 7, 8, 94, 98, 99, 100, 101, 104, 106, 107, 108, 110, 111, 112, 113, 114, 115, 116, 122, 123, 126, 127, 128, 132, 133, 137, 140, 141, 142, 143, 144, 146, 147, 149, 150, 151, 152, 153, 154, 156, 157, 158, 159, 160, 161, 162, 166, 168, 170, 171, 172, 177
Nile 141, 194
niʿma (favour, benefit) 62, 63, 65, 66, 67, 68, 70, 71, 72, 73, 74, 78, 79, 80, 81, 82, 85, 86, 88, 90, 91, 97, 98, 103, 105, 108, 111, 112, 113, 123, 129, 136, 138, 139, 140, 146, 147, 149, 157, 163, 171

opportunism, opportunistic 79, 92, 136, 140, 146
Ottoman 95, 97

palace (*qaṣr, iṣṭabl, dār*) 17, 20, 97, 118
patron (patronage) 57, 58, 59, 60, 61, 62, 63, 64, 65, 67, 68, 69, 70, 71, 72, 73, 74, 75, 76, 77, 78, 79, 82, 83, 85, 86, 87, 88, 89, 90, 91, 93, 94, 95, 98, 100, 101, 102, 103, 104, 105, 106, 107, 108, 109, 110, 111, 112, 113, 115, 117, 118, 119, 120, 122, 123, 124, 128, 129, 130, 132, 133, 134, 136, 137, 138, 139, 140, 141, 142, 143, 144, 146, 147, 148, 149, 150, 151, 152, 153, 154, 155, 156, 157, 158, 159, 160, 161, 162, 163, 164, 165, 166, 167, 168, 170, 171, 172, 189, 191, 192
plague 2, 36, 79, 117, 154, 169
portrayal 140, 142, 146, 147, 159, 171
promise 63, 64, 66, 67, 103, 138, 139, 141
promotion (to promote) 27, 28, 37, 38, 39, 44, 61, 63, 64, 65, 67, 68, 69, 70, 71, 85, 90, 93, 94, 96, 97, 99, 102, 103, 104, 105, 106, 107, 111, 112, 114, 116, 121, 123, 137, 139, 153, 161
protection 62, 67, 69, 70

Qajmas al-Ṣāliḥī 82
Qalāwūn, al-Manṣūr 23, 34, 135, 175
Qalāwūz al-Nāṣirī 59
al-Qalqashandī 35, 36, 49
Qarābughā, Sayf al-Dīn 56, 75
Qarābughā al-Abūbakrī 99
Qarābulāṭ 99
Qarākasak 99
Qaraṭāy al-Ṭāzī 29, 64, 84, 117, 118, 120, 138, 139, 142, 164, 165, 166, 184, 195
Qawṣūn 3, 4, 17, 28, 29, 43, 55, 63, 66, 69, 71, 72, 73, 74, 78, 81, 82, 89, 91, 98, 104, 116, 118, 119, 120, 124, 130, 133, 134, 137, 138, 141, 142, 144, 145, 147, 148, 150, 167, 184, 189
Qawṣūnī 116
Qazdamur al-Ḥasanī 168
Qubbat al-Naṣr 118, 126
Quruṭ al-Turkumānī 126
Quṭlūbak al-Niẓāmī 99
Quṭlūbak al-Sayfī 99
Quṭlūbughā al-Fakhrī 63, 66, 70, 87, 88, 140, 141, 143, 148
Quṭluqtamur al-ʿAlāʾī 184
Quṭlūqujāh 118

Ramaḍān b. Muḥammad b. Qalāwūn 135, 140, 145
raʾs nawba 40, 44, 50, 54, 72, 165, 168, 179, 180, 181, 184, 185, 186
Robert, *see dawādār*
rumours 134, 136, 142, 144, 145, 189, 190, 191, 192, 194, 195, 196

Safad 35, 42, 62
al-Ṣafadī, Khalīl b. Aybak, 10, 11, 59, 61, 80, 93, 100, 111, 153
al-Ṣāliḥ Ayyūb, *see* Ayyūb, al-Ṣāliḥ
al-Ṣāliḥ Ḥājjī b. Shaʿbān b. Ḥusayn b. Muḥammad b. Qalāwūn, *see* Ḥājjī b. Shaʿbān b. Ḥusayn b. Muḥammad b. Qalāwūn, al-Ṣāliḥ
al-Ṣāliḥ Ismāʿīl b. Muḥammad b.

Qalāwūn, *see* Ismāʿīl b. Muḥammad b. Qalāwūn, al-Ṣāliḥ
Ṣāliḥīya (mamluks of al-Ṣāliḥ Ismāʿīl) 152
Ṣāliḥ b. Muḥammad b. Qalāwūn, al-Ṣāliḥ 29, 63, 72, 115, 116, 117, 119, 155, 175, 192
Sanjar al-Jāwulī, ʿAlam al-Dīn 61, 62, 69
Sarāy al-ʿAlāʾī 112
Ṣarghitmish 165
Ṣarghitmish al-Nāṣirī 60, 61, 115, 125, 132, 133, 154, 155, 156, 157, 185, 192, 193
sāsa 54
sayyid 124
service, *see khidma*
Shaʿbān 59
Shaʿbān b. Ḥusayn b. Muḥammad b. Qalāwūn, al-Ashraf 3, 4, 17, 25, 30, 31, 32, 33, 35, 56, 61, 65, 66, 69, 72, 75, 84, 85, 95, 97, 102, 107, 109, 110, 111, 117, 119, 120, 124, 129, 131, 132, 136, 138, 139, 142, 143, 144, 159, 160–161, 162, 163, 164, 165, 175, 185, 194, 195
Shaʿbān b. Muḥammad b. Qalāwūn, al-Kāmil 23, 24, 29, 32, 56, 70, 84, 102, 104, 105, 107, 113, 119, 132, 135, 137, 140, 145, 150, 151, 152, 175, 185, 190
Shaʿbān b. Yalbughā 96
shafāʿa (intercession) 67, 68, 69, 70, 94, 100, 108, 109, 116, 130, 131, 149, 160, 189, 194
Shaykhū al-ʿUmarī 33, 44, 54, 55, 58, 59, 60, 67, 73, 74, 85, 89, 96, 99, 100, 109, 114, 115, 116, 119, 125, 131, 133, 145, 154, 155, 156, 157, 167, 186, 191, 192, 193
al-Shujāʿī 12, 69, 74, 79, 87, 91, 94, 113, 142, 143, 148
signature (sultan's) 28, 39, 68
socio-political practice, socio-political conduct 7, 10, 22, 23, 51, 53, 56, 57, 62, 70, 75, 77, 92, 93, 98, 101, 122, 123, 127, 137, 141, 150
stables (of the sultan) 40, 41, 43, 97, 120, 126, 166, 168, 195
struggle (for power) 101, 123, 124, 125, 127, 128, 130, 133, 146, 171, 172, 189–196
al-Subkī, Tāj al-Dīn 70
succession (to the sultanate) 23, 24, 25, 125
Sūdūn Bāshā 99
Sūdūn al-Shaykhūnī 168
sultanate 6, 15, 19, 20, 22, 27, 34, 38, 41, 49, 50, 53, 54, 97, 98, 107, 113, 120, 121, 122, 134, 135, 136, 138, 164, 168, 190, 193
Sulṭān Shāh b. Qarā 112
Sūsūn 81

tadbīr, see dabbara
Tamurbughā al-Sayfī 99
Tamurbughā al-Shamsī 99
Ṭanbughū 81
Tankiz, Sayf al-Dīn 62
Tankiz al-ʿUthmānī 99
Tankizbughā al-Māridānī 106
Ṭānyariq al-Yūsufī 54, 75
taṣarruf 54, 61
Ṭashtamur al-ʿAlāʾī al-Dawādār 61, 69, 84, 109, 112, 124, 131, 135, 144, 145, 166, 167, 186, 194, 195, 196
Ṭashtamur Ḥummuṣ Akhḍar 70, 81, 113, 115, 119, 130, 131, 147, 148, 149, 186, 189
Ṭashtamur al-Laffāf 139
Ṭaybughā al-Majdī 54
Ṭaybughā al-Ṭawīl 74, 79, 125, 132, 158, 159, 193, 194
Ṭaydamur al-Bālisī 83
Ṭāz al-Nāṣirī 29, 54, 66, 83, 85, 88, 106, 116, 117, 118, 119, 120, 125, 131, 141, 154, 155, 156, 165, 187, 191, 192, 193
tension 23, 123, 124, 127, 128, 129, 130, 133, 134, 139, 140, 142, 143, 147, 150, 151, 152, 154, 156, 157, 159, 163, 167, 170, 171, 192, 193
thawra (eruption) 127
Timur (Lenk) 19
Tripoli 35, 39, 67
Ṭughaytamur al-Najmī 191
Ṭughunjaq 81
Tuḥfa al-Saniya 31, 35, 36, 47
Tūjī al-Ḥasanī 99
Ṭulubāy 96
Ṭulūdamur 88
Ṭulūtamur al-Aḥmadī 99
Ṭuqtamur al-Ḥasanī 112
Ṭuqṭāy al-Nāṣirī 59, 83
Ṭuquzdamur al-Ḥamawī 70, 85, 103, 148

Ṭurghāy al-Nāṣirī 145
Ṭurṭuqā b. Sūsūn 81

ukhūwa (brotherhood) 86, 87, 88, 89
ʿulamāʾ 17
Uljāyhīya (mamluks of Uljāy al-Yūsufī) 112
Uljāy al-Yūsufī 80, 85, 89, 111, 112, 131, 143, 144, 187, 194
Uljībughā al-Muẓaffarī 54
Urumbughā al-Kāmilī 75
Urus al-Bashtakī 83
ustādār 40, 50, 87, 126, 183
ustādh 56, 89, 90, 91, 104, 114, 139, 143, 160, 161, 163, 164, 171
ustādhīya (vertical loyalty) 88, 89, 90, 91, 92
usurpation 23, 24, 121, 168

viceroy, *see nāʾib al-salṭana*

walad al-nās, see awlād al-nās
wālī 40, 73, 177
waqʿa (incident, encounter) 127
waqf (religious endowment) 62, 80
wazīr 40, 54, 87, 177, 183, 192

Yalbughā al-Khāṣṣakī 56, 61, 64, 69, 74, 80, 81, 89, 91, 96, 107, 109, 117, 118, 123, 128, 131, 132, 133, 135, 136, 138, 139, 141, 144, 158, 159, 160, 161, 162, 163, 164, 165, 167, 171, 188, 193
Yalbughā al-Manjakī 99
Yalbughā al-Nāṣirī 99, 126, 133, 145, 165, 166, 167, 188, 195, 196
Yalbughāwīya (mamluks of Yalbughā al-Khāṣṣakī) 17, 66, 107, 109, 110, 112, 117, 120, 129, 138, 161, 162, 163, 193, 194
Yalbughā al-Yaḥyāwī 59, 73, 78, 88, 144, 190, 191
Yūnūs al-Nawrūzī al-Dawādār 72, 127, 168
Yūsuf b. Shādhī 99
al-Yūsufī 12, 13

al-Ẓāhirī 35
zuʿr 17